CONTROVERSIAL ISSUES IN SOCIAL WORK RESEARCH

Edited by

Walter W. Hudson

Arizona State University

Paula S. Nurius

University of Washington

Series Editors

Eileen Gambrill

Robert Pruger

University of California, Berkeley

ALLYN AND BACON

Boston London Toronto Sydney Tokyo Singapore

Senior Editor: Karen Hanson
Editorial Assistant: Sarah Dunbar
Production Administrator: Susan McIntyre
Editorial-Production Service: Ruttle, Shaw & Wetherill, Inc.
Cover Administrator: Suzanne Harbison
Manufacturing Buyer: Louise Richardson

A Division of Paramount Publishing
160 Gould Street
Needham Heights, MA 02194

Library of Congress Cataloging-in-Publication Data

Controversial issues in social work research / edited by Walter W. Hudson, Paula S. Nurius.
p. cm.
Includes bibliographical references.
ISBN 0–205–15615–0
1. Social service—Research. I. Hudson, Walter W. II. Nurius, Paula.
HV11.C7186 1994
361--dc20 93–28671
CIP

Printed in the United States of America

10 9 8 7 6 5 4 3 2 1 98 97 96 95 94

Contents

Preface

In 1992, Allyn and Bacon published a book titled *Controversies in Social Work* (Gambrill & Pruger, 1992). The book was so well received and the number of issues that it raised in readers' discussions was so numerous that several books focusing on different aspects of social work have been spawned. Our mission has been to focus on points of issue and concern about social work *research.* Our most obvious purpose is to present different perspectives on a number of current issues related to this research. However, in so doing, we hope to foster an appreciation that controversy—even when the issues are deeply heartfelt—can be explored in a respectful and constructive manner.

It is unfortunate that debate is sometimes viewed as destructive—in the sense that debates are seen as a forum in which debaters attack each other as people. Debate can be instructive and constructive, however, when positions are focused on the issues at hand and not on the person who delivers or presents a specific idea or position. Debates can be particularly useful in consolidating and providing immediate contrast of key points that undergird a controversy. For most, if not all, of the controversies in social work research found here have been addressed in the professional literature—through journal articles, editorials, books, and conference presentations. But rare is the opportunity to have knowledgeable writers "cut to the chase" so that the bare bones of opposing views are illuminated side by side. The downside, of course, is that debates are time (and space) limited.

Who is this book for? It is for all who are intrigued, confused, interested, or even infuriated about one or more controversial issue in social work research. We believe this collection of debates provides useful information and meaty, controversial ideas for students, educators, practitioners, and researchers across our profession. It could easily be used in introductory B.S.W. and M.S.W. research courses as a supplementary text, to deepen an appreciation and understanding of the "sticky wickets" of research in social work. It could galvanize stimulating discussions in doctoral research courses or seminars. (In fact, in the process of reading the early stage debate topics, the editors found themselves rethinking and retooling their own research-related courses and trying to influence their faculty colleagues.) As you will see, these are not just boring, esoteric research topics. They speak to vital issues that touch the field. Thus, we see this book as a potential resource to agency in-service training programs (e.g., for new employees who need an informative exposure to research and its relationship to service delivery and practice; to facilitate staff discussion of the pros and cons of various forms of research in practice or agency life). For the most seasoned of practitioners, educators, and researchers, it is likely to be useful for revisiting some of the issues that one has not examined recently.

The topics selected for this book are by no means exhaustive. Our goal was to select a representative set of issues that concern an array of professional interests, and to provide a broad "snapshot" of current debates (with references for further reading). In selecting topics for this book, we drew upon a combination of methods: generating topics that we were aware of from our own tenure and battle wounds in this arena, soliciting topics from colleagues, undertaking and reviewing library searches of recent articles in social work journals on research topics, and seeking input as to which topics were seen by others as both interesting and true controversies. We also made a concerted effort to entice a diverse set of contributors to "sign up": diverse with respect to gender and race as well as ideological backgrounds. We are delighted to have recruited a splendid group of contributors in this book.

Each author prepared a position statement arguing for or against a position and, in addition, prepared a rebuttal to the opposite side. Authors were asked to keep their statements brief, to get to the heart of their argument quickly, and to strive to be thought-provoking and forward-looking. This format allows for an engaging exchange that offers readers an opportunity to raise questions such as: Are the assertions persuasive? Does the reply really speak to the opposing points? Is evidence provided to support claims made? Have important points been neglected? Is the author relying on tactics (such as overstatment, creating false dichotomies, using inuendo or emotionalism, and appeal to status or authority) at the expense of substance?

The book contains twenty-three debate topics that are organized into six major sections or parts. *Part I: Debates about Research and Epistemology* contains five debates that examine the fundamental quesiton of "how do we know?" These fundamental issues form the foundation upon which subsequent decisions are built about what research tools are (and are not) useful, toward what objectives, and within what contexts. A vital concern, indeed, for a profession that aspires to embrace plurality and to also base its practice on as solid and credible a knowledge base as possible. *Part II: Debates about Research and Direct Practice* contains four debate topics. Questions about how (and if) to integrate the realms of research and direct practice date back to the inception of social work. The topics here speak to some of the more contemporary questions in hot debate. *Part III: Debates about Research and Administrative Practice* contains four debate topics that parallel some of the discussion concerning the relationship between research and direct social work practice. Parts II and III together serve to highlight the practice-based nature of our profession and the sense of relative tension or complementarity between research and practice. *Part IV: Debates about Research and Education* contains four debates that address some knotty issues about what we should be teaching with respect to research across degree programs. These issues reflect questions about research influencing *how* we think as well as what we *do. Part V: Debates about Research Methods, Analysis, and Publication* contains four debates that focus on methodology and the ways research ''should'' be used in evaluating the relative merit of findings and claims. This is yet another area rich with stormy controversy. *Part VI: Debates about Research and The Future* contains two debates intended to end the book on a forward-looking note, because the topics of this book and many others will be debated for many years to come.

Before turning to the debates themselves, we wish to caution you against the assumption that each author is ideologically committed to the debate position and arguments she or he has taken. In some cases this may be true. In others—not at all! There are several instances in which authors accepted the challenge of investigating and articulating a position that they had some reservations about or felt had good arguments on both sides.

As collaborators who have literally debated with one another for many years, seeking a complement of our different perspectives that is more complete than our individual parts, we (the editors) can speak from experience that there are few exercises that help clarify one's thinking and understanding as effectively as a respectful debate. Nor should you assume that opposing authors will bear animosity toward one another for having participated in the rigor of debate and retort. To the contrary, many of our opposing debaters have ongoing relationships as colleagues and friends. This is neither the first nor the last time that they will express their differnces. An environment that encourages constructive expression of differences is an essential ingredient to the continuous process of inquiry, reflection, and growth.

We want to thank all of the contributors for preparing debate positions and writing rebuttal statements to their counterpoint authors. We have been impressed by and are most grateful for the interest and enthusiasm shown by all. As editors, we have had the benefit of a ''sneak preview'' of the book and of feedback from our students. We are happy to report that both have been very stimulating, indeed. The ultimate test lies with you, the reader. Do these debates stimulate new ways of looking at the issues? Are you willing to suspend favored positions and defensiveness; to seriously work to understand, appreciate, and possibly be influenced by differing perspectives? We hope you find these discussion useful, and we hope to be a part of ongoing dialogue. If you have a perspective to share—write us!

Walter W. Hudson
Paula S. Nurius

University of California, Berkeley

Introduction

The purpose of this book is to stimulate thought: questioning, weighing of new information, and reexamining that which has been considered previously. Controversy and debate can be excellent devices for getting right to the heart of issues and gaining a better understanding of various perspectives. As such, debates can serve as an important learning resource.

We see this form of learning as continuous across both the varied roles in social work and within our professional lives. That is, our goal here is not to present learning content in the same fashion as a text on research methods. To varying degrees, the debate authors do refer to specifics about research tools and methods to support their arguments. Learning related to issues is much tougher and much less likely to be "completed" in any single reading or step.

Truly controversial issues tend to involve differences in conception and perception, values, world views, and sense of purpose and professional identity. For all of us, it is far too easy to reach a point where we would just as soon not keep going back over our thinking and feelings about complex issues. We would like to invite you, however, to approach this book as an opportunity. That is, an opportunity to tune into feelings of internal brakes being applied and to use any sense of unease (whether it be confusion, annoyance, disdain, or anxiety) as a reminder to look again: to be open to challenging perspectives, thoughtfully weigh the strengths and weaknesses of the debate positions, and allowing room for change.

The Crisis in Social Work Research

For some, it may be difficult to think in terms of a crisis in social work research. Crisis in social-welfare problems and the lack of resources, yes, but in social work *Research?* For many social workers, research seems like some rather distant phenomenon that doesn't have much to do with their work or concerns. Yet research, much like policy, has many levels of influence on the world of practice, which often go relatively unnoticed.

The relationship of research to practice was the focus of an National Institute of Mental Health (NIMH) sponsored Task Force on Social Work Research. According to the findings of this task force, the contributions of practice-relevant research to the knowledge base of social work practice is seriously lagging, with significant consequences for individuals using social work services, practitioners, and the credibility and viability of the profession.

"As never before, social work needs better, more demonstrably effective intervention technologies to use with client populations that present increasingly chronic and difficult problems. Professional practitioners simply require more usable information about what works with whom, under what circumstances" (McMahon, Reisch, & Patti, p. 5, as quoted by Task Force on Social Work Research, 1991). Few who have worked in the challenging arena of social work would argue with the assertion that we sorely need more and better information to guide decision making, strengthen services, and open up helping options. We would and do, however, argue energetically about just *how* we "should" go about getting better answers to our practice and service questions, and what the relationship of research to policy and practice should be. Indeed, these issues are the focus and catalyst for many of the debates that you will encounter here.

The concepts of "scientific philanthropy," "natural experiments," and "social engineering" can be found in the annals of social work's inception. Yet debates about the roles and forms of research and the relationship of research to the profession have taken place throughout the life of the profession. Many controversial works and exchanges have provided an enormous stimulus to develop new theory, devise new methods of practice, and create new methods of research and evaluation. We do not mean to suggest here that debates or controversy are *necessarily* productive or healthy, nor that we have truly "solved" many of the most complex issues. These require an ongoing, long-term commitment. However, our ability to effectively respond to our crisis of research is predicated upon our willingness to be self-critical as a profession. Debate is one device we use to grow, mature, and diversify.

The Topics of Debate

In the *Preface,* we described the organization of the debate topics into six parts: epistemology, direct practice, administrative practice, education, methodology and dissemination, and a look to the future. This organization is intended to pull together clusters of related issues and assist the reader in thinking about controversies relative to differing professional domains. You will see, both within and across these groupings, however, that there are very different ways of viewing the nature of conflict. One major division is a conflict between paradigms of investigation. One of the great divisions of the past decade has concerned many arguments about the preference for, even the "rightness" of, qualitative or quantitative research methods. Another important debate arises with respect to recognizing diversity issues, such as gender differences in life experiences and the roles played in the knowledge development enterprise by men and women, as well as differing experiences and perspectives of people of color and other minority groups, who have had limited opportunities to participate in and define the realm of research.

Naturally there are enormous debates around the methods of research design, data collection, and data analysis; and another large series of debates involves the conflicts among theories of practice and their research validation. The point is that debate and controversy can be shaped and engaged from many different perspectives and those conceptions influence the nature and format of controversy. Some conceptions will likely be more productive than others because they shed more light on possible solutions or better ways of resolving differences.

When you turn to the debate topics themselves, it may be helpful to have some guideposts for your reading and thinking, and we would like to offer some tools and suggestions as a basis for analyzing the debate materials. Yet, you should be acutely aware of the fact that the number and types of tools or guideposts that we offer are themselves open to debate. This book is not about clean and simple answers as much as it is about complex and messy questions and objectives. Think of your efforts here as a start down a road loaded with signs and commercials, which you must sort through in order to continue on your way without getting detoured or lost. We will be pleased if you find the following materials useful, but you should remember that there are many other ways to examine readings. It is simply not possible to provide an extensive coverage of such materials and we encourage you to look long and widely for conceptions that will aid your future study and analysis of research evidence and debates about research.

Six Social Work Languages

Before turning to the specific guideposts that we offer, we want to draw upon a recent analogy of social work as being essentially multilingual. Bloom, Wood, and Chambon (1991) describe social work as having at least six different languages: "the lay language of the client, the abstract language of the theorist, the empirical and often quantitative language of the researcher, the categorical language of the information scientist, the technical terminology or jargon (minus its pejorative sense) as used by helping professionals, and the preferential language that conveys values'' (p. 530). The challenge for all of us is to become fluent, or at least reasonably conversant, in each of these and other languages and we urge you to further investigate this area of social work theory. For now it may be useful to ask which languages are being used in the debates and to note that the following materials rely heavily on concepts and abstractions that might well be seen as a seventh language (or meta-language)—the use of language to discuss language.

Ways of Knowing and Claims-Making

What is ''the truth'' and how do we know it when we see it? A definitive answer to these questions would be very reassuring indeed! It is hardly news that people vary enormously in their opinions and characteristic ways of looking at things. However, it is clearer today than ever before that reality is far less a factually based entity than an interpretation that each of us constructs in our efforts to establish meaning and sustain a sense of order. We draw naturally on our constructions to explain the past, predict the future, function in the present, and, as you will see in these debates, make claims and pose arguments about what is and what should be (Best, 1989).

Part of your job as a reader is to evaluate the merits of the arguments and constructions or premises on which the debate claims are based. Different constructions will contain and reflect differing experiences, understandings, goals, and values. Part of your challenge is to try to temporarily suspend some of your own presumptions and commitments to enable you to see and appreciate legitimate differences in the *content* of these arguments. Another part of your challenge is to distinguish the content from the *style* in which the claims, conclusions, and positions are presented, and to critically evaluate the merits of these two components. For example, a claim can be elementally weak (e.g., have little to no evidence to back it up; be inappropriate to a context) yet be so eloquent, dramatic, and charismatic that we get swept up by the compelling style and lose track of the weak foundations. By the same token, a solidly supported argument that labors under a colorless delivery has limited chances of influencing us, despite its merits.

Although we strive to value differences, this does not mean that all arguments are created equally. Are the arguments equally valid? Equally viable or sustainable? There are a number of good descriptions of how to go about analyzing arguments (Gambrill, 1990; Gibbs, 1991; Nickerson, 1986; Scriven, 1976; Toulmin, Rieck, & Janik, 1979). It is beyond the scope of this book to review this literature in detail. However, we urge you to do some background reading. Some of this can be fun; like the list of ''dishonest tricks commonly used in argument'' that Gambrill and Pruger (1992) cite in their appendix, drawing on Thouless' (1974) notions of straight and crooked thinking.

Two Classes of Knowledge Used in "Construction"

Let us now take a closer look at the idea that virtually all of what we call "knowledge" is a construction. We build this construction completely by using our body, its sensory mechanisms, and our tools of language—which we also construct. While not the whole story, there are two simple classes of knowledge that we draw on in our ongoing construction efforts (Johnson & Pennypacker, 1980, pp. 5–40):

1. Discovered knowledge
2. Invented knowledge

These categories are useful. We note, however, that there are many other ways to approach the examination of debate positions.

As defined by Johnson and Pennypacker (1980), *invented knowledge* is created by social groups as "a basis for formulating rules or codes by which to manage themselves." Thus, invented knowledge is indispensable to us. It is a basic fabric of social organization and social order. Invented knowledge is often used to enrich aesthetics, expand a sense of culture, enhance understanding of one another, provide entertainment, formulate boundaries and bases of exercising social control. The entire corpus of legal knowledge exemplifies the use of invented knowledge to define and enforce social control. The canons of professional ethics and behavior constitute bodies of invented knowledge that are aimed explicitly at the control of persons who chose to become members of professions and professional societies.

We can state the matter more directly, and in doing so suggest how the concept of invented knowledge may be useful in reading this book. That is, invented knowledge consists of our ethics, values, "shoulds," "oughts," wants, needs, desires, and wishes. Thus, it may be useful to ask, as you read the debates, whether the core issues of argument, conflict, and controversy are rooted in disagreements about ethical positions and values (which are aspects of invented knowledge) or whether they focus on different kinds of material. This often helps clarify the nature and scope of the debate.

Discovered knowledge is constructed from our ability to make and analyze observations about objects and their relations in the real world. When people speak of "scientific knowledge," they are generally referring to the realm of discovered knowledge; or at least to some components of discovered knowledge. Unfortunately, the very notion of "scientific knowledge" lacks crisp definition. Some tend to define it in very broad terms, while others use rather narrow constructions. The keynote here, for us, is that discovered knowledge refers to efforts to understand objects by drawing on patterns and events in the observable world. Naturally, many will be eager to debate vigorously the notions of what is "scientific," but we encourage a broad view of the matter. We highlight the fact that people continuously engage in *observing* and rendering interpretations about their world. From this vantage point we are all inveterate data gatherers and analyzers—and in this sense, we are all scientists. We constantly seek to observe the world about us and to understand how it ticks. It is this large body of observation and analysis that leads to what we describe here as "discovered" and scientific knowledge in the broadest sense of these terms.

The acquisition of discovered knowledge is important to all of us. It is certainly one of the primary purposes for pursuing a professional education and professional credentials—to gain more discovered knowledge. We want to know what causes people to have the problems that they bring to us as "clients." Moreover, we want to know what to do about those problems. We want to discover and validate which interventions, treatments, and services will affect the problems most fruitfully. This is not to suggest that invented knowledge is any less important in pursuing a professional education. Indeed, we want to know as much as we can about the ethics and values of our profession and about theories (another type of invented knowledge) or problem causation and intervention.

Clearly, these two classes of knowledge are not independent of one another. When reading the research debates in the book, it may be helpful to ask whether a debate seems to be more focused on invented knowledge (theories, beliefs, values, etc.) or whether it involves arguments about discovered knowledge (observations, methods, findings, etc.)—or both. While this may be a useful way to consider various debate positions, it is also important to recognize that a very old saw, "The facts speak for themselves," is simply not true. To the contrary, the facts never speak for themselves. This means that the "facts," (observations) must always be interpreted—and they are interpreted by using the constructions we describe as "invented knowledge." It may be useful, therefore, to break the concept of "knowledge" into some additional constructs, which may help further in understanding and evaluating the debates you will encounter.

Three Kinds of Knowledge

Knowledge can also be conceived as being of three different "kinds," known as 1) *intentional or deontic knowledge*—the values, shoulds, oughts, needs, and wants that we assert for our maintenance and welfare; 2) *analytic knowledge*—our theories, propositions, and assertions about how the world "works"; and 3) *contingent knowledge*—observed relationships among objects and energies in the physical world. The latter is judged as being valid, contingent on the amount of real-world evidence amassed to support their veracity. It may be useful to ask which of them is being offered or used as the basis for the debates in this book.

Building on the foregoing material, we can see that a theory about client problems or methods of practice is a form of analytical knowledge. When we subscribe to a theory, we are adopting it as one of our belief systems and our theory-driven belief systems can influence our practice activities powerfully.

(Nurius & Hudson [1993, pp. 121–199], have much to say about the delicate balances in using, yet restraining, our systems of belief in practice judgment.) We cannot act responsibly as professional practitioners unless we have a set of organized beliefs about how to engage in problem description, diagnosis, and practice. Indispensable as our values, theories, and beliefs may be, they are not facts or evidence *per se* and, alone, they do not constitute contingent knowledge. Here we begin to better see the advantage of multilingualism with respect to multiple forms and aids to creating, communicating, testing, and modifying "what we know" and "how we know what we know."

When you engage the debates in this book, we hope it will be useful for you to consider whether, when, and how each debate focuses on deontic, analytical, and contingent knowledge and to remember that theories, values, and beliefs are beginning points more than ending points. Reality is indeed relative—and contingent. Theories, values, and beliefs are the driving force that motivate the conduct of research which, in turn, often has the goal of testing belief and theory to determine whether it, along with its supporting evidence, indeed constitutes contingent knowledge.

We offer these language or meta-language constructions in the hope that you can better recognize the nature of the conflict that is embedded within these debates. We hope that the nature of the argument becomes clearer once you recognize that it focuses on disputes around values (deontic knowledge), theories and beliefs (analytical knowledge), or research findings (contingent knowledge). If these devices are helpful, they may assist you in forming your own belief system more carefully, devising your own theories and propositions, and then perhaps in conducting research or seeking the results of other research to determine whether we can enhance a pluralistic and integrative knowledge base of our profession.

Research as an Ethical Safeguard

For many of us, it is often easy to scrutinize the knowledge-development sins of the remote past, simply because we did not participate in its folly. It is much more difficult to be self-critical in the present. Yet, we must engage in such self-examination and scrutiny in order to improve the knowledge base that we use as practitioners, teachers, and scholars. It is for these reasons that the National Association of Social Workers (NASW) places such great emphasis on the use of research in its "Code of Ethics." The conduct of research and inquiry toward enriching our foundation of contingent knowledge helps us to mature as individuals and as a profession.

Conclusion

Debate is only one form of organized self-examination. However, it is an important device for testing ideas, confronting issues, and clarifying beliefs and our positions concerning them. Yet, debate positions must be understood and analyzed in order to profit from them. There are many tools for engaging in such analysis and examination and we have offered a very small number for you to consider. There are other, similar books about controversial issues in social work (practice, mental health, administration, policy, etc.) and others may follow. Each will contain suggestions and ideas for engaging the use and analysis of debate positions, and we urge that you consult those works.

References

Best, J. (1989). *Images of issues.* New York: Aldine of Gryer.

Bloom, M., Wood, K., & Chambon, A. (1991). The six languages of social work. *Social Work, 6,* 530–534.

Gambrill, E. (1990). *Critical thinking in clinical practice.* San Francisco: Jossey-Bass.

Gambrill, E., & Pruger, R. (Eds). (1992). *Controversial issues in social work.* Boston: Allyn & Bacon.

Gibbs, L.E. (1991). *Scientific reasoning for social workers.* New York: Merrill.

Johnston, J.M., & Pennypacker, H.S. (1980). *Strategies and tactics of human behavioral research.* Hillsdale, NJ: Lawrence Erlbaum Associates.

McMahon, M.O., Reisch, M., & Patti, R. (1991). Scholarship in social work integration of research, teaching, and service. Washington, D.C.: National Association of Deans and Directors of Schools of Social Work.

Nickerson, R.S. (1986). *Reflections on reasoning.* Hillsdale, NJ: Erlbaum.

Nurius, P.S. & Hudson, W.W. (1993). *Human services practice, evaluation & computers: A practical guide for today and beyond.* Pacific Grove, CA: Brooks/Cole Publishing.

Scriven, M. (1976). *Reasoning.* New York: McGraw-Hill.

Task Force on Social Work Research (1991). Building social work knowledge for effective services and policies: A plan for research development. Publication contact: David Austin, University of Texas at Austin, School of Social Work.

Thouless, R.H. (1974). *Straight and crooked thinking: Thirty-eight dishonest tricks of debate.* London, England: Pan Books.

Toulmin, S.E., Rieke, R., & Janik, A. (1979). *An introduction to reading.* New York: Macmillan.

DEBATE 1

Does Emphasizing Accountability and Evidence Dilute Service Delivery and the Helping Role?

Roy Ruckdeschel is a professor at the school of Social Services of Saint Louis University, where he teaches a variety of human behavior and environment and research courses. His primary writing and research interests are in the area of qualitative methods and their role in social work.

Mary Lou Balassone is an associate professor at the University of Washington School of Social Work, where she teaches health care and research courses. Her research is in the areas of adolescent reproductive health and prenatal care, focusing on the development of prevention interventions.

YES

ROY RUCKDESCHEL

Although I am arguing the yes side of this debate, I would quickly add that I am not opposed to the general notion of accountability and evidence. Who could be? Accountability suggests that one should be responsible and committed—this certainly is not the issue. Rather, the problem lies with the way in which accountability generally has been framed and the way it has been discussed in the social work research literature. Accountability has been presented as a solution, an answer, and an alternative.

If I accepted this logic in the context of the present debate, my opposition to accountability would then imply that I believe that the de-emphasis or elimination of accountability would strengthen service delivery and the helping role of the practitioner. This is clearly silly.

We might better ask—if accountability is the answer, what then is the question? In this yes paper, I will explore the following: the difficulties of posing accountability in measurement and evaluative terms, the utility of reframing the argument, the relevance of a political organizational perspective, and the costs of accountability.

Accountability as Measurement and Evaluation

The presentation and operationalization of accountability in the social work research literature has focused largely on measurement concerns and the use of quantitative evidence. It has also been linked closely to issues of research use and the evaluation of practice. Thus framed, accountability is the answer to the question, "How can we improve practice?" This is particularly the case at the clinical level, where the single-system design has been presented as the design of choice to evaluate practice and to become accountable. Typical of this approach is the way in which Bloom and Fischer (1982) bundle the issues:

> Single system designs involve approaches and procedures that demonstrate how research an practice can be integrated, thus offering an excellent opportunity for practitioners to demonstrate their accountability.
>
> The fundamental step in becoming an accountable professional is to start counting with the A–B design. (p. 385)

We might well wonder with Meyer (1984), why research on effectiveness—and effectiveness in a way that can be counted—is a substitute for other measures of accountability. But even taking this proposed solution at face value, one is left struggling with the meaning of it all. At the risk of being facetious, it would appear that one begins to become accountable by learning to count. The more one counts, the more one becomes accountable. If we all learn to count and become accountable, will not the profession as a whole become more accountable? Dare one ask what we should count and why?

It should be noted that practitioners have been rightly suspicious about the way in which accountability has been posed in clinical practice. There is, for example, little evidence of the voluntary acceptance of single-subject designs in the world of practice. By way of contrast, the "accountability as measurement/solution" point of view has made its greatest headway in the realm of education. The Council on Social Work Education has mandated that students be taught skills to evaluate their own practice. Given the seeming reluctance of the present crop of practitioners, the students are apparently to be the accountable professionals of the future and the spearhead of change. They are, as students, essentially a captive audience with little power and even less say in the matter (although some faculty may have a similar feeling).

One implication of the above is that the accountability equation might be stated thusly: accountability = evaluation-of-one's-practice = counting. Needless to say, this has ramifications for both research and practice. It seems to lead to a preference for particular kinds of research designs at the cost of others and for practice modalities that lend themselves to counting rather than those that do not. Does this not also lead to a preference for brief over long-term therapy, for universal languages of discourse in therapy over divergent and diverse languages, and for behavioral as opposed to phenomenological approaches to practice? For that matter, does this formulation have much of anything to say about macropractice, or about social change?

Reframing the Issue

Despite the argument above, I do not really think the problem lies with single-subject design, evaluation, or quantitative data. Nor does it lie with the complex and cumbersome accountability and performance evaluation procedures that increasingly confront social workers in human-service organizations. All of these can be and sometimes are useful. What I do not find at all useful or helpful is the posing of accountability as a question and evidence of accountability as the "answer," and its equivalence with measurement.

In point of fact, the terms, "accountable" and "evidence," have no meaning without a referent. The terms at best suggest questions, not answers. To say that one should be accountable or that one should use evidence is no more meaningful than to say that one should use more or less thinking to solve a problem. The problematic issues lie at a different level. Perhaps the real questions are "Accountable to whom?" and "For what purpose?" The research literature has dealt almost exclusively with issues of instrumentation and has been relatively silent on the questions as framed above. The research texts generally and briefly explain that social workers need to be accountable to themselves, their clients, their organizations, and the profession. The purpose is to improve practice or programs. Who should argue with this? However, does an answer at such a level of generalization really engage the issues of to whom and for what purpose?

Accountability and the Political Organizational Perspective

For some insight into this matter, it is useful to turn to the literature on human-service organizations. Much of social work practice takes place in organizational and institutional settings. In some settings, social work is the dominant profession; in others, it is one among many. As such, accountability mechanisms, particularly performance evaluations, are likely to be part of organizational life. By implication, any formulation of accountability that emphasizes measurement is also making assumptions about the legitimization and use of these mechanisms in the organizational environment. It also presupposes at least some degree of professional control of these mechanisms.

In essence, many organizational theorists would characterize organizations that have such a means–ends relationship as rational in nature (Gummer, 1978; Hasenfeld, 1992). More specifically, the conditions that must be obtained for rationality to apply are the existence of clear goals that are widely accepted by the major actors within the organization. The same must also apply to means; a variety of distinctive means must be available and their effectiveness must be possible to determine or predict. The organizational structure or programs will, in turn, reflect an orientation toward rationality. To the extent that this model applies to any organization (there is some debate on this point), it seems to best fit a business-type structure wherein profits are the prime organizational goal and the main measure of effectiveness. This is all well and good if the assumptions are met. But what if they are not? What implications might this have for the ways in which accountability mechanisms are actually used?

Hasenfeld (1992) has argued that the types of organizations in which social workers function, or what he terms human-service organizations are distinctive in a number of ways, not the least of which is that they "process" people. They also tend to be characterized by multiple and sometimes conflicting goals and indeterminant technologies or means. It follows that the key conditions for rationality are not generally met in human-service organizations and that other factors must be considered when analyzing such organizations and their effectiveness.

Although there are a variety of contemporary models, each of which shed light on the human-service organization, the approach that I find most useful is the political-economy model of Hasenfeld (1992), who feels it is particularly important to pay attention to the organizational environment and to political processes. The latter refers to the processes of bargaining, negotiation, coalition building, and the ways in which interest groups struggle for control of resources in order to set the organizational agenda. Following from the above, I would argue that goals and means are better understood as functions of political processes than as functions of the norms of efficiency and rationality.

Viewed in this fashion, accountability mechanisms are only one among many factors to consider when appraising the performance of the organization as a whole or of the individuals within the structure. The use, nonuse, or misuse of accountability results, and indeed other forms of data, have to be viewed in the context of the overall organizational environment. In fact, I would maintain that it is likely that the environment and the attendant political processes will define the role of accountability rather than the other way around.

This does not negate the importance of research and data as part of the process. Rather, I believe it is important to put research and data into the proper context. In the case of analyzing the role of accountability in a particular situation, it is important to raise such critical questions as "accountable to whom?" and "for what purpose?"

This is not to suggest that these are the only important questions to ask, or that one must subscribe to a political view of organizations. Rather, the point is that we as social workers would be better off adopting a critical, as opposed to an instrumental, view of accountability. Put another way, it is more important to begin asking the right questions than to begin counting.

The Costs of Accountability

Gummer (1978, p. 359), in his critique of organizational theories, claims that the rational model provides little insight into the real world of human-service organizations and is, in that sense, irrelevant. I would suggest that the same is true of the contemporary discussion of accountability in social work. It has generated little insight into the real issues of practice and therefore is irrelevant to their solution. In fact, contrary to the hopes of some researchers, I fear that the emphasis on instrumentation in the guise of accountability is more likely to widen rather than narrow the gap between research and practice.

I believe there is also a cost in the educational arena. Accountability as instrumentation begets designs that are appropriate for counting. As has been noted, the advocacy of such designs has been bolstered by the Council on Social Work Education accreditation requirements. Given the relatively limited amount of coursework devoted to research by most schools of social work, this inevitably results in a disaproportionate emphasis in the curriculum on a narrow range of designs. It also pushes an already pressured group of research educators into teaching the crucial research basics in a superficial fashion. At times, it surely does seem like we are losing sight of the forest for the trees.

The manner in which we have discussed accountability in social work has side-tracked us for too long. It's time for a change! Bloom and Fischer, writing in 1982, noted that the decade of the 1980s was the age of accountability. Paraphrasing a former president of the United States, we might ask; "Who among you is better off now than you were before the age of accountability?"

References

Bloom, M. & Fischer, J. (1982). *Evaluating practice: Guidelines for the accountable professional.* Englewood Cliffs, NJ: Prentice Hall.

Gummer, B. (1978). A power-politics approach to social welfare organizations. *Social Service Review, 53,* (3), 349–361.

Meyer, C. (1984). Integrating research and practice. *Social Work, 29,* (4), 323.

Hasenfeld, Y. (ed). (1992). *Human services as complex organizations.* Newbury Park, CA: Sage.

Rejoinder to Dr. Ruckdeschel

MARY LOU BALASSONE

It is difficult to write a rebuttal to Dr. Ruckdeschel's YES position because our positions with regard to accountability and evidence are more similar than different. I understand Dr. Ruckdeschel's argument to be that accountability should not be thought of as interchangeable with measurement and that the most important questions that social workers need to ask themselves are; "Accountable to whom?" and "Accountable for what purpose?" Those are the same questions that I deal with in my NO statement. Both of us make a plea for a broad definition of accountability and adequate evidence.

I agree that the simplistic equation of "accountability = evaluation of one's practice = counting" would have serious, negative influences on social work practice and reserach. But I do not think this equation is an accurate presentation of accountability's current role. This sort of reductionism causes the profession as many problems as the assumption that there are "good" and "bad" sorts of evidence. These dichotomies keep us arguing rather than searching for common ground on which to build appropriate practice evaluation techniques.

I also agree with Dr. Ruckdeschel's observation on the importance of organizational environment and politics in determining sources of evidence and the role of accountability in practice. These realities provide the basis for my saying that social workers need to be able to adapt various sources and types of evidence to a range of the different audiences. Social workers need to be able to illustrate their activities and the effects in ways that are understandable and acceptable to others. If we can not do this, those to whom we are accountable will define legitimate sources of evidence and types of accountability. Then, we truly do run the risk of being told "evidence equals counting."

Finally, I believe the implications of the various definitions of accountability and evidence have an impact that is not restricted to social work research education. As long as we continue to see accountability as connected only to research, we will fall short in educating effective social work practitioners. Accountability and evidence are integral parts of practice and are issues that should be part of practice courses. As I argue in the NO statement, social workers cannot act without answering innumerable practice questions. I think educators need to spend time in practice classes teaching students how to think consciously about their practice questions and how to investigate the sources of their knowledge about the answers to those questions. This is more than just the job of a research course or two; this should be one of the major goals of M.S.W.-level education.

NO

Mary Lou Balassone

Requirements for accountability and evidence are an integral part of professional practice. As social workers, accountability has to do with being answerable to a wide range of audiences for the services we deliver. Evidence has to do with being able to show outward signs or proof of our functioning in our helping roles. Both ideas are central to a practitioner's ability to provide professional and effective services to clients.

This chapter reviews the various audiences to whom social workers are accountable and then discusses the range of sources and types of evidence that can be used to establish accountability. I argue that social workers cannot perform their jobs without the use of evidence in making practice decisions and that an emphasis on accountability and evidence enhances social work practice. Finally, the specific tasks that social workers must perform in adapting various sources and types of evidence to the different audiences to whom they are accountable are reviewed.

Audiences to Whom Social Workers Are Accountable

There are a number of different audiences to whom practicing social workers are accountable. These include themselves (in making practice decisions), administrators and boards that oversee service programs, clients, other social workers, other professionals, policymakers, and service funders. Each of these groups can be thought of as having different requirements about the types of evidence and process of establishing accountability that is acceptable to them. Administrators may want evidence of program implementation, while funders may demand proof of a program's effectiveness. The social worker may be interested in gathering evidence of a particular intervention's impact on a number of clients, while individual clients are concerned with seeing that their situations have improved.

Perhaps the best place to start in building an understanding of the requirements of these various audiences is with a discussion of the individual practitioner's reliance on evidence in performing his or her job.

Practice Decision Making

Social workers are constantly faced with making decisions about the services that they provide and the approaches that they will use in their practice. These practice questions are wide ranging and include: What is the presenting problem of this client (client system)? What intervention(s) will work best? What program or policy changes are necessary to better meet the needs of clients? Who are the community leaders that should be involved in any change efforts? How should gaps in the current delivery systems be addressed?

A professional social worker cannot function without an ability to answer the constant flow of practice questions such as these. In fact, practitioners do constantly ask and answer these questions and their answers guide the actions they take in their social work practice. For example, the social worker who asks herself, "What program changes are needed to better meet this client's needs?" may use her own prior practice experiences in answering. On the other hand, she may gather input from some clients or look at the results of prior studies.

An emphasis on accountability and evidence requires that all social work practitioners be conscious of both the process used to answer practice questions and the types information used to arrive at these answers. Not surprisingly, most social workers do not always think consciously about their practice questions, nor do they typically investigate the sources of their knowledge about the answers to these questions. But think about the example presented above: the social worker needs to be clear about the source and type of information that is used to answer the practice question, because these sources may vary in terms of providing appropriate and adequate evidence for the decision. (As will be discussed later, the assessment of appropriateness and adequacy depends on the audience for the information.)

Attention to the ways in which practitioners "know" answers to practice questions is central to social workers' ability to perform their job tasks and cannot be separated from the professional practice of social work. That is, social workers would be unable to act without answering the series of practice questions that face them. I think the controversy arises not so much in agreeing that there is a need for accountability and evidence, but rather in the definition of what constitutes adequate sources of evidence and what are appropriate techniques for establishing accountability.

Sources of Evidence

There seems to be a distinction between "acceptable" and "unacceptable" sources of information for answering practice questions. As noted earlier, the audiences to whom the social worker is accountable may differ with respect to the acceptability of the various sources of evidence. Some of these sources are beliefs, theories, value choices, practice wisdom, tradition, authority, common sense, and empirical study. While none of these are inherently superior, each has a limited ability to provide viable answers to practice questions.

For example, knowledge based on adherence to a set of value choices or beliefs will not be acceptable to many audiences because such knowledge is seen as based solely on ideologies that various groups may not be agreed upon. On the other hand, knowledge from empirical study is not acceptable to some because of the artificial circumstances under which the information is gathered.

Types of Evidence

As social work has increased in professional status, the pressure for an empirical basis for answers to practice questions has grown. Unfortunately, this push for empirical answers has been interpreted by some as meaning there is a distinction between "good" and "bad" types of evidence. From some perspectives, good evidence is that which is quantitative, based on objective observations, and includes the experiences of large numbers of people. Less acceptable is evidence that is qualitative, based on subjective meanings and context, and includes the experiences of some smaller number of people.

Both of these definitions suffer from limitations. Quantification requires the reduction of information and experiences to numerical form and may result in the loss of the richness inherent in contextual data. For example, quantitative information might not be the best source of knowledge about a particular client's interpretation of a problem. Qualitative information is often viewed as being more susceptible to bias and, therefore, is discounted as an inappropriate source of evidence. For example, this type of information would probably not be used as a source of knowledge about the incidence and prevalence of a particular problem.

Obviously, these "good versus bad" and "acceptable versus unacceptable" distinctions are not value free, but rather rest on deeply held beliefs and assumptions about the world and how best to "know" things in this world. A discussion of these different approaches to knowledge, evidence, and accountability are beyond the scope of this paper.[1]

Adapting Sources and Types of Evidence to Various Audiences

I take a rather pragmatic view of the above debates and argue that because social workers are accountable to a range of audiences, we are probably best served by rejecting ideas about the absolute correctness or superiority of any one position regarding acceptable sources and types of evidence. A more relativistic stance will probably best meet the needs of the profession.

There are two tasks that social workers must be able to perform in order to adopt this more relativistic stance. First, they need to be able to match practice questions with reasonable techniques for gathering evidence and showing accountability. Second, social workers need to be able to translate the meaning of various methods and sources of evidence (be it practice wisdom or scientific study) to their different audiences.

Let me provide an example. You are a social worker in a newly funded project to provide services to women and children with AIDS. You have developed a case-management referral system to ensure that these clients receive the range of services that they need. Now funders want to know if the interventions work; is their money being used effectively? It is unlikely that either your "practice wisdom" (intuition) or information derived from a single client will be acceptable to the funders as evidence of effectiveness. Your job is to show the funders how you "know," from these and other sources of evidence, that the service works. You need to examine the process you used to know about the service's effectiveness and make the process a conscious and explicit one. This will probably involve showing quantitative evidence of the intervention's effectiveness (number of people served, number of services received, percentage of clients with improved health and mental health status, etc.); evidence that is understandable and acceptable to the funder.

Another audience interested in the effectiveness of this case-management system may be the clients whom it is intended to serve. They may be interested in a different sort of evidence. That is, they may want evidence of the case manager's intimate understanding of their unique situation and needs. This information is of a more interpretative and qualitative nature. Another way of showing evidence of effectiveness to clients is to involve them in monitoring and collecting information regarding the services that they receive and the progress they make over time.

As the social worker, you may be interested in a variety of types of evidence and might draw on a range of information (anecdotal accounts, surveys of providers, reports from clients) in accumulating evidence of the intervention's effectiveness. For example, knowledge regarding service gaps that impede effective service delivery might be inductively derived from your practice experience. In addition, you may also be interested in assessing the case-management system's effectiveness with clients of diverse ethnic backgrounds. You should collect evidence for this assessment by using qualitative case studies.

So, as this example shows, there is a range of types of evidence and of ways of accessing evidence that can be useful in answering practice questions. The skilled practitioner becomes adept at matching evidence needs to practice questions and then translating the answers to the various audiences to whom the worker is accountable.

Conclusion

It seems to me that social workers are constantly involved in asking and answering practice questions in order to perform the tasks of their jobs. The answering of these questions requires the use of evidence and, although it is not always an explicit process, social workers perform their jobs by relying on various sources and types of evidence. They, in fact, cannot meet the goals of service delivery without an ongoing process of asking and answering practice questions. The process of answering these questions is in many ways an accountability process; a process that leads to being answerable and responsible professionals.

Social workers need to be able to show others how we arrived at various practice decisions. The challenge to each of us is to be clear about the process and nature of the evidence we use in making those decisions. There is inherently no good/bad evidence or acceptable/unacceptable accountability process. Rather these vary, depending on the nature of our practice questions and the audience for our evidence of effectiveness.

Notes

1. A discussion of different approaches to knowledge development is an ongoing one that fills many books and articles in a range of disciplines. For a review of these issues from a social work perspective, please see the following articles: Fraser, Taylor, Jackson, and O'Jack (1991); Haworth (1984); Heineman (1981); and Peile (1988).

References

Fraser, M., Taylor, M.J., Jackson, R. & O'Jack, J. (1991). Social work and science: Many ways of knowing? *Social Work Research and Abstracts, 27,* 5–15.

Haworth, G.O. (1984). Social work research, practice, and paradigms. *Social Service Review, 58,* 343–357.

Heineman, M. B. (1981). The obsolete scientific imperative in social work research. *Social Service Review, 55,* 371–397.

Peile, C. (1988). Research paradigms in social work: From stalemate to creative synthesis. *Social Service Reveiw, 62,* 1–19.

Rejoinder to Dr. Balassone

Roy Ruckdeschel

Dr. Balassone's defense of accountability is both interesting and somewhat unusual. She departs from the more typical instrumental approach to accountability and instead begins to move in the direction of raising questions about the importance of audiences. However, the argument lacks the kind of critical perspective needed to fully engage the issues and to ground the arguments and give them meaning. Dr. Balassone frames accountability in terms of the necessity for social workers to be answerable to a range of audiences through providing evidence of functioning. She characterizes her position as pragmatic and relativistic, with the task of the social worker being that of mediating/translating between evidence and audience. Thus, it seems that her argument and her defense of accountability rest on the nature of that relationship. Accordingly, one must examine her views about the nature of evidence, practice, and audiences.

Dr. Balassone suggests that much of the controversy surrounding accountability has to do with the debate over what constitutes adequate evidence. She "resolves" the matter by stating that there is inherently no superior or acceptable (versus unacceptable) sources of evidence nor any good (versus bad) types of evidence. Unfortunately, her distinction between type and source of data is somewhat vague, as is the grounding for this position, because she notes that the debate over evidence is beyond the scope of the paper. Despite this disclaimer, I presume she is asking us to accept her "relativistic" stance at face value. However, I would suspect that many advocates and some opponents of accountability would not agree with this position. The problem lies with the fact that Dr. Balassone ignores the crucial issue of the rules of evidence. While perspectives may differ on the nature of evidence, each has its own internal rules for what constitutes good or bad data. The effect of Balassone's "anything goes" approach is contradictory in that, on one hand, she maintains that the use of evidence is a critical part of accountable practice, but, on the other hand, she suggests that there are no valid criteria for judging the adequacy of the evidence. Having stripped the notion of evidence of any meaning, she suggests that choice of evidence also depends on the nature of practice questions and the audiences to whom we are answerable.

Alas, the author never really specifies the nature of these practice questions, nor how these questions would filter the choice of evidence. Instead, we are simply told that one of the main advantages of accountability procedures is that they make the decision-making process more conscious and more overt. Nor does her example of the AIDS project shed much light on the issue, because the only practice question addressed is that of effectiveness. The significance of practice context is not at all discussed; in fact, both in text and in example, one senses the image of an autonomous, free-floating accountable practitioner. This is an interesting image, but of doubtful relationship to practice reality.

Given the above, one is left with the conclusion that the linchpin for Dr. Balassone's advocacy of accountability must be her claim that social workers are accountable to various audiences, which have "different requirements" for the acceptability of evidence, and that it is the task of the social worker to match/translate the evidence with the audience. I would certainly agree with her that the issue of varying audiences must be addressed if accountability is to have any meaning. It is not clear, however, how the task is to be accomplished. Not only is her view of evidence ambiguous, but Dr. Balassone also paints an overly rational and consenusal view of these different audiences. Perhaps this is why the accountability issues in her illustrative discussion of an AIDS program seem so nonproblematic. This picture runs contrary to what we know about human-service organizations. It is not always clear who constitutes the relevant audiences. Likewise, audiences differ not in terms of evidence requirements, but more fundamentally, in terms of interests—interests which are frequently in conflict. Importantly, audiences also differ widely in the amount of power that they have to define a situation. Her example is an ironic one because the provision of services to deal with AIDS has been politically and emotionally charged. If one views such a project more critically, would there not be more than the three audiences identified, would there not be the possibility of conflicting interests among the audiences, and would not different audiences (both known and unknown) have different amounts of power to affect both the program and its evaluation?

In conclusion, what is presented as a pragmatic defense of accountability is in fact neither pragmatic nor do-able. It is an argument without a referent. The need for a critical questioning of accountability remains.

DEBATE 2

Are Traditional Empirical Research Methods Inherently Biased against People of Color?

Sung Sil (Sue) Sohng is an assistant professor at the School of Social Work, University of Washington, Seattle, where she teaches advanced research and social work practice in the M.S.W. program. Her current research and writing interests concentrate on chronic mental illness, empowerment practice, and participatory action research. She also consults with community agencies in cross-cultural practice, homeless, and mentally ill programs.

José B. Ashford is an associate professor at the Arizona State University School of Social Work and Interdisciplinary Doctoral Program in Justice Studies where he teaches human behavior and the social environment, pyschopathology, social work and the law, and social science in law courses. His publications and research interests focus on discretionary justice and social science in law and in law-like systems of the criminal, mental-health, and juvenile-justice systems. He is an expert witness in capital mitigation cases and provides consultation and program evaluation services to child-abuse and substance-abuse prevention agencies and to agencies involved in the criminal-justice and mental-health interface.

YES

SUNG SIL (SUE) SOHNG

Historically, social work has participated in the "discovery" of numerous social problems, from domestic violence, teen-age pregnancy, and sex abuse to welfare dependency, substance abuse, and delinquency. Many of these social problems have been brought to public attention through research documenting their incidence and impact on individuals and society. While empirical research has played an important role in advocacy and social reform for the oppressed and disadvantaged, it often has brought negative consequences to these communities. Although these limitations are present in research with all oppressed groups, I will restrict my concern to communities of color.

Research in minority communtities has been criticized because it has not directed sufficient attention to unique conceptual and methodological problems endemic to the study of people of color. Criticisms focus on the use of culturally biased measures, stereotypic interpretations, inattention to the effects of community history and institutional discrimination, and lack of accountability to the community studied. These criticisms raise a renewed doubt about research methodology that is grounded in positivist assumptions and that emphasizes rationality, impersonality, and "value-free" objectivity. Through an explicit "ethnic lens," troubling aspects of this dominant model of social work research are examined and an emerging minority perspective is presented in the conduct of research with people of color.

The Myth of "Value-Free" Objectivity

Why in recent years is research on minority communities plagued with charges of racism and elitism? This is partly because traditional empirical research fails to recognize issues of value influence embedded in research methodology. This dominant research model is grounded in the belief that knowledge can be objectively derived and verified, primarily by preventing the researcher's influence from affecting the observed outcome. Methodologically, this means researchers can and should stand outside and apart from the phenomena being studied.

This belief has been seriously challenged over the past few decades by members of oppressed groups (i.e., people of color, women, and the poor). They reject the conceptual validity of the detached outsider, on the grounds that the researcher is a member of a society and a culture and has a position within a collectivity of colleagues, which affects the way in which he or she sees the world. The values that researchers hold and the ideological perspectives that guide them exert powerful influences on choices they make in the course of inquiry: from the problem that they selected for study, to the instruments and the analytic modes used, to the interpretations, conclusions, and recommendations made (Guba & Lincoln, 1989).

Such an ideological and value context is particularly salient in research on racial minority communities. Until now, research on minority communities has been produced by members of the dominant majority. These researchers are in every respect—politically, economically, socially, and culturally—more powerful than the members of the minority community whom they studying. An unfortunate consequence has been the neglect and exclusion of minority perspectives. The prevailing visions, accounts, and conceptualizations of minority issues are shaped and influenced by a dominant perspective. As Popkewitz (1990) points out, the appearance of "detached outsider" is easy to maintain when researchers' values reflect society's dominant views. There then seems to be no reason to scrutinize the concepts an theories that researchers employ. This posture is consistent with the logic of empirical research, which tends to define research problems as apolitical, asocial, and ahistorical, and to remove social and historical aspects of minority concerns from the construction of research procedures. A common pursuit in early race and ethnic studies, for example, was the comparison of races by means of "intelligence" tests and other sorts of tests. Attention was directed to "intelligence differences," while ignoring social, economic, and cultural differences between blacks and whites, which are so much a part of the problems in race relations. Likewise, Native Americans are seen as prone to alcoholism and suicide; Hispanics are described as exhibiting tendencies toward criminal behavior and undependability (Zane & Sue, 1986).

Research that documents only differences between races offers no understanding of why those differences exist or how such differences may be attenuated; and therefore, it tends to reinforce (or create) any negative stereotypes. Furthermore, this approach implicitly promotes an understanding of minority issues as residing within individuals, despite social work's commitment to a "person-in-environment" approach. Such research generally concludes that the problems encountered by people of color are the result of their personal deficits and of their cultural tradition, which deviate from those of the majority. This frame of reference, bolstered by "scientific" findings, has a kind of institutionalized legitimacy that may discredit minority views and disempower minority communities.

Concerned with generalizability, prediction, and control, researchers use standard concepts, instruments, and procedures developed for a majority population group. But these devices can be inappropriate in the study of minority peoples, whose cultural perspective and historical experience differ from the majority. Standard designs in previous survey studies, for example, seldom include enough people of color, resulting in minority members being "statistically invisible" in most public opinion data (Smith, 1987). Too often, the emergent body of knowledge in social research excludes people of color and neglects their histories and life situations. The paucity of crucial information on most minority communities may lead to their disenfranchisement by limiting the presence of their perspectives, visions, and accounts in the construction of social work knowledge.

At another level, Rogler (1989) voiced a similar concern for the appropriateness of methods and procedures across different populations. Traditional empirical studies have typically assumed that ethnic minority behaviors should be judged according to established norms. However, this becomes problematic when ethnic relations are conceptualized in terms of the Western perspective which is then applied as universal. For example, one of the constructs that Rogler examined in his study of families of schizophrenics in Puerto Rico was family decision making. This topic is easily measured among whites by asking respondents to indicate who makes decisions, such as where to go on a vacation, or which schools students should attend. Initial data on Puerto Rican respondents indicated that the concept of decision making measured by the same items was irrelevant to them because their financial situation never required those types of decisions. The concept of decision making was later discarded and replaced with that of division of labor, which was appropriate and relevant to the understanding of these family dynamics.

As Marin and Marin (1991) observe, social research is a human, not entirely objective, process. Methods and procedures used reflect ‘‘the culturally based world view of those individuals doing the research, including their perceptions, norms, values, and biases’’ (p. 66). Lack of appreciation for cultural and historical sensitivity often yields biased information, masks important relationships, and prevents valid interpretations of the findings.

An Emerging Minority Perspective

What we have, then, is the recognition of science as a social institution and as a social practice, dependent for its warrant on the often tacitly held beliefs within particular social and political communities. This recognition is the starting point for an emerging minority perspective. This viewpoint recognizes social problems and concepts as political claims instead of granting them privileged status as universal truths. Implicit in this stance is that many issues concerning race and culture consists of paradoxes in which two or more cherished principles or ideals are valid, but contradictory. For example, one perplexing and complicated issue is the current impact of racism. If ethnic minority groups fail to achieve equality, who should be held accountable? A self-determinism perspective praises society for changes and holds ethnic minorities solely responsible for their respective difficulties. A racism viewpoint claims that, despite changes, society is still largely implicated in racial problems.

A minority perspective holds that many ethnic minority issues are conflicts in which the clash of values has not been clearly recognized. More often than not, such practice results in the following: 1) one side of the conflict is dominant at the expense of the other; 2) the dominant side is perceived by many as universal truth; and 3) the dominant perspective is one that fails to recognize the legitimacy of minority views (Zane & Sue, 1986).

A minority perspective rejects ‘‘the one story,’’ ‘‘the one reality—one description’’ notion as an adequate rendering of the objective of science. The minority perspective is to search for differences and distinctions that can lead to divergent perspectives in understanding human behaviors and interests. The argumentation, debate, and cross-fertilization concerning these interests have a complementary quality, which makes for a more serious debate about knowledge building in social work. It also enables a certain humility, as we are continually made aware of the precarious quality of our knowledge and agendas.

This minority perspective does not specify particular research designs, measures, or data analysis techniques. It is more relevant to the basic frame work of research. Specifically, three dimensions shape the minority research perspective. First, a rigorous analysis and critique of dominant perspectives and institutions that affect ethnic and racial minorities. This perspective rarely presents minority peoples' behavior without attention to the conditions of social regulations, unequal distribution, and power that shape their lives. Their perception of choices and their place in society becomes a critical analytic framework.

Second, a cultural–critical approach that fosters diversity. Ethnic cultural heritage—folklore, popular knowledge, or popular wisdom—remains outside the formal scientific structure and is constantly being devalued and suppressed by the majority culture. An emerging interest in ethnic cultures, a distinct sense of peoplehood, means of survival, and the role of creative expressions in sustaining minority communities' self-valuation are important dimensions in countering the devaluation of their histories and life situations by the dominant society. This approach helps re-appraise minority issues and reduce the distortion and fragmentation of knowledge about the minority experience.

The third dimension is ethical. Making ethical reasoning conscious and explicit is a powerful means for improving all phases of the research process. Questions can help to make imbedded values explicit, such as, "Who does the content of this research empower?" "What does this method of research empower?" "Whose point of view does it champion?" "If I were in that person's situation, would I be satisfied with having this done to me?" This process—seeing how others with alternative views see and reason through the ethical implications—keeps one aware of hidden influences and unexamined political and cultural assumptions.

Social scientists and researchers play an increasing role in social, economic, and public policy. Important in this is their status as scientists. What they recommend has the force of knowledge, and not mere opinion. In studying minority communities, social scientists have a special responsibility to examine basic assumptions, develop culturally sensitive conceptual models, and empirically determine the meaningfulness of substantive concepts for minority people under study.

References

Guba, E., & Lincoln, Y. (1989). *Fourth generation evaluation.* Newbury Park, CA: Sage.

Marin G., & Marin, B. (1991). *Research with Hispanic populations.* Newbury Park, CA: Sage.

Popkewitz, T. S. (1990). Whose future? Whose past? Notes on critical theory and methodology. In E. Guba (Ed.), *The Paradigm dialog,* (pp. 46–66). Newbury Park, CA: Sage.

Reason, P., & Rowan, J. (Eds.). (1981). *Human inquiry: A sourcebook of new paradigm research.* NY: John Wiley & Sons.

Rogler, L. H. (1989). The meaning of culturally sensitive research in mental health. *American Journal of Psychiatry, 146,* 296–303.

Smith, A. W. (1987). Problems and progress in the measurement of black public opinion. *American Behavioral Scientists, 30*(4), 441–455.

Zane, N. & Sue, S. (1986). Reappraisal of ethnic minority issues. In E. Seidman & J. Rappaport (Eds.), *Redefining social problems* (pp. 289–304). New York: Plenum Press.

Rejoinder to Dr. Sohng

JOSÉ B. ASHFORD

Dr. Sohng's paper is a solid review of recent issues raised in the social work and social-science literature about biases in the measurement of phenomena involving people of color. She also presents a biting account of the social and the structural barriers to the inclusion of minority voices in the practice of science. Because this account is consonant with many widely held views in the sociology of science, I have minimal disagreement with the general thrust of her arguments. However, I do disagree with some of her reasoning about the role of traditional empirical methods in studying minority concerns.

Although Dr. Sohng challenges the legitimacy of a research methodology grounded in assumptions of positivism, she offers no alternative methodology. Instead, she provides a compelling outline of the kind of minority perspective needed to guide the use of traditional empirical methods. In this perspective, she presents several assumptions that clarify the components of a minority lens that she deems appropriate for scientific practice. In my opinion, this implies that she supports traditional methods and is merely offering a needed perspective to combat the exclusion of minority views in the practice of science. If this is her position, then we have no fundamental disagreement. However, I am not confident that this is her entire position.

In a number of places in Dr. Sohng's paper, she implies that unique methods are needed to study the problem of persons of color. However, no unique methods were proffered. This raises a number of questions about the reasoning underlying these statements. If these statements are being used to challenge the inherent insensitivity of traditional empirical methods, then I am puzzled as to why she did not clarify what such an approach would look like.

Some of my strong reactions to a view of her comments about empirical methods were triggered by her glib use of the term ''unique.'' Although I admit this may be somewhat of an over-reaction, I believe that comments of this nature have contributed to substantial confusion in our literature about the factors reinforcing insensitivities in social work research. In my view, ideology plays a far more important role in biasing our knowledge about minorities than does the use of empirical methods. Are empirical methods the issue or is the issue better framed as a problem of ideology? Many disputes about methodology have evolved into what I consider irrelevant controversies about empirical assumptions. This is not to suggest that I am opposed to alternative modes of knowledge inquiry that are capable of transcending male-Eurocentric justificationism (Bartley, 1964, 1962; Joseph, Reddy & Searle-Chatterjee, 1990) in Western social science and epistemology. Moreover, I believe that nonjustificational or non-authoritative approaches to knowledge inquiry are an inevitability in a post-modern and global village. In my view, much of the fault for the insensitivities to ethnic and racial realities lies with the concepts and theories of scientists and not with their methods of measurement. That is, I would support the contention that minority issues require conceptualizations that are ''unique'' to minority perspectives, but not that they require unique methods of observation.

Because Dr. Sohng concludes her arguments with remarks that imply that she supports the use of traditional empirical research to document minority perspectives, I was unable to identify her position on the general issue being examined in this debate. That is, it is unclear whether she was advocating against the use of traditional empirical methods in studying persons of color. I attribute some of these inconsistencies in her reasoning to her failure to make clear distinctions in her arguments between issues involving inherent biases in methods and issues involving inherent biases in the policies and the ideology of the social scientists.

In summary, I believe Dr. Sohng's arguments offer substantial support for the conclusion that the community of scientists participate in a social institution that perpetuates the hegemony of dominate group perspectives on minority concerns. Her paper also clarifies how suspect ideology held by scientists contributes to findings that are inherently biased. However, her arguments fail to provide a coherent justification for the proposition being debated in this controversy on inherent insensitivity in traditional empirical methods. That is, I believe that the problem is not with the methods, but with the social institutions of the scientists.

References

Bartley, W. W. (1962). *Retreat to commitment.* New York, NY: Alfred A. Knopf.

Bartley, W. W. (1964). Rationality versus the theory of rationality. In M. Bunge (Ed.), *The critical approach to science and philosophy* (pp. 3–31). New York: Free Press.

Joseph, G. G., Reddy, V., & Searle-Chatterjee, M. (1990). Eurocentrism in the social sciences. *Race & Class. 33,*(4), 1–26.

NO

JOSÉ B. ASHFORD

The general issue addressed in this paper is whether traditional empirical methods and findings of scientific research are inherently biased or insufficiently sensitive to concerns of people of color. In response to this issue, I will argue that any assertion of inherent biases is predicated on a number of specious assumptions that ignore important realties about the use of traditional empirical methods. These unfounded assumptions ignore an important distinction in philosophy of science between the methods of science and the "administration" or "policy" of science (Radnitsky, 1988; Weinberg, 1988).

In this brief paper, I will affirm the proposition that there is not a distinct methodology of science for studying the concerns of minorities and women. This does not mean that I am opposed to nontraditional approaches to knowledge inquiry (Ashford, 1990), or that I dispute the need for female and minority voices in the practice of science. Instead, my fundamental aim is to confront many of the glib assertions in the social work literature about concepts such as "traditional" and "empirical." These facile assertions can be a significant barrier to future social change and reform efforts.

Preliminary Remarks

Before presenting this apology for traditional empirical methods, I need to clarify a number of key assumptions underlying my arguments against the proposition being examined in this controversy. First of all, I need to articulate my views on traditional empirical science and how these views are being threatened by a number of factious arguments in the social work literature. These arguments involve a number of false claims about ethnographic and other qualitative research methods. That is, some scholars in social work imply in their writings that qualitative methods and ethnographic principles of research are inherently less biased toward racial and ethnic concerns than are quantitative methods. They also imply that qualitative methods do not involve the measurement or the enumeration of qualitative phenomena. In my view, this rhetoric has obscured many of our important advances in eliminating perverse forms of scientific research on ethnic and racial phenomena.

Lessons from the Sociology of Deviance

In my formal research training on crime and deviance, ethnography and qualitative research methods were considered traditional approaches to studying all facets of deviant behavior. In fact, they were widely promoted by several mainstream traditions in sociology: the Chicago school of symbolic interactionism, labelling theory, social phenomenology, and ethnomethodology. Although these traditions have had substantial support in the social-science literature, they also have been criticized widely by Marxist and other critical theorists from the Frankfort School. In fact, these traditions were perceived by many critical theorists as supporting fundamental traditions in Western philosophical thought that maintain a number of questionable ethnocentric assumptions (Taylor, Walton, & Young, 1973)

Thus, in my view, qualitative methods are not necessarily as nontraditional as some social work scholars have implied. In fact, the National Institute of Justice, a relatively conservative and traditional research institution, has advocated for the use of ethnographic reserach in studying a variety of substantive issues in the field of crime and delinquency. Qualitative research is recognized widely in the social-science community as a key component of doing good science. It is distinguished from quantitative methods, in terms of its ontological assumptions: subjective versus objective approaches to measuring the essence of social reality (LeCroy, Ashford & Macht, 1989; Mullen, 1985.)

Still, ''subjective scientists'' are just as likely as ''objective scientists'' to adhere to epistemological assumptions from empiricism or positivism. That is, some scholars tend to ignore the fact that qualitative research can be as empirical in its measurement approaches as approaches to science that focus on objective aspects of reality (Athens, 1984b). Glib characterizations of ethnographic and other qualitative research methods ae also disturbing because they ignore their highly ignoble relationship with numerous examples of scientific racism (Joseph, Reddy, & Searle-Chatterjee, 1990; TAWA, 1983). For instance, most early anthropological studies relied heavily on ethnographic methods to document many ethnocentric and racist assumptions. In my view, racism and ethnocentrism are not fundamental products of specific methodologies, but products of concepts and theories that consciously or unconsciously seek to assert the superiority of one group over another. These biased assumptions about ethnic and racial phenomena require much closer scrutiny from members of the scientific community than do the debates about the inherent sensitivity of quantitative versus qualitative research methods.

The Scientific Community and the Role of Qualitative Methods

In traditional science, it is widely recognized that qualitative methods are most effective for describing previously ''under-described'' facets of social reality (Athens, 1984a; Taylor, Walton & Young, 1973). That is, they help us to guard against the reification of false conceptions by outside observers of unfamiliar social realities. These well recognized principles of good science do not imply that empirical measurement is inappropriate or inherently insensitive to minority concerns. Furthermore, few scientists, whether subjectivist or objectivist, would assert that ''numbers have the capacity to speak to us without prior interpretation'' (Grove, 1989, p. 81). This is not to suggest that historical figures in science were free from making such claims. Grove (1989) clarifies this point in his examination of Karl Pearson's invalid belief in the objectivity of numbers:

> The idea that a number produced by a measurement is of necessity objective—''hard fact''—is obviously fallacious since the measurement may itself be affected by subjective factors: desires, prejudices, biases, which may often be unconscious. Pearson seems to have been wholly unaware of this possibility. (p.81)

Although Pearson's view was accepted in early scientific circles, it has been vigorously repudiated in current philosophy of science disputations.

This brings me to my next important argument. Science is a collective activity that limits knowledge to those observations on which independent observers can agree (Grove, 1989). Independent observers have not agreed about the views of Pearson and other naive empiricists. Furthermore, the literature is replete with instances in which minority and majority members of the scientific community have questioned empirical findings that lead to racist and ethnocentric conclusions. Most of these identified biases have been associated with studies seeking to discern racial, cultural, or group differences. In my view this speaks directly to one of the most important ethical issues confronting research in social work. Are racial-difference or cultural-difference paradigms appropriate frameworks for guiding social work researchers?

Difference Paradigms in Social Work Research

Unlike some of the social-science disciplines, social work did not uniformly abandon individual-difference and cultural-difference hypotheses in the 1960s. For instance, many researchers involved in the sociology of crime and deviance were opposed to personality, cultural-value, and individual-difference research. Schur (1973) and Matza (1964) are excellent examples. These popular theorists voiced strong opposition to studying value, personality, and biological differences in persons who had been labeled deviant by society. Their position has come under close scrutiny in recent disputes on individual-difference research in the study of crime (Andrews & Wormith, 1989, Gibbons, 1989). It is assumed by anti-difference researchers in criminology that studying differences tends either to marginalize natural variations in behavior or to perpetuate societal reifications that have no scientific basis in reality. Comparable views are evident in the works of Ryan (1971) and Valentine (1968) on poverty and culture. Is this tradition among scientists trained in the 1960s and early 1970s likely to perpetuate insensitivity to important cultural differences?

In my view, there is an urgent need for a response from our profession to this issue. Many of our present-day researchers were exposed in their academic training to various anti-individual and group-difference hypotheses. This training has contributed to a definite skepticism in some scientific circles about the legitimacy of cultural-difference and racial-difference research. Their philosophical position supports a ''universalism'' that in many instances ignores important cultural realities contributing to socially meaningful differences or variations in behavior. In other instances, this bias toward universalism is useful in debunking invalid forms of social imagery that have no scientific basis in reality. For instance, universal principles about race in the biological sciences have helped to dispel many myths supporting the superiority of one racial group over another (Tawa, 1983). This point is discussed at length by Grove (1989):

> All human beings belong to the same natural species and all human groups are mutually fertile . . . Biologically, then, there is very little to be said for race. The basic mistake made by many of our nineteenth century forebears, was in thinking that the major groupings of humankind (conceived in terms of their distinctive, visible and mainly physical characteristics) constituted separate species. This is not to say that races have no existence; but they exist only as socio-cultural entities, not as biologically meaningful aggregations (p. 79)

This universalistic conceptualization of race was valuable in early scientific research in dispelling assumptions asserting an inherent inferiority in the biological nature of various racial classifications. It was also useful in challenging legal convenants against racial and ethnic minorities in housing law. Thus, it is not possible to summarily dismiss universalistic images in social work research. Besides, there are equally inherent dangers in adhering to a cultural determinism that foreshadows clear evidence of universal aspects of nature. Some form of comprise is obviously warranted. This compromise needs to strike not only a balance between these extremes, but provide a clear set of guidelines that will not deny the important role played by ideology and morals in scientific policy.

In summary, I believe that traditional empirical science is an instrument that can be used for purposes of liberation or oppression. Traditional empirical science has been very helpful in litigation campaigns in school desegregation and capital punishment cases (Loh, 1984). It can also be useful in other areas of modern life that are of concern to minority persons. For this reason, I believe that the most important issue for our consideration is how to clarify the ideological, social, and moral underpinnings of the profession's current research agenda. Like Thomas Kuhn, I am reducing the development of science and knowledge in social work to a sociological problem (Munz, 1988). This sociological problem is the result of inherent biases in the social structure and policy of science in social work. These biases influence and maintain inherent structural inequalities within the scientific institutions of social work. The upshot of this problem of stratification in science (see Cole & Cole [1973]) is that a variety of minority voices are being excluded from the practice of science. In order to rectify this real issue of inherent insensitivity to minority groups, we will need to reform our current science policies and theories of culture (Rogler, 1989). As Grove (1989) has pointed out:

> Science will not be much affected by those intellectuals who attack its methodological and epistemological foundations on humanist grounds. The more substantial threat to science . . . comes from trends in its organization and practice. (p. 177)

References

Andrews, D. A., & Wormith, J. S. (1989). Personality and crime: Knowledge destruction and construction in criminology. *Justice Quarterly, 6,* 289–309.

Ashford, J. B. (1990). Penetrating the veil of appearance in empirical clinical practice. In L. Videka-Sheraman, & W. J. Reid, (eds.). *Advances in empirical clinical practice.* Silver Spring, MD: NASW Press, 352–348.

Athens, L. H. (1984a). Blumer's method of naturalistic inquiry: A critical examination. *Studies in Symbolic Interaction, 5,* 241–247.

Athens, L. H. (1984b). Scientific criteria for evaluating qualitative studies. *Studies in Symbolic Interactionism, 5,* 259–258.

Cole, J. R., & Cole S. (1973). *Social stratification in science.* Chicago, IL: University of Chicago Press.

Gibbons, D. C. (1989) Comment—Personality and crime: Non-Issues, real issues and a theory and research agenda. *Justice Quarterly, 6,* 313–332.

Grove, J. W. (1989). *In defense of science: Science, technology, and politics in modern society.* Toronto: University of Toronto Press.

Joseph, G. G., Reddy, V., & Searles-Chatterjee, M. (1990). Euro-centrism in the social sciences. *Race & Class, 31,*(4), 1–26.

LeCroy, C. W., Ashford, J. B., & Macht, M. W. (1989). A framework for analyzing knowledge utilization in social work practice. *Journal of Sociology and Social Welfare, 16,* 3–17.

Loh, W. D. (1984). *Social research in the judicial process.* New York: Russell Sage.

Matza, D. (1964). *Delinquency and drift.* New York: Wiley.

Mullen, E. J. (1984). Methodological dilemmas in social work research. *Social Work Research & Abstracts,* 12–20.

Munz, P. (1988). The philosophical lure of the sociology of knowledge. In G. Radnitsky (Ed.), *Centripetal forces in the sciences.* New York: Paragon House.

Radnitzky, G. (1988). Introduction. In G. Radnitsky (Ed.), *Centripetal forces in the sciences.* New York: Paragon House.

Rogler, L. H. (1989). The meaning of culturally sensitive research in mental health. *American Journal of Psychiatry, 146,* 296–303.

Ryan, W. (1971). *Blaming the victim.* New York: Pantheon Books.

Schur, E. M. (1973). *Radical non-intervention: Rethinking the delinquency problem.* Englewood Clifs, NJ: Prentice Hall.

Tawa, E. (1983). Historical aspects of the question of science and racism. In Unesco (Ed.), *Racism, science and pseudo-science.* Vendome: The United Nations.

Taylor, I, Walton, P., & Young, J. (1973) *The new criminology.* London; Routledge & Kegan Paul.

Valentine, C. A. (1968). *Culture and poverty.* Chicago, IL: University of Chicago Press.

Weinberg, A. M. (1988). Values in science: Unity as a value in administration of pure science. In G. Radnitzky (Ed.), *Centripetal forces in the sciences.* New York: Paragon House.

Rejoinder to Dr. Ashford

SUNG SIL (SUE) SOHNG

Dr. Ashford and I agree on a number of points, perhaps most importantly that racism and ethnocentrism are not products of specific research methods, but "products of concepts and theories that consciously or unconsciously seek to assert the superiority of one group over another." In my YES paper, I refer to such concepts and theories as *ideology.* Although there are divergent theories of ideology, I use the term to mean a combination of beliefs, attitudes, and interpretations of reality that are derived from one's experiences, knowledge of what one presumes to be facts, and one's values.

The relevance of ideology to research arises from the fact that every research tool or procedure is embedded inextricably in commitments to particular versions of the world. To use a questionnaire, use an attitude scale, take the role of a participant observer, select a random sample, measure IQ, and so on, is to be involved in conceptions of the world that allow these instruments to be used for the purposes conceived. In other words, research instruments and methods are formed through the interrelation of questions, concepts, and procedures. The questions at hand, the concepts brought to bear on the investigation, and the particular contextual variations contain ambiguities and complexities that researchers work through to shape their methods and inquiry. It is in this matrix of research that racism and ethnocentricism can be properly discussed.

Two collateral issues about research methods emerge from the consideration of this interplay. One is the overcommitment to the method of science in established social work research practices. For example, Rubin and Babbie

(1989) mentioned that values, subjective views, ideology, and personal politics may infiltrate social research endeavors, but accepted research techniques should enable the same results to emerge when different subjective views are used:

> Many of the established techniques of science function to cancel out or hold in check our human shortcomings, especially those we are unaware of. Otherwise, we might look into the world and never see anything but ourselves—our personal biases and beliefs. (p.66)

Similarly, Borowski (1988) has stated:

> Social workers with quite different ideas, beliefs, motives, attitudes, and values can, in fact, achieve similar results if they employ scientific procedures and techniques. (p. 52)

It is in this sense that social work research has become procedural, technical, and one-dimensional. The development of knowledge and science tends to be separated from social movements, historical conditions, or political interests, except in terms of a technical issue to control bias and prejudice. Increasingly, however, such conventional practices of science have been criticized by feminists, critical theorists, and nonorthodox researchers. They argue that history contains stories of grave injustices perpetrated by leading scientists operating with what they thought to be the best research methods of their day. As Namenwirth (9186) writes:

> Repeatedly, in the course of history, the pronouncements of scientists have been used to rationalize, justify, and naturalize dominant ideologies and the status quo. Slavery, colonialism, laissez faire capitalism, communism, patriarchy, sexism, and racism have all been supported, at one time or another, by the work of scientists, a pattern that continues unabated into the present . . . By draping their scientific activities in claims of neutrality, detachment, and objectivity, scientists augment the perceived importance of their views, absolve themselves of social responsibility for the applications of their work, and leave their (unconscious) minds wide open to political and cultural assumptions. (p. 29).

A second collateral issue is the influence of dominance and power in the production of knowledge. Science cannot be properly understood as solely one of the conflict of ideas without locating the practices of science within its social conditions. The power of traditional empirical research in social work derives not from its explanatory power, but from the effect of human, capital, and ideological orthodoxy, which controls the direction and leadership of the social work profession. Issues of dominance, apparent in our society, are reflected in what Dr.

Ashford refers to as ''stratification . . . in which a variety of minority voices are being excluded from the practice of science.'' The introduction of minority questions challenges that dominance. Acquiring a critical consciousness of method or knowledge is unlikely when different human interests and different dispositions toward the world are suppressed or unavailable. What is pervasive often goes unexamined.

Despite our opposing point of departure to the debate, we arrive at a similar conclusion. I agree fundamentally with Dr. Ashford's position that '' . . . to rectify this real issue of inherent insensitivity to minority groups, we will need to reform our current science policies and theories of culture.''

References

Borowski, A. (1988). Social dimensions of research. In R. M. Grinnell, Jr. (Ed.) *Social work research and evaluation* (pp. 42–64). Itasca, IL: F. E. Peachock.

Namenwirth, M. (1986). Science seen through a feminist prism. In R. Bleier (Ed.), *Feminist approaches to science.* New York: Pergamon.

Rubin, A., & Babbie, E. (1989). *Research methods for social work.* Belmont, CA: Wadsworth.

DEBATE 3

Are Practitioner Intuition and Empirical Evidence Equally Valid Sources of Professional Knowledge?

Paula Allen-Meares is Dean and Professor at the University of Michigan, Ann Arbor, School of Social Work. Her teaching and research interests are in social work services in schools, social work practice, services to at-risk children, and adolescent sexuality. She also consults with state, national, and international agencies and organizations.

Yosikazu S. DeRoos is a lecturer at the University of Illinois at Urbana-Champaign School of Social Work, where he teaches research, statistics, and psychopathology. His current research and writing interests include computer-assisted instruction, distance learning, clinical judgment, and item-response theory.

Deborah H. Siegel is an associate professor at the Rhode Island College School of Social Work, where she teaches social work practice, research, and evaluation. Her current research and writing focus on open adoption and issues in adoptive families. She maintains a clinical practice and consults with agencies involved in single-subject and program evaluations, and political advocacy on behalf of low-income populations.

YES

PAULA ALLEN-MEARES
YOSIKAZU S. DEROOS

It is our position that practitioners' intuition and empirical evidence are equally valid sources of professional knowledge. We argue that our position has existed since social work's initial attempts to develop a knowledge base, and it has continued into the current debate about appropriate research methodology for the profession.

Definition of Concepts

Intuition may be considered as one mode of knowing. The various operations that are labelled *intuition* include: 1) the immediate, noninferential apprehension of something, 2) innate or instinctive knowledge not based on sensory or intellectual activity, and 3) that which is immediately provided to and organized by the mind (Angeles, 1981). Our definition of intuition is equivalent to Schön's (1983) concept of "knowing-in-action." Schön writes, "Although we sometimes think before acting, in much of the spontaneous behavior of skillful practice we reveal a kind of knowing which does not stem from *a prior* intellectual operation" (p. 49). This definition recognizes the relevance of sensory experience, but does not wholly subsume it under such experience.

The term, *empirical evidence,* refers to evidence gained through a formal, systematic process of research or evaluation, often called *scientific.* We choose to define empirical evidence as a product of a formal, systematic process because this is the definition used in discussions within social work research. We argue, however, that social work knowledge extends beyond data validated through scientific methods, and in some areas, beyond what can be validated by scientific means. Nonetheless, such "unscientific" knowledge has validity and use for the profession. This is not to discount the relevance of formal theories and systematic research, but to argue that these are not the only means by which professional knowledge is derived.

Harrison (1987) suggests that social workers often make decisions that are based on partially "known factors [empirical evidence] and unclear contingencies" (p. 396). They develop a representation of what has occurred and how events might unfold in the future. Often, knowledge from intuition, unclear contingencies, and known facts are integrated and brought to bear on practice situations.

Professional knowledge in social work is practical knowledge, that is, knowledge that is useful for practice. It is important that we not define too narrowly this knowledge base. Barker (1991) includes in the knowledge base of social work: accumulated information; scientific findings; value and skills; and methodology for acquiring, using, and evaluating what is known. This knowledge base may be derived from systematic research, formal theories, personal experiences, intuition, sociocultural institutions, society generally, and so forth.

For our discussion, knowledge is defined as that which is learned. The most important distinction is between "knowing *about* something" (secondary knowledge) and "knowing something" (primary knowledge). Action transforms secondary knowledge into primary knowledge. For example, a social work student gains secondary knowledge about casework from reading casework textbooks, observing role plays, and so forth. However, that student does not have a primary knowledge until she or he has participated in casework activity. Such participation is not sufficient alone to guarantee the student's gaining primary knowledge of casework, but it is a necessary activity for such knowledge. It is through such activity that knowledge about casework becomes internalized (incorporated into the thoughts, feelings and behavior of the student); that is, it becomes primary knowledge (Schön, 1983).

For practical activities, this distinction is paramount. In social work, knowledge is not simply a compilation of facts and figures, but a transformation of knowledge into practical activity; primary and secondary knowledge distinguishes knowledgeable social workers from those who are not. One may also argue that the conceptual bifurcation of knowledge and skill does not exist in practice. It is the synthesis of knowledge and skill that constitutes what we often label as professional knowledge (DeRoos, 1990).

Our Position

Given this conception of professional knowledge, we ask how one may gain such knowledge. Toulmin (1982) has written that it is the transparency and intelligibility of the world of nature that has served as the cornerstone for the development of knowledge about the world. Somehow, human beings and their mental equipment are adapted to that world. Although over a more restricted sphere, this definition can be applied to social work. And securing and acting on such knowledge is not limited to an approach built on a model requiring 1) conscious appraisal of available information, 2) the conscious selection of the seemingly best available alternative and 3) the conscious performance of some action. Ryle (1949) writes, "What distinguishes sensible from silly operations is not their parentage but their procedure, and this holds no less for intellectual than for practical performances. 'Intelligent' cannot be defined in terms of 'intellectual' or 'knowing *how*' in terms of 'knowing *that*'; 'thinking what I am doing' does not connote 'both thinking what to do and doing it.' My performance has a special procedure or manner, not special antecedents" (p. 20). In social work practice, knowing and doing are one thing, not two.

When assessing individuals who are skillful in some activity, a similar response is usually received from them about how they are able to perform skillfully. Whether it is a skilled athlete or a skilled therapist, they seldom characterize their activity as one in which they are thinking about what they do as they are doing it; their work is characterized simply as something that is done. It can be surprising or disconcerting that the sincere answer to "How did you do that?" is often "I don't know," or "I just do it." It is not that the person does not know how something is done, but that 1) the action is not easily translated into linguistic description, and 2) the cognitive activity involved in the action is difficult to make conscious.

Such an argument has special relevance for a profession such as social work, in which all knowledge must become "knowledge for practice" in order to be characterized as social work knowledge. For example, nomothetic knowledge about normal human growth and behavior becomes part of social work knowledge only when it becomes knowledge for practice. Otherwise, it remains psychological or sociological knowledge.

Thus, the issue is how knowledge in other fields, such as psychological, sociological, or economic knowledge, becomes social work knowledge. The answer is that all knowledge becomes transformed into social work knowledge when it can be used in practice. This transformation invokes methods of knowing and acting that can be characterized, to some degree, as intuitive or as a process of incipient induction.

Nonlogical (but not irrational) factors play a role in the development of social work knowledge. Because knowing and doing become one activity, it is reasonable to speak of social work knowledge in terms that denote action. It is appropriate to say that to be knowledgeable in social work means to be able to use knowledge in a skillful way. Thus, technical skill, although not sufficient in itself, must be considered part of social work knowledge. Schön (1983) writes, "Often we cannot say what it is that we know. When we try to describe it, we find ourselves at a loss, or we produce descriptions that are obviously inappropriate. Our knowing is ordinarily tacit, implicit in our patterns of action and in our feel for the stuff with which we are dealing. It seems right to say that our knowing is *in* our actions." Obviously, this applies to social work practice.

In social work practice, a practitioner may not have to think about actions, recognitions, and judgments prior to or during a performance (Schön, 1982). An example is the ability of an experienced social worker to "read" body language and to react appropriately without resorting to conscious reflection on the meaning of the client's posture or movements. Not all nonconscious thought is intuition, but all intuition is grounded in nonconscious mental activity.

Although we argue that, in general, practitioners' intuition and empirical evidence are equally valid sources of professional knowledge, we also argue that in specific areas, practitioners' intuition is more useful or may be the only viable resource of the two.

This superior usefulness of intuition may be illustrated. In social work direct practice, the basic unit for work and analysis is often the case. Whether the case concerns a person, community, family, or a group, primary practice knowledge is gained through such work. Through repeating such work, one develops primary knowledge in the form of information and practice principles, which may be expanded by other means and experiences. Through repetition, one gains an intuitive sense of what works, of what to do, and how and when to do it. Such knowledge gains veracity through its successful re-application. When problems arise in the application of this intuition knowledge, one may resort to a conscious appraisal of the situation and possibly to the use of secondary knowledge to illuminate the nature or source of the problem at hand.

Other areas of knowledge are left unaddressed by conventional scientific means and intuition may be the only viable alternative. One of these areas is that of practice ethics. Social work's knowledge base includes not only scientific knowledge, but also knowledge about what is right or wrong, and good or bad. Science can answer questions about what is; it cannot answer questions about what ought to be. It is generally accepted that the is/ought or fact/value dichotomies are valid ones. There is a distinction between "is" questions, related to factual claims, and "ought" questions, which are related to normative claims; one cannot derive normative conclusions from factual premises. Thus, social work must turn elsewhere for knowledge about these other areas. Intuition may be a means by which ethical questions in social work are answered.

Intuition in issues of practice ethics operates similarly to intuition in other spheres of social work activity. Practice ethics involves a type of knowing that does not stem from *a priori* intellectual operation. Such knowledge is immediate and prereflective, but is grounded nonetheless in prior ethical knowledge and experience (Hare, 1981). This recognizes the relevance of sensory experience but does not wholly subsume it under experience.

The various professional codes of ethics found in social work are analogous to the body of classically developed knowledge used in social work. In both cases, they characterize what is general. A code of ethics specifies general normative guidelines; classical science develops general descriptions. Although one is prescriptive and the other descriptive, there is a similar difficulty encountered in translating the general to specific practice situations. Given such generality, one resorts to methods that more effectively evaluate a specific practice situation. Ultimately, intuition may effectively serve that purpose.

Hartman's (1990) recent editorial, "Many Ways of Knowing," captures the central theme that is advocated here. She does not advocate that any one way of knowing is better than another, but that the profession of social work, as complex as it is, requires "many ways of knowing and many kinds of knowers . . . and that we must not turn our backs on any opportunities to enhance our knowledge" (p. 4).

References

Angeles, P. (1981). *Dictionary of philosophy.* New York: Barnes & Noble.

Barker, R. (1991). *Social work dictionary.* Washington, D.C.: National Association of Social Workers.

DeRoos, Y. (1990). The development of practice wisdom through human problem-solving processes. *Social Service Review, 60,* 276–287.

Hare, R. (1981). The philosophical basis of psychiatric ethics. In S. Bloch, & P. Chodoff (Eds.), *Psychiatric ethics.* Oxford, England: Oxford University Press.

Harrison, D. (1987). Reflective practice in social care. *Social Science Review, 37,* 394–404.

Hartman, A. (1990). Many ways of knowing [editorial]. *Social Work, 35,* 3–4.

Ryle, G. (1949). *The concept of mind.* London, England: Hutcheson.

Schön, D. (1983). *The reflective practitioner: How professionals think in action.* New York: Basic Books.

Toulmin, S. (1982). Evolution, adaptation, and human understanding. In M. Brewer & B. Collins (Eds.), *Scientific inquiry and the social sciences.* San Francisco, CA: Jossey-Bass.

Rejoinder to Drs. Allen-Meares & DeRoos

DEBORAH H. SIEGEL

Clearly, Drs. Allen-Meares and DeRoos and I agree that empirical evidence and practitioner intuition are both essential, valuable, and sometimes inextricable sources of information. While I agree that neither way of knowing "is better than another," it is not clear to me that the arguments they offer adequately support their assertion that both ways of knowing are equally *valid* sources of professional knowledge. In order to make this argument convincing, one would have to produce persuasive re-definitions of the terms "valid," "empirical evidence," "practitioner intuition," and "professional knowledge." Drs. Allen-Meares, DeRoos, and I use similar definitions of these terms. According to Drs. Allen-Meares and DeRoos, because empirical evidence and intuition are both important, knowing and doing are linked, and professional knowledge includes skill, the different ways of knowing in social work must somehow be equally valid sources of professional knowledge. That conclusion seems to be unsupported by the arguments presented.

For example, Drs. Allen-Meares and DeRoos point out that in specific areas, practitioners' intuition is more useful or may be the only viable alternative to empirical evidence. This, of course, is true. It does not follow, however, that intuition must then be an equally *valid* source of professional knowledge. Because the superior usefulness of intuition in a given situation can only be determined by means of empirical evidence, empirical evidence must have greater validity.

Drs. Allen-Meares and DeRoos argue that skilled practitioners seldom characterize their activity as one in which they are thinking about what they do as they are doing it. When skilled persons are asked, "How did you do that?" they report that the sincere answer is often, ''I don't know,'' or ''I just do it.'' Allen-Meares and DeRoos assert that this phenomenon demonstrates the equal validity of empirical evidence and intuition as sources of professional knowledge. I, however, believe that practitioners who are unable to explain cogently the reasons for their behaviors may be poorly trained and potentially dangerous, rather than models of professionalism. Assessments and interventions that spring unchecked from the gut, and are not filtered through a screen of knowledge derived from research, empirically tested theory, and the Code of Ethics, are more prone to error.

I also disagree with Drs. Allen-Meares' and DeRoos' assertion that ''intuition may be the only viable alternative'' to ''conventional scientific means'' for resolving ethical dilemmas. While empirical evidence often does not, and cannot, tell us what is right in a moral sense, intuition itself is only one of many alternative ethical decision-making tools available (Reamer, 1990). Many other ethical decision-making frameworks exist and are used within the social work profession.

NO

DEBORAH H. SIEGEL

Practitioner intuition and empirical evidence, by definition, cannot be equally valid sources of professional knowledge. Intuition can be a notoriously inaccurate source of information and, thus, does not provide a suitable foundation for professional knowledge. Consider the tale of a fellow who spent his days constantly snapping his fingers. When asked why he did so, he replied, ''It keeps rampaging elephants away.'' His companion responded, ''That's ridiculous!'' The fellow replied, ''Oh yeah? Do you see any rampaging elephants around here?'' His intuition was certainly not a valid source of knowledge.

Intuition may, on occasion, happen to be consistent with knowledge that has been confirmed by empirical evidence. But to be considered valid, knowledge must be well grounded, sound, cogent, and convincing. It must be ''supported by objective truth or generally accepted authority,'' be ''based on flawless reasoning and on solid grounds,'' and have ''the power of overcoming doubt . . .'' (Webster's Seventh New Collegiate Dictionary [Webster's] 1965, p. 980). Professional knowledge can be ''reliably communicated and is verifiable by scientific procedures'' (Gordon, 1962). Gordon (1965), has also stated that ''knowledge refers to what, in fact, seems to be established by the highest standards of objectivity and rationality, of which [people] are capable'' (p. 34). An intuition that conforms with valid knowledge does not meet the criteria for empirical evidence. Evidence is empirical when it is gathered and analyzed according to a systematic, structured plan that adheres to the canons of inductive and deductive logic. Experimental and quasi-experimental designs, and qualitative and quantitative research methods yield empirical evidence and provide the most valid sources of professional knowledge.

Flexner (1915), in his statement of criteria that define a profession, stressed that professional practice must be based upon a ''systematic body of knowledge and theory'' (quoted in Humphreys & Dinerman, 1984, p. 181). Intuitive knowledge is not systematic; it is by definition ''without rational thought and inference,'' it is a ''quick and ready insight'' (Webster's, 1965), which, because of its immediacy, has not been validated by systematic testing. Our intuitions, however humans, are a ''blind force'' (Richmond, 1917). Intuition is not practice wisdom (Siporin, 1989), which is a ''shared consensus'' (Hartman, 1990) that synthesizes intuition, experience, theory, and empirical evidence. Practice wisdom incorporates rational elements; intuition is more primitive, ''preconscious'' (Carew, 1987), springing unchecked from the gut, an ''uninformed hunch'' (Gambrill, 1990). Thus, practitioner intuition and empirical evidence are not equally valid sources of professional knowledge. To assert that they are is to reject commonly held notions of what constitutes a profession. Palm reading and astrology, highly intuitive realms, are generally not recognized as professions in the same ways as are medicine and law, although intuition also plays a role in the latter fields.

Intuition is, of course, an enormously useful and inescapable source of information for professional practice (Hartman, 1990). Without intuition there would be no practice wisdom, and our search for empirical evidence would be seriously impaired, for many hypotheses for empirical testing begin as intuitions. As Salomon (1967) notes, social work processes are based upon two elements: ''one is personal, intuitive, sympathetic and empathic; the other is scientific, abstractive, and generalizing'' (p. 26). Intuition plays an inherent, integral role in all areas of social work practice. The social work administrator, clinician, policy analyst, community organizer, and researcher often have intuitions that end up shaping accurate assessments and effective interventions. This does not, however, mean that as a source of professional knowledge, intuition equals empirical evidence.

Consider the following example: A client enters the clinician's office, plops into a chair, and appears to scowl at the worker. ''Oh my,'' thinks the worker to herself. ''He's really angry at me.'' This is an intuitive response that may or may not be accurate. The apparent scowl could mean many things—perhaps the client is squinting as his eyes adjust to the light indoors, he has a headache, feels hassled at work, is depressed, or is playfully teasing the worker. The worker's intuition, her spontaneous reaction to the client's facial expression, may be an inaccurate assessment of the client's feelings because it stems not from the client's experience, but from the worker's. Perhaps her analysis springs from her feelings of inadequacy in her role, her acute discomfort with anger, countertransference issues with scowling men, projection because her husband was angry with her that morning, or some other aspect of this worker's intrapsychic dynamics and life circumstances.

Thus, the worker's intuition, her quick and ready insight uninformed by rational thought, could be wrong. Clinical theories and practice wisdom tell this worker to check out her intuition by gathering empirical evidence. She might, for example, ask questions to probe for more information in order to gather data to test the accuracy of her intuition that he is angry at her. The worker's intuition in this example is rooted in an empirical observation—the client's facial expression. The intuition itself, however, does not qualify as empirical evidence. Once the worker has systematically, validly, and reliably measured the accuracy of her intuition, the intuition becomes empirical evidence and is intuition no longer.

Clearly, intuition and empirical evidence are interwoven, yet they remain two very different kinds of knowledge. Practitioner intuition, although often vital, is not as valid a source of professional knowledge as empirical evidence because it more easily falls prey to logical fallacies and is more impervious to contradictory evidence. While empirical evidence may also be tainted by bias, and by the epistemological limitations of the five human senses and available research technologies, intuition is even more tainted.

Intuition can, for example, be based upon false information. Our grandparents warned us to stay out of the rain so we wouldn't catch a cold. Today we know that colds are caught, not by exposure to rain, but by exposure to viruses that enter the body when the eyes or nose are touched by contaminated hands. Misinformation about the causes of colds has been passed down through so many generations that it still has the power of truth, despite its speciousness.

For years, social workers believed that childhood autism was caused by unresponsive, rejecting parenting (Kanner, 1943; Eisenberg & Kanner, 1956). Some recommended that parents place their children in residential treatment facilities for children who had autism and refrain from all contact with the child (Bettleheim, 1967). Parents, distraught with guilt and grief, complied. Today we know that autism has biological roots and is not caused by parental behavior (Konstantareas, 1990). There are many other disturbing examples of how social workers' beliefs, assumptions, and gut reactions, when untested by systematic research, have led to client anguish.

As the tale of the fellow who snapped his fingers to keep rampaging elephants at bay illustrates, intuition can lead to superstitious behavior that is based upon spurious correlations. In the autism example, practitioners observed lack of warmth between parents and their children, and inaccurately concluded that parental behavior had a causal relationship with the autism, rather than being the end result of complex interactions with the child. Parents, whose efforts to cuddle, make eye contact with, and converse with their children were typically rebuffed, and they learned to back off, giving their child the space that she or he seemed to demand.

Similarly, we often implement an intervention, see the desired outcome, and conclude that the intervention was effective without having used either a nomothetic or idiographic design to test our conclusion. On the basis of our intuition, we continue to use ineffective or iatrogenic methods, screening out contradictory evidence. In addition, we may sometimes apply increasing amounts of ineffective interventions in difficult cases, believing that more is better. It is not uncommon, for instance, for a clinician to recommend that a severely depressed client come more often for appointments. It is possible, however, that the clinical intervention may be causing or exacerbating the depression. When the client suggests this, the worker may believe that transference, projection, or some other dynamic accounts for the client's point of view. The practitioner's intuition is that more of the same intervention is needed.

Intuitions are often distorted by wishful thinking. A dieter may be genuinely perplexed by his lack of weight loss when he is eating so little. Only when he starts writing down each morsel that he consumes does he realize that "so little" is actually quite a lot. Social workers who earnestly want to believe that they're helping their clients can fall prey to similar self-deception.

Intuitive knowledge is questionable also because one person's intuition is not necessarily the same as another's. In the absence of empirical evidence, it is impossible to determine whose intuitions are more accurate. It is not very informative to call in a third party to add her or his intuitions to the debate, for one ends up simply with a stew of competing intuitions, whose validity has not been proven. For example, one policy analyst may believe that eliminating the General Assistance program (which provides income support for childless adults) will force recipients to find employment; another policymaker believes the elimination will have no effect on unemployment and will lead to more homelessness, disease, and despair. Only empirical evidence, not intuition, can meaningfully inform the debate.

It is true that the virtues of empirical evidence are sometimes extolled too highly (Heineman, 1981; Pieper, 1985; Reamer, 1993; Rodwell, 1987). Nonetheless, rational thought that is grounded in empirical evidence is a major protection against seductive self-deception and impulsive, irrational decision-making. The kinds of knowledge derived from intuition and empirical evidence are different and not of equal validity. While empirical evidence may be flawed, intuition is more prone to logical fallacies (Ingle, 1976). To be a profession, social work must be based upon knowledge that is generated by systematic empirical research. The practitioner's intuition, or "gut sense," by its very nature is not systematic, and is more susceptible to bias and distortion.

References

Bettleheim, B. (1967). *The empty fortress: Infantile autism and the birth of the self.* New York. Free Press.

Carew, R. (1987). The place of intuition in social work activity. *Australian Social Work, 40*(3), 5–10.

Eisenberg, L., & Kanner, L. (1956). Early infantile autism. *American Journal of Orthopsychiatry, 26,* 556–565.

Flexner, A. (1915). Is social work a profession? In *Proceedings of the national conference of charities and correction.* Chicago, IL: Hildman Printing.

Gambrill, E. (1990). *Critical thinking in clinical practice: Improving the accuracy of judgments and decisions about clients.* San Francisco, CA: Jossey-Bass.

Gordon, W. E. (1962). A critique of the working definition. *Social Work, 7*(4), 7.

Gordon, W. E. (1965). Knowledge and value: Their distinction relationship in clarifying social work practice. *Social Work, 10*(3), 34.

Hartman, A. (1990). Many ways of knowing. *Social Work, 35*(1), 3–4.

Heineman, M. (1981). The obsolete scientific imperative in social work research. *Social Service Review, 55*(3), 371–396.

Humphries, N., & Dinerman, M. (1984). Professionalizing social work. In M. Dinerman, & L. Geismar (Eds.), *A quarter-century of social work education.* Copublished by National Association of Social Workers, ABC-CLIO, and Council on Social Work Education.

Ingle, D. (1976). *Is it really so?* Philadelphia, PA: Westminster.

Kanner, L. (1943). Autistic disturbances of affective contact. *Nervous Child, 2,* 217–50.

Konstantareas, M. M. (1990). A psychoeducational model for working with families of autistic children. *Journal of Marital and Family Therapy, 16*(1), 59–70.

Pieper, M. N. (1985). The future of social work research. *Social Work Research and Abstracts, 21*(4), 3–11.

Reamer, F. G. (1990). *Ethical dilemmas in social work practice.* New York: Columbia University Press.

Reamer, F. G. (1993). *The philosophical foundations of social work.* New York: Columbia University Press.

Richmond, M. (1917). *Social diagnosis.* New York: Russell Sage.

Rodwell, M. K. (1987). Naturalistic inquiry: An alternative model for social work assessment. *Social Service Review, 61*(2): 231–246.

Salomon, E. L. (1967). Humanistic values and social casework. *Social Casework, 48*(1), 26–32.

Siporin, M. (1988). Clinical social work as an art form. *Social Casework, 69*(3), 177–183.

Webster's Seventh New Collegiate Dictionary, (1965). Springfield, MA: G. & C. Merriam.

Rejoinder to Dr. Siegel

Paula Allen-Meares
Yosikazu S. DeRoos

Dr. Siegel has taken a very interesting position in the NO paper. She writes that, by definition, intuition and empirical evidence cannot be equally valid sources of professional knowledge. Unfortunately, she defines neither intuition nor empirical evidence, thus leaving unclear what is being discussed. The examples do little to clarify the concepts. Fingersnapping as an act to keep away rampaging elephants, while spotlighting an example of superstitious behavior, is not an argument against intuition. Also, the logical error that leads one to assume a spurious correlation, and that underlies the superstitious behavior is commonly found in all spheres of life's activities, including formally scientific activities, not only those involving intuition. Her example is unfortunate because she is operating definitionally. In her example, she "defines" the behavior as superstitious; that is, she knows the behavior does not keep rampaging elephants away. How does she know this? Because she knows fingersnapping does not cause the desired outcome and, therefore, a spurious correlation exists, and, thus, the behavior is superstitious. She falls victim to her own logical error, that of making a circular argument.

She argues that for knowledge to be considered as valid, it must be developed in a particular way and take a particular form. We believe, however, that there is more than one scientific method that may serve as a means for generating knowledge and that these methods may take different forms. One can argue effectively for logical, systematic procedures that may produce knowledge without arguing too narrowly on what those procedures ought to be. Further, Dr. Siegel argues for adherence to canons of deductive and inductive logic. Although deductive logic in its several forms is highly codified and has proven useful, inductive logic is much more problematic. Induction has proven a difficult subject, from Francis Bacon's seminal attempt to John Stuart Mill's "method of induction" to Rudolf Carnap's system employing probability functions. The very influential philosopher Karl Popper has even argued that induction performs no role at all in scientific activity. Clearly, what induction is and what role it plays remains an open question. Also, one often finds that even among the most successful scientists, strict adherence to deductive and inductive principles is often tenuous.

Dr. Siegel states that intuitive knowledge is not systematic. We argue that it is, but because of its nonconscious dimension, its internal coherence or external correspondence is not always evident. To argue that intuitive knowledge has not been systematically validated is to negate all that we do as beings in a world in which we, in our daily lives and professional activities, are continuously testing our assumptions, beliefs, and expectations against the template of reality. Whether we do or do not formally practice as scientists in our professional lifes, we may be legitimately characterized in our daily lives as "lay scientists." Children, even infants, test the world, through trial and error, systematic observation, gathering evidence, and experimentation, to develop knowledge of themselves and their role as actors in that world. Such activity serves as the basis for the development of our intuition. In other words, intuition is the accumulation of observations, experiences, and professional training. It is an informed reflex.

Dr. Siegel acknowledges the importance and usefulness of intuition, stating that it plays an integral role for the profession. She characterizes it, however, as a basis for, or as a precursor to, empirical evidence. While its use in this way is appropriate, we argue that there is also a complementary process. Social workers can take empirical evidence and through its use develop heightened intuition.

A problem with examples, such as the one in which the clinician misreads the client's scowl, is that Dr. Siegel uses them to equate intuition with being wrong. Every example she gives is meant to show the error of intuition. She does acknowledge that the worker "could" be wrong. We don't profess infallibility for intuition, however, and neither does she for empirical knowledge. That is, she allows for the possibility of empirical evidence also being wrong. She indicates that while empirical knowledge may be less likely than intuition to suffer from illogic or to be based on false information, it nonetheless may have these failings. The fingersnapping, social worker, and cold-catching examples bear no weight on the veracity of intuition. Unless one argues that intuition is infallible, which we do not, fictional cases such as these do not effectively argue against intuition. In fact, given her argument that her method is less fallible, such instances weigh more heavily against her position. Such examples are not difficult to find. A good example of the failings of empirical knowledge is the case of autism. The research on childhood autism has gone through several phases of development, undergirded by "empirical evidence," which was later rejected by new findings. Perhaps by the year 2000, we will learn that childhood autism, which was thought to have biological roots in the 1990s, is caused by other factors. Further, we know all too well the shortcomings of empirical research.

What is missing is discussion about certain methods being useful for drawing general conclusions and other methods for drawing specific conclusions. In our sphere of activity, one without the other would be highly limiting. We believe that no social worker takes general conclusions that were secured through formal empirical procedures, such as classical research methods, and simply applies them in practice. Nor should we use intuition without checking continuously other information sources to validate our activity. The checks and balances possible in employing the two approaches argues for maintaining the use of both.

Finally, we don't argue against the veracity or utility of Dr. Siegel's position. We object to the dichotomization of intuition as unsystematic, irrational, and ungrounded and of empirical knowledge as systematic, rational, and grounded. Our two positions are much more similar. Each approach has benefits, each has its deficits. The two have often worked in complement, buttressing the work of the other, doing so in its own way, as a way of knowing, as a way of knowledge development, both used to pursue truth. They can and should continue to do so.

DEBATE 4

Are Exploratory *Post Hoc* Models Better Suited for Social Work Research Than Hypothesis Testing Approaches?

Michie N. Hesselbrock is a professor at the University of Connecticut School of Social Work, where she teaches courses on research and psychopathology. She directs the faculty development program and is a grant reviewer for National Institute of Alcohol Abuse and Alcoholism and for the Veterans Administration. Her research interests are in gender differences and co-morbidity in alcohol and substance abuse.

Victor M. Hesselbrock is a professor in the Department of Psychiatry, School of Medicine, University of Connecticut, where he teaches courses on statistics and epidemiology. He directs the postdoctoral training program in alcohol studies. His research interests are in the genetics of psychiatric disorders and psychosocial risk factors associated with psychopathology.

William J. Reid is a professor at the School of Social Welfare, University of Albany, State University of New York, where he teaches research methods and task-centered practice, and directs the doctoral program. His most recent book is *Task Strategies: An Empirical Approach to Clinical Social Work,* published by Columbia University Press, 1992.

YES

MICHIE N. HASSELBROCK
VICTOR M. HESSELBROCK

A principal assumption of our YES position is that the exploratory, *post-hoc* model can be both quantitative and qualitative. The quantitative method of the exploratory *post-hoc* model is used in epidemiological approaches to the study of disease in communities, while grounded theory and the ethnographic methods used in anthropological studies often employ a qualitative approach. In both, the emphasis is placed on observation and description of the occurrence of social conditions or behaviors, often in the absence of a guiding theoretical framework.

An exploratory research design is often the first step used in the process of knowledge building. It is a fact-gathering procedure, often conducted when little is known about the phenomenon or situation. Thus, the purpose of conducting exploratory research is to obtain new information, new insights, ask questions, and assess phenomena from a different perspective (Adams & Schvaneveldt, 1991). The researcher who conducts exploratory research begins with very general questions and identifies several potentially important variables to be examined. By identifying variables that may relate to the problem of interest, the research systematically describes the phenomenon in terms of several relevant variables and the distribution of their values. One example of this type of research was the determination of the worldwide prevalence of AIDS and the patterns of transmission in samples at high risk for the disease (Piot, Plummer, Mhalu, Lamboray, Chin, & Mann, 1988).

The *post-hoc* research design attempts to answer questions about phenomena that have already occurred (i.e., ''after the fact'') and to explain relationships between the condition and variables identified as ''important'' in a descriptive study. A frequently used example of the *post-hoc* design in mental-health research is the case-control study. In this type of study, persons with a particular condition, problems, or characteristic are compared with persons in whom the condition or problem is absent in relation to the putatively important factors. For example, parents who abuse their children are compared with parents who do not abuse their children, and they are compared in terms of their own history of being abused and other areas of psychosocial development.

All of the above-mentioned research methods (exploratory, descriptive and *post-hoc* designs) are classified as nonexperimental (or quasi-experimental) research designs. While nonexperimental research designs do involve systematic empirical inquiry, inference about relationships among the variables of interest remains at the level of association. Casual inferences cannot be made. Further, manifestations of the independent variables are often measured retrospectively or are not inherently manipulable (e.g., gender), thus the identified independent variables cannot be directly controlled or manipulated.

Exploratory, descriptive, or *post-hoc* research models are especially suited for social work practice research. Social work practitioners are ''front-line workers'' in the community, regardless of the practice methods in which they are engaged. Social workers are often the first human-service and health-care professionals to observe the effects of a new policy, of a policy change, and the occurrence of new health, social, and psychological problems. Often the social condition observed by an agency social worker is unique and the observation requires a qualitative approach that seeks information from several sources. By doing so, the social worker must assesses the situation without preconceived assumptions. Often these observations result in more innovative interventions. These types of research approaches are not unique to social work practice. Public-health professionals have been using similar approaches based on epidemiological methods to study health problems in the community for several centuries. Further, ethnographic and grounded theory approaches have been used to study society in different cultures and in primitive societies (Glaser, 1978; Glaser & Strauss, 1967).

Exploratory, descriptive designs offer several clear advantages to social work practice researchers. First, exploratory designs are flexible and allow researchers to observe, talk, listen, and ask questions without being locked into a fixed theoretical approach or a fixed method of data collection, permitting a given situation to be evaluated from several different approaches. The development of DSM-III-R is an example of the use of a nontheoretical, descriptive approach. Mental-health researchers and clinicians from various theoretical orientations collaborated to describe a variety of psychiatric disorders without invoking different etiologic explanations (i.e., learning theory, psychoanalytic theory, etc.). By documenting only observable signs and behaviors, they were able to reach a consensus on the description of each disorder that is relevant to both clinicians and researchers, regardless of their own theoretical orientations.

A common area of social work research is "needs assessment." Exploratory, descriptive research designs can be used to identify the needs and characteristics of target populations to be served by social work intervention. By integrating social work research into policy planning and practice, social workers can better serve their clients and community by a systematic identification of program goals and objectives, monitoring of the services provided, and evaluating the effectiveness of the applied interventions. Thus, a methodologically sound "needs assessment" is essential to the proper planning of social work policy and practice. Such studies, when correctly conducted, can provide social work planners and practitioners with exciting opportunities to be imaginative and innovative when planning social policies and services.

Social workers who attempt to pursue exploratory types of research often encounter difficulties because of their lack of training. The research training of social workers often comes out of a tradition based on theory-derived hypothesis testing approaches. Rigorously controlled hypothesis-testing designs often are conducted in a laboratory, where many extraneous factors can be controlled or manipulated, permitting a direct test of the hypothesis under investigation. Social work practitioners, however, often find it difficult for several reasons to conduct a research study that imposes systematic controls. First, social work practitioners often need to study clients in their natural environment rather than in a laboratory setting. A basic tenant of social work practice posits that clients are constantly interacting with their environment (an ecological perspective). A client's behavior and attitudes are influenced, in part, by environmental conditions. The client's behaviors, in turn, affect the environment. Thus, the condition that is the object of investigation is constantly changing and the study hypotheses may need modification accordingly, making rigorous control of the confounding factors difficult. Further, studies of clients often make it difficult to identify an appropriate control group because it is unethical to withhold services if the service that is the focus of the investigation is beneficial. Rather than imposing strict experimental controls on the situation under investigation, the services offered and client change are monitored closely to examine the effectiveness and quality of the ongoing programs or interventions.

Secondly, social work practitioners often encounter new social conditions or social phenomena not experienced by the majority of society. For these new social phenomenon or conditions, no existing theories of etiology are available. Thus, social workers are often expected to provide interventions before the condition is fully understood. When the clients affected by these conditions seek assistance, social workers are often the first professionals confronted with having to provide some type of intervention. Thus, a systematic study to accurately describe the phenomenon is necessary in order to obtain information that is relevant to practice.

Because social workers traditionally serve and research persons living in the community, their practice focus on social problems is similar to the epidemiologists, who must study the occurrence of diseases in a community. Epidemiological traditions were developed in the 17th century to identify sources and possible interventions for infectious diseases. This methodology has been expanded to examine a variety of mental-health problems, alcohol and substance abuse, and other social problems (i.e., child abuse, homelessness, etc.). In order to provide an effective intervention with little theoretical background, a systematic description of the social problem in terms of the characteristics of persons involved, the environmental conditions, geographical locations, time of occurrence, and the time sequence of events connected to the phenomena is necessary. A recent example of the application of the exploratory model of research is the study of the outbreak and spread of HIV infections and AIDS. In the early 1980s, few people were affected with the HIV virus. An initial exploratory, descriptive study found that persons affected by the AIDS virus appeared to live only in large urban areas (e.g., New York and San Francisco). That descriptive study also revealed that the majority of persons who were affected were homosexual or bisexual men, while others appeared to have become infected through a blood transfusion. As the disease spread to other communities, the characteristics of affected persons became more diverse and included intravenous drug users, their sexual partners, and infants born to HIV-positive mothers (Curran, Morgan, Hardy, Jaffe, Darrow, & Dowdle, 1985). The etiology of the disease was examined by description of those persons identified over time as having AIDS. Although information regarding the AIDS disease process has increased, social worker practice with AIDS patients was conducted early in the epidemic without knowledge of the disease's etiology, transmissibility, or course.

Different approaches were taken by basic scientists and by social workers in the study of this social and medical problem. The basic scientists identified a virus and then tried to grow the virus in the laboratory. By contrast, social workers dealt directly with HIV-infected persons. They could not wait until more was known about AIDS, because persons affected with the disease required professional assistance in a variety of areas. Social workers needed information about the social implications of the disease: how can an affected person live in the community without infecting others? how long can an affected person be gainfully employed? what can be done to prevent an infected person from developing AIDS symptoms? how should family support be provided? and how can the clients be made more comfortable?

As part of their intervention, social workers not only had to educate clients and family members about what was known about the disease, but they also had to provide emotional support for the clients' family members. Social workers also had to be concerned with the legal and ethical issues regarding AIDS, such as confidentiality, information and referral services. A theory was not available to guide social work research on this topic. Much of the descriptive information came from the observations of social workers who had worked directly with clients affected with AIDS. Thus, relative to traditional hypothesis testing approaches, exploratory models can be more flexible and are more useful for providing the data necessary to plan appropriate social work interventions. This is not to say that social work research should not use theory-driven hypothesis testings. Exploratory types of research should be used to build the foundation required for more rigorous hypothesis testing studies and for theory building.

Another advantage of the *post-hoc* model for social work research is that it can use existing information. The condition of interest can be explained by linking existing data from various sources to illuminate the association between relevant variables and the condition which is the focus of the study. For example, a *post-hoc* comparison design might be used to examine the prevalence of substance abuse among delinquent and nondelinquent teenagers in terms of the prevalence of substance abuse in their parents, using information obtained from court documents, social workers' intake information, records of arrests, and so forth. Because sufficient information may already be available from existing records, a more costly and time-consuming study involving direct interviews of the subjects may be unnecessary.

Further, the *post-hoc* design can be an effective research tool for building social work knowledge because the social conditions in which social work is practiced are changing constantly (e.g., changes in employment levels, changes in local, state, and federal policies, etc.). For example, changes in unemployment compensation coverage will affect the financial condition of the long-term unemployed. In order to study the effects of unemployment, a *post-hoc* type of design may be the only research design available because employment levels cannot be manipulated by the researcher. Because such information is readily available, large data sets can be easily obtained without the investigator having to wait for the condition to occur.

A limitation of relying on theory-driven hypothesis testing is the rapidity with which new information is being generated. As new scientific evidence becomes available, existing theories need to be modified quickly. An example is the case of the disease concept of alcoholism. This widely held belief regarding the nature of persons with alcohol problems was proposed by Jellinek in 1960. However, scientific evidence gathered over the past 10 years suggests the importance of genetic factors in both the etiology and course of alcoholism, casting considerable doubt on Jellinek's original "disease" conceptualization.

Often only an experimental design in which the independent variable is manipulated and the dependent variable is measured pre-experimental and post-experimental manipulation is considered to be scientifically rigorous. However, the *post-hoc* design has no less scientific rigor. While no strictly controlled manipulation of the independent variables are applied, the designs are purposeful and flexible. The researcher must be alert and be a keen observer in order to adapt and be willing to change and be open to the impact of the study's findings (Adams & Schvanevelt, 1991). The flexibility of the exploratory study does not imply a lack of direction or consistency. Rather, the exploratory study is a systematic process of moving from a broad focus of the problem to a more specific and focused view of the relevant variables. Thus, researchers can learn a great deal and be innovative by being keen observers and identifying conditions or situations that seem odd or interesting. By questioning previously held beliefs and by being open to a critical study of their practice observations, the exploratory design would enable researchers in social work practice to keep abreast of a changing world and enhance the service delivered.

The exploratory descriptive research design has its limitations. Kerlinger (1986) cautions that the *post-hoc* model may lead to erroneous and misleading interpretations of research findings. It should be remembered that the purpose of the descriptive study and *post-hoc* design is to explain phenomena that have already occurred, not to examine causal relationships. Further, these designs should not be used exclusively. Rather, findings from studies employing exploratory *post-hoc* research designs should form the basis for more rigorously controlled experimental research. The social work profession is in an important position to contribute to scientific knowledge and theory building by more fully using the practice knowledge and research skills that are unique to its professional practice. The findings of this unique type of research could be invaluable for improving the human condition.

References

Adams, G. R., & Schvaneveldt, J. D. (1991). *Understanding research methods* (2nd ed.). New York: Longman Publishing.

Curran, J., Morgan, M., Hardy, A., Jaffe, H., Darrow, W., & Dowdle, W. (1985). The epidemiology of AIDS: Current status and future prospects. *Science, 229,* 225–231.

Glaser, B. (1978). *Theoretical sensitivity: Advances in the methodology of grounded theory.* Mill Valley, CA: Sociology Press.

Glaser, B., & Strauss, A. (1967). *The discovery of grounded theory.* Hawthorne, N.Y.: Aldine Publishing.

Jellinek, E. M. (1960). *The disease concept of alcoholism.* New Haven, CT: New Haven College and University Press.

Kerlinger, F. N. (1986). *Foundations of Behavioral Research,* (3rd ed.). New York: Holt, Reinhart and Winston.

Piot, P., Plummer, F., Mhalu, F., Lamboray, J., Chil, J., & Mann, J. (1988). AIDS: An international perspective. *Science, 239,* 573–579.

Rejoinder to Drs. Hesselbrock

William J. Reid

My main objection to the YES argument is that it downplays the importance of experimentation in social work. Early in the paper, Drs. Hesselbrock argue that "*because of the nature of social work practice,* exploratory, descriptive, and *post-hoc* designs are more appropriate for social work research" (emphasis added). My conception of social work practice would lead me to quite a different conclusion. Social work practice consists of activities performed through interventions, programs, and so forth. Such activities, often innovative and usually lacking in evidence for their effectiveness, need to be developed and evaluated within the context of experimental research strategies.

This does not mean simply the use of controlled experiments using group designs, as important as they may be. It means use of a multifaceted experimental approach that includes single-system designs, exploratory experiments (Reid & Smith, 1989; Schön, 1983), quasi-experiments, such as pre–post designs, and methods of developmental research (Thomas, 1984). Much social work research is already experimental in this broad sense and more should be, in my opinion.

Drs. Hesselbrock might well see much of this kind of research as "exploratory," but, if so, the point is not apparent in their paper. Rather they create what I regard as a false dichotomy between their preferred approaches and the controlled experiment. The dichotomy ignores the exploratory nature of much experimentation. Experiments, in the form of single-case studies, pilot projects, preliminary trials of innovations, and the like, can be as "exploratory," if not more so, than the AIDS studies that they cite.

This is not to deny the importance of the kinds of investigations that they advocate. We need more, not less, of them. But we also need a view of experimentation in social work that highlights rather than obscures vital areas of inquiry.

In addition, I was also puzzled by their statement later on that a "limitation of relying on theory-driven hypothesis testing is the rapidity with which new information is being generated." They give as an example, challenges from research "over the past ten years" to Jellinek's "disease concept of alcoholism." Obviously research accumulating over a ten-year period could lead, and in fact has led, to rival theories and hypotheses and, of course, to hypothesis testing. I could have added this to my own examples illustrating the *value* of hypothesis testing.

References

Reid, W. J., & Smith, A. D. (1989). *Research in social work.* New York: Columbia University Press.

Schön, D. (1983). *The reflective practitioner.* New York: Basic Books.

Thomas, E. J. (1984). *Designing Interventions for the Helping Professions.* Newbury Park, CA: Sage Publications.

NO

William J. Reid

In developing my NO response, I have interpreted "*post-hoc* models like grounded theory" to mean methods formally designed as "grounded theory" (Glaser, 1978; Strauss & Corbin, 1990). These approaches are not guided by theoretically derived hypotheses, but rather are oriented towards the discovery of theory and its "grounding" through data obtained by qualitative methods. Basically what I shall have to say about grounded theory can be applied to similar *post-hoc* models that use qualitative methods.

A key term of the question is "better suited," which I will interpret to mean "preferable" or "should receive major emphasis." Although I am convinced there is need to make *greater* use of grounded theory in social work research, I do not think it should supplant traditional hypothesis testing.

Hypothesis Testing

Over many years and in many fields, hypothesis testing has proved to be a powerful means of building knowledge. The reasons why can be briefly summarized. First, it makes use of existing theory to direct investigations: theory can identify and organize those conjectures that are most likely to pay off in additions to knowledge. For example, a theory of the impact of divorce on children suggests that effects are different for boys than girls (Zaslow, 1989). Inquiry is guided accordingly. In short, theory tells you where to look and what to look for when searching.

Second, it seeks the most rigorous evidence possible to verify the hypotheses tested. Thus, researchers attempt to base their evidence on precise measures and to control for bias and spurious factors. Finally, it results in a cumulative, self-corrective process of knowledge building. With repeated testing, theories become more inclusive and discriminating. Theories supported by evidence eventually win out over those for which evidence is lacking.

A familiar argument is that this paradigm may work well in the natural sciences, but is less applicable to the social sciences and to social work research because it cannot adequately capture the elusive complexities of psychological and social phenomena. A better way of putting it is that *any* research approach has difficulty doing justice to such phenomena. The real questions are: 1) can hypothesis testing produce valid knowledge about these complexities? and 2) can other approaches do a better job?

In most areas of concern to social work, one can find bodies of reasonably valid and useful knowledge that have resulted from hypothesis testing. To be sure, what has been produced is only a tiny fraction of what is needed, but there are signs that the pace is quickening. A leading example in the past two decades has been the development of a wide range of effective methods of intervention based on learning theory.

Two inter-related examples of hypothesis testing will be examined in detail. The first example is the rise and fall of the "double-bind" theory of schizophrenia. Originally proposed by Bateson, Jackson, Haley, & Weakland (1956), the double-bind theory posited that paradoxical and confusing communication sequences involving parents and offspring were influential in the subsequent development of schizophrenia in the offspring. Hypotheses generated by the theory were tested in a number of studies (Olson, 1972). These tests generally failed to support the hypotheses and, as a result, the theory "lost ground," as Lakatos (1972) would put it, to rival explanations of the etiology of schizophrenia. The example shows how hypothesis testing can prevent speculative theory from becoming established as knowledge.

However, a series of studies suggested that families did have an impact on the post-hospital adjustment of their schizophrenic members. Schizophrenics who returned to families who reacted with criticism, hostility, and over-involvement (referred to as "expressed emotion") were more likely to relapse than those whose families did not react in these ways (Brown, Birley, & Wing (1972); Leff & Vaughn, 1981). The theory of "expressed emotion" has led to subsequent studies that have not only confirmed its impact, but have also altered its definition and specified activating conditions (Hogarty et al., 1986). This body of hypothesis-testing research has provided a base for demonstrably effective psychoeducational approaches in work with schizophrenics and their families (Leff, Kuipers, Berkowitz, Eberlein-Vries, & Sturgeon 1982; Hogarty et al., 1986).

Grounded Theory

Although it has potential for enhancing social work knowledge, grounded theory lacks the requisites to become the dominant approach to knowledge development for the profession. I shall present only four of the many reasons why I believe this to be so.

First, in grounded theory, emphasis is on discovery of theory and on extending such theory to new situations. It does not make systematic use of existing theory to identify likely regularities that can then be thoroughly studied. As Glaser (1978) has said, the investigator is "to enter the research setting with as few predetermined ideas as possible—especially . . . *a priori* hypotheses" (p. 3). Thus, to gain fresh perspectives, grounded theory purposely forsakes the power of established theory to guide and focus inquiry. It is a critical trade off, one that puts grounded theory in the role of a specialized and subsidiary methodology. For example, a major purpose of social work research is to evaluate the effectiveness of service programs. This kind of research is hypothesis-driven. It is hypothesized that a program will have certain effects and then the hypothesis is tested. This kind of testing is not within the province of grounded theory, even though it may be useful in generating theory about phenomena addressed by service programs or about how such programs work.

Second, while grounded theory may be adept at discovering possible relationships, it lacks the methodology to verify them rigorously. Without control groups, statistical controls, tests of significance, and other devices to establish the strength of associations among variables and to rule out the influence of extraneous factors, the grounded theory approach has difficulty in determining the likelihood of causal connections between variables of primary interest.

Third, in grounded theory, the researcher studies small samples in depth. Although the samples may be carefully selected, they may not offer an adequate base for generalization. Grounded theorists have argued that the context surrounding the events studied necessarily limits one's ability to generalize. However, to develop knowledge of general application, one needs to specify aspects of context that are critical and to make these aspects a subject of study. In using this strategy, hypothesis-testing approaches have been able to build differentiated theories that specify the contingencies that may affect generalizations. An example is provided by the theory of the impact of divorce on children cited earlier: "boys tend to show more pervasive effects of divorce [than girls], *except in the post-divorce family form in which a step-parent is present*" (Zaslow, 1989, p. 137; emphasis added).

Finally, words alone may offer the best tools for understanding many complex situations, but there is much that is important about the human condition that can be captured more precisely through quantitative instruments and analysis. The well developed field of "objective" measurement can provide tools of empirically tested validity that are reasonably free from the biases of the investigator. For the "human instrument" of qualitative methodology, investigator bias is extraordinarily difficult to control and virtually impossible to identify.

Conclusion

In conclusion, my view of the place of grounded theory in social work research echoes the modest observation made by Glaser himself (1978) about the place of grounded theory in his discipline, "Our perspective is but a piece of a myriad of action in Sociology, not the only right action" (p. 3). Grounded theory should indeed have a piece of the action in social work research. It is a superb method for developing theory in areas where adequate theory is lacking. It can serve not only as a precursor to quantitative approaches, but often can produce insights that cannot be extracted by quantitative techniques. But all these utilities of grounded theory are best seen as subordinate to hypothesis testing. Grounded theory may augment traditional approaches in social work research, but it would be a grievous error to cast it into a leading role.

References

Bateson, G., Jackson, D. D., Haley, J., & Weakland, J. H. (1956). Toward a theory of schizophrenia. *Behavior Science, 1,* 251–264.

Brown, G. W., Birley, J. L. T., & Wing, J. F. (1972). Influence of family life on the course of schizophrenic disorders: A replication. *British Journal of Psychiatry, 121,* 241–258.

Glaser, B. (1978). *Theoretical sensitivity.* Mill Valley, CA: Sociology Press.

Hogarty, G. E., Anderson, C. M., Reiss, D. J., Kornblith, S. J., Greenwald, D. P., Javna, C. D., & Madonia, M. J. (1986). Family psychoeducation, social skills training, and maintenance chemotherapy in the aftercare treatment of schizophrenia. *Archives of General Psychiatry, 43,* 633–642.

Lakatos, I. (1972). Falsification and the methodology of scientific research programs. In I. Lakatos, & A. Musgrave (Eds.). *Criticisms and the growth of knowledge.* Cambridge, England: Cambridge University Press.

Leff, J., Kuipers, L., Berkowitz, R., Eberlein-Vries, R. & Sturgeon, D. (1982). A controlled trial of social intervention in the families of schizophrenic patients. *British Journal of Psychiatry, 141,* 121–134.

Leff, J. P., & Vaughn, C. E. (1981). The role of maintenance therapy and relatives' expressed emotion in relapse of schizophrenia: A two-year follow-up. *British Journal of Psychiatry, 139,* 102–104.

Olson, D. H. (1972). Empirically unbinding the double bind: Review of research and conceptual reformulations. *Family Process, II,* 69–94.

Strauss, A., & Corbin, J. (1990). *Basics of qualitative research.* Newbury, CA: Sage Publications.

Zaslow, M. J. (1989). Sex differences in children's response to parental divorce: 2. Samples, variables, ages, and sources. *American Journal of Orthopsychiatry, 59,* 118–140.

Rejoinder to Dr. Reid

Michie N. Hesselbrock
Victor M. Hesselbrock

Dr. Reid, in supporting the traditional hypothesis-testing approaches to social work research seems to begin his discussion with slightly different assumptions. His argument focuses on a discussion of hypothesis testing versus exploratory/*post-hoc*/grounded theory approaches to social work research. Exploratory/*post-hoc* approaches were equated with grounded theory. We use, however, a rather broader definition of the exploratory or *post-hoc* designs that includes both quantitative and qualitative research methods. In our view, qualitative designs (e.g., grounded theory, ethnography) compose only a small proportion of the researches conducted on the human condition. Rather, the majority of exploratory and *post-hoc* designs conducted are quantitative in nature, using the most current research technology (i.e., epidemiological studies, use of computers, etc.)

Further, our argument for use of exploratory, *post-hoc* designs was focused only on their applicability to problems in social work research, not to science in general. Because social work is an applied science, not a basic science, our argument is that the *post-hoc* model is quite relevant. As we have stated earlier, however, the validation of possible causal associations and theoretical propositions must be achieved by using hypothesis testing with tightly controlled experimental or quasi-experimental designs.

Dr. Reid states that the theory-based hypothesis-testing model is a powerful means of knowledge building. However, social work practice knowledge often does not come from the established theory of social science; rather, it is in large part based on practical experience. The knowledge gained by theory-based research endeavors remains abstract and impractical until its applicability to social work practice is made explicit. Alternatively it could be argued that *post-hoc* exploratory research findings of client behavior or social conditions, although atheorectical, are directly relevant to social work practice.

An example of the appropriate use of an exploratory design comes from the "rise and fall of the 'double-bind' theory of schizophrenia." When the hypotheses generated by that theory failed, alternative theoretical explanations of the etiology of schizophrenia were sought. In this situation, investigators explored the role of the family, not only on the etiology, but also on the course of the illness. This is a prime example of the usefulness of exploratory, *post-hoc* designs to seek alternative explanations. When hypothesis-testing efforts failed to support the theory, it would have been more efficient to conduct exploratory studies to gather additional information, rather than seeking for another theoretical explanation, because an exploratory study may offer more than one explanation.

Another advantage of the exploratory design for social work research is that sometimes established theories do not change over time, and available scientific evidence contradicts widely known theory. One example is the importance of ''moral weakness'' in the etiology of alcoholism. Current evidence indicates a strong genetic influence on the development and the course of alcoholism. Thus, hypotheses based on the ''moral weakness'' theory are not relevant to clinical practice or prevention programs of alcohol abuse. Another example can be found in the changes in the theory of mental illness. The discovery of psychotropic medications provided a range of effective treatment modalities for the mentally ill. Biological theories of mental illness are based, in part, on the clinical experience of effective administration of psychotropic medications for different psychiatric conditions.

While the exploratory, *post-hoc* models have practical applications to social work research, the limitations stated earlier should be recognized. Effective knowledge building in social work must use both methods appropriately to conduct the most efficient, methodologically sound research studies possible.

DEBATE 5

Is Feminist Research Inherently Qualitative, and Is It a Fundamentally Different Approach to Research?

Liane V. Davis is Associate Professor and Associate Dean for Academic Programs at the University of Kansas School of Social Welfare, where she teaches social work practice courses. Her passion is applying feminist thinking to all aspects of the social work profession and the social work curriculum.

Jeanne C. Marsh is Professor and Dean of the School of Social Service Administration at the University of Chicago, where she teaches courses in practice research and program evaluation. Her current research and writing interests are knowledge use in practice and program decision making, social welfare program and policy evaluation, and mental-health service delivery. She serves on the editorial boards of *Social Service Review, Journal of Social Work Practice, New Directions for Program Evaluation,* and *International Applied Social Sciences Index and Abstracts.* She recently authored, with Sharon Berlin, *Informing Practice Decisions* for Merrill Macmillan (New York).

YES

LIANE V. DAVIS

At this moment in history, feminism requires qualitative research that is directed at challenging and transforming the patriarchal construction of reality. To understand why I believe this, I must first ground my readers, if only superficially, in the intersection between contemporary feminism and epistemology. In the early

1970s, feminism emerged as a strong social and intellectual force. Over the past twenty years, as feminists realized that no one perspective could adequately speak for all women, the singular concept of *feminism* has been replaced slowly by the pluralistic construct of *feminisms.*

''Liberal feminism'' is what most people think of when they hear the term, *feminism.* This approach is represented by the National Organization for Women's (NOW) dedication to achieve equality for women in all spheres of life. As with any liberal agenda, NOW directs its energies toward political change, fighting for laws that extend to women the same rights as men and that extend to men the same responsibilities as women. If I identified myself as a liberal feminist, I would be on the other side of this debate, advocating for more and better quantitative research that corrects the historic neglect of women and demonstrates, among other things, the continued inequities in their lives.

The more radical feminists, and I include myself in this diverse group, demand far deeper and more encompassing changes that go to the heart of the knowledge-making enterprise itself. Joining with other constructivists in the critique of the prevailing epistemology, these feminists argue that it is people who construct and legitimate society and its institutions. Over time, however, people act as if what has been constructed by previous generations has a life independent of its human creators. But while many versions of reality may be constructed, only those of the powerful are ''legitimated'' (Berger & Luckmann, 1967). Until now, those in power have been a small group of privileged white men who have ''generalized from themselves to all, established their sex/gender, their race, their class, as norms and ideals for all, while also maintaining their exclusivity'' (Minnich, 1990, p. 68). It is these elitist definitions of society and its institutions (which includes its theories, arts and sciences, forms of governance and economic structures, the roles assigned to people and the behaviors expected of them, as well as the rules for determining what constitutes acceptable knowledge) that become normative standards against which everyone and everything is judged. There is a pernicious cycle. First, women (and members of other marginalized groups) are marked as lesser beings, which justifies their exclusion from the knowledge-making enterprise. Then, they are further judged deficient by the elitist standards developed by those in power. Finally, as they judge themselves against the ideal standards, they internalize the belief that they are not good enough. Thus, their exclusion from power continues. Through this process, defining reality (and morality and truth) becomes the private domain of a powerful elite.

If all of this sounds far-fetched, think about how we are all socialized 1) to devalue and discredit our own knowledge and experience, and 2) to rely instead on experts to define reality for us (Weick, 1994). As an example, think of the millions of women whose experience of having been battered, raped, and sexually abused by some man has been so powerfully defined by others that they hold themselves responsible for the assaults on their bodies and minds or deny the reality of their experiences.

From this more radical perspective, feminist research has an over-arching and far-reaching goal: to develop versions of reality that more accurately reflect the experience of women, versions that affirm women's strengths and value and can transform society itself. Clearly for this to occur, research must be able to convert the elitist reality that has been imposed on us into the multiple realities of the many persons whose voices have thus far been silenced. It is my belief that only qualitative research is capable of such a monumental remaking of reality.

Why Qualitative Research?

There are five reasons that this more radical feminism requires qualitative methodologies. These are discussed briefly below. Many other equally important interconnections between feminism and qualitative methodologies are explored more fully elsewhere (see, for example, Belenky, Clinchy, Goldberger, & Tarule [1986]; Mies [1979]; Reinharz, [1992]).

The Potential to Allow Women to Tell Their Stories in Their Own Voices

Describing why they chose intensive, open-ended interviews in their study of women's ways of knowing, Belenky, Clinchy, Goldberger, & Tarule (1986) write:

> . . . because we wanted to hear what the women had to say in their own terms rather than test our own preconceived hypotheses, particularly since we included a number of disadvantaged and forgotten women whose ways of knowing and learning, identity transformations, and moral outlook have seldom been examined. . . . We proceeded inductively, opening our ears to the voices and perspectives of women so that we might begin to hear the unheard and unimagined. (p. 11)

The Potential to Allow Participants and Researchers to Come to a Common Understanding of What They Are Creating

Despite claims to the contrary, we all come to see the world through the glasses that we wear. Those glasses are colored by our gender, class, and race—forces so powerful that as hard as we try, we can never completely free ourselves of our biases. Only through interactive dialogue where we actively work to come to a common understanding can we hope to capture and create new realities.

The Potential to Allow the Researcher to Encourage the Silenced to Speak

Stifling any public admission of discontent is a successful survival strategy for oppressed persons. Feminist scholars have written extensively about the selflessness of women, the abnegation of their own needs while devoting themselves to the care of others (Miller, 1976). Yet if we, as researchers, are to document the lives of those who have been silenced and selfless, we must be able to get beneath their well guarded secrecy and give them permission to become "self-ed." Why should a woman, assaulted as a child and an adult, believe that a stranger posing as a researcher is going to be *the* person who finally listens to her story? Qualitative methods allow the researcher to sensitively explore what lies behind the shrugs, smiles, and scowls, to probe the inconsistencies that we hear, see, and feel.

The Potential to Allow for the On-Going Construction of Complex Realities

Too often, we assume or look for ready-made and simple answers to complex life issues. We are taught to search for generalities and for parsimonious explanations. But the world is a complex place inhabited by diverse people. What Flax (1987) has written about feminist theories applies equally to feminist research:

> Feminist theories . . . should encourage us to tolerate and interpret ambivalence, ambiguity, and multiplicity as well as to expose the roots of our needs for imposing order and structure no matter how arbitrary and oppressive these needs may be. If we do our work well, reality will appear even more unstable, complex, and disorderly than it does now. (pp. 56–57)

Women don't stay in abusive relationships because they have dependent personality disorders. They stay because nobody believes in them or in their story. They stay because their church and government fathers tell them it is their god-ordained responsibility to keep their families intact. They stay because the alternatives of poverty and stigmatization appear far worse. They stay because they love their children too much to leave. Then they leave because they love their children too much to stay (Davis & Srinivasan, 1992). These are complex realities that can only be portrayed through qualitative methods.

The Potential to Empower Women

Women have internalized the message that they lack knowledge about even the most intimate details of their lives. Women have internalized the message that their subjective experiences are not trustworthy sources of data. We can begin to empower women by using research to affirm their knowledge and wisdom and to teach them that they are, indeed, the best sources of data about themselves, that they know best what paths to take.

Knowledge is not out there waiting to be discovered by our increasingly sophisticated research methodologies. Rather, we are all constructing it on a daily basis. As Bruner (1986) has put it so well:

> It is not that we initially have a body of data, the facts, and we then must construct a story or theory to account for them. Instead . . . the narrative structures we construct are not secondary narratives about data but primary narratives that establish what is to count as new data. (p. 143)

Take "date rape" (or sexual harassment, or incest, or wife abuse) as an example. Ten years ago, "date rape" didn't exist. It was not that women weren't being assaulted by the men they dated; it was just that women accepted unwanted sexual intercourse as a necessary (and shameful) part of the dating and mating ritual. They accepted their responsibility for being "cock teasers"; they accepted their responsibility for taking care of their date's sexual "needs." Women had to create a different story about themselves and about their male partners before "date rape" could become new data. And yet, even at this point in history, I suspect that most women do not define unwanted sexual intercourse as rape. Their socialization is still too powerful; they still fear that they will not be believed; and they still will not be believed.

Only qualitative research *has the potential* to transform the patriarchal construction of reality. Yet qualitative methods, in and of themselves, are not feminist. To fulfill *the potential,* the researcher must be committed to using her research tools to provide women the opportunity to name their oppression, to speak out about their realities, and to transform society. This requires that researchers reach out to previously silenced persons (e.g., women of color, lesbians, women who are impoverished), provide them with opportunities to come together to share their experiences and wisdom and develop ways to act upon their knowledge, and then to support them as they use that knowledge to transform their lives and the society in which they live.

References

Belenky, M. F., Clinchy, B. M., Goldberger, N. R., & Tarule, J. M. (1986). *Women's ways of knowing: The development of self, voice, and mind.* New York: Basic Books.

Berger, P. L. & Luckman, T. (1967). *The social construction of reality: A treatise in the sociology of knowledge.* New York: Anchor Books.

Bruner, E. (1986). Ethnography as narrative. In V. Turner, & E. Bruner (Eds.), *The anthropology of experience.* Chicago, IL: University of Illinois Press.

Davis, L., & Srinivasan, M. (February 29–March 3, 1992). *Listening to the voices of battered women: What helps them escape violence.* Paper presented at the 38th Annual Program Meeting of the Council on Social Work Education, Kansas City, MO.

Flax, J. (1987). Postmodernism and gender relations in feminist theory. *Signs, 12,* 621–643.

Mies, M. (1979). Toward a methodology for feminist research. Occasional Paper of the Hague, The Netherlands.

Miller, J. B. (1976). *Toward a new psychology of women.* Boston, MA: Beacon Press.

Minnich, E. K. (1990). *Transforming knowledge.* Philadelphia, PA: Temple University Press.

Reinharz, S. (1992). *Feminist methods in social research.* New York: Oxford University Press.

Weick, A. (1994). Overturning oppression: An analysis of emancipatory change. In L. V. Davis (Ed.), *Building on women's strengths: A social work agenda for the 21st century.* New York: Haworth Press.

Rejoinder to Dr. Davis

JEANNE C. MARSH

If our goal as feminist researchers is to ''transform the patriarchal construction of reality,'' then we need all the knowledge-building tools available—and then some. Dr. Davis sets before us an ambitious and absolutely appropriate task. And if we are to make a dent in the patriarchal construction of reality, we should not waste intellectual energy quibbling about whether the best brand of feminism is ''liberal'' or ''radical,'' or whether the change that we seek is ''superficial'' or ''deep.'' Rather, we should grab the knowledge-making enterprise, make it our own, and with our considerable talent and energy, illuminate the perspectives, experiences, and knowledge of women. Evidence abounds that this is happening already to a very positive extent.

If we discuss the issue of rape raised by Dr. Davis, the social construction of this topic (i.e., how we generally understand it) has shifted significantly in the last fifteen years. The work of female social scientists and social workers has contributed enormously to the shift. In Ann Arbor, Michigan, in the early 1970s, the prevailing wisdom about rape was captured in the phrase, ''If rape is inevitable, lie back and enjoy it.'' Then women began to write on the walls of restroom stalls at the University of Michigan about their personal horrors as victims of rape, including what we now know as ''date rape.'' This led to the Michigan Task Force on Rape, a group eventually responsible for the passage of legislation that would serve as a model for legislative reform in the area of criminal sexual conduct in states across the country. The impact of the Michigan legislation was evaluated (Marsh, Geist, & Caplan, 1982) as was the impact of other reforms. The evaluation of the Michigan law was a quantitative study, but overall research on victim experiences, as well as on remedies, legislative and other subjects, have employed both qualitative and quantitative tools (c.f., Russell [1975]; Holmstrom & Burgess [1978]; Estrich [1987]; Gordon & Riger,

[1989]). Starting with statements on bathroom stalls, the perspectives of women have been expressed and analyzed and critiqued, using a variety of methodological tools, and the way we think about rape and respond to victims of rape is very different now than it was fifteen years ago.

Despite evidence of progress, there is no question that there is significant work to be done to transform the "patriarchal construction of reality." And I say let us get to work—with all the energy and tools at our disposal.

References

Estrich, S. (1987). *Real rape.* Cambridge, MA: Harvard University Press.

Gordon, M., & Riger, S. (1989). *The female fear: The social cost of rape.* New York: The Free Press.

Holmstrom, L. L., & Burgess, A. W. (1978). *The victim of rape: Institutional reactions.* New York: Wiley.

Marsh, J. C., Geist, A., & Caplan, N. (1982). *Rape and the limits of law reform.* Boston, MA: Auburn House.

Russell, D. E. H. (1975). *The politics of rape: The victim's perspective.* New York: Stein & Day.

NO

Jeanne C. Marsh

I reject the position that feminist research is based inherently on qualitative methodologies, and that it represents a fundamentally different approach to science relative to mainstream, empirical research methods. I reject this narrowly constructed definition because it focuses only on *how* to study the subject matter. While various definitions available in the literature focus both on *what* to study and *how* to study it (Stanley & Wise, 1983; Collins, 1986), I take the position that 1) understanding and illuminating the events and experiences in women's lives is a central and difficult aspect of feminist research, and 2) in this enterprise, it is necessary to rely on all existing methods of inquiry, as well as to depart from them. This definition of feminist research focuses on the *purpose* of the enterprise.

Implicit in the definition is recognition that knowledge is socially constructed and that what we know is heavily determined by the social and cultural context. The significant influence of social context, norms, and expectations on women's behavior and on self-descriptions is illustrated by Heilbrun (1988) in her book, *Writing a Women's Life.* She documents how, until very recently, women's public descriptions of their lives conformed to society's expectations, while their true experiences and perspectives remained invisible to all but close confidants. She illustrates the point by using the example of early social worker Jane Addams. By her own public accounts (i.e., books and papers prepared for a wide audience), Jane Addams lived a dull, passive, and conventional existence: her career found her; her ideas enjoyed general acceptability; and financial support for Hull House appeared at the necessary times. In her private letters to other women, she provides a starkly different picture. In her communication with intimates, she paints a picture that includes struggle for recognition, struggle for accomplishment, and struggle to pursue reformist ideals through detached, systematic, scientific methods.

The contrast between the public and private writing of Jane Addams illustrates Reinhartz' (1983) suggestion that in order to find out what we know about being women, we must constantly question what we know and how we know it. Du Bois (1983) makes a similar point when she articulates the difficulties of feminist research that attempts to break out of the influence of the dominant culture and states that "women have been barred from experiencing [their] experience; it takes enormous effort, enormous consciousness to be able to feel our own feelings."

Even if one accepts the position that the primary task for feminist research is to create broad, public understanding of women's perspectives and experiences, one still could contend that qualitative methods provide the best vehicle for this purpose. There are at least two arguments that support this position. Both stem from an ongoing debate in virtually all social sciences about the merits of quantitative versus qualitative research. One aspect of the debate relies on the perspective that human behavior is too complex to be measured. A second and related argument suggests that all measurement efforts are efforts to control and dominate—activities antithetical to feminist philosophy and perspective.

These arguments can be countered in the following ways. First, accepting that all measurement strategies are fallible, it is possible to point to enormous progress made in the social sciences in recent years in the development of valid and reliable measures of attitudes, feelings, beliefs, and behaviors. Secondly, systematic scientific study traditionally has been used to meet the objectives of explanation, as well as prediction and control. That is to say, social science research methods can be aimed at different kinds of research questions: those related to understanding and explaining phenomena (e.g., what are the characteristics of informal helping in rural communities? what are the social and emotional sequelae for victims of sexual assault?), as well as those related to prediction and control (e.g., what is the perceived benefit of a Victim Assistance Program for victims of sexual assault?) Those who equate quantitative approaches only with studies involving prediction and control ignore an entire domain of applications for these methods.

The position taken here that qualitative and quantitative methods both have something to offer feminist research is based on three recognitions of fundamental importance.

First, tools available under the labels of qualitative and quantitative approaches are numerous and varied. It is useful to discuss specific research methods that fall under the broad labels of "qualitative" and "quantitative." It is sometimes argued that qualitative methods are preferred because their philosophical orientation and underlying value stance is more consistent with feminist ideals. However, qualitative methods themselves vary enormously in their philosophical origins and specific character. Indeed, included under the label of qualitative methods are *ethnography,* deriving from anthropological traditions; *phenomenology,* deriving from philosophy; *ethnomethodology,* from sociology; and *hermeneutics,* from theology, philosophy, and literary study (Patton, 1989). Similarly, quantitative methods incorporate a range of tools emerging from a broad spectrum of disciplinary traditions that include *randomized experimentation* and *quasi-experimentation* and *single-case analysis* from psychology; *survey interview methodology,* from sociology; and *cost-benefit analysis* from economics. Every tool mentioned has specific contributions to make. As feminist researchers attempt to break out of prevailing conceptualizations of their experience and perspective and pursue a range of research questions, all available tools are potentially useful.

Second, every tool offers the possibility of addressing a particular set of issues and questions. In general, qualitative tools are useful for providing detailed, rich descriptions of phenomena with minimal influence of preconceptions or pre-existing prevailing frameworks. They are useful for determining new insights and understandings. And, for this reason they are useful for scholars who are attempting to sort out the "true" experiences and perspectives of women from the "publicly acceptable" ones. Quantitative tools, in comparison, have significant utility for distilling overall trends and patterns from such rich, detailed information, thus, painting representative pictures. And because quantitative tools offer highly meaningful indicators that can summarize detail (i.e., cost-benefit ratios, effect sizes, and ratings of functionality), they are convenient, manageable, and "handle-able." For social workers who believe that research evidence should be used to inform practice and policy decisions, the products of quantitative tools can be particularly useful because of their accessibility.

Third, the selection of any tool depends on the research question. As indicated above, various kinds of research questions, whether aimed primarily at understanding a phenomenon or seeking to predict an outcome, require different tools. Restricting feminist research to one set of tools or another necessarily limits the types of questions that can be asked and answered. If we take on the issue of sexual assault, do we want to understand only the emotional and social impact of the experience on the victim (which might be addressed most appropriately through qualitative methods), or do we also want to know the impact of sexual assault legislation or other remedies for reducing the number of such assaults (a question that would lend itself most readily to quantitative techniques)? Cook and Reichardt (1979) suggest that often the most effective strategy for addressing a research question involves a combination of qualitative and quantitative tools.

Proceeding on the notion that *purpose,* rather than *content* or *method* should define feminist research, it is possible to identify examples of feminist research that derive from both quantitative and qualitative perspectives. One of the earliest examples of research on sex differences attempted to counter the idea, widely accepted in the late 1900s, that women are intellectually inferior to men and, indeed, that intellectual activity is detrimental to their reproductive capacity and general physical health. Marion Talbott, the first female professor and Dean of Women at the newly formed University of Chicago, organized the first systematic analysis of this theory. Using survey techniques emerging from the developing discipline of sociology, she found little evidence of difference in the fertility or general health of educated and uneducated women. This was the beginning of a strong tradition of female researchers at the University of Chicago, such as Edith Abbott and Sophinisba Breckenridge (who ultimately established the School of Social Service Administration). These women insisted on seeking solutions to poverty, crime, and family disruption through systematic, quantitative methods (Rosenberg, 1982). More recently, the work of Gilligan (1982) in her book, *In a Different Voice,* provides an example of the use of qualitative methods to establish distinct patterns of moral development among young women.

The research of female social scientists and social workers past and present illustrates and supports the idea that inquiry into the experience, perspectives, and preoccupations of women is a central aspect of feminist research. It is an endeavor that requires us to think in new ways about what constitutes knowledge and how we find it, an arduous task that cannot be limited to one or another set of methodological tools.

References

Collins, B. G. (1986). Defining feminist social work. *Social work, 31*(3), 214–220.

Cook, T. D. & Reichardt, C. (Eds.). (1979). *Qualitative and quantitative methods in evaluation research.* Beverly Hills, CA: Sage.

Du Bois, B. (1983). Passionate scholarship: Notes on values, knowing and method in feminist social science. In G. Bowles, & R. Klein (Eds.), *Theories of women's studies.* London, England: Routledge & Kegan Paul.

Gilligan, C. (1982). *In a different voice: Psychological theory and women's development.* Cambridge, MA: Harvard University Press.

Heilbrun, C. (1988). *Writing a woman's life.* New York: Ballantine.

Patton, M. Q. (1990). *Qualitative evaluation and research methods.* Newbury Park, CA: Sage.

Stanley, L., & Wise, S. (1983). Back into the personal or: Our attempt to construct ''feminist research.'' In G. Bowles, & R. Klein (Eds.), *Theories of women's studies.* London, England: Routledge & Kegan Paul.

Reinharz, S. (1983). Experiential analysis: A contribution to feminist research. In G. Bowles, & R. Klein (Eds.), *Theories of women's studies.* London, England: Routledge & Kegan Paul.

Rosenberg, R. (1982). *Beyond separate spheres: Intellectual roots of modern feminism.* New Haven, CT: Yale University Press.

Rejoinder to Dr. Marsh

LIANE V. DAVIS

As I stated in my YES position paper, feminism is not a monolithic way of understanding or responding to the societal oppression of women. Only from the outside can one speak of feminism; from the inside we recognize and value the diversity amongst ourselves. Therefore, it is difficult, if not impossible to argue with Dr. Marsh's position. From *her* feminist perspective, rejecting the inherent qualitative nature of feminist research is appropriate. In fact, forcing us to choose one side or the other in this debate is, I would argue, inherently antithetical to the way I have come to think of feminism. For me, feminism succeeds in bridging such dualistic thinking, embracing as it does ambivalence, ambiguity, and contradictions.

As I sat down to write this rejoinder, I found myself in a situation that illustrates the complexity and the contradictions of being a feminist researcher. On behalf of NASW's National Committee on Women's Issues, I had taken on the task of looking anew at the issue of gender disparities in our own profession. I had obtained a large data set and was cranking out statistic after statistic on my office computer. Using this quantitative research method, I was once again demonstrating that female social workers earn less than male social workers, even when controlling for important relevant variables (their primary job function, years of post-degree experience, etc.) Clearly this is a task that can only be accomplished with quantitative methodology. Furthermore, it was a feminist research project. While such research has been undertaken in the past by persons whom I presume would not have identified themselves as feminists, I had agreed to undertake it as a feminist with the goal of stimulating NASW to develop strategies to counteract the continuing discrimination against women in this women's profession.

And yet, at the same time that I cranked out the statistics, I was writing this rejoinder on a laptop computer that I had brought into the office. Am I not being duplicitous, arguing one thing while doing another? How can I live with such contradictions?

Over the years of my developing feminist consciousness, I have come to think of myself as living simultaneously in two worlds. One is the world as it is; the other is the world as I would like it to be. In the world as it is, there is a white-male power structure that defines reality and sets the rules for playing the game. In this world, women continue to be discriminated against just because they are women. I have learned that if we (and by "we," I mean feminists) are to achieve any short-term success, we have to play by the rules that have been imposed upon us. Thus, I sit at my computer grinding out statistic after statistic to prove, in the only language that those in power respect, a truth that almost all women know intimately.

Yet, I also know that if I play only by these traditional rules, the most I can ever hope for is that women may someday be equal players in the world as it is. For example, if we play by their rules, some day women may earn the same salary as men when they perform the same job function. The world as I would like it to be is a different place entirely; it has new games and new rules, which we have developed collaboratively. For example (and it is only one small example), we can acknowledge and value (monetarily) the immense amount of caring and caregiving that is provided to children, elders, people at home, and in the community. In this new world, we might even value (monetarily) the work that social workers do. To transform the world as it is into the world as I would like it to be requires the kind of radical transformative research I have described. In the meanwhile, I may have to occasionally play by the rules of the game, but I don't have to like them.

DEBATE 6

Is a Scientist–Practitioner Model Appropriate for Direct Social Work Practice?

Richard F. Dangel is Professor of Social Work and Director of the M.S.S.W. Program at The University of Texas at Arlington. He has published numerous books and articles about behavior modification, parent training, and residential treatment. He serves as consultant to many agencies, including the YMCA, Boy's Town, and Sesame Street. His newest book, *User Friendly Program Evaluation,* will be published by Sage in 1993.

Denise E. Bronson is an assistant professor in the College of Social Work at The Ohio State University, where she teaches research, clinical practice, and child welfare at both the undergraduate and graduate levels. She is involved in developing and implementing innovative practice evaluation methods for agency settings, such as the use of computers to assist clinical practice. Recently, she has also written articles on social work in Poland and on risk assessment for child abuse and neglect.

YES

RICHARD F. DANGEL

Social work, like psychology and medicine, contains numerous examples of beliefs and practices that sooner or later are proven incorrect. Not too long ago, obstetricians chastised their patients for gaining more than fifteen pounds during pregnancy. Subsequent research demonstrated that weight gains of over twenty-five pounds produced babies with fewer respiratory and cognitive developmental delays. For decades, psychologists told mothers that too much or too little hugging produced homosexual or autistic children, respectively. Subsequent research demonstrated that too much or too little hugging produced neither homosexual nor autistic children. A few years ago in Canada, the press reported that a social worker, using an innovative group-therapy technique called ''stomping,'' successfully freed a patient of his inhibitions. The social worker placed the patient between two mattresses and instructed the group members to ''stomp out'' the patient's inhibitions. They did, along with his ability to breathe. No subsequent research was conducted.

Aims of the Scientist–Practitioner Approach

The scientist–practitioner approach aims to reduce the number of incorrect beliefs and practices employed by social workers, to increase the effectiveness of social work practice, and to allow social workers to be accountable to their clients for what they do. The approach requires social workers to put their practice behavior under the control of data, either data that they collect themselves or data that they consume from the professional literature, to be skeptical of methods with weak or nonexistent empirical support, and to favor parsimony in explanation and operationalization in description.

Merits of the Scientist–Practitioner Approach

Not too many years ago, a colleague of mine, then the department chairperson, was asked by a long-time, social work field instructor why the school stopped requiring students to spend a year studying differential diagnosis. My colleague replied, ''For the same reasons that medical schools stopped teaching blood-letting.'' The scientist–practitioner approach distances social work practice from blood-letting, sorcery, and all-purpose-tonic salesmen and positions it more competitively with psychiatry and psychology.

The NASW Code of Ethics offers another compelling reason for the use of the scientist–practitioner approach. The Code requires that the social worker ''. . . take responsibility for identifying, developing, and fully utilizing knowledge for professional practice. The social worker should base practice upon recognized knowledge relevant to social work. The social worker should critically examine and keep current with emerging knowledge relevant to social work. The social worker should contribute to the knowledge base of social work and share research knowledge and practice wisdom with colleagues. Furthermore the Code requires that the social worker should terminate service to clients and professional relationships with them when such service and relationships are no longer required or no longer serve the clients needs or interests.'' The scientist–

practitioner approach facilitates compliance with these requirements. Fundamental principles of ethics dictate that social workers base their activities on evidence. The scientist–practitioner approach can contribute significantly to the evidence.

More than does a set of, say, techniques for marriage counseling or methods of relaxation training, induction into the scientist–practitioner model of practice teaches social workers a broadly generalizable set of skills that transcend any particular field or method of study. The scientist–practitioner approach teaches social workers a way to think. Instead of basing decisions, sometimes decisions with life-threatening consequences, on fad or fancy, the approach trains social workers to base decisions on the cumulative findings of research, and to doubt, ask the hard questions, and look for a better way. No other set of social work skills cuts as wide a swath across all fields and methods of practice, and with such wide-ranging implications.

In the late 1960s, for about one hundred dollars, an undergraduate student could free herself from her slide rule and purchase a somewhat bulky, battery-operated calculator that could *even* do square roots. Less than thirty years later, second graders routinely use pocket calculators that now do many more functions, faster, and for a fraction of the cost. Unfortunately, thirty years of practice advances in the social services have not yielded as impressive a record of progress. Take a social worker in the 1960s, change her dress, put out the cigarette, up the cost, and you've got a social worker in the 1990s. An engineer at Ford Motor Company in Dearborn, Michigan, can send a set of blueprints for a car to an engineer at Ford Motor Company in Mexico City, with relative assurance that the two cars built at entirely different locations would look alike and operate in the same manner. Such technological accomplishments are far too rare in social work. Those areas that have shown the greatest advancement, such as biofeedback, treatment of phobias, and parent training, are those most closely wedded to a research base. The resistance of social work to the scientist–practitioner model has significantly delayed the much needed technological advancements in the field.

A final rationale in favor of the scientist–practitioner approach concerns the increasing demand for accountability at the micro and macro levels. Insurance companies now routinely require evidence that clients are making progress. In one large county in Texas, United Way requires agencies to establish outcome objectives and performance standards, design and implement evaluation systems, and demonstrate how the findings are used to strengthen program effectiveness. Agency funding is contingent on evaluation outcomes. At the national level, most major entitlement programs are under careful scrutiny by the Democrats and Republicans because taxpayers are demanding that ineffective programs be stopped. In each example, social work stands to either benefit or suffer. If social work education programs equip social workers with the skills to contribute to these evaluation processes at the micro and macro levels and to interpret and apply research findings in program applications, social work can take the lead, simply by virtue of its numbers. If not, social workers will continue to be the poorest paid and least respected of the helping professions.

In summary, social work needs the scientist–practitioner approach for five reasons. First, the approach elevates social work to the rank of a science and away from the camps of witchcraft and superstition. Secondly, the NASW Code of Ethics requires social workers to identify, develop, and use knowledge for professional practice. Third, scientist–practitioners use a set of generalizable, critical-thinking skills that encourage them to be skeptical and to base decisions on facts rather than fad or fancy. Fourth, the approach facilitates the development of technological advances in practice that parallel those in engineering and the other hard sciences. Finally, the scientist–practitioner model permits the field to take the lead in the increasing demand for accountability at the micro and macro levels.

Why Arguments against the Model Fail

Critics of the scientist practitioner model generally put forth a handful of arguments as to why the model does not, has not, or will not work. The first argument is that not many social workers are ''cut out'' for research: you know, all those numbers and stuff. Social workers are best, they claim, at *really helping people.* This argument frames social workers as the idiots on the block, unable to conceptualize, quantify, critique, or analyze. Any social worker who would accept this, probably is.

The second argument is that social workers have only so much time to spend in school: any time spent studying research is time taken from studying particular practice theories and procedures that may be needed immediately. Certainly, the judicious use of time in training programs makes sense. All the more reason to concentrate on teaching generalizable skills that cut across fields and methods of practice and theories. The list of practice theories and procedures that have come and gone grows almost by the minute, recall: ''I'm O.K. You're O.K.,'' transactional analysis, and primal screaming.

The next argument concerns the adequacy of the available research methodology for the complex practice issues faced by social workers. Current research methods are inadequate and incomplete. Many require huge samples of clients or tremendous resources or control groups or simple client problems that respond quickly and dramatically to treatment. Likewise, current treatment methods for cancer are inadequate and incomplete. However, not many people advocate abandoning them. Instead, scientists advocate continuing to use what is available, while intensifying the refinement of existing methods and the development of new ones.

The final argument presented against the scientist–practitioner approach concerns the complexity of humans and the intricacies of the social work process.

Humans and human problems are, the argument goes, much more complex than a Ford or a pocket calculator, or for that matter than anything else. Because of this complexity, each and every human must have an individually designed treatment. Just like snowflakes, no two humans are alike and therefore no two treatments can be alike. This thinking all but eliminates any standardized or replicable treatment, a critical component of the scientist–practitioner approach. Similarly, the social work process, with its untold complexities and its mysterious blend of art and science, belies definition or operationalization. Practice wisdom is passed down from the generations, from the old social worker to the new. And, it must be passed down in a certain way, like a secret family recipe: if you spell out the ingredients, it just won't taste the same.

Yes, humans, and human problems, and social work practice methods, are complex. However, this statement far too often serves as an explanation when social work practice fails. "Those multi-problem families certainly are complicated to work with," social workers can be heard to say, "That's why they keep having one problem after another." Human complexity should not stop the search for effective solutions: it should intensify it.

Summary

The scientist–practitioner model of social work practice falls short of the panacea that many had hoped it would be. Nevertheless, the model provides a framework for social work practice that is necessary to carry social work into the next decades as the demand for accountability increases. The Council on Social Work Education should amplify its curriculum requirements to mandate that all Schools of Social Work require their students to evaluate systematically their practice and that education programs give them the skills to do so. The refreshing move towards more competency-based education in social work should facilitate greater research competency in students. And, social work faculty should be encouraged to develop training methods that help social work scientist–practitioners apply scientific methods to real-world problems in practical ways.

Rejoinder to Dr. Dangel

Denise E. Bronson

The debate about the appropriateness of the scientist–practitioner model for social work centers on the ability of workers to conduct research while providing good service. This discussion is complicated by poorly defined terms and, at times, a failure to understand the realities of practice settings. In order to bring some closure to this issue, these problems need to be addressed.

One place to start is to identify exactly what is required of the scientist–practitioner. Dr. Dangel states in the YES paper that the scientist–practitioner model emphasizes the importance of data-driven practice, the use of empirically tested interventions, critical thinking skills, and attention to practice effectiveness. These skills are critically important to effective, accountable social work practice, and should be part of social work practice, whether or not the practitioner is also a scientist.

Unfortunately, the scientist–practitioner model places additional responsibilities on the practitioner. In this model, it is not enough for social workers to document client improvement, they are also asked to contribute to the social work knowledge base by employing research designs in their clinical work that allow them to explore the causal relationship between the intervention and the outcomes. This is akin to asking a family physician not only to establish that a patient's fever has dropped, but also to determine that it was the aspirin that was responsible for the reduced fever rather than a host of other possible explanations for the change. Establishing the causal link between aspirin and fever reduction is left to medical researchers, who are trained in research methodology and whose primary objective is knowledge development.

Although medicine and psychology are often used as examples of professions in which practitioners are also scientists; this is a gross misrepresentation of what actually happens in these fields. With few exceptions, advances in medical and psychological technology come from research labs and practice research centers. Patients or clients of physicians and psychologists hope that they are receiving service from practitioners who are familiar with the current empirical literature, able to evaluate the research findings, and interested in helping them resolve or manage the problem for which they sought assistance. These professionals should use a treatment method that has some proven effectiveness for the problem, but if their clinical measures (e.g., temperature, white blood cell counts, etc.) indicate that the first intervention did not successfully alleviate the problem, they are expected to try another and another until the treatment goal is achieved. Although they are monitoring the outcomes, this is not research . . . just good clinical practice. With fewer years of formal education, how can we expect more from social workers?

Citing the NASW Code of Ethics, Dr. Dangel also argues that social workers have an ethical obligation to engage in scientific practice. In addition to using empirically derived methods and research results, the Code of Ethics calls for social workers to contribute to social work knowledge. It does not specify, however, how this contribution should be made. Enhancing social work knowledge can be accomplished in many ways other than engaging in rigorous practice-based research. For example, practitioners can identify trends based on their systematic evaluation of practice and share this information with practice researchers for further study. This would enable researchers to study questions which are guided by practice experience and which will be relevant to future social work practice. Rather than expecting practitioners to conduct this research, we need to develop better vehicles for getting practice questions and service data to trained researchers, and subsequently, for getting the results of their studies back to the practitioners.

Once social work abandons the notion of the scientist–practitioner, we will be in a better position to explore new directions in practice evaluation and practice-based research. Empirical studies over the past fifteen years have shown us that there are important problems with implementing the scientist–practitioner model in social work settings. Isn't it time to let the data guide our behavior? If we want M.S.W.-level practitioners to 1) develop critical-thinking skills, 2) systematically evaluate their practice, 3) critically read current practice research articles, and 4) implement empirically based interventions, then let's restructure social work education to guarantee that those skills are acquired. At the same time, let's provide doctoral-level training in practice-based research and develop better mechanisms for practice to inform research and for research to inform practice. As Dr. Dangel notes in his conclusion, "The scientist–practitioner model of social work practice falls short of the panacea that many had hoped it would be." It is time to better define our terms and expectations in order to develop a new approach; one that better serves both practice and science.

NO

DENISE E. BRONSON

The time has come to abandon the scientist–practitioner model for social work practice in favor of one that better suits the realities and objectives of service settings. The scientist–practitioner model of social work calls for greater reliance on empirically supported interventions and the use of research methods to evaluate service outcomes. When this approach was first presented, nearly twenty five years ago, it highlighted the need for more systematic and objective research on practice effectiveness and called on practitioners to provide this information through the experimental evaluation of practice outcomes. Wide acceptance of this model has had an important influence on social work education, and many schools now provide courses in single-case research methods for practitioners. Unfortunately, numerous studies indicate that few social workers can be called scientist–practitioners and that there are significant problems with using research techniques in a practice setting. It is becoming increasingly clear; the scientist–practitioner model is not, and never has been, an appropriate model for direct social work practice. A new model for evaluating social work service is needed that is consistent with service objectives and feasible in practice settings.

Review of the Scientist–Practitioner Model

The scientist–practitioner model of social work is often equated with empirical practice. This approach calls for workers to use practice methods for which there is sound empirical support, whenever possible, and to evaluate their own methods empirically (Ivanoff, Blythe, & Briar, 1987). Using empirically supported methods requires practitioners to read current research literature, evaluate the quality of the research, generalize the results to their own cases, and be willing to alter their treatment procedures in the light of changing (and sometimes contradictory) empirical outcomes. Social workers who adopt the scientist–practitioner model must also engage in a variety of activities that will allow them to empirically evaluate their own practice. They must 1) systematically collect information during assessment, intervention, and follow-up; 2) document the interventions that they are using with enough specificity to allow for future replication; 3) compare their results across clients and problems; and 4) communicate their findings to others (Ivanoff, Blythe, & Brian, 1987). To successfully perform these activities, social workers must have a strong background in research methods, sound analytic skills, sufficient time, and an environment which supports these activities.

Problems with the Scientist–Practitioner Model

The problems with the scientist–practitioner model have been covered extensively elsewhere (Thomas, 1978; Gingerich, 1988). The earliest criticism of this model focused on the conflicting objectives between scientific research and practice (Thomas, 1978). Thomas noted that the methods required to establish a causal link between an intervention and the observed outcomes often interfere with service delivery as, for example, when collecting baseline data delays services. Similarly, when service objectives take precedence, the rigor of the research is likely to be compromised.

The methods (primarily single-system research designs) associated with the scientific practitioner have also been criticized as being inapplicable to many types of social work practice (Gingerich, 1988). Questions have been raised about whether these techniques can be used with nonbehavioral practice. Single-case designs may also be difficult or impossible to implement with very short-term cases, those for which there are no change objectives, crisis situations, or cases in which the social worker is functioning as an advocate or mediator with the external environment (Ivanoff, Blythe, & Briar, 1987).

A third problem with the scientist–practitioner model is indicated by the difficulties that social workers report in trying to use single-case evaluation methods. Evidence to date suggests that few social workers have adopted an empirical approach to practice. Those that have, selectively use the techniques with only a small percentage of their total caseload (see Gingerich [1988]).

Social workers report that rigorous evaluation is time-consuming and that there are a host of difficulties (i.e., obtaining reliable client self-reports, collecting data during an interview, deciding how much information to collect and on which goals, etc.) that interfere with their use of practice evaluation techniques. Furthermore, agencies are not reimbursed for time spent on scientific inquiry or knowledge development. Social workers often engage in these activities on their own time and with little administrative or collegial support.

A fourth problem is that most M.S.W.s do not have the prerequisite research skills and knowledge to function as a scientist–practitioner. The scientist–practitioner role requires social workers to have the ability to 1) formulate research questions, 2) develop reliable and valid data collection procedures, 3) analyze their results, and 4) present their results in such a way that social work knowledge can be advanced. In addition, they are to do this in one of the most difficult research settings (i.e., the natural environment), where even the most skillful researcher has difficulty controlling the various threats to internal validity. To assume that M.S.W.-level social workers have the skills to conduct meaningful research in applied settings overestimates the training that social workers receive and underestimates the complexity of agency-based research. Conducting scientific investigations without adequate training can result in erroneous or misleading results that might prove to be detrimental to clients and knowledge development.

Finally, the technology has not been sufficiently developed as of yet to allow scientist–practitioners to make significant contributions to knowledge development. Methods for comparing single-case results across cases, problems, workers, or settings need to be developed. Intervention replicability continues to be a significant problem in practice settings, and questions remain on the appropriateness of statistically analyzing single-case data. There are many issues that need to be addressed concerning practice research, and it is unlikely that practitioners have the time or training to address them.

The Self-Evaluative Practitioner Model

In light of these significant problems with the scientist–practitioner model, it is time to develop a new model of practice. This would be the self-evaluative practitioner, which retains the systematic evaluative approach to service delivery, but uses methods that are better suited to the realities of the practice world. The self-evaluative practitioner can best be defined by several characteristics. First, self-evaluative social workers will continue to have service as their primary objective, but will place a strong emphasis on monitoring progress toward their service goals. They will also have the ability to think critically and to identify the ways in which their own judgmental biases might influence their decisions about client progress and will try to overcome those biases. The self-evaluative social worker will also have a willingness to assess failures and look for ways to improve service delivery. As in the scientist–practitioner model, they will systematically collect information and use measures that will inform them about their client's progress, and they will use this information to make clinical decisions about whether to change or continue with the intervention plans. Finally, the self-evaluative practitioner will have an interest in developing social work knowledge to the extent that they are willing to identify practice issues and trends that might be worthy of more intensive and rigorous research by those who are trained to engage in such activities.

There are several steps that need to be taken in developing this model. First, the differences between clinical research, outcome evaluation, and practice assessment/monitoring need to be described clearly, including the objectives of each set of activity and the methods that are best suited to it. Recent articles by Gingerich (1988) and Proctor (1990) have made important contributions in this area. Gingerich notes that "the purpose of *research* is to develop scientific knowledge. . . . *Evaluation* refers to the determination of whether a desired outcome was achieved." Furthermore, he argues that social workers should be able to determine whether their clients have benefitted from treatment, but not to provide evidence of a causal connection between their intervention and the observed changes. Proctor (1990) has further refined this distinction and proposed four levels of evaluation and research: 1) assessment and monitoring of client behavior, 2) monitoring change in relation to treatment, 3) testing treatment effectiveness, and 4) comparing the outcomes of two or more interventions. She suggests that the question to be answered will determine the best level of evaluation for both practitioners and researchers. Both of these articles have made significant contributions to defining the activities of practice research and practice evaluation in a way that will foster the development of the self-evaluative practitioner and techniques better suited to a practice environment.

Once a clear distinction is made between research and evaluation in social work practice, it will be possible to focus greater attention on developing evaluative tools that are better suited to the diversity and constraints of practice settings. It is important to do more than just adapt research tools to practice. Instead, evaluation methods need to be developed in the settings in which they will be used and with the help of those who will be using them (Robinson, Bronson, & Blythe, 1987). As Gingerich (1988) has stated, "We should abandon the 'uniformity myth' of single-case evaluation and begin to develop practice-specific methods and techniques" (p. 11). This will not happen until we recognize the differences between research and evaluation, and begin to acknowledge practice evaluation as a valuable activity in its own right, rather than a weakened version of research.

Social work education needs to be revised, if we adopt the model of the self-evaluative practitioner for direct service. Many schools of social work currently teach evaluation as part of their research sequence. Case-evaluation projects are undertaken as research theses and students feel unsuccessful if their clients fail to provide reliable data, if their research design is interrupted by the client terminating treatment, or if the measures they select at the beginning of service turn out to be invalid indicators of client change. By abandoning the scientist–practitioner model, social work research courses can begin to focus greater attention on understanding published research, critically evaluating reports of new intervention techniques, and, in short, learning how to be consumers of research. Practice evaluation can be offered as part of practice methods courses, using texts that place service objectives first and offer evaluation strategies for the various roles and settings in which social workers are employed. This requires a recognition that it is impossible to teach M.S.W.-level social workers how to conduct research in a two-year program, given the other areas of expertise they are expected to acquire. Research training can then be offered in advanced courses for doctoral students, with the expectation that practice research will be conducted by those with intensive training in this area. Practice researchers may be affiliated with universities or, as Thomas (1978) suggests, with practice research centers. By restructuring social work education, it will be possible to separate the roles of research and evaluation and develop teaching methods appropriate for each. The self-evaluative practitioner can be instrumental in helping practice researchers identify interesting areas for exploration, but only if social work education helps them to recognize this as an important part of being a self-evaluative practitioner.

Finally, once we recognize that it is not the responsibility of practitioners to add to social work knowledge, it is important to identify who is responsible for conducting the experimental analysis of treatment effectiveness and comparative research on alternate intervention strategies. Practitioners need to know that it is their responsibility to determine if change is occurring (practice evaluation skills), but it is not their responsibility to establish what caused the change (research skills). The responsibility for determining what produced the change belongs to practice researchers, who have the resources, training, and time to undertake an experimental analysis. In an ideal world, practice research will be informed and guided by interesting trends and patterns that are observed in practice settings by those who systematically evaluate the services they deliver. A cooperative model in which the evaluative practitioner and the practice researcher work together to identify important service questions and advance social work knowledge is a more realistic and efficient way to proceed.

As long as we harbor the notion that social workers can be scientists doing research in practice settings, we are committed to finding ways to make research methods fit practice settings. Let's stop trying to force a square peg into a round hole! It's time for a new approach, one which recognizes the importance of both evaluation and research, the complexity of each endeavor, the distinct objectives of service and research, and the need for techniques specific to each. More importantly, one that recognizes social workers' first priority—to serve clients.

References

Ivanoff, A., Blythe, B., & Briar, S. (1987). The empirical clinical practice debate. *Social Casework, 65,* 290–298.

Gingerich, W. (1988, August). Rethinking single-case evaluation. Paper presented at the Conference on Empiricism in Clinical Practice: Present and Future, Great Barrington, MA.

Proctor, E. K. (1990). Evaluating clinical practice: Issues of purpose and design. *Social Work Research & Abstracts, 26,* 32–40.

Robinson, E., Bronson, D., & Blythe, B. (1988). An analysis of the implementation of single-case evaluation by practitioners. *Social Service Review, 62*(2), 285–301.

Thomas, E. J. (1978). Research and service in single-case experimentation: conflicts and choices. *Social Work Research & Abstracts, 14,* 20–31.

Rejoinder to Dr. Bronson

Richard F. Dangel

The bad news is that Dr. Bronson has outlined five faulty arguments to support abandoning the scientist–practitioner model of social work practice. First, she asserts, "We [should] recognize that it is not the responsibility of practitioners to add to social work knowledge . . . ." "Why not?" we might ask. With every client, practitioners see intervention effects, or lack of intervention effects. How much can social work knowledge advance if its major data base—feedback from practitioners—is deemed worthless? In fact, a much stronger case exists to assert just the opposite: practitioners should be critical partners in the development of social work knowledge. Their experience, their close proximity to the data, and their professional commitment to effective practice make them second to none in terms of the importance of their contributions.

In her second argument, Bronson denigrates social workers' capabilities, "Most M.S.W.s do not have the prerequisite research skills and knowledge to function as a scientist–practitioner." Instead of criticizing social workers' capabilities, perhaps the criticism, if it is correct, should prompt graduate training programs in social work to re-tool their curricula for the current century. When physicians lacked the skills and knowledge to use sutures, medicine did not conclude that patients should be left to bleed to death. Instead, medical schools trained their students to sew.

Dr. Bronson fears turning social workers loose in the research community because they could produce "erroneous or misleading results that might prove to be detrimental to clients and knowledge development." This argument resembles the one used by the Chinese emperors to prohibit women from learning to read:

no telling what they might do! Oh, if only it were so easy to make changes in clients or in knowledge development. All social scientists know that a single piece of research, however beautifully or poorly executed, rarely produces profound effects.

Fourth, Dr. Bronson hitches her wagon to the oft used argument of incomplete methodology, "The technology has not been sufficiently developed as of yet to allow scientist–practitioners to make significant contributions." The first section of this paper addresses this criticism. However, another example may prove illustrative. Had the Wright brothers followed Dr. Bronson's logic, we would still be travelling by foot because we would be waiting for the complete technology of air travel. *Only* by repeated trial and error, and persistence, following much the same path as the Wright brothers, will improved technologies for applied research be developed.

Finally, Dr. Bronson suggests reverting to the old-fashioned shoot-from-the-hip model because of "difficulties social workers report in trying to use single-case evaluation methods." Bronson notes that research activities may be time consuming and social workers may receive little administrative or collegial support. Social work is committed to organizational change when organizational characteristics interfere with the objectives of the profession. If social workers find themselves in organizations that impede their ability to deliver quality and effective services to their clients, they have the professional responsibility, ethical obligation, and technical capability to promote organizational change.

The good news is that Dr. Bronson, herself, recognizes the weaknesses of her arguments and spends more than half of her paper defending the scientist–practitioner model. Sure, she changes a few words: scientist–practitioner becomes self-evaluative practitioner. She acknowledges that not all research theses will be brilliant. And, she argues for the virtues of highlighting the differences between research and evaluation, rather than for noting their respective points on the same continuum. Beneath it all, however, Bronson really supports the underlying principle of the scientist–practitioner model: that research and practice must feed each other to thrive. As Bronson puts it, ". . . practice research will be informed and guided by interesting trends and patterns that are observed in practice settings by those who systematically evaluate the services they deliver. . . . [working toward] a cooperative model in which the evaluative practitioner and the practice researcher work together to identify important service questions and advance social work knowledge. . . ."

A rose by any other name. . . .

DEBATE 7

Should Systematic Assessment, Monitoring, and Evaluation Tools Be Used as Empowerment Aids for Clients?

Srinika Jayaratne is Assistant Dean for Research and Professor at the University of Michigan School of Social Work. He teaches in the research and interpersonal practice areas. His current research interests include agency-based studies on practice evaluation, and studies on job stress and strain among social workers.

Jill Doner Kagle is a professor at the University of Illinois at Urbana-Champaign School of Social Work, where she teaches social work practice and human behavior in the social environment. She writes, presents workshops, and consults on recordkeeping, professional ethics, and the relationship between practice and research. An active member of NASW, she currently serves as President of the Illinois Chapter (1993–1995) and is a member of the Editorial Board of *Health and Social Work* (1991–1994).

YES

SRINIKA JAYARATNE

Someone once said that you learn from your failures as well as your successes. I can think of no other arena in which this truth is more salient than in clinical practice. All clinicians will attest to the emotional rollercoaster associated with clinical work—the grand successes and the grand failures. It will be the rare clinician who can brandish the badge of success and ignore interventions that failed. Rather, most will dwell on the failures, trying to find an answer by asking themselves, their supervisors, and their colleagues, what else could have been done?

How Do Practitioners Make Clinical Decisions?

Ironically, we know little about "how" clinicians judge or make decisions about client change. What criteria do clinicians bring to bear in making decisions about success and failure? According to the literature, few clinicians use any form of systematic data collection, and even fewer employ clinical instruments or measures. How, then, is change detected and recorded, and who decides? For the most part, this aspect of practice appears to be defined *completely* by the practitioner. It is the practitioner who assesses change by virtue of what she or he observes in client behaviors, interprets in client attitudes, infers from client statements, and synthesizes from feedback from the environment. In other words, change is what the practitioner says, reports, and records. The client is a parenthetical party, a mere informant to this judgment.

Little empirical research is available on the issue of the client's role in this process. For years, we have been told, and the data have generally supported the contention, that clients view treatment and therapists positively at the end of treatment. Therefore, to ask clients about treatment outcome is simply reconfirming what we already know. These conclusions merely supported the practitioners' decisions to stay away from client-generated data and to rely more on their own clinical observations. An alternate vision portrayed the practice scene as imbued with complexity and almost immune to measurement. I am of the opinion that *all* practitioners and *all* clients evaluate progress and change. We just don't know how they do it. The use of systematic data collection procedures and relevant practice tools may provide a cogent and common ground on this issue. The direct beneficiaries would be the client and the worker.

Campbell (1988), in one of the few studies that address the issue of client preferences on clinical outcome, concluded the following, "Clients overwhelmingly preferred the use of some type of systematic data collection over reliance on practitioner opinion as the sole means of evaluating practice effectiveness" (p. 22). While Campbell does not speculate on why clients express this view, one can argue that the clients are simply asking for their voice to be heard or for a verification of their perceptions. This perspective is placed within the context of empowerment by Kopp (1988). After an exhaustive review of the self-monitoring literature, she concluded that, "A client's perceived sense of self-efficacy, the belief that one can change, may be enhanced through the worker empowering the client to self-record" (p. 15).

While it is argued that the client and significant others are a part of the clinical process, and, therefore, a part of this judgment process, the legitimacy of such a perspective can be questioned. If, for example, the client has a different view of treatment progress, how systematically is this recorded? The absence of systematic data collection or the failure to employ measurement tools is simply a reification of the practitioner's base of power. It is in this context that I propose the adoption of "fourth-generation evaluation" as the basis for systematic evaluation and client empowerment (Guba & Lincoln, 1989).

Fourth-Generation Evaluation

According to fourth-generation evaluation, the claims, concerns, and issues of the different parties involved (stakeholders) serve as the methodological foci. In clinical practice, the client and worker will together decide on both the form and type of data collection and use this information to guide the intervention. All participants in the process of evaluation will be empowered. Each party is given an opportunity to provide systematic feedback on the nature and quality of information as well as its interpretation. A caveat, of course, is that not all clients will be capable and competent to be a full participant. Under these circumstances, fourth-generation evaluation will suggest the maximum use of significant others.

Such an approach to assessment is entirely consistent with the professional code of ethics and the use of treatment contracts, as well as the considerable literature on empowerment that emphasize the sharing and transfer of power. Gutierrez and Ortega (1991), who identify three levels of empowerment (personal, interpersonal, political), note that "what unifies these three levels of empowerment is a belief that the goal of social work practice is to help individuals to develop the capacity to change their situations" (p. 25). But, in order to exercise power in any social context, one must possess the necessary skills and self-efficacy. What better context is there for the modeling and learning of such skills than the context of practice? Pratt and Gill (1990), who advocate the sharing of research knowledge with mentally ill patients, note that the practice environment provides an excellent venue for teaching the jargon, developing realistic expectations, and for the client's taking a more pro-active stance in collaboration with the practitioner. If one accepts the principle that the client is not only a part of the treatment process, but is also a part of the evaluation process, then the notion of client empowerment has been put in place.

All workers gather information from their clients and sometimes from significant others, and they then proceed to use this information for treatment purposes. A worker may request clarification and ask for additional information from the client or others during the course of treatment. The extent to which the worker is willing to share *both* the data and interpretations of the data becomes a critical feature in empowerment. Typically, what is shared is the interpretation and not the data, because the so-called data are notes or other nonsystematic information gathered by the worker. In such a situation, the client has little to work with, other than what the worker says. If the client disagrees or remembers the situation somewhat differently, it is simply her or his perspective versus that of the professional. If, on the other hand, there is "hard evidence," and this is not necessarily objective evidence, a more relevant and clinically beneficial dialogue can occur.

A Case Example

Consider the following case example from Freiband, Jayaratne, Talsma, and Tommasulo (1993). In a marital treatment situation, the wife comes in and requests help for sexual problems. In an attempt to gather data, the worker asks her to keep track of the frequency of sexual activity between the couple on a simple frequency graph. The worker independently tracks progress as well, based on her interpretation of client verbal reports. After six weeks of data collection, the worker perceives the situation as getting significantly better, and the client reports the situation as considerably worse. Sharing the data and discussing the information reveals that the worker and client were employing essentially different criteria for the assessment of success. In this example, the worker gave the client an opportunity to independently assess the situation and, more importantly, to bring in this "evidence." This strategy empowered the client to use data on behalf of her perception of the problem and, thereby, better understand her situation. It also allowed the worker to correct a misunderstanding she had of the situation. Her original assessment was simply wrong. In my opinion, the absence of data in this instance would have led to clinical failure, client drop-out, or, at best, treatment of considerably longer duration.

If the above scenario were pushed even further, the worker and client could have employed a reliable and valid instrument of sexual satisfaction. Presumably, such an instrument would provide a more general, and perhaps more accurate, global representation of the nature of the problem as perceived by the client. Will this result in even more client empowerment—because the data gathered here will be somewhat more "objective"? A data collection strategy in which the nature of the data being collected and questions being asked are under the control of the client, is likely to provide a more positive basis for empowerment. On the other hand, as noted earlier in Campbell (1988), any kind of data collection may be preferable over worker opinion alone. While this is an empirical question, the use of a research tool by definition does not necessarily result in empowerment. What is critical is how the data are used.

The type of instrument or data collection tool may be less important than the act of data gathering *per se*. The collection of systematic data and the sharing of such data for purposes of clinical practice and evaluation should have a significant impact on treatment. While there is no empirical evidence to support these observations, I will argue that systematic data collection will result in 1) far fewer drop-outs from treatment, 2) treatment of a shorter duration, and 3) more efficacious behavior on the part of clients and workers. To collect systematic data and to share this information for purposes of decision making is, by definition, the very crux of empowerment.

References

Campbell, J. A. (1988). Client acceptance of single-system evaluation procedures. *Social Work Research & Abstracts, 24,* 21–22.

Freiband, D., Jayaratne, S., Talsma, E., & Tommasulo, C. (1993). Counseling update: A flexible monitoring method for the client and practitioner. *Research on Social Work Practice.*

Gutierrez, L. M., & Ortega, R. (1991). Developing methods to empower Latinos: The importance of groups. *Social Work with Groups, 14,* 23–31.

Guba, E. G., & Lincoln, Y. S. (1989). *Fourth generation evaluation.* Newbury Park, CA: Sage Publications.

Kopp, J. (1988). Self-monitoring: A literature review of research and practice. *Social Work Research & Abstracts, 24,* 8–20.

Pratt, C. W. & Gill, K. J. (1990). Sharing research knowledge to empower people who are chronically mentally ill. *Psychosocial Rehabilitation Journal, 13,* 75–79.

Rejoinder to Dr. Jayaratne

Jill Doner Kagle

Dr. Jayaratne, a noted advocate of empirical practice and research, clearly believes that the use of systematic measures will not only empower clients, but will have beneficial effects on service delivery. In his view, because few social workers are using systematic measures in their practice, practitioners must be relying on their own judgment, and disregarding the client's perspective in evaluating services. Practitioners may observe the client and may receive feedback from the environment, but without systematic measures, they retain too much responsibility for interpreting, synthesizing, and recording information. Dr. Jayaratne argues that clients will be empowered when they are actively involved in the measurement process and can contribute to the evaluation of services. They will be able to influence the worker because they will have ''hard evidence'' to support their views. He envisions an environment in which clients and workers can be equal partners in data collection and interpretation. Moreover, he believes that using systematic measures will prevent clients from dropping out, and will make services more efficient and effective. What more could we ask?

Unfortunately, Dr. Jayaratne himself presents no "hard evidence" to support his argument. Indeed, his quotations from four studies are misleading. The first two studies examine related issues, but the findings do not confirm Dr. Jayaratne's position. Campbell (1988) asked thirty clients to rate the use of four different evaluation methods in hypothetical cases. His subjects preferred self-monitoring to practitioner opinions as the sole means of demonstrating to clients that services are effective. Although the study suggests that clients might be receptive to self-monitoring procedures, it does tell us if or under what conditions, systematic measurement procedures are empowering. Kopp (1988) reviewed the findings of twenty three studies on the reliability, accuracy, and effect on target behaviors of client self-monitoring. She found that self-monitoring generally produced significant changes in target behaviors and that this occurred in unmotivated as well as motivated subjects. Her findings suggest that self-monitoring procedures are powerful intervention tools; however, they also showed that these procedures can be used to control as well as to empower clients. The other two articles that Dr. Jayaratne cites do not even address the issues in question. Gutierrez and Ortega (1991) defined three forms of empowerment (personal, interpersonal, and political) and studied the influence of group processes on Latino college students' sense of political empowerment and willingness to participate in political activities. Pratt and Gill (1990) recommend sharing research findings with chronic mentally ill clients, adapting a standard psychoeducational technique to direct practice. The authors of these two articles did not investigate or produce findings on the use of systematic measures and their impact on empowerment.

Dr. Jayaratne's presentation of case material from his own research (Freiband, et al., in press) is intended to demonstrate that clients can use the data that they collect as a means to empower themselves. The case actually provides an example of an assertive client coping with the effects of poor clinical practice. As I understand the case, a wife seeks marital counseling because of sexual problems. She is told by the worker to keep track of the frequency of sexual activity (presumably with her husband), while the worker is keeping track of the client's verbal reports. After six weeks, the worker and client have distinctly different opinions of the effectiveness of services. Only after the reviewing the client's data do the worker and client recognize that they were using different criteria for evaluating improvement. I have many questions about this case: What had the worker and client been talking about? on what kind of "verbal reports" had the worker based judgments? why hadn't the worker and client examined the client's data before? and, most important of all, where was the husband? What is truly remarkable about this case is not the use of systematic measurement to empower a client, but the fact that the client chose to remain in treatment and believed that she benefited from services with a practitioner who clearly was not listening to her.

Dr. Jayaratne admits that his commitment to the use of systematic measurement is based more on faith than on fact. If he and other advocates of empirical practice and research are to convince nonbehavioral practitioners that these measures empower clients, they will need to address the political, methodological, and transactional issues that I have identified. They will also need to demonstrate that these tools are effective in assisting clients in making decisions and taking action, shifting the locus of control to the client, and strengthening the client's influence both inside and outside the treatment relationship.

References

Campbell, J. A. (1988). Client acceptance of single-system evaluation procedures. *Social Work Research & Abstracts, 24,* 21–22.

Freiband, D., Jayaratne, S., Talsma, E., & Tommasulo, C. (1993). Counseling update: A flexible monitoring method for the client and practitioner. *Research on Social Work Practice.*

Gutierrez, L. M., & Ortega, R. (1991). Developing methods to empower Latinos: The importance of groups. *Social Work with Groups, 14,* 23–31.

Kopp, J. (1988). Self-monitoring: A literature review of research and practice. *Social Work Research & Abstracts, 24,* 8–20.

Pratt, C. W. & Gill, K. J. (1990). Sharing research knowledge to empower people who are chronically mentally ill. *Psychosocial Rehabilitation Journal, 13,* 75–79.

NO

Jill Doner Kagle

Since the mid-1970s, a small but influential group of social work educators have sought to convince practitioners to adopt empirically based approaches to practice. Members of this group, advocates of empirical practice and research, argue that the best way to establish social work's standing as a scientific profession, enhance accountability, and improve service delivery is for practitioners to incorporate the findings and methods of quantitative research into their practice. The cornerstones of an empirically based approach to practice are: 1) defining problems, processes, and goals that are susceptible to measurement; 2) selecting intervention techniques that have some empirical evidence of effectiveness; and 3) using systematic, repeated measures, single-system designs, and quantitative methods of analysis to evaluate movement toward goals and service effects.

The Empirical-Practice-Research Agenda

At first, the advocates of empirical practice and research hoped to replace traditional practice with a revolutionary new paradigm and a new breed of practitioner: the scientist–practitioner. Eschewing practices that had not been proven effective, notably those of psychosocial casework, the scientist–

practitioner would choose instead cognitive, behavioral, and other empirically validated techniques. The scientist–practitioner would also use the scientific method to evaluate his or her own practice and develop new technology for the field.

Through the 1980s, the advocates for this change wrote prolifically and argued cogently for their point of view. Their paradigm received considerable attention in the literature, at professional meetings, and at all levels of the social work curriculum. Yet opposition grew in both the academic and practice communities. Before the 1980s were over, the data were in. The scientist–practitioner model was not gaining wide acceptance; the goal of replacing traditional practice with a new paradigm had largely failed.

In the light of these findings, these advocates have shifted their agenda. Rather than entirely replacing traditional practice, their goal in more recent years has been to infuse psychosocial, family-systems, ecological, and other non-behavioral approaches to practice with elements of empirical research. They argue that practitioners need not be logical positivists or adopt the role of scientist–practitioner in order to use the tools of science in their practice. At the very least, practitioners should use systematic, repeated measures to assess problems, monitor progress, and evaluate their practice. Any practitioner can and should use rapid-assessment instruments and other scales to inform their practice (Blythe & Tripodi, 1989; Corcoran & Fischer, 1987; Hudson, 1982). They argue that although this modified agenda may not add substantially to the knowledge base of the profession, it can make practice more effective and practitioners more accountable. Further, adopting the rhetoric of the 1990s, they contend that these measures actually empower clients by giving them a more active role in the service process.

Empowerment or Control?

Theoretically, any technique may be used to empower or to control a client. The key to evaluating whether a technique is being used for empowerment is to look at its impact on the process and outcome of services. If a technique is used to empower, it will offer the client authority in decision making and action taking, shift the locus of control from others to the client, alter interpersonal and environmental systems to make them more responsive to the client, and strengthen the client's influence both inside and outside the treatment relationship. If a technique is used to control, it will be used to direct the process or outcome of services, limit the client's autonomy in decision making and action taking, consolidate and strengthen others' influence over the client, and increase the client's compliance with others' authority.

In gauging whether a technique is empowering, the issue is not what decisions and actions that the client chooses to take; it is whether the client is permitted to make the choice. Empowering the client means that the practitioner, the agency, and others in authority must relinquish control over the process and outcome of services. They become the client's agent rather than agents of social control. For this reason, empowerment may have unforeseen consequences; an empowered client may not make the "right" decisions or take the "appropriate" action. Indeed, permitting clients to make only the "correct" decisions is like giving citizens the right to vote for only one candidate. Empowerment means giving clients the freedom to make their own decisions, even when those decisions are self-destructive, antisocial, or simply not the ones that those in authority would make. The process of empowerment is turbulent; its outcomes are unpredictable.

Systematic assessment, monitoring, and evaluation tools might be used to empower clients. However, for political, methodological, and transactional reasons, such tools are more likely to be used to influence and control clients than to empower them.

Political Issues

In today's political climate, social-service agencies and practitioners act more often as agents of social control than as agents of the client. Social problems are transformed into personal problems; their solutions involve change in those individuals who are most affected by social conditions, rather than in the social order that produce them. Those in authority, rather than the client, decide that there is a problem, what that problem is, how that problem is to be solved, and what is a "successful" outcome. The problem is usually defined as some personal characteristic or behavior of the client that requires remediation.

In programs as diverse as family preservation, substance-abuse treatment, and job training, for example, the problem, the process, and the goal are defined by others "on behalf of" the client, who becomes the likely target of change. Of course, the client is offered a choice: participate in the program and accept its contingencies or reject services and accept the consequences, which may involve losing one's child, job, or income. Under such conditions, using scales to assess, monitor, and evaluate services does little to empower clients, although it may appear to do so. Quantifying the problem and movement toward the goal can make the practitioner more accountable and services more effective. However, that accountability is directed toward goals set by the agency and community, and those effects are achieved not by empowering clients but by assisting them in adapting to the rules and expectations of family, organization, community, and those in authority.

Methodological Issues

The method itself tends to reinforce institutional and subjective biases that focus the service process and its outcome on changing the client, rather than on changing the client's circumstances. Although systematic measurement is supposed to be an objective process as a component of the empirical practice and research paradigm, it is actually grounded in a series of subjective decisions (Garfield & Bergin, 1986). The practitioner must decide what to assess, what instruments to use, and how to evaluate the results.

Like all observers, social work practitioners are influenced in these decisions by attributional bias. That is, in their analyses of client situations, practitioners tend to attribute the source of problems to personal traits and actions, and overlook the role of environmental factors (Kelley, 1972). These attributions can lead practitioners to concentrate their attention on client characteristics and behaviors, making them the focus of assessment and the target of change. Moreover, practitioners may find measuring personal characteristics more feasible, efficient, ethical, and prudent than measuring interpersonal or environmental factors. Not only is the client accessible; he or she may be persuaded to participate in the measurement process, while others in the situation may be unavailable or refuse to take part. Involving outsiders in the measurement process may unnecessarily compromise the client's privacy. Practitioners might also face sanctions within the organization or in the community if they seek to assess, monitor, and evaluate the behavior of those who were not part of the client situation.

Rather than counteracting these biases, systematic measurement may actually strengthen the tendency to neglect interpersonal and environmental issues. With a few notable exceptions, almost all of the instruments that are currently available measure individual traits or behaviors. Even those instruments that appear to measure relationships, really measure personal perceptions of interpersonal relationships or individual behaviors in interpersonal contexts. Simply put, systematic measures only answer the question: Has the client changed?

Standardized measures may also place clients who are members of oppressed, minority, and discredited social groups at risk (Witkin, 1991). Most scales that are now available have been designed, tested, and normed for use with white, middle-class individuals. Even scales that show relatively high reliability coefficients when administered to college students are probably neither reliable nor valid when administered to clients from other socioeconomic and cultural groups. The concepts, language, and experiences used in questions may be unfamiliar to these populations or incongruent with the situations that they encounter. In addition, norms based on traditional, white, European-ancestry, middle-class, heterosexual attitudes and expectations are likely to make members of racial, ethnic, economic, and sexual minorities, as well as other oppressed and discredited social groups, appear more troubled or deviant.

Transactional Issues

Systematic, standardized measures alter the balance of power in the worker–client transaction, strengthening the worker's position at the expense of the client. The use of assessment instruments offers the practitioner the credibility of science and the status of expert. By contrast, the client's personal perspective, couched in a less scientific vernacular, may be less compelling. Who could argue with the results of a "scientific test?"

Moreover, using such measures shifts attention from "where the client is." Beginning early in the process of service, the client's search for meaning in the complexity of his or her subjective experience gives way to the worker's attempts to simplify, quantify, and objectify that experience. These measures, whether or not they are valid, become a prism through which the client situation is viewed. For nonbehavioral practitioners, the shift in emphasis from "where the client is" to the technology of measurement is most disturbing. Worker and client must define the purpose of service when they know little about each other and have not yet begun to understand the problem. The process of systematic measurement takes precedence over the process of growth and discovery. Furthermore, this approach not only reifies method over meaning, the measures themselves are reductionistic and seem to miss the point. They calibrate responses, rather than explaining them, and isolate experiences, rather than connecting them to their historic emotional and social contexts.

If the advocates of empirical practice and research are to convince traditional practitioners to adopt systematic assessment, monitoring, and evaluation tools, they must find a strong and cogent argument. Their contention that the use of such measures empower clients is not persuasive.

References

Blythe, B. J., & Tripodi, T. (1989). *Measurement in Direct Practice.* Newbury Park, CA: Sage.

Corcoran, K., & Fischer, J. (1987). *Measurement in Clinical Practice.* New York: Free Press.

Garfield, S. L., & Bergin, A. E. (1986). *Handbook of Psychotherapy and Behavior Change* (3rd ed). New York: Wiley.

Hudson, W. (1982). *The Clinical Measurement Package.* Chicago: Dorsey.

Kelley, H. H. (1972). Attribution in social interaction. In E. E. Jones, D. E. Kanouse, H. H. Kelley, R. E. Nisbett, S., Valins, B. Weiner, (eds.) *Attribution: Perceiving the Cause of Behavior.* New York: General Learning Press, 1–26.

Rejoinder to Dr. Kagle

Srinika Jayaratne

While Dr. Kagle makes some important observations, she has also based her arguments on several false premises.

Dr. Kagle makes an unfortunate statement in arguing that the cornerstone of empirical practice is identifying problems and goals that are susceptible to measurement. Nothing could be further from the truth. Problems and goals are *not* defined by the ability to measure. Specification of problems and goals and the ability to monitor progress systematically is good clinical practice. If good research practice can be assimilated by employing reliable measurement strategies, it can only benefit the clinical process.

To argue that those who support ''empirical practice and research'' advocates only *quantitative* research is to invoke outdated ideology. Over the nearly two decades that have elapsed since the emergence of this literature, there has been a broad range of ideas about the meaning of practice evaluation. If there is consistency, it is in the notion of systematic assessment and evaluation, and the ability to elucidate one's practice procedures. While Dr. Kagle acknowledges this shift, she also argues against the value of systematic measurement, primarily on the basis of values and political ideology.

According to Dr. Kagle, systematic assessment is unlikely to benefit the client. For political and other reasons, such strategies are inherently biased toward maintaining the status quo and possibly are harmful to the client. She further argues that such monitoring by outsiders compromises client privacy. In principle, we agree. Both the environment and the individual often need change. However, these statements reflect political ideology, not clinical reality. The client must often live with others that are a part of their environment, possibly the same others who have now identified an individual as a client; and client and worker must work within existing legal and social guidelines. Granted, we may disagree with many of these realities, but to argue against helping an individual ''adjust,'' if necessary, to a not-so-ideal environment creates as many ethical questions as Dr. Kagle's arguments for changing an unjust environment.

On one issue I agree with Dr. Kagle, and that is the normative base of many measures essentially reflects the experience of white, middle class men. These measures may indeed lack cultural and gender sensitivity. But, it is also important to point out that the empirical model vehemently argues against the use of group norms and argues for within-case assessments. What matters, for example, is how much improvement the client reports, not a comparative improvement with some unknown group. To then push this argument even further, and state that measurement alters the balance of power is not at all compelling. Data, like any other bits of information (yes, even qualitative information) can be misused and misunderstood. Good practice depends on good assessment. Sharing data is good practice and can only lead to a better understanding of the situation. Implicit interpretations of practitioner-selected data could be far more biased than any form of empirical clinical practice.

Growth and discovery is indeed relevant, but not enough. The rubric of empirical practice asserts the importance of problem and goal specification for the very reasons cited by Dr. Kagle. It allows the worker and the client an opportunity to fully discuss and identify the nature and context of the problem. Only then is systematic data collection possible.

DEBATE 8

Is There an Ethical Responsibility to Use Practice Methods with the Best Empirical Evidence of Effectiveness?

Waldo C. Klein is an assistant professor at the University of Connecticut School of Social Work, where he teaches research and gerontology. His current scholarly interests include aging families, alcohol use among the elderly, and the area of social work knowledge development. He is actively involved as a consultant with a number of community-based human-service organizations.

Martin Bloom is a professor at the University of Connecticut School of Social Work, where he teaches research and practice. He is well known as the author of many books and has recently published, with Joel Fischer and John Orme, the second edition of *Evaluation Practice: Guidelines for the Accountable Professional* (Prentice-Hall, 1994).

Susan Meyers Chandler is a professor at the School of Social Work, University of Hawaii. She teaches in the area of social policy, community organization, and mental health, and currently is chair of the Ph.D. program. Her current research and writing interests are in the areas of mental health and substance abuse. She is currently working on a needs-assessment study with incarcerated persons.

YES

WALDO C. KLEIN
MARTIN BLOOM

Are practitioners ethically responsible for using practice methods with the best empirical evidence of effectiveness? Yes, of course; to do otherwise would be unethical and probably inefficacious as well. If we knew that an ethical practice method was 100 percent effective and would succeed at minimal social costs, we would be foolish not to use the method. If we know that another method was completely ineffective, we would be stupid to employ such a method. But relatively few cases of social work practice lie in either extreme of this continuum of knowledge about effectiveness. Thus, in this YES paper, we argue that the most ethical stand for social work practice is characterized by the phrase "acting on the basis of the best available information." It is necessary, therefore, that we clarify what is meant by the best available information in the context of scientific practice.

The "best available information" refers to knowledge that has emerged by means of the scientific process. This process contains a number of interactive elements: 1) empirically observable results (i.e., results available to the senses of any qualified observer); 2) a conceptual framework that provides a context of meaning for any empirical result; 3) possibly some technology or instrumentation that offers some exactness of what is known; 4) a valuational framework that indicates the practitioner's preferences regarding goals and means of actions related to the project; and 5) openness to the critical response of the scientific community to the product of this scientific effort, which will permit corrective modification. These five elements are the larger context of any piece of knowledge that a practitioner might use. To identify empirical practice only with the first element (observable results) is to impose too narrow an interpretation of "best available information." Thus, we interpret the terms of this discussion on empirical practice to refer to the broader meaning of the "best empirical evidence of effectiveness."

This broader meaning of empirical practice is especially important in social work, an applied social science. Students invest a great deal of time and energy learning about theories of behavior and of behavior change at individual and collective levels, research methods, values and the profession's code of ethics, and methods of practice. We do not propose to discard any of this educational experience when it comes time to use this knowledge/skill/value base in action.

Personal Knowledge

Part of the on-going nature of social work practice includes the empirical experiences from practice itself, both from one's colleagues and from one's own experience. These experiences are "empirical–conceptual–valuational" in nature; that is, they provide sensory confirmations of the conceptualized relationship among value-laden events of one's immediate actions (or the indirect knowledge as told to one by colleagues). We will call this experience *personal knowledge;* and we hypothesize that such personal knowledge is derived largely from and combined with one's professional training—the theories, empirical generalizations, values, instruments, and critical commentary of one's social work education. Personal knowledge does not come out of nowhere; nor does it stand alone as a self-confirming source of wisdom. It fits into a professional context for meaning, as well as direction. How this knowledge is used is a matter of personal artistry or the style of individual workers. Yet, if the idea of professional education has any meaning, it represents the common core of knowledge on which each individual builds. As a certified professional, the social worker is expected to use the scientific knowledge so far as it is practical to do so. As the NASW Code of Ethics (1980) expresses it:

> V. O. 1. The social worker should base practice upon recognized knowledge relevant to social work.
> V. O. 2. The social worker should critically examine, and keep current with, emerging knowledge relevant to social work. (p.)

The NASW Code (1980) offers ". . . general principles to guide conduct . . . in situations that have ethical implications. . . . Specific applications of ethical principles must be judged within the context in which they are being considered." Social work practice necessarily involves actions directly or indirectly affecting the lives and circumstances of people. Such person-affecting actions are moral relationships and are thereby to be guided by the Code of Ethics. This discussion addresses the knowledge context of ethical practice. As described above, we address the middle range of contexts, when we have only partial information on both the projected effectiveness of a method and a guess as to its ethical and other costs.

Securing the Best Available Knowledge

Within this middle range of contexts, there is variability in the amount of information available. We would presume that practitioners would use the "best available information" to guide their practice until there was enough uncertainty of outcome to make it difficult to decide whether to go with some established approach or to consider an alternative method guided by unique client information. Such an alternative would try some experimental method that seemed to offer hope of success. There are two main senses of the word "experimental." First, there is the explicit experiment, which involves standardized methods, randomization, use of control groups, and such. A second usage of experimental refers to little innovations applied to a situation at hand that might be called the testing of practice hypotheses. ("If I do X, the client is likely to do Y.")

Experimentation in the first sense (formal research) is not the focus of this discussion. The practitioner may know an empirically supported method exists, but choose to use another method—with unknown or less empirical support—as part of a research project in knowledge building in a new context. The entire experiment is circumscribed in time, structure, and process; its goals are for knowledge building, not the use of knowledge as is the goal of experimentation in the second sense.

We will focus on experimentation in the second sense, because this becomes a critical test for using the "best available information." With on-the-spot practice innovations, the practitioner can try out almost any idea, with the potential for prompt feedback and rapidly instituted changes. But in fact, people cannot be turned on and off like light switches, and more time must be given to an on-the-spot innovation. The practitioner has to plan the intervention, being careful of unintended side effects as well as main effects. Thus, even on-the-spot innovations have to be based on something other than the practitioner's hope and intuition. These innovations must be developed from the best available information, including ideas from the literature, reports by colleagues, other empirical information, conceptual frameworks, and the original thinking of the practitioner. These reflect the elements of the best empirical information as we have defined it.

At no point in this discussion should social workers depart from the use of critical thinking. The process of critical thinking begins by being open to innovative ideas, sorting many "floating fragments" until one is chosen because it is hypothesized to be effective within some frame of reference. Then social workers will try these on-the-spot hypotheses and make use of its logical structure to test them for continuing use, based on their *observed outcomes*. Finally, they incorporate these supported ideas (or discard the unsupported ones) according to our scientific frame of reference. To do otherwise would be to wander aimlessly in a dream world rather than perform professional practice in an ethical manner.

Single-system evaluation offers a special case of this on-the-spot innovation testing. Single-system evaluations are, by definition, an approximate method of receiving rapid feedback on operationally defined interventions affecting operationally defined targets. Yet, even here, the Code of Ethics binds the practitioner in choice of practice methods. What grounds would there be for selecting a less efficacious method over a more efficacious one? We would suggest that these grounds are no different than in any other practice situation—that the social worker should always be using the best available information to guide practice.

Applying the Best Available Knowledge

Thus, when the presenting case may differ to some degree from the existing body of research, we have to make a decision on whether or not to draw inferences from the research to the new situation. The greater the degree of difference between the current situation and the body of knowledge, the more risky that inference is likely to be. The less similar the knowledge that we have to apply to the new situation, the more free we are to experiment with new methods—and the greater our obligation to report our findings for those who follow us. In this way, we contribute to the "best available information," another ethical imperative of the Code of Ethics (NASW, 1980, Section V. O. 3.).

In all cases, ethical practice calls upon the social worker to be accountable for his or her practice. According to the Code of Ethics, social workers should terminate services to clients ". . . when such service and relationships are no longer required. . . ." (Section F. 9.). The only way that a practitioner would be able to tell if the client's problems had been corrected—or that no further progress would be made toward the elimination of the client's problems—is through an objective comparison of the client's current status with that which existed before the intervention. Observed differences would then need to be interpreted within a value context that established a preferred state or desired direction for change. These decisions rest at the core of professional accountability. To make such a comparison professionally requires that the practitioner engage in empirical research or evaluation so as to control for alternative explanations for the visible outcomes. While empirical checks on one's own practice differ from the general empirical studies intended to assess the effectiveness of a specific method across a number of practitioners and clients, both contribute directly to the state of empirically validated practice knowledge. Both involve using the best available information, that which we borrow and that which we contribute.

Effective practice methods are those that enable clients to solve their problems or achieve their goals, without causing significant harm to themselves or others. Again, we learn that a practice method is effective only through performing empirical research. The practitioner chooses a practice method for reasons of predicted efficaciousness under conditions of acceptable ethical and practical costs. Professional training provides workers with a perspective that honors the hard efforts of other social scientists in generating knowledge about human behavior and methods of behavior change. Such hard-won knowledge is not to be lightly rejected. Yet, there is value in the sensitivities of the worker for a given case situation, her or his inside knowledge may recognize nuances that differ from the existing knowledge base and suggest that some method other than the empirically established ones might be used with greater success (e.g., efficacy, humaneness, and cultural sensitivity). But the burden of proof is on the practitioner who makes this choice. It is not one to be made lightly, on a whim or an intuition that cannot be logically and systematically argued before a review board or a court of law. The latter point is very important because helping professionals are held accountable for their practices and practice methods in courts of law.

Summary

In summary, the ethical mandate to use practice methods with the best empirical evidence of effectiveness implies using empirically tested, conceptually guided, value-sensitive information from the fund of professional common understanding. When the demands of a particular client situation exceed the general knowledge base, the social worker is thrown back onto his or her personal knowledge, applied to on-the-spot hypothesizing. At no time is the social worker ever free from the ethical mandate to use the best available information as defined in this paper. What is the best available information will vary, however, according to the circumstances. The client and, ultimately, society demand nothing less than our acting on the best available information, either the general empirical foundation of the profession or the personal empiricism set within that professional context. Ethical social workers must strive to provide clients with practice that reflects a commitment to such information.

Reference

National Association of Social Workers. (1980). *Code of ethics of the National Association of Social Workers.* Silver Springs, MD: Author.

Rejoinder to Drs. Klein & Bloom

Susan Meyers Chandler

Drs. Klein and Bloom begin their discussion by begging the question of this debate. They say, and I agree, *''If we knew''* (italics mine) that an ethical, social-work-intervention practice method was 100 percent effective, indeed, we would be foolish not to use it. Conversely, if we were debating whether social workers should use a practice intervention based on ''the best available information,'' as opposed to the title of this chapter, ''best empirical evidence of effectiveness,'' I would ask two questions: what is their definition of ''practice effectiveness,'' and who is deciding what is ''best?''

Drs. Klein and Bloom attempt to design an ethical standard based on their five-part ''scientific process.'' Their description of the scientific process, while not very precise, interestingly includes practice wisdom, which they explain as ''personal artistry,'' ''style,'' and ''personal knowledge.'' They choose to exclude explicitly ''experimentation'' in their discussions of formal research; this usually requires standardized methods, randomization, use of controls, and so forth. Rather, they encourage practitioners to conduct ''on-the-spot innovations'' to determine practice effectiveness, when new situations occur. They suggest that single-system evaluation designs offer an exemplar mechanism for this type of innovation testing. I suggest that this methodology, by its very design, artificially limits the scope, range, and context of social work practice, and it is an unrealistic burden for practitioners to shoulder alone.

The scientific process that will have most utility for the profession of social work will have to move beyond context-stripping positivism and toward a collaboration between researchers and practitioners, bridging the gap that exists now. The goal of social work research should be to fully explore and understand the context of social work practice and expand our knowledge base for effective practice.

Ethical practitioners and researchers must consciously examine if it is appropriate to generalize across studies in an effort to find a more culturally and gender sensitive, humane, and effective practice. When are the conditions really similar? What is the "transferability" of an empirically supported method reported in a study, and who should be included in the knowledge building in the new context?

This debate originally rested on the definition and scope of social work practice and whether a requirement of ethical practice should be constrained to an existing body of empirical evidence of effectiveness. Softening the question as Drs. Klein and Bloom did to using the "best available information," broadened with "little innovations" avoids most of the important issues. The newer collaborative, developmental approaches to research, which include practitioners, consumers, and policymakers in the designs and which focus on transferring knowledge to new practice situations and contexts, will result in a strong, ethical practice standard that will move our profession ahead.

NO

Susan Meyers Chandler

Social work practitioners have a profound responsibility to individuals, couples, families, and communities. Interventions must be carefully planned and implemented because they are designed to change behavior. Professional social workers must be knowledgeable about the currently available evidence on effective practice interventions, and they must systematically evaluate their own practice. Ethical practice must not be constrained, however, to the use of only those methods with empirical evidence of effectiveness.

Social workers intervene in a complex array of social problems in a variety of settings. Their tasks range from voluntary counseling to surveillance and from support to involuntary monitoring. Some interventions pit family members against one another, as in child protection cases. Social work practitioners struggle daily with difficult ethical issues. Their day may include decisions such as when (or whether) to terminate parental rights, leave a child "adrift" in foster care, or if (or whether) to encourage a battered woman to go forward with a case against her husband when there is little protection for her from his wrath. The problem for the social worker is that there is not very good empirical evidence of effective practice in these situations, nor even much guidance . . . yet they must intervene.

The NASW Code of Ethics (1980) guides social workers' practice, while respecting each practitioner's style. It describes and prescribes rules for practitioner behavior. It requires that clients are treated with loyalty and self determination, and it also requires that social worker practice be based upon the recognized, current knowledge relevant to the field. Should the Code of Ethics also include a requirement that practitioners *use* the best empirical evidence of effectiveness?

While there should be no debate about the proposition that social workers need to know what they are doing, Thyer (1989) suggests that:

> . . . for the determination of social work effectiveness there is no substitute for controlled experimental research guided by the philosophy of science known as logical positivism. (p. 320)

Clearly, if this is the standard, then much of what social workers do has not been, and probably can never be, researched adequately. The experimental design requirements required by this proposition will by necessity, narrow the scope of what can and will ever be researched. In addition, because this type of research is expensive, it is most often designed and implemented only by well funded academic institutions (Cheetham, 1992). Academic researchers, with their focus toward the goal of publication in refereed journals, tend to be quite conservative in their choice of topics. Negative results, nonsignificant statistical findings, and qualitative findings are rarely published, so the empirical evidence actually disseminated to the field may be somewhat biased.

Let's assume, however, that this new ethical standard was advisable. How could this be accomplished? Would each new study be beamed to all social workers in the field? Which empirical studies would be selected? What if there were a question about the appropriateness of the research design, methodology, statistics used, or the interpretation of the data? Would there be a national monitoring office of compliance to ensure that each practitioner was indeed using the newly deemed effective practice technique? Would clients be informed of the new evidence?

If two studies demonstrated that social skills training was an effective intervention for adults with severe mental illness, would that be sufficient for practitioners to be ethically bound to use this technique? Should they wait until twenty studies confirm these initial findings? What if another study using similar methods reported different results for a rural setting? Or when the sample was more ethnically diverse? Or when more women were included? What would the ethical practitioner be expected to do if the study samples were composed of diagnosed schizophrenic patients in state hospitals, but her caseload was primarily out-patients? Would a practitioner be held accountable to apply these "best" techniques to other "similar" populations or be charged with unethical practice?

What if a practitioner with years of clinical experience, who had been using Rothman's (1989) research and development model, to monitor her clients with careful contracts and evaluation/feedback mechanisms, noticed that based on her practice wisdom, the published evidence of effectiveness didn't fit with her experience? Perhaps the empirical evidence was primarily based on multiple samples of white, college men (a common phenomenon), and this practitioner's caseload was primarily Chicana? Would this person be in violation of the new ethical Code by questioning whether the "best" evidence was culturally biased, gender biased, or just inadequate?

Should social workers be ethically constrained to practice only those rather limited and narrow range of techniques that have (to date) been empirically tested? Fischer (in press) lists sixteen techniques that meet the criteria of having empirical evidence of effectiveness. For those clients who have clearly identified behavioral problems, these training techniques and problem-solving skills are useful and should be used. But, as social work practitioners know, what researchers often fail to acknowledge is that social work practice is broader than "training" clients. The person-in-environment is a deeply held value among the social work profession and engaging clients in an empowering relationship in which substantial progress takes place, not only on a researcher's scale, but in the client's life, is the goal of most social work practitioners. Social work activities deal with the rights and obligations of vulnerable people, and with issues of justice and equity. These constructs are not easily scaled nor empirically validated.

What Are Social Work Practice Methods?

Perlman (1979) describes social work practice as:

> The interchange between a human helper and help seeker . . . demonstrat[ing] a bonding between one member of society who needs a hand and another member of society who represents its concern that a hand is available. . . . This is what the human services in all their forms are for—to meet human needs. (p. 53)

Jayarante and Levy (1979), in stark contrast, call for the social worker to use empirically based interventions to alter objectively measured problems in order to establish cause–effect relationships. Fischer (in press) wants a revolution in social work that would entail:

> A move away from a vague, unvalidated and haphazardly-derived knowledge traditionally used in social work toward a more systematic, rational

and empirically-oriented development and use of knowledge for practice. (p. 1)

He notes, however, that ''there is little or no evidence at this time that the empirically-based practitioner is more effective than the non-empirically based practitioner'' (in press). If the social work practitioner who uses empirically based methods is no more effective than the ''nonempirically based'' practitioner, how can the former type of practice become an ethical responsibility?

So, what is a social work practitioner to do? What interventions should a child protective services (CPS) worker use that are not ''vague and unvalidated?'' What cause and effect interventions should be offered to a battered woman? What empirically based interventions should be used to assist a person dying of AIDS? Would it be ethical to wait until such evidence is available? If ever?

The Practitioner and Researcher Chasm

If the effectiveness evidence currently being produced was helpful and useful in guiding practitioners in their interventions, why is it not being used? Why do studies continue to find that M.S.W. graduates don't use most of what they read in school? Could it be that the ''best'' empirical evidence in the past has turned out to be rather suspect? Could it be that the ''best'' empirical evidence focuses on only a subset of the real issues that occupy social work practitioners? Could it be that the debates in the research literature about what exactly is the best research design for the specific problem being studied have become so strident that social work practitioners prefer to keep their heads down and do their work? Social work practitioners often criticize academic researchers for reductionism when published studies appear using an elaborately designed research methodology that has focused on a narrowly defined problem, traditionally conceptualized, that has little applicability to the cases that social workers see in their practice. And even these studies rarely conclude with definitive directions that a line worker can follow. Conversely, innovative studies, which attempt to break new ground, such as examining the social work ''process,'' ''interactions,'' or ''relationship'' are criticized for lacking scientific rigor.

Perhaps there is a shared ethical responsibility between practitioners and researchers to collaborate more closely, so that the evidence of effectiveness being provided to the field is really relevant to the field. Much of the methodological debate in the social work journals has become so abstract that the studies provide little direction for social work practitioners. Is it solely the ethical responsibility of the practitioner to evaluate each study's design and critically judge its strengths and weaknesses in order to weigh its utility? Isn't it also the ethical responsibility of the researcher to understand fully the broad array of techniques that comprise social work practice, work with practitioners to better conceptualize their strategies of intervention, and design culturally sensitive and gender-sensitive evaluations of effectiveness?

Of course, all social workers (practitioners and researchers) should be well read, knowledgeable about the current lines of research on interventions, and vigilant about updating their practice skills. All social workers need to clearly define and describe their package of interventions, and monitor and carefully evaluate their client's progress (or lack of it). But currently, it would be impossible, impractical, ill advised, and premature to call for mandating practitioners to use only those practice methods that some agree have the "best" evidence of effectiveness.

Conclusions

Social work is moving ahead in designing new, culturally competent, gender-sensitive, practice techniques. New forms of research are being tested that examine interventions across different ethnic and cultural groups, cognizant of the gender and age divides and spanning ideological gulfs. Davis (1985) suggested that:

> When the prevailing scientific paradigm is applied to studying what social workers do, the essence of what researchers seek to understand is destroyed, as rich subjectively experienced phenomenon are reduced to isolated bits of objective data. (p. 107)

She explains that the "female voice" that values connection, relationships, intuition, context, and interactions has been silenced by the male-dominated academic publishing voice, whose objective truth resides "more in what the community of scholars agrees to be truth than it does in some objective verifiable aspect of reality" (p. 107).

Thus, when faced with the complexities and breadth of the social problems that social workers contend with each day, and the inadequate research base that covers what social workers really do, should practitioners be ethically responsible for using practice methods with the best empirical evidence of effectiveness? NO.

References

Cheetham, J. (1992). Evaluating social work effectiveness. *Research on Social Work Practice, 2,* 265–287.

Davis, L. (1985). Female and male voices in social work. *Social Work, 30,* 106–13.

Fischer, J. (in press). Empirically based practice: The end of ideology? *Journal of Social Service Research, 17.*

Jayarante, S., & Levy, R. (1979). *Empirical clinical practice.* New York: Columbia University Press.

National Association of Social Workers. (1980). *Code of Ethics of the National Association of Social Workers.* Silver Springs, MD: Author.

Perlman, H. H. (1979). *Relationship: The heart of helping people.* Chicago, IL: University of Chicago Press.

Rothman, J. (1989). Intervention research: Application to runaway and homeless youths. *Social Work Research & Abstracts, 25,* 13–18.

Thyer, B. (1989). First principles of practice research. *British Journal of Social Work, 19,* 309–323.

Rejoinder to Dr. Chandler

WALDO C. KLEIN
MARTIN BLOOM

Dr. Chandler raises several points that require clarification. First, is the use of practice evaluation an ethical issue at all? Evaluation may or may not be useful, but Dr. Chandler argues that surely it is not an ethical issue. We argue that evaluation is an ethical issue because it is vital to setting goals and knowing if goals have been attained. Social workers are, as Dr. Chandler notes, making important decisions that affect others—this is at the heart of the meaning of ethical acts. Thus, these considerations are, *ipso facto,* ethical ones. Without scientific evaluation, social workers would have no objective way to know where they were headed and when, if ever, they arrived.

The second point is whether research is the only or best way of knowing objectively what is happening in a case situation. It is easy in the short run to lambaste those who uphold the purity of the controlled experiment. But for the long run, we argue that the strong methods used by caring researcher–practitioners will produce the kinds of knowledge and methods that will approximate a true scientific practice.

There are many ways of knowing, however, including some quasi-experimental methods, that may provide practitioners with immediate feedback on practice. Dr. Chandler does not consider the rapidly expanding area of evaluation—in distinction to research on basic knowledge. Yet it is here that she will find that "other voice" that connects values and relationships to the practice situation. Out of the mutual exchanges that define the tasks for resolution and the methods by which they will be addressed comes an objective and caring practice, in which adaptations are made to the uniqueness of client situations.

A third point raised by Dr. Chandler concerns the strength of the knowledge base that we urge practitioners to use. Is it a science fiction—"Beam up the new study, Scotty''—to make use of the ''best available information'' as we propose? We believe that this is a current reality. Electronic information retrieval, expert systems, and computer aids in practice are mind-boggling—but are not to be discarded for that reason. A sensitive profession must make effective use of these tools. The future will bring more efficient mechanisms, through which all social workers can be informed of the best available information. To use or not use this information, we assert, is the ethical issue at question.

Another point concerns the limited focus of research compared to the broad range of client needs. Certainly, teachers have to provide instruction on the translation of good ideas to related areas. This relates to another point, regarding the exclusive use of ''Great Research'' with ''Great Statistical Findings.'' There is far too little great research. We only proposed that practitioners use the best available knowledge. Again, teachers must enable students to use these modest ''islands of knowledge,'' as they explore and evaluate how this best available information can lead them to efficacious and humane outcomes.

We reject a ''Big Brother or Big Sister is watching'' approach to monitoring the use of the best available knowledge—this is a basic ethical stance that students should learn as part of their training. Schools offer curricula to supply this knowledge and the skills to locate new knowledge and incorporate it into practice. The Council on Social Work Education has mandated that students be able to evaluate their practice.

The last point we can address (given space limitations) concerns Fischer's quotation that there is little evidence that empirically based practitioners are more effective than nonempirically based ones. This is true in a strict sense—we lack controlled experiments of the issue. But there are many approximations of this situation. Reid & Hanrahan's (1982) review suggests that empirically oriented studies typically yield better outcomes than those that are not empirically oriented. Further, many evaluation studies support empirical practice, although without a direct comparison to the nonempirical (cf. Reid [in press]), and social work graduates are increasingly using evaluation methods or components in their practice (Blythe, 1983).

With this available knowledge base, we again assert that it would be unethical not to make as full use of the information for practice as possible. We have so much to gain by an open-minded, and yet critical, look at the best available evidence, its artful application, and its objective on-going evaluation.

References

Blythe, B. (1983). *An examination of practice evaluation among social workers.* Unpublished dissertation. University of Washington, Seattle, WA.

Reid, W. J. (in press). Fitting the single-system design to family treatment. *Journal for Social Service Research.*

Reid, W. & Hanrahan, P. (1982). Recent evaluations of social work: Grounds for optimism. *Social Work, 27,* 328–340.

DEBATE 9

Lacking Evidence of Effectiveness, Should Single-Case Evaluation Techniques Be Encouraged in Practice?

William R. Downs is Professor of Social Work at the University of Northern Iowa in Cedar Falls, Iowa. He is also Director of the Center for the Study of Adolescence. He teaches courses and conducts seminars in human behavior, research, family violence, and substance abuse. His research interests include the inter-relationship of alcohol and drug problems with family violence and gender-related differences in juvenile-justice service delivery.

Allen Rubin is a professor at the University of Texas at Austin School of Social Work, where he teaches research methods and coordinates the social work doctoral program. He has co-authored (with Earl Babbie) the text, *Research Methods for Social Work,* second edition (Wadsworth Publishing, 1993), and he is currently evaluating the effectiveness of a program to prevent child abuse and preserve families.

YES

WILLIAM R. DOWNS

In a past life, when I taught research methods to graduate social work students, I eventually arrived at the point in the syllabus where "ethics in research" was the topic. The class launched into a spirited criticism of the experimental design: "random assignment to a no treatment control group." The class concluded that this particular design was clearly unethical because researchers were (cruelly) experimenting with clients by withholding treatment from half the clients (and apparently based on a coin flip no less).

To be equitable, the next topic was concerned with circumstances under which it is instead unethical to *provide* treatment, still under the condition of random assignment to a no treatment control group. The following questions were discussed: What if we learned that the treatment group fared no better than the no treatment group? Would this be evidence that, at best, we had wasted time, money, and other precious resources? How ethical is it to accept funding and then fail to help clients when other social workers or agencies might have performed better? Or even worse: What if we learned that the treatment group fared worse than the no treatment group? Would this be evidence that we had harmed our clients? Would it be more ethical, in this case, to assign clients to the no treatment group where at least they aren't harmed by treatment? Would it be unethical to assign them (cruelly) to a treatment where they had fared so poorly?

Having already covered the evidence from early reviews of evaluation studies indicating that some interventions are indeed ineffective, or even harmful, for some clients under some conditions, this discussion took on a certain poignancy: Is it ethical to provide treatments that don't work? If not, then should we as professionals know which ones do work and which ones do not work? Do we as professionals have the responsibility to know whether or not our interventions are working?'' The implicit and potentially dangerous assumption underlying social work practice seemed to be that our interventions do work, until proven otherwise, and that our clients therefore are helped.[1] Instead, the burden of proof should be on ourselves and we should assume the opposite: our interventions do not work, and our clients are not helped, until we have demonstrated otherwise.

Fortunately, thanks to a number of later evaluation studies and synthesizing reviews of the same, social workers are now able to choose among a wide range of interventions that have empirically demonstrated efficacy. Can we conclude, therefore, that the battle for accountability is over and the social workers won? Can we conclude that if we select one of the empirically verified interventions that this intervention really is working for our client? Unfortunately, we cannot make these claims. Instead, we need to realize that the battle for accountability must now move to a different level.

Published Evaluation Studies Cannot Be Generalized to Practice

Because of the ecological fallacy, individual differences are not discernible in group statistics. Therefore, group level evaluation studies have little, if any, external validity when extrapolated to interventions performed at the individual level. Group level statistics provide no information about how individual clients change, only how the group itself changes. While the group means may be used to show that one interventive method is on average statistically superior to a different method, or to no treatment at all, in fact some individual clients that received the "inferior" treatment, or no treatment at all, may have actually fared better than if they had received the "superior" treatment.

Hawkins (1989) has further criticized group designs as artificial due to their standardization of treatment, outcome measures, and settings across clients, none of which exist in the real world. Even the random assignment of clients, necessary to control for several threats to internal validity, rarely exists in the real world of service provision. These criticisms lead to the conclusion that the very attributes of group design that maximize the internal validity of a given study also reduce the external validity of the same study, for the purposes of generalization to the individual level interventions that so many social workers provide for their clients.

The larger the group the less useful the data are for individual level conclusions. Conversely, the smaller the group, the more useful the data are for individual level conclusions. The limit in this direction is single case evaluation.[2] Compared with group level studies, single case evaluations provide much better information on the direction, pattern, speed of effect, and level of final effect, for each individual client (Hawkins, 1989).

However, even published single case evaluation studies have restricted generalizability to practice. The ecological fallacy can be extended to the generalizability of results across client characteristics, an example being the gender of the client. A certain intervention that worked well for a male client may not work at all for a female client. There are no controls for client characteristics such as gender, race, and developmental stage (to name just a few), that may that affect the intervention reported in a single case evaluation study. It would be difficult for a given social worker to match their client to clients in reported studies on all such characteristics.

Even if this matching were possible, there is the subsequent issue of generalizability to the social worker providing the intervention. The social worker(s) in published single case evaluation studies may be better, worse, or simply different in some way from social workers elsewhere at implementing the treatment being evaluated. Finally, there are the interactions between client and worker characteristics that may affect the intervention in unknown ways as compared with the results in published single case evaluation studies.

Are then the published evaluation studies useless for social workers? No, published evaluations have been valuable in providing guidelines for social work practice. We know that certain interventions are likely to work with certain clients under certain conditions, and can therefore make probabilistic statements about the effectiveness of such interventions. Social workers can use published studies on practice effectiveness as guidelines for selecting interventions that will "probably be successful" with a given client under given conditions and with a given presenting problem. However, social workers cannot use published studies as evidence that their *own* interventions are successful with clients. Only by incorporating single case evaluation techniques into practice can social workers have evidence that their own interventions with clients are indeed successful, and therefore engage in competent and ethical practice.

Benefits of Single Case Evaluation for Practice

Practice evaluation can be defined as "making decisions about whether our clients' problems are actually changing, and also whether or not it was our interventions that helped them change" (Corcoran and Fischer, 1987: 5). Besides the accountability so necessary for ethical practice, Ivanoff, Blythe, and Briar (1987) have listed two additional benefits for single case evaluation designs: First, it bridges the gap between practice and research; and second, the social work intervention itself will be improved via continuous and more systematic data collection.

Social work practice and research share several common steps, including problem specification and data collection. Selection of an intervention automatically involves the hypothesis that the intervention (the independent variable) will cause change in the presenting problem (the dependent variable). Therefore, social workers are automatically experimenting with clients by selecting and performing their interventions with clients. The question becomes how systematically the social worker is engaging in his or her experimentation with clients. Social workers can either systematically experiment with clients (i.e., by using single case evaluation techniques) or social workers can arbitrarily experiment with clients by failing to evaluate whether their interventions are actually working.

Given the similarities of research and practice, single case evaluation can help bridge the "gap" between social work practice and research. In fact, this "gap" is a fallacy in the real world, existing as a construct mostly to explain unsuccessful efforts at applying large sample research to practice situations. Research classes can emphasize single case evaluation techniques and minimize content on group and survey methods, or place this content in a separate course. The research course can then be taught from the perspective of showing the utility of "research" concepts and strategies (i.e., single case evaluation) for practice. The alternative is to teach research strategies that perhaps 95 percent of B.S.W. and M.S.W. students will never use because these strategies are beyond the resources of most social work practitioners.

Practice classes can be taught from the perspective of the social worker using "research" concepts and strategies (i.e., single case evaluation techniques) to collect data systematically, specify and operationalize the presenting problem, select interventions based on maximum likelihood of success with the given client, continue to collect data systematically, select the best design strategy to evaluate the intervention (decide if the client is changing and if the intervention is causing the change), and continue to collect data systematically to perform the evaluation.

In the second benefit, social work practice will be improved via the use of single case evaluation techniques. To monitor practice has been defined as to "keep track of our clients' problems over time and, if necessary, make changes in our intervention program if it is not proceeding as well as desired" (Corcoran and Fischer, 1987: 5). Both practice monitoring and evaluation involve systematic data collection concerning the client's situation, the dependent variable. In collecting data continuously and systematically, social workers will be able to determine whether clients are improving and change the intervention if they are not. This state of affairs alone would be an improvement for much of social work practice where it is unclear precisely what is happening with clients.

However, practice monitoring controls for no threats to internal validity, and therefore cannot be used as evidence that it was the intervention itself that caused change in the client. Practice evaluation techniques add this new dimension to the improvement of social work practice. Practice evaluation involves systematic manipulation of the intervention (the independent variable) to make the best decisions about practice effectiveness. Thus, practice evaluation involves maximizing internal validity by controlling for as many threats to validity as possible. With these controls, social workers will be able to decide whether in fact it was their intervention itself that caused change in the client. By keeping track of the intervention itself, social workers will over time be able to decide which interventions, and which elements of interventions, are the most successful for them with their clients, ultimately improving their practice. Social work practice will be improved as social workers become more systematic in their selection, use, and subsequent evaluation of their own interventions.

Clinical realists have argued that single case evaluation techniques must be adapted to the constraints of practice situations. There is a tradeoff here. At worst, the social worker will have controlled for no threats to internal validity but he or she will have at least monitored client outcomes. However, if we continue to say that "practice comes first" and if we continue to adapt research to practice as opposed to the reverse, we will not be able to determine whether it was our interventions that were successful. Instead, we will be in the position of the students who said experimentation using "no treatment control" is unethical.

We will feel good about providing the client with the treatment that we think he or she needs and will have seen improvement (we hope) in the client, but *we will not know* if it were our interventions that helped (or harmed) clients. We will not know whether clients would have improved (or deteriorated) in the absence of our interventions. We will not know whether to attempt the intervention, or elements of it, or which elements to attempt, or instead attempt a different intervention with other clients who have similar characteristics and similar presenting problems.

The published evaluation studies have provided excellent guidelines for selection of interventions, but cannot be used to demonstrate successful practice for a given social worker. Practice monitoring is an excellent next step in the process of improving practice at the end of the dependent variable, client outcomes, but also cannot be used to demonstrate successful practice. Even with practice monitoring, it is impossible to conclude that absence of an intervention would have resulted in similar or even more improvement for the client.

In the final analysis, it is simply not enough to know whether clients are improving or not. If we as professionals cannot state with confidence that it was our intervention that helped our clients change, then others might legitimately question whether we should be in business at all. Therefore we, as social work professionals, must know which of our interventions are successful at the level of our own professional practice. To accomplish this, we must incorporate single case evaluation techniques into our practice.

Notes

1. An even more dangerous assumption is that social workers will somehow "know" whether their interventions are successful and don't need single case evaluation to tell them this. Threats to internal validity (e.g., history, maturation) alone discredit this assumption. Even worse, social workers making this assumption typically do not see the need to specify in advance exactly what level of change constitutes progress or engage in systematic data collection. Given the human foible of selective attention to favorable data, such social workers are likely to delude themselves and their clients.

2. For the purposes of this paper, the author is using single case evaluation to refer to evaluations of interventions with systems of all sizes, for example individual, group, family, and organization. Other terms that have been used synonymously with single case evaluation include single system design, single system research, and single system experimentation.

Acknowledgments

The author would like to express his sincere appreciation to Dr. Denise Bronson of The Ohio State University College of Social Work, and Drs. Howard Doueck and Nancy Smyth, both of the State University of New York at Buffalo School of Social Work, for their many informative discussions of this topic and their very helpful editorial suggestions on earlier versions of this article.

References

Corcoran, K., & Fischer, J. (1987). *Measures for clinical practice: A sourcebook.* New York: The Free Press.

Hawkins, R. P. (1989). Developing potent behavior-change technologies: An invitation to cognitive behavior therapists.'' *The Behavior Therapist, 12*(6), 126–131.

Ivanoff, A., Blythe, B. J., & Briar, S. (1987). The empirical clinical practice debate. *Social Casework: The Journal of Contemporary Social Work, 68,* 290–298.

Rejoinder to Dr. Downs

ALLEN RUBIN

Dr. Downs and I seem to disagree about the extent to which group evaluation studies have provided social workers with ''a wide range of interventions that have empirically demonstrated efficacy.'' Group evaluation studies are beginning to identify some effective interventions. But many more such studies will be needed before we are anywhere near the point at which we can afford to shift accountability to the level that Dr. Downs advocates. This would require a shift from a focus on group evaluations that attempt to test what interventions are generally effective, to a focus on single-case evaluations that test whether interventions found to be effective in group studies are effective when applied by a particular practitioner to a particular client. (Readers can examine the major reviews of group-level evaluations and decide for themselves whether they agree with Dr. Downs or me on this point.) Fortunately, this is not an either/or issue; we can continue to do both nomothetic (group) and idiographic (single-case) research. That is, we can encourage single-case evaluation without having to discourage group-level evaluations.

My main thesis is that ambiguity in the interpretation of graphed data patterns too often impedes our ability to infer whether it was the intervention or some alternative explanation that accounts for improvement in the target problem. My unstated premise was that single-case evaluation is being conducted primarily on interventions that have not yet amassed adequate group-level evidence that indicates that they are probably effective. The need to rule out alternative explanations is greater when practitioners are testing interventions with unknown effects than when testing interventions that have already received adequate testing and are known to be generally effective. In the latter case, practitioners would know at the outset that they were applying a well tested and generally effective intervention, and, therefore, they would not need to worry as much about ambiguity in the visual data pattern or the timing of the improvement. As long as improvement commenced at some point in a way that supported the mere *plausibility* of intervention efficacy—even if the timing of the commencement of improvement was not dramatic—it would seem reasonable to suppose that the intervention, because it already had been shown to be generally effective, appeared to be a sound choice for the particular case with the particular practitioner. In other words, if the graphed data were ambiguous as to whether the intervention or some alternative explanation were causing the improvement, it might be reasonable to give the benefit of the doubt to the intervention, since it had already been shown to be effective in previous evaluations. Thus, if we are encouraging single-case evaluation merely to see if interventions with demonstrated efficacy seem to fit a particular practitioner or a particular case, then my concerns are largely irrelevant. But I think my concerns are relevant because Dr. Downs and I disagree about this premise.

Moving on to another point of disagreement, Dr. Downs cites an article by Hawkins that argues that single-case evaluations are better than group-level studies in providing information on several aspects of intervention effectiveness. It is noteworthy that the Hawkins article is geared to behavior therapists. My qualms about the potential utility of single-case evaluation, however, concern its likely payoff in settings that do not emphasize cognitive or behavioral interventions. I do not disagree with Dr. Downs' (or Hawkins') points regarding the utility of single-case evaluation for cognitive or behavioral therapy. The data analysis problems that I cite in my statement, however, do leave me with much less optimism than Dr. Downs expresses regarding the extent to which encouraging the use of this technology in noncognitive and nonbehavioral settings will result in social workers knowing ''which interventions, and which elements of interventions, are the most successful for them with their clients.''

In advocating more emphasis on single-case evaluation, proponents correctly argue that the findings from group research only give us probabilities. They point to the uniqueness of each case and the uniqueness of each practitioner–case interaction; and they correctly argue that different cases will respond to tested interventions in idiosyncratic ways. But if each case is unique, and if different cases respond to the same intervention in idiosyncratic ways, then it seems far-fetched to suppose that single-case evaluations of effective interventions (other than cognitive and behavioral ones) are likely to produce data patterns containing consistent, *unlikely* coincidences in the timing of improvement from case to case.

NO

Allen Rubin

In the late 1970s and early 1980s, single-case evaluation was expected to bridge the perennial gulf between social work research and practice, increase the production of research evaluating the practice effectiveness of social work, and ultimately make social work practice more empirical. These hopes resulted in the adoption in 1984 by the Council on Social Work Education (CSWE) of new accreditation standards, implying the need for all schools of social work to prepare students to use single-case evaluation techniques to evaluate their practice.

Only a handful or two of single-case evaluations have appeared in our professional literature since then. During the same time period, another handful of studies have reported disappointing findings about the extent to which practitioners who learn about single-case evaluation as students eventually use it in their professional practice. These studies suggested that even when practitioners are trained in single-case evaluation techniques, they are very unlikely to use them, and that this is due in part to the large amount of time it takes to formulate and carry out single-case evaluations.

Arguments for Continued Emphasis on Single-Case Evaluation Despite Its Limited Use

Did the profession go overboard in embracing of single-case evaluation methods? Many remain steadfast in their advocacy of this methodology, despite the dearth of evidence so far that it is living up to its billing. Three arguments have been proposed to support their position.

One argument is that the field expected too much of this technology. Even if only a small cadre of social workers produce single-case evaluations, some argue, the investment that the profession has made in this methodology will have been worthwhile. A second argument is that it is too early to pass judgment on this issue. More time may be needed before practitioners who have been trained in single-case study become predominant in practice agencies and create agency environments that provide the level of support required for it to become feasible. A third argument is that even if our embracing of this technology does not lead to a significant improvement in the production of practice-relevant research, it will have been worthwhile because merely using case-monitoring techniques will make practice more effective.

Each of these arguments is plausible. Over time, as we accumulate more research evidence about the use of single-case evaluation and its impact, we will be in a position to respond empirically to the possibility that the profession has been too quick to encourage its use in practice. I am skeptical about what we are likely to find. My doubts are based primarily on previously neglected problems in the analysis of single-case evaluation data.

Ambiguous Data Patterns

The main data-analysis problem that I see involves ambiguity in interpreting the visual significance of the graphed data patterns in single-case evaluations. (For the sake of simplicity, and to stay within given space limitations, my comments will refer primarily to AB designs, those most feasible in social work practice. However, the same argument can be made in regard to more complex designs.)

Graphed results are deemed visually significant when they clearly support intervention efficacy as the most plausible explanation for improvement in the target problem. This requires unlikely coincidences in which stable improvement in the target problem commences consistently after the onset of intervention. If we are considering only one single-case evaluation, the improvement must commence almost immediately. This enables us to rule out the plausibility of alternative explanations, such as history. If we are interpreting a series of replications, then improvement can commence later during the intervention period, but only if it occurs in a dramatically consistent manner from case to case.

Graphed results of single-case evaluations will have clear implications that suggest the ineffectiveness of an intervention, only if virtually no sustained improvement occurs during the intervention phase. If some improvement appears late during intervention, we may wonder about delayed treatment effects. If some improvement appears early during intervention, but then trails off later during intervention, we may wonder whether some extraneous factor is causing a temporary setback.

Will Replications Resolve the Ambiguity?

We can attempt to reduce ambiguity and sort out whether the intervention or some alternative seems to be the most plausible explanation by extending our evaluation of a particular case over a much larger number of data points and then replicating the evaluation over a large number of similar cases. Aside from the practical obstacles to obtaining many data points and many similar cases, however, what happens if we replicate across a large number of cases and find that for many cases improvement commences at very different points after the intervention, while many others do not improve at all?

Target problems can improve without treatment in many cases, because of a variety of potential factors outside of our interventions. If we just conduct a one-group, pretest–postest design, therefore, we cannot infer that an intervention was effective just because a certain proportion of the cases improved. Comparison or control groups are necessary for such causal inferences, in order to rule out the plausibility of alternative explanations. In single-case evaluation, however, we rely on obtaining numerous data points and replication in the hope of finding unlikely successive coincidences in which sustained improvement in the target behavior commences at about the same time after the onset of intervention across replications. But if, for many cases, improvement commences at very different points after intervention begins, while many other cases do not improve, then we have not established a consistent series of unlikely coincidences that would provide the basis for arguing that the improvements observed are unlikely to have been due to alternative explanations. Thus, if across our replications, we find that, say, 60 percent of the cases improve at various points during intervention, for all we know a similar percentage of untreated controls may have improved to the same extent. In a group design, we would know the extent of improvement among untreated controls and be able to compare it to the extent of improvement among treated cases. In order for the results to support the efficacy of intervention, we would need only to show that the extent of improvement among treated cases significantly exceeded the extent among controls. The precise timing of the onset of improvement from case to case would not matter, as long as the aggregate degree of improvement occurring after the pre-test was greater for treated than for untreated cases. Neither would we need to show that almost all, or even a majority, of treated cases improved. Even if less than half of the treated cases improved, treatment efficacy might be indicated—if a much smaller proportion of untreated controls improved. But because we lack comparison rates in single-case evaluation, we are forced to look for dramatic, unlikely coincidences in the timing of improvement—coincidences that replicate consistently from case to case.

Is it realistic to expect to find dramatic coincidences in the timing of improvement from case to case? Perhaps it is when we use cognitive or behavioral interventions. It seems reasonable to suppose that many people change their behavior almost immediately, once they start employing cognitive techniques, are taught new skills, or start earning rewards for the changed behavior. But practitioners with other orientations, might deem it unrealistic to expect dramatic coincidences in the timing of improvement, perhaps citing the variable amount of time it takes from case to case to overcome problems like denial. Although it is not impossible to obtain useful single-case evaluation results with noncognitive and nonbehavioral practice approaches, as a few studies have illustrated, the *probability* of obtaining unambiguous graphed data patterns seems slim. Thus, the extent to which we should emphasize single-case evaluation techniques may vary. This variation depends on the intervention methods and practice orientations being emphasized and upon the extent to which we expect the target problems being treated to begin improving immediately at the onset of intervention or at about the same time from case to case.

Will a Statistical Analysis Reduce Visual Ambiguity?

Some might argue that visual ambiguity in graphed data patterns can be offset by augmenting the analysis of visual significance with an analysis of statistical significance. One problem with this argument is that statistical significance refers only to statistical conclusion validity—that is, to ruling out chance—and says nothing about the plausibility of various threats to internal validity (i.e., whether it was the intervention or something else that caused the statistically significant change.)

Another problem is the low statistical power inherent in single-case evaluations. It is difficult to obtain much more than 10 data points in each phase of an AB design in social work. Assuming an alpha of .05 (two-tailed) and a medium effect size (r = .30), the power of tests of significance with two groups of 10 data points is approximately .25. Even with an alpha of .10, the approximate power would be only .37. That means we are likely to take a huge risk of a Type-II error when we calculate statistical significance in single-case evaluations. This large risk means that knowing that results are not statistically significant is virtually no help at all in reducing the ambiguity of graphed data patterns that offer unclear visual evidence about whether an intervention is effective.

Should We Take an Inductive Approach?

Do I worry too much about obtaining unambiguous results that support causal inferences? Why not instead consider each single-case evaluation as a tiny exploratory step in a very long process of accumulating many replications and using inductive logic to tease out some useful working hypotheses about the conditions required for a particular intervention to begin showing desired effects? This is a powerful argument in the context of pursuing a very long-range and time-consuming research agenda—an agenda that might require more resources and much more data gathering than would be required by a research strategy involving traditional group designs. But I find it unrealistic to suppose that the elusive long-range payoff of this scenario would motivate practitioners to produce single-case evaluations in their practice. If they did produce some of these evaluations, I suspect they would soon long for the days when we relied on researchers to build knowledge through pre-tests and post-tests in group designs, rather than asking practitioners to collect many repeated measures with each case—measures yielding ambiguous data and thus little payoff for their immediate practice.

Will Single-Case Evaluation Enhance Practice Regardless of Data Analysis Problems?

Some may argue that practitioners will find that collecting and graphing repeated measurements is worthwhile because it gives them more clinical information and a better empirical basis for gauging when a target problem has been sufficiently resolved or when it is time to try a different intervention. But I suggest that such clinical decisions are complicated by visually ambiguous graphs. I also suggest that the need to collect many repeated measures forces practitioners to rely primarily on client self-reports (perhaps using rapid assessment instruments) and client self-monitoring for their data. These measures are highly vulnerable to bias, and may be perceived by practitioners who understand measurement problems as not adding much more useful information beyond what they already observe in clinical interviews with the client. The use of rapid-assessment instruments does not solve this problem. The validity of such instruments tends not to be tested in the context of repeated measures gathered by a client's practitioner to gauge client progress. Moreover, these instruments generally require at least a few days, or perhaps a week, between each measure with the same client. Thus, stable trends can be established only over the course of long baseline and intervention periods.

Despite the potential bias inherent in self-monitoring, perhaps it will prove to be a useful clinical technique that helps make a variety of forms of social work practice more effective. As I suggested earlier, that is a plausible hypothesis that can be verified empirically. If it is verified, then we can teach it as a practice technique regardless of where we stand on the issue being debated in these papers.

Conclusion

I am not arguing against the use of single-case evaluation techniques in practice or against teaching them in research courses. I do not see this technology as intrinsically harmful or worthless. Indeed, I believe single-case evaluation techniques should be encouraged in settings that have a clear orientation toward cognitive or behavioral practice. I am merely questioning whether we have gone overboard in the extent to which we are emphasizing this technology in other settings, because its likely payoff does not seem to justify the emphasis that it is getting. When we focus on nonbehavioral and noncognitive practice, I recommend that we teach single-case evaluation as a very long-range, labor-intensive, inductive research strategy and that we give it no more emphasis than we give other research strategies.

Rejoinder to Dr. Rubin

WILLIAM R. DOWNS

Single-case evaluation should be measured against its alternatives: performing no evaluations or only group evaluations. In the final analysis, I suspect we will eventually decide that some combination of group and single-case evaluations will be optimal for improving social work practice.

Single-case evaluation has not yet been given a thorough trial. Field educators and social workers who are uneducated in single-case evaluation may not support its use in practice. Thus, to maximize the use and fair testing of single-case evaluation, social work educators need to extend the training for this technique to both of these groups. Doueck and Kasper (1991) and Doueck and Bondanza (1990) have reported some promising results in these areas.

However, the major issue raised here is the ambiguity likely to be obtained in the graphed data, because of problems such as cyclicity, which may render impossible the aggregation of data across cases. However, the very purpose of collecting baseline data is to rule out alternative hypotheses. The major uncontrolled threat to internal validity, assuming an adequate baseline, consists of events extraneous to the intervention that improve the target problem. Collecting supplemental data on such events, itself often motivated by changes in the target problem, can help rule out (or rule in) such competing hypotheses. One can hope for immediate improvement in the target problem, but this is not necessary in order to infer improvement resulting from the intervention. With adequate controls, several graphic patterns can be used to infer treatment success, including a delayed effect or even gradual change in the target problem.

Replication of the results or aggregation of data across clients to achieve *group-level* conclusions are not the primary purposes of single-case evaluation, but of group designs. The purpose of single-case evaluation is to focus on individual-level conclusions, specifically whether the intervention performed by social worker X with client Y is working or not. In a similar manner, with practice monitoring, the social worker tries to determine whether there has been consistent improvement for client Y, not whether clients A, B, C, and Y all improved in the same manner. The client is his or her own control, and change in the target problem after introduction of the intervention is compared to (presumably) the lack of change before the intervention. In this sense, the social worker focuses on only one graph at a time, as opposed to trying to make sense out of several graphs simultaneously.

Finally, I would like to point out that all data is subject to validation issues, even that of behavioral observation. Social workers already rely heavily on both self-report and observational data, given that the social work interview is probably the major data source for most practitioners. Single-case evaluation based on self-report data is congruent with this tradition. In addition, most research data is self-report data, including that for group-evaluation studies. Bias due to self-report data is not a problem inherent only in single-case evaluations. In fact, the use of instruments, such as rapid-assessment scales (e.g., Hudson [1982]) should reduce this bias.

In closing, I would like to propose that both group and single-case evaluations are necessary for the improvement of social work practice. Both methods have advantages and disadvantages that tend to complement each other. Practitioners rarely have the resources to perform group evaluations, but can perform single-case evaluations with clients, and should be doing so.

References

Doueck, H. J., & Bondanza, A. (1990). Training social work staff to evaluate practice: A pre/post/then comparison. *Administration in Social Work, 14*(1), 119–133.

Doueck, H. J., & Kasper, B. (1991). Teaching practice evaluation to field instructors: A comparative study. *Journal of Teaching in Social Work, 4*(2), 105–125.

Hudson, W. W. (1987). Measuring client outcomes and their use for managers. *Administration in Social Work, 11*(3/4), 59–72.

Robinson, E. A. R., Bronson, D. E., & Blythe, B. J. (1988). An analysis of the implementation of single-case evaluation by practitioners. *Social Service Review, 62,* 285–301.

DEBATE 10

Is a Scientist–Practitioner Model Appropriate for Social Work Administrative Practice?

Tony Tripodi is Associate Director and Professor in the Department of Social Work at Florida International University. He directs the Ph.D. program and is on the editorial board of *Social Work Research & Abstracts* and *Evaluation and Program Planning*. His current research and writing interests are in program evaluation and research methodology. He consults with Boysfille of Michigan and the Zancan Foundation, Padova, Italy.

Leonard E. Gibbs is Professor of Social Work at the University of Wisconsin-Eau Claire. His interests concern ways to transfer principles of scientific thinking to everyday social work practice through critical thinking, taxonomies for matching client types to treatment, and measuring ability to reason scientifically about practice.

YES

TONY TRIPODI

This YES position paper asserts that a model of administrative practice, infused with scientific attitudes and methods as reflected in research technologies, is viable for many administrative tasks and functions. Three inter-related conditions support this thesis:

1. clear delineation of responsibilities for administrators of human service organizations;

2. a conception of a continuum of administrator–scientist functions with respect to the application and development of levels of knowledge, and the resulting hypothesis that the viability of the administrator–scientist role is inversely proportional to the level of knowledge being developed in the organization; and
3. an illustration of administrator–scientist functions by level of knowledge pursued with respect to a particular responsibility: program planning, implementation and evaluation.

Administrative Responsibilities

Typical of statements in the social work literature on administration is this exhortation by Sarri (1987):

> Dynamic leadership in administration is critical to the survival and enhancement of human service organizations in a hostile social environment. This leadership must be based on empirically derived knowledge of effective administration as well as on subjective judgment. . . .'' (p. 38)

The context of social administration is a turbulent environment in which sociopolitical and budgetary constraints interact with societal values and demands, as well as the values and priorities of social workers, their clients, and related professionals. Yet, within that environment there are administrative responsibilities that must be met.

Administrators, first of all, are responsible for their administrative organizations. Specific responsibilities depend, in part, on the nature, complexity, and size of the organization. In large, complex organizations, for example, an administrator might be responsible for a team, of which separate members have different functions, such as budgeting, program operations, research and development, and so forth. In smaller organizations, however, there may be only one person responsible for administration.

In general, administrative responsibilities include a range of activities: development of proposals for funding programs; interactions with governing boards; preparation of budgets; allocation and re-allocation of resources as a function of budget increases or reductions; training, supervision, and evaluation of staff performance; management of the operations of the organization, including its information system; development and maintenance of inter-organizational and community relationships; justification of expenditures in regard to cost effectiveness of the organization's programs; determination of organizational goals and an evaluation of the extent to which they are attained; assessment of client and staff training needs; management of crises that affect the organization's performance and morale, and so forth.

To perform their responsibilities, administrators must make critical decisions. Some decisions require quick, immediate action; others involve more thoughtful deliberation. In crisis management, for example, there is little time to gather new information; and administrators make decisions based on subjective judgments, their experiences of similar situations, and on immediately available knowledge. Contrariwise, a budget planning process may involve much more time for the collection of relevant data. In concert with the organization's staff, administrators decide on the primary goals that the organization wishes to achieve, how to evaluate goal attainment, what information should be gathered routinely to describe the organization's costs and services, and so forth. Administrators make personnel decisions, as well as decisions about what programs or portions of programs should be cut or expanded in relation to budgetary changes. Moreover, administrators are increasingly involved in raising funds. It is obvious that effective administration requires a great deal of knowledge and technical skills. Not surprisingly, it has been noted that most administrators of social welfare organizations are not trained in social work (Sarri, 1987); they have training in business administration, public administration, and other fields. A cursory review of catalogues of schools of business administration reveals that substantial portions of education are devoted to technical functions and competencies, such as computer usage, information-system design, budgeting and accounting, elementary and advanced statistical methods, and research design and analysis. Furthermore, there is an increasing relationship between technical business skills and program evaluation. Bradenburg (1989) indicates that business issues and decision making can be linked profitably to the evaluation of training programs in business and industry. In addition, it is noteworthy that many social welfare administrators who do not have technical competencies enroll in training seminars and part-time degree programs devoted to managers of nonprofit organizations. Hence, it is assumed, for purposes of this presentation, that many, if not most, administrators of social welfare organizations have or desire technical expertise, or employ staff capable of performing technical functions.

A Continuum of Administrator–Scientist Roles

Scientific method involves the display of objective, rigorous attitudes in describing and making inferences from empirical (i.e., quantitative and qualitative) data; its central components are observation, hypothesis formulation, and hypothesis verification. When an investigation employs all aspects of the scientific method, its pursuit is the development of causal relationships. Correspondingly, when fewer aspects are involved, there is a pursuit of lower levels of knowledge. A continuum of knowledge levels ranges from the development of hypotheses, to systematic descriptions, to associations among variables, to the verification of causal hypotheses and the explanation of social phenomena. The extent to which an administrator uses scientific method in practice can be inferred from the degree to which she or he incorporates substantive and methodological research knowledge. Substantive knowledge refers to the results of previous research studies, while methodological knowledge is the application of research concepts, principles, and procedures for generating knowledge levels within the context of the organization (Tripodi, 1993).

Research knowledge can be employed by the administrator as administrator–scientist for many administrative functions that correspond to different levels of knowledge. For example, results of previous studies from the literature or in the organization are used to generate program hypotheses represented in proposals for funding. Sampling, information processing, survey research, and accounting procedures are employed for producing descriptive knowledge about the organization's staff, costs, services, and clientele. Quasi-experimental and multivariate statistical procedures can be employed to show associations among program costs, technologies and indicators of effectiveness; while field experimentation, cost–benefit analyses, and developmental research can be used for verifying program cost effectiveness. In general, the higher the level of knowledge pursued, the greater are the time, costs, and technical knowledge required by the administrative team. Hence, it is postulated that the extent to which an administrator or administrative team can incorporate methodologies based on scientific method is inversely proportional to the level of knowledge that is being developed. For example, it is believed that administrators are more likely to engage in the process of articulating program goals and anticipated outcomes (hypothetical knowledge) and to describe agency services and client needs (descriptive knowledge) than in generating knowledge about causal relationships among program contents, their costs, and program outcomes and benefits.

The application of systematic research procedures takes time and requires planning. Research tools, strategies, and analyses can be used to provide information as inputs for administrative decisions involved in budget planning, evaluation of staff performance, allocations and re-allocations of resources based on effective services for clients, and so forth. Administrative responsibilities, however, such as crisis management or conflict resolution, are less amenable to the incorporation of scientific technologies than are other administrative functions that require systematic data for proper inferences.

Program Planning, Implementation, and Evaluation

The degree to which it is possible for an administrator to perform an administrator–scientist role can be illustrated in reference to a vital responsibility in human-service organizations: program planning, implementation, and evaluation (Epstein & Tripodi, 1978).

Comprehensive program planning entails knowledge about the needs of potential and current clientele; information on resources in the organization and in the community; development of program hypotheses regarding particular practices and strategies that might result in need reduction and problem resolution for clientele; selection of empirically based programs or practices, if available; and so forth. Levels of knowledge pursued in program planning are typically hypothetical and descriptive, and can be obtained by methodologies such as needs analysis based on census, survey, and quantitative and qualitative data gathering techniques; resource surveys involving sampling, questionnaire construction, and interviews; or assessment of reports regarding programs and their cost effectiveness. These data can be obtained by one or more members of an administrative team. They are used for various activities: developing grant proposals, planning for staff training needs, allocation of resources, and specification of data needed for the organization's information system, among others.

Program implementation is the process of making all the necessary arrangements to render a program fully operational. It includes such activities as contacting potential clientele, engaging clients in the delivery of the program's services, and maintaining contacts until termination and follow-up activities occur. The administration should monitor these activities to determine the barriers to program delivery; location of resources to carry out the program; extent to which there is adherence to requirements to ensure program quality and integrity; sufficient amounts and types of information to keep track of clients, services, and costs. Monitoring and information-processing strategies can be employed to provide descriptive and associational levels of knowledge.

Questionnaires, check lists, budgeting sheets, and other types of forms are used to gather data; and computer software packages are employed for analyzing them. Data are assessed in regard to program standards for implementation. For example, if the program requires a specified amount of time in which there are intensive and extensive contacts with clients, collateral sources, and others (as in a family-preservation program), the administrator can use data to indicate whether changes in programming should be made to adhere to quality control standards.

Program evaluation involves a determination of the extent to which a program attains its goals and objectives. Often, data are desired on the relative cost-effectiveness of two or more programs; and the information is used for making decisions about program allocations. Knowledge may also be pursued regarding explanations for relative degrees of success or failure. Summative evaluations are much more difficult and costly to implement than formative evaluations that are geared to the specific organization's development.

Knowledge levels obtained from evaluations are basically associational, and sometimes approximately causal. Associational knowledge is procured by quasi-experimental procedures, such as those that entail measurements of client status before and after a program is instituted or time-series designs. Controlled field experiments, analyses of cost effectiveness, and benefit–cost analytic procedures are used to infer causal relationships between the program, its costs, and changes in clientele and other expected outcomes.

Conclusion

The practitioner–scientist model is appropriate for some but not all, parts of administrative practice. I maintain that many administrative responsibilities in human-service organizations require knowledge of technical skills that incorporate research methods. Furthermore, I hypothesize that there is an inverse relationship between the degree to which an administrator incorporates research methods in practice and the level of knowledge that is pursued within the organization. Administrators are more likely to generate hypothetical and descriptive program knowledge and possibly associational knowledge obtained from formative evaluations; and are less likely to routinely develop associational and causal knowledge based on field experiments, cost effectiveness analyses, and benefit–cost analyses.

References

Brandenburg, D. C. (1989). Evaluation and business issues: Tools for management decision making. In R. O. Brinkerhof (Ed.), *Evaluating training programs in business and industry: New directions for program evaluation,* No. 44, 83–100. San Francisco, CA: Jossey-Bass.

Epstein, I., & Tripodi, T. (1977). *Research techniques for program planning, monitoring, and evaluation.* New York: Columbia University Press.

Sarri, R. C. (1987). Administration in social welfare. In *Encyclopedia of social work* (18th ed., vol. 1). Silver Spring, MD: National Association of Social Workers.

Tripodi, T. (1992). Differential research utilization in macro and micro social work practice: An evolving perspective. In A. J. Grasso, & I. Epstein (Eds.) *Research utilization: A decade of practice.* New York: Pergamon Press.

Rejoinder to Dr. Tripodi

Leonard E. Gibbs

I had assumed when writing the NO paper that we were to confine our thinking to the here-and-now—the present—not to an ideal state that might exist someday. Consequently, I based my conclusions on surveys of social workers, the Task Force on Social Work Research's (1991) findings, and informal conversations with leaders of social work administrators. These sources led me to the conclusion that, currently, those who occupy administrative positions in human-service organizations are insufficiently trained in scientific thinking to conduct research. I think that Dr. Tripodi has been arguing that in an ideal world, they should be capable. I agree with him in the ideal, but cannot agree in the practical here-and-now.

We seem to differ on another assumption. Dr. Tripodi seems to assume that "... most administrators of social welfare organizations are not trained in social work ..." and that these administrators, because they are trained in, "... business administration, public administration and other fields ..." are sufficiently competent in the methodology of science to conduct program evaluations. In regard to the question of the proportion of administrators in social welfare organizations who are trained in social work, I don't have sufficient evidence to agree or disagree. Tripodi cites Saari (1987, p. 29) who says, "... professionally trained social workers continued to compose only a minority of all administrators in these agencies." Saari gave no data regarding this point, but referenced Gummer (1979). Gummer cited figures from an unpublished paper given by Neugeboren about the decline in the numbers of social work majors who specialize in administration. I was unable to contact Neugeboren to see if he had data about the proportion with social work degrees. A representative from the NASW's Center for Social Policy and Practice told me that the Center has no data regarding the proportion of administrators within social welfare agencies who have social work degrees. Without survey data we are only guessing.

As for the second part of this assumption, Dr. Tripodi argues that those trained in disciplines other than social work (because their college bulletins include courses in "statistical analysis, research design and analysis") are sufficiently trained to perform the technical functions required of a scientist–administrator. Even if we assume for a moment that most administrators in social welfare agencies have such training, they may not be able to apply scientific reasoning to evaluation functions within their agencies. I have unrepresentative data regarding this transference problem. My data consist of a file containing over 300 questions posed by administrators and workers in human-service agencies regarding the effectiveness of their programs. None of these questions are posed with sufficient methodological precision to get a clear answer (Gibbs, 1991, pp. 109–133), including those posed by persons trained in other disciplines.

References

Gibbs, L. E. (1991). *Scientific reasoning for social workers: Bridging the gap between research and practice.* New York: Macmillan.

Gummer, B. (1979). Is the social worker in public welfare an endangered species? *Public Welfare, 37*(4), 12–21.

Sarri, R. C. (1987). Administration in social welfare. In *Encyclopedia of social work*. 18th ed., vol 1, pp. 27–40. Silver Spring, MD: National Association of Social Workers.

Task Force on Social Work Research. (November 1991). *Building social work knowledge for effective services and policies: A plan for research development.* Austin, TX: National Institute of Mental Health, Capital Printing.

NO

LEONARD E. GIBBS

Before stating why administrators of social welfare agencies generally should not involve themselves in research within their agencies, here are conceptual definitions for terms used in this NO position: *social welfare agencies* typically refer to organizations that seek to maintain or improve the personal care, nutrition, clothing, shelter, health, and safety of society's members (e.g., a mental-health clinic, hospital, prison, or child protective service [CPS] agency); *administrators* are persons who oversee the work of others and set policy in such agencies; *conducting research* refers to procedures for objectively, systematically, and logically gathering data to answer specific questions that concern decision making within the social welfare agency.

An Example of Research Within a Social Welfare Agency

Assume that an administrator heads a county CPS agency in a metropolitan area, whose clients have, or may have, abused or neglected a child. The administrator's staff must gather information to determine, against criteria laid out in state statutes and agency procedures manuals, whether abuse or neglect has occurred among persons referred to the agency, and, in cases in which the investigation's results are positive, the staff member must see that something is done to prevent a reoccurrence, paying particular attention to high-risk cases. In other words, the agency's mission concerns risk assessment and treatment for child-abuse cases.

Assume that the administrator wants to help staff to sharpen their ability to accurately identify those cases where re-abuse is most likely. The administrator has read reviews of research that shows the superiority of statistical prediction over clinical prediction in many contexts (Dawes, Faust & Meehl, 1989). Clinical prediction in the administrator's agency would involve workers interviewing clients, conducting assessments, interviewing collateral sources, and intuitively predicting which cases will most likely involve re-abuse. Statistical prediction, on the other hand, involves measuring salient features of the case (e.g., stress level of caregivers, number and severity of prior abuses, appropriateness of expectations for the child's behavior given the child's age), following up at-risk persons to see which salient features are most statistically associated with later re-abuse, constructing a risk-assessment scale, and testing the scale's ability to predict re-abuse in another sample of the agency's clients.

The administrator hopes that vigorous preventative action among high-risk cases can reduce re-abuse rates. To test hypotheses, the administrator tests the predictive efficiency of staff's predictions versus that of the prediction scale; then the administrator randomly assigns high-risk cases to intensive treatment, or to standard treatment within the CPS agency to see if intensive treatment for high-risk clients reduces re-abuse.

Reasons for Not Conducting Research

Does the scenario above sound realistic? Is this the way that administrators in social welfare agencies typically conduct themselves? I think not. Why not? The reasons that make research uncommon about such vital issues are the very reasons that administrators should not and typically do not conduct research. The reasons relative to this example, are explained in the arguments below. All arguments below concern what is now generally true—not what can be argued by citing atypical case examples.

Argument #1: presently, most human-service administrators lack the necessary training to conduct research. Incredible as it may sound, not until 1984 did the Council on Social Work Education (CSWE) first mandate that students in social work courses should be able to evaluate their own practice! According to the *Handbook of Accreditation Standards and Procedures* (1984), CSWE then mandated that:

> The professional foundation context in research [within social work curriculum] should thus provide skills that will take students beyond the role of consumers of research and prepare them systematically to evaluate their own practice. (p. 127)

Given the lateness of this standard's initiation, even if we assume that this policy was immediately implemented, it still will not have been in effect for long enough to affect the capabilities of most administrators.

Argument #2: most administrators in the foreseeable future will lack the training necessary to conduct research. Just recently, a Task Force on Social Work Research (1991), supported with funds from the National Institute of Mental Health, did an extensive study of research in social work. The Task Force, composed of prominent research leaders, were asked to identify problems and potential solutions within the profession. Here is their conclusion with regard to research training in social work at the present time:

> There are critical problems in how research is taught at every level of social work education. In general, the teaching of methods is separate from and unrelated to the teaching of professional practice methods. The basic texts used to teach practice methods do not convey information about the relation between research and practice. (p. 13)

Given the above, how could one argue that administrators in human-service agencies should conduct research within their own agencies? As a general rule—though there are likely to be a few exceptions—administrators are not sufficiently trained to conduct research regarding practice within their agencies. In the child-welfare example above, the typical administrator would not understand how to locate relevant literature, systematically select prognostic indicators, reliably measure these indicators, keep follow-up data, analyze the data to construct a statistical risk-assessment instrument, compare the predictive efficiency of staff predictions versus the instrument, and conduct a randomized evaluation of intensive versus standard treatment for high-risk cases.

Argument #3: it would be unethical for administrators, who generally are insufficiently trained in research, to try to conduct research within their own agencies. Federal guidelines for the protection of human subjects requires that human subjects participate in experiments only when the experiment's potential benefits outweigh potential risks to subjects. One source of unreasonable risk to subjects occurs when poorly designed experiments produce only trivial or uninterpretable results. Therefore, if poorly trained administrators conduct poorly done experiments, they subject their agency's clients to unethical practices.

Relative to the substantive example from child-welfare above, if the administrator believed that a re-abuse scale's predictive efficiency was high, and the opposite were true, then decision making within the agency that was based on the scale could error seriously. High-risk children might be misclassified as ''low-risk,'' with disastrous results. Furthermore, ignorance of the need for random assignment, and consequently a potential selection bias in the administrator's experiment could lead to harmful effects. For example, if the administrator unknowingly placed clients with good prognosis into one treatment group disproportionately, and inferred that post-treatment differences favoring that treatment were causal with the treatment, then an ineffective or even harmful treatment might gain favor or continue in use.

Argument #4: administrators who want to retain their jobs and maintain the goodwill of their workers will not conduct research. Any administrator who contemplates conducting research should know about widespread resistance, ambivalence, and even hostility, toward research in the social work profession. There have been numerous reviews regarding attitudes toward research and knowledge of research principles among social work practitioners and students. Recently, Lazar (1991) looked into this relationship between social work and research. Lazar examined fifteen studies that explored the profession's orientation toward research and the attitudes toward research that exist among different groups within the social work community. Lazar reports that studies done through 1976 reflected a predominately negative attitude toward research. Respondents to surveys reported a lack of concern for and interest in research and a belief that research can counter the values of casework. More recent surveys reflect ambivalence. Some studies report increased interest and knowledge in research; some reported more negative attitudes toward research after research training.

If negative or ambivalent attitudes prevail toward research within the rank and file of human-service professionals, then any administrator who tries to initiate or support research within a human-service organization risks getting tangled up in an administrative buzz saw. Any administrator bold enough to try to initiate research in an organization proposes something potentially new, and new ideas invariably generate tension. A research-minded administrator might have to fight an appeal to tradition, that is, the belief that the agency has survived previously without research; so why start now? For example, in the hypothetical CPS agency above, workers might argue, "I have been judging which cases are high risk for over a decade now. No prediction instrument can possibly replace my years of personal experience." The tendency of persons to misinterpret truth-seeking as being an attack on them personally presents another obstacle to an innovative and far-sighted research advocate. Workers in the CPS agency might say essentially, "You really have the nerve coming in here to snoop around about my work." Another particularly devastating obstacle to research is the "soft-hearted, therefore also soft-headed fallacy." This argument posits that only two kinds of human-service workers exist: those who are warm, caring, empathic, socially skilled; and those who are rational, scientific, analytical, and data-based. The implied question is, "Which are you?" Perhaps the most devastating obstacle to research in a human-service agency is the "aloneness" that a scientific thinker experiences. Because research is unfamiliar, research-minded persons might get a response from staff along the lines of "Which planet are you from?" Where the research-minded see the need for reliable measures (e.g., of re-abuse, or high-risk status); the conventional thinker is content with traditional and often vague notions about these terms. Where the research-minded sees questions (e.g., can a risk-assessment instrument out-predict clinicians?), practitioners may feel confident in their personal judgments. Where the researcher carefully notes and examines failures, others may attribute incidents of re-abuse to vague, indistinct dynamics, including a lack of client "motivation." These are only a few of the tripping mechanisms that threaten to throw a scientific-thinking administrator into an organizational buzz saw.

Argument #5: administrators do not have the time to conduct research. A search for studies that quantify how administrators of social welfare agencies use their time uncovered nothing; so data cannot clarify how many hours administrators work per week, nor how those hours are allocated by task. Such data would probably document the long, extra hours that administrators spend at their jobs and the many immediate demands on their time. I did speak with Hal Benson, Head of the Network of Social Work Managers, who gave two reasons that administrators do not become involved more often in research. First, he pointed out that administrators are "... up to their eyeballs in other non-research tasks. ..." His second reason underscores ideas presented above. He said that administrators of social welfare agencies often rise to their position within the agency from a clinical position and, thus, do not have the expertise in research that one formally trained in administration might have. I also spoke with Robert Maslyn of the Department of Health and Human Services, in the Office of Assistant Secretary for Management and Budget. Maslyn underscored Benson's concerns. Additionally, Maslyn said that if an administrator were to get involved in research, it should be in the role of overseer—one who sees that the research question is of importance to the agency and that it is conducted within the agency by someone trained in research.

Conclusions

I have not discussed whether or not expertly applied, rigorous, analytical, data-based research methodology can answer questions of importance to administrators; it can. I argue that, as a general rule, most administrators should not hold the role of researcher within their own agency: they lack the time to do the job themselves; they face insurmountable odds in many agencies in which the tenets of scientific thinking are completely foreign; typically, they have not been nor are they now sufficiently trained to conduct their own research; and because they tend to lack the necessary training, they should not, for ethical reasons, conduct their own studies.

Hopefully, in the future, administrators and staff in social welfare agencies will be sufficiently trained in scientific reasoning to conduct or oversee methodologically sound research. Though presently, and for the immediate future, administrators generally should not become involved in research within their own agencies, there are isolated examples to the contrary. Wil Johnson and his outstanding team of protective service workers in Alameda County, California, are one such example. They conducted the hypothetical study presented above by comparing predictions by child-welfare workers versus predictions by statistical means (Johnson, Clancy, Robinson, & Wong, 1989). Johnson and his colleagues are an exception to the rule.

References

Council on Social Work Education. (July 1984). *Handbook of accreditation standards and procedures.* 111 Eighth Avenue, New York 10011: Author.

Dawes, R. M., Faust, D., & Meehl, P. E. (1989). Clinical versus actuarial judgment. *Science, 243,* 1668–1673.

Johnson, W., Clancy, T., Robinson, E., & Wong, E. (February 14, 1989). Letter to Alameda County Board of Supervisors. Alameda County Social Service Agency, Oakland, CA.

Lazar, A. (1991). Faculty, practitioner, and student attitudes toward research. *Journal of Social Work Education, 27*(1), 34–41.

Task Force on Social Work Research. (November 1991). *Building social work knowledge for effective services and policies: A plan for research development.* Austin, TX: National Institute of Mental Health, Capital Printing.

Rejoinder to Dr. Gibbs

TONY TRIPODI

My rebuttal to Dr. Gibbs will be organized according to his five arguments.

Arguments #1 and #2: the argument is made that administrators lack the training to do research, and they are not likely to receive the training soon. It should be noted that not all administrators of human-service agencies are social workers; many have received their education in business administration or public administration and related fields, and they have been trained in computers, data processing, quantitative analysis, forecasting, decision theories, and research methods. Increasingly social work administrators have been requesting and attending seminars on management and administrative methods by business schools. Moreover, a careful reading of the report of the Task Force on Social Work Research (1991, November) indicates that all levels of social work education should increase the competence of their students in using research to develop knowledge and to evaluate practice, including that of administrators.

Argument #3: this argument implies that the conduct of research by administrators not adequately trained in research will be harmful to workers and clients. There is no empirical evidence to substantiate this claim. As a part of their ethical responsibilities, administrators must see to it that effective and efficient services and interventions are provided. To know whether or not there is organizational effectiveness, administrators must plan for the selection of effective technologies as well as the evaluation of services and interventions.

Argument #4: this argument says that "administrators who want to retain their jobs, and maintain the good will of their workers will not conduct research." There is no empirical evidence to substantiate this claim. Furthermore, in these times of budget reductions and tight budgets, administrators often seek funding from granting agencies to bolster their budgets based on needs and resource surveys.

Argument #5: Dr. Gibbs argues that administrators do not have the time to do research; yet, he says he does not really know what administrators do with their time because no empirical data are available. Obviously, he refutes his own assertion. So long as administrators are responsible for organizational effectiveness, they and their staffs must find the time to do the necessary research.

References

Task Force on Social Work Research (1991, November). *Building social work knowledge for effective services and policies: A plan for research development.* Austin, TX: National Institute of Mental Health, Capital Printing Co.

DEBATE 11

Should Program Decisions Be Based on Empirical Evidence of Effectiveness?

Peter Gabor is an associate professor at The University of Calgary, Faculty of Social Work, where he has taught a variety of research and practice courses. He is also Director of the Lethbridge Division of the program. His current research and writing interests are in the area of child welfare and evaluation. He co-authored, with R. M. Grinnell, the text, *Evaluation and Monitoring in Social Work,* to be published by Allyn and Bacon (1993).

Richard M. Grinnell, Jr., is Professor and Associate Dean at The University of Calgary, Faculty of Social Work. He is author of (or has co-authored) over fifty professional journal articles and twenty book chapters. He is co-author of *Research in Social Work: A Primer* (2nd Ed.) (with M. Williams, & L. Totty, 1995, F. E. Peacock), two editions of *Statistics for Social Workers* (with R. Weinbach, Longman, 1987 & 1991), *The Social Work Practicum: A Student Guide* (with D. Collins & B. Tomlison, Peacock, 1992), *Student Study Guide* for the fourth edition of *Social Work Research and Evaluation* (with J. Krysik & I. Hoffart, Peacock, 1993), and *Evaluation and Quality Improvement in the Human Services* (with Peter Gabor, Allyn and Bacon, in press). He is also the editor of four editions of *Social Work Research and Evaluation* (Peacock, 1981, 1985, 1988, & 1993), and the current editor of *The Canadian Journal of Program Evaluation.*

Merlin A. Taber is Professor Emeritus at the University of Illinois. He studies information management and policy planning problems as a consultant.

YES

PETER GABOR
RICHARD M. GRINNELL, JR.

Ideally, decisions about programs should be based on empirical evidence of effectiveness. Effectiveness is the degree to which a program meets its objectives; and these objectives may address such matters as the type of problems and needs served, number of clients served, and the results achieved. To the degree that a program meets its objectives, it can be considered to be effective.

At their best, programs are dynamic entities, which continually evolve and develop. Program decisions impact program development; some decisions may result in routine, day-to-day fine-tuning, while others will occasion major changes in practices and structures, or may even effect the existence of a program.

On what basis should such decisions to be made? Few would argue that program decisions should be made on the basis on idiosyncratic whims or personal preferences. Most would agree that relevant information should be obtained, considered, and then synthesized into the decision.

There is, however, controversy in social work about the *type* of information required for such decisions. It is our opinion that, to the extent possible, decisions should be based on information that is as accurate and unbiased as is possible. Historically, empirical methods, relying on systematic observation and measurement, have been the preferred method of obtaining such information.

Typically, program decisions are based on information relating to a variety of variables. Substantive variables relating to client outcomes, program activities and structures are one group to be considered; contextual variables such as history, experience, professional norms, community expectations, and political pressures are another.

Because many contextual variables cannot be measured empirically, impressions, intuition, and global judgment are relied upon to provide the requisite information. In short, subjective data frequently are used to provide information about contextual variables. Substantive variables, on the other hand, usually can be measured through empirical methods. Questions relating to the number of clients served, demographic characteristics of the clients, types of presenting problems, numbers of staff members employed, total hours of service provided, and changes in selected problem indicators can be answered empirically. How would a program manager know the number of clients served if empirical data were not kept on this variable? The manager might base an estimate on impressions formed during walks through the waiting room and from discussions with social workers, but such an estimate would not likely be very accurate. Empirical data can provide the required information with precision.

Although questions relating to client outcomes and other matters relating to program effectiveness often can be settled on the basis of empirical data, it is frequently the case that a program resorts to subjective data to answer these types of questions. Suppose that a key objective for an outreach program for adolescent boys is the reduction in problems with self-esteem. If the program is of sufficient size, dozens of young people and several staff members may be involved. Individual workers may feel that they have a handle on the progress of the young people with whom they are working, but no staff member is likely to have contact with all the young people. A manager who wishes to assemble a program-wide picture of how clients are doing would have to collect these individual impressions and form them into a composite picture regarding client progress. Of course, some workers' impressions and reports will be more accurate than others' because workers are likely to have different levels of accuracy in judging client progress and in assembling such judgments across their own caseload. Moreover, workers' judgments will be subject potentially to a variety of biases because of such things as a genuine desire to see clients progress, a belief in the efficacy of the program, and, in some cases, a desire to present themselves in the best light possible.

A picture built on impressions may or may not be accurate. It is impossible to know, in any given case, to what degree it is accurate. To augment such a picture, the manager may rely on other indicators: feedback received from parents, the community, and other professionals, the apparent level of motivation and enthusiasm among staff, the smooth functioning of various program components, and so forth. Out of all these sources of information, the manager may come to a conclusion about the effectiveness of the program. Even if it should happen to be accurate, such a picture will hardly be convincing to outside stakeholders, such as funders and program sponsors. Moreover, the picture is likely to have limitations for internal use as well. The estimate will lack precision because the degree to which the program reached its objectives is not quantifiable. Thus, it will be of limited use in attempting to compare current status with past performance. Again, the manager may have some ideas that the program is doing "better" or "not quite as well" as previously, but the amount of change cannot be determined with any degree of precision.

The discussion above, highlights some of the limitations inherent in subjective data. Impressions, intuition, and global judgments come to the mind already formed and the process by which they were formed cannot be readily examined. Consequently, such data are prone to inaccuracies and biases, and the extent of such errors cannot be readily assessed.

In contrast, the main advantage of relying on empirical data for decision making lies in its relative objectivity and precision. In the case of the program described above, changes in the level of self-esteem problems of clients can be measured empirically. A number of excellent instruments are available for such purposes. Suppose that Hudson's Index of Self-Esteem (ISE)[1] is used to measure these changes. When the data are aggregated for a client group discharged during a six-month period, it is found that problem scores have declined from a mean of

55 at the time of entry into the program to a mean of 43 at discharge. Such data confirm the impression that clients are improving. However, these empirical data have considerable advantages over impressions based on subjective data:

1. Individual changes are assessed by the use of an instrument that has been demonstrated to be reliable and valid. It is reasonable, therefore, to have confidence in the accuracy of the scores.
2. Because standardized measurements are used, the biases inherent in individual judgments are reduced, if not eliminated.
3. All participants' results are used in determining client group status at the beginning and end of the program.
4. The resulting data provide information not only on whether or not clients have improved on the average, but also on the amount of improvement. This information is useful in addressing questions about the adequacy of the improvement and in comparing outcomes in this reporting period with results from other periods.

How should empirical data be used in decision making about programs? Many people in social work are suspicious of empirical data, fearing that reliance on it will reduce or eliminate human judgment from social work. We would like to make clear that we are advocating nothing of the sort. We recognize that empirical data represents only part of the information that must be considered in arriving at most program decisions. For example, what is a manager to make of the results described above? Is a 12-point mean improvement in self-esteem problem levels indicative of program effectiveness, keeping in mind that the mean score at program conclusion was still well above the clinical-cutting score? The data should help inform such judgments, but certainly do not dictate them. In assessing the adequacy of results, the manager should take into consideration a variety of contextual variables. Some of the variables that may be taken into the decision-making equation include the following: the levels of improvement that have been demonstrated in the past; levels of improvement found in similar programs elsewhere; stage of development of the program; costliness of the program; adequacy of resources provided to the program; feedback from clients after discharge; feedback from other community members; and other factors. Most of these factors will not be measured empirically; rather, the answers to such contextual questions will be made on the basis of impressions and judgment. Ultimately, subjective data relating to these contextual factors and the empirical data will be combined into a decision. The specific contextual variables used for the decision and the weight they are to be given in relation to the empirical data is, again, a matter for judgment.

Clearly, much of the decision-making process relies on data that are not empirical. However, certain variables, particularly those relating to program effectiveness, can best be measured through empirical methods. The resulting data are likely to be free of bias and distortions, and be more representative and accurate than information about effectiveness acquired through subjective methods.

Empirical data will not remove human judgment from decision making. It will serve, however, to bring more accurate and complete information to the decision maker, thereby improving the quality of decisions. Consequently, program decisions should be made, to the degree possible, on the basis of empirical data.

Notes

1. Hudson's ISE is a standardized instrument measuring problems in self-esteem. The possible range of scores is 0–100, with higher scores indicating greater problems. The clinical-cutting score is 30; scores below that number indicate the absence of a clinically significant problem. This instrument has been shown to have excellent reliability and validity.

Rejoinder to Dr. Gabor & Grinnell

Merlin A. Taber

My debators, in their YES paper, say decisions should be based ideally on evidence of effectiveness. I agree. My mother in her 80s often told me we could have world peace if Baha'I teachings were widely followed. I always agreed with my mother then, and I agree with Gabor and Grinnell now. In the ideal world, there would be universal love and there would be scientific measures of everything. Looking at my debators' final sentences, I find further grounds for agreement. They conclude that "more accurate and complete information" would be desirable for decision making, and again I agree.

It is in between the first and last sentences where I find much to question. The terminology used by Drs. Gabor and Grinnell is overly general and vague. In their rush to occupy the high ground, they brush past inconvenient questions about the real world. Their main topic shifts from decision making to measurement technology.

A brisk walk down my opponents' line of argument will show why I object to the general and vague nature of their arguments. Program decisions, for them, range all the way from fine tuning to program termination. Any administrative action is a program decision. A dichotomy is posed between "relevant information," on the one hand, and "idiosyncratic whims," on the other, as a basis for such decisions. This dichotomy is neither clear nor helpful. Next, variables relating to program operations, which I would call program data, are called "substantive" for reasons that are not clear. Other data are called "contextual," and we are told that contextual data tend to be ''subjective.'' I do not see any basis for this claim. Any objective, they say, may show ''effectiveness.'' I have thought effectiveness meant outcomes that realize central program aims and not such things as bigger caseloads or higher fee collections. In the last third of the paper, the term ''empirical'' data become observations with numbers attached. Such observations are said to be more unbiased and more accurate than ''impressions and judgment.'' Thus do the authors use vague and idiosyncratic definitions to argue their case. If they limited and defined their terms, then their argument might not reach the same end.

By noting a ''rush to occupy the high ground,'' I was objecting to the heavily loaded nature of my partners' diction and their shifting semantics. They favor using data that are empirical, unbiased, accurate, systematic, relevant, substantive, precise, and quantifiable. Who does not? Unfortunately, however, all of us in social work are forced to use much the same data. Assignment of numbers or claims to ''objectivity'' change neither the data nor the processes creating the data. My debators do not examine such matters, rather they repeatedly invoke the adjectives of science without examining their application to social work.

A more serious problem—more serious than loaded terminology—is the structure of their argument. Where does it go? The last third of their paper is an argument for attaching numbers to observations. At the end, ''empirical'' has been given a new meaning: quantified measures of program data and outcome indicators. I, too, am eager to use measures with such properties as equal intervals over their range, meaningful zero point, and the like. But I differ from Drs. Gabor and Grinnell in my ideas about ''social work variables.'' The field as a whole has not clearly defined main outcomes or modeled their relations to other variables, much less shown them as interval scales. More accuracy is always welcome, but the real problems of program analysis and design are matters of helping process, program model, and the like, rather than measurement technology.

In short, I believe Drs. Gabor and Grinnell avoid the difficult, real problems of our field in favor of presenting a version of the standard philosophy of science. Here is my offer to them. I will agree that, ideally, decisions about programs should be based on empirical evidence of effectiveness, if they will agree that in the real world most program decisions cannot be made that way now, and many should never be made that way at all.

NO

MERLIN A. TABER

I was dubious about taking the NO position on this question of knowledge. I've long been an advocate for guiding practice by observation (Taber & Shapiro, 1965), for professional theory development (Taber, Quay, Mark, & Nealey,

1969), for ransacking research findings for new knowledge (Taber, 1980), and for careful approximation to experimental design (Taber & Proch, 1987). The question itself sounds suspiciously like a booby trap. How could there be a negative side? The editors said I could have fun with this question, so I agreed to try. The intellectual excursion led me to unexpected places and I will try to retrace my steps and offer my conclusion. First some definitions are necessary.

"Program Decisions" Are Central to Social Work

Personal social services are remarkable in that the benefit is produced by interaction between helper and helped. The program defines for all three parties (client, worker, societal sponsor) parameters for the creative helping relationships. The social-service program defines rights and obligations, paths through the program, and reasonable expectations and goals for each participant.

What are "program decisions?" Examples of program decisions, in my understanding of the subject (Taber & Finnegan, 1980; Taber, 1987), are questions of eligibility, appropriate interactions, goals, and time frames for the interaction. Case decisions, in contrast to program decisions, refer to specific time-limited objectives, exceptions to agency rules, and the like. Program decisions then serve to design a system of social services.

Effectiveness of Program Decisions Can Be Defined

How might evidence about effectiveness be used in program decisions? If only those program features that produced better outcomes on average were adopted. One would insist on evidence that a program design element (charging a fee, or limiting intake to first-time offenders, or employing more experienced workers) leads to better outcomes. Thus would program decisions be based on outcome research.

What is meant by effectiveness? Which outcomes are better? My answer is that reasonable kinds of goals for clients are part of the program design. What is empirical evidence of effectiveness? According to the *Oxford English Dictionary,* evidence might be "that which manifests or makes evident" or better perhaps, a "ground for belief" (Simpson & Weiner, 1989, p. 469). From the same source, we learn that with respect to a physician, empirical means ". . . bases his methods of practice on the results of observation and experience, not on scientific theory," or even, ". . . that is guilty of quackery" (p. 188) In our field, we are advised, empirical indicates an art or practice "that is guided by mere experience, without scientific knowledge." Those who framed this debate, I believe, wanted to stake the issue on positivistic methodology, not on the "empirical" nature of evidence. Therefore, I take evidence of effectiveness to be the result of theory-relevant and hypothesis-focused research that uses positivist methodology.

The question under debate then is whether administrators, program directors, and others should use research findings on effectiveness to design personal, social service programs. I will not argue that factual data, program statistics, program descriptions, and research on related questions should not be used; of course they should all be used. But facts, numbers, and related findings are not empirical evidence on effectiveness of program design—achieving case goals under that program.

I was reluctant to take on the NO position on this question. After surveying literature and thinking about it, however, I believe the negative has a good case.

Experts on Program Management Do Not Cite Empirical Evidence

The first problem with use of research findings to guide program decisions is that there are no such research findings. The array of research findings is so limited, the research designs so incomplete, and the sampling of problems and situations is so slight that persons doing program design cannot use research as a guide. Let us see how empirical evidence is brought to bear in textbooks. Weiner (1982) will be discussed first, not as a model, but because his coverage of ideas and sources is exhaustive.

Weiner promises to present an integrated set of management science and behavioral science philosophies, theories, and concepts . . . and I believe Weiner delivers. He presents concepts, principles, and technology in every area of management functions. He emphasizes the need for factual data about operations. He does *not* however mention any findings on the effectiveness of different ways to design human-service programs. None of the 200 or so items in his bibliography are research reports on programs or on outcomes of service programs.

The collections of essays by Slavin (1985), and the text by Weinbach (1990) are similar to Weiner's volume in their focus on organization, use of terms and technologies from many sources, and stress on the need for good data to make daily decisions. They are also like Weiner's volume in their reliance on essays and ideas from other fields. Research on programs is used neither for developing arguments nor for codifying management procedures.

The texts by Gates (1980), by Lewis, Lewis, and Souflee (1991), and by Rapp and Poertner (1992) are different from these in that the concept of a program is given a more central place in organizing each book and in defining professional tasks. Lewis, Lewis, and Souflee (1991) treat program evaluation extensively and make it an administrative task. The creation, design, and implementation of programs is not included in their discussion. Gates (1980) conceptualizes a continuum within policy, program, implementation, and results; and his book provides a good catalogue of program features, in which each is treated as a problem for development by administrators. Rapp and Poertner (1992) have developed a general approach to administration in which the concept of a program is central. I find their approach especially congenial, which is not surprising because they studied and worked with me, and because "Part 2" of their text is organized around my ideas. Despite my respect for these works, and despite the contributions of all three, it must be noted that research findings are not significant in any of the three texts for development of the arguments presented. All three recognize the need for empirical guidance for practice. None of them, however, cite research that is relevant for program decisions, nor do any of them adduce research findings to shape their frameworks.

It may be objected that research findings do exist, but that these particular authors did not cite them, or that useful research is just beginning to be published. To see if these objections might be valid, a further search was made.

Research Activity on Program Decisions Is Not Apparent

To discover current research that is relevant to program decisions, recent issues of seven journals were examined (*Administration in Social Work, 15,*(1/2–4), 1991; *Clinical Social Work, 19*(1–4), 1991; *Evaluation Review, 15*(1–6), 1991; *Sociology and Social Research, 57*(1–4), 1991; *Social Service Review, 65*(1–6), 1991; *Social Work, 36*(1–6), 1991; *Social Work Research & Abstracts, 27*(1–4, 1991). The search was most enlightening. My method was to use author and title indexes to find articles that might be relevant. Twenty four articles were found that had some relevance to program decisions. Only two were accounts of systematic research that reported outcomes under specified program conditions. Of these articles, one (Rosenthal & Rosenthal, 1991) reported that juvenile delinquent recidivism was lower under certain placement conditions, and those findings led to actual program changes. The second article concerned a service program, but not a personal social service. In summary, current journals provided only one report of empirical evidence on effectiveness of personal social-services program decisions.

A number of studies examined outcomes in terms of factors other than program characteristics, for example: agency affiliation, worker characteristics, or agency philosophy. There were numbers of interesting, though fragmentary, program descriptions, especially in *Social Work.* A tendency to discuss, "How I would *like to do* research," rather than, "How I *did* some research," was apparent; eight of the pieces that sounded promising turned out to be research designs recommended, but not carried out. All of these essays and reports could be very useful to program decisions, but cannot be counted as empirical evidence on effectiveness of program design practice.

Believers in a positivist methodology may argue that we must try harder to apply proper research methods to our problems. Is a payoff likely from such continued devotion? I think not, for several reasons.

We Do Not Have the Equipment for Research on Personal Social Service Programs

Why is there not more program research? One problem, I think, is cost; program research is very costly. Large scale attempts in the 1960s and 1970s were not regarded as worthwhile in results. This problem—lack of funding—has become worse. But if funds were available, could we do program research? I think not, at least for some time.

It seems likely that, even if funds were freely available, research useful to program decisions would still not be undertaken. Concepts, ideas about entities and connections, measuring procedures, and so on are not available. It appears that we are not equipped to perform research on programs.

We see that program decisions are made every day by using precedent, common sense, humanistic values, political feasibility, and professional experience—not empirical evidence. Is this a deplorable situation? Perhaps not.

Research Findings Cannot Guide Program Decisions

Were a well tested theory of personal social-service programming available, should it be used to guide program decisions? No, except in company with, and subordinately to, other considerations.

Consider these social work programming decisions: priority given to more versus less seriously dysfunctional among severely mentally ill clients; information to be given to young women asking for abortions; rights of terminally ill persons to refuse treatment or choose a suicidal course of action; extent of participation of abusive parents in decisions about their children. Program-design questions (professional qualifications needed, per unit of service costs, intake procedures, and others) hinge on each of these questions. Yet none of these questions can now be answered by empirical evidence. If they could be, should they?

Political interests, value conflicts, and even conceptual difficulties are central in social work programming. Persons answerable for outcomes in the political or community sectors and persons understanding the stakes and pressures involved must make these decisions. Certainly factual data are central; but factual data are not "empirical evidence of effectiveness."

It may be objected that some social work program decisions are subject to rational analysis and use of research evidence. True, but knowledge or theory is built around well understood problems and familiar technologies. Social work by its nature (Taber, 1970) deals with emergent and poorly defined problems.

Another problem overlooked by those who advocate "application of research findings" is that such application is an art, not a science. Debates over meaning of the income experiments and the public-aid "service" trials of the 1960s dramatize the difficulties of application. All analysts seem to find what they want to in research findings, just as they do in anecdotal evidence.

Conclusion: Let Social Administration Be Social Administration

We do not have research findings to guide the important decisions about program design. Even if we did, precedence should still be given to humanistic, political, and professional matters. I believe that evidence is to program decision making what seasoning is to a good beef stew. Use moderately. Do not add 'til the last twenty minutes. And always remember that seasoning can never substitute for good beef.

References

Gates, B. L. (1980). *Social program administration: The implementation of social policy.* Englewood Cliffs, NJ: Prentice-Hall.

Lewis, J. A., Lewis, M. D., & Souflee, F. (1991). *Management of Human Service Programs* (2nd ed). Pacific Grove, CA: Brooks Cole.

Rapp, C., & Poertner, J. (1992). *Social administration: A client-centered approach.* White Plains, NJ: Longman.

Rosenthal, J. A., & Rosenthal, D. H. (1991). Logit and probit models: A juvenile justice program evaluation. *Social Work Research and Abstracts, 27*(3), 9–15.

Selznick, P. (1957). *Leadership in administration: A sociological interpretation.* Berkeley, CA: University of California.

Simpson, J. A., & Weiner, E. S. C. (1989). *The oxford english dictionary* (2nd ed., vol. 5). Oxford, England: Clarendon Press.

Slavin, S. (Ed.). (1985). *Social administration: The management of the social services* (2nd ed., vol. 1). *An Introduction to Human Services Management.* New York: Haworth.

Taber, M. A. (1970). A knowledge base for social work: Three positions. In *Modes of professional education: Functions of field learning in the curriculum* (pp. 143–152). New Orleans, LA: Tulane University.

Taber, M. A. (1980). *The social context of helping: A review of the literature on alternative care for the physically and mentally handicapped* (DHHS Publication, no. ADM 80-842). Washington, D.C.: U.S. Government Printing Office.

Taber, M. A. (1987). A theory of accountability for the human services and the implications for program design. *Administration in Social Work, 3–4,* 115–126.

Taber, M. A., & Finnegan, D. J. (1980). The social service program developer: A new role in social work. *Journal of Education for Social Work, 16,* 27–32.

Taber, M. A., & Proch, K. (1987). Placement stability for adolescents in foster care: Findings from a program experiment. *Child Welfare, 66,* 433–445.

Taber, M. A., Quay, H. C., Mark, H., & Nealey. (1969). Disease ideology and mental health research. *Social Problems, 16,* 349–357.

Taber, M. A., & Shapiro, I. (1965). Social work and its knowledge base: A content analysis of the periodical literature. *Social Work, 10,* 100–107.

Weinbach, R. W. (1990). *The social worker as manager: Theory and practice.* New York: Longman.

Weiner, M. E. (1982). *Human service management: Analysis and applications.* Homewood, IL: Dorsey.

Rejoinder to Dr. Taber

PETER GABOR
RICHARD M. GRINNELL, JR.

We agree with Dr. Taber that there is a paucity of published research findings that relate to program outcomes. We also agree with Dr. Taber that other considerations, in addition to empirical findings, are important in guiding program decisions. However, we part company with him with respect to a number of other points that he makes while reaching his conclusion that program decisions should not be based on empirical evidence of effectiveness.

In his paper, Dr. Taber defines effectiveness in a very restrictive manner: he seems to argue that effectiveness is a concept that is relevant only in relation to outcomes. Our view of program effectiveness is much broader. We see effectiveness as the extent to which a program meets its objectives. These objectives need not be restricted to outcome objectives, but may well include process objectives, such as the types and numbers of clients served. Even if empirical evidence relating to outcomes is unavailable, it is appropriate to rely on empirical data to determine whether process-related objectives are being met. For example, many programs have objectives related to how quickly the intake process should be completed and services initiated. Surely, it is only through collecting the appropriate empirical data that program managers and administrators can know to what degree this objective is being met. If the objective is not being met satisfactorily, a responsible program manager would undoubtedly move to adjust the intake process—in other words, make a program decision on the basis of these empirical data.

Dr. Taber makes the point that published outcome research is unavailable because of its high cost and because theory and research technology are not yet well developed. The type of research implied by such considerations is large-scale program evaluation. As Dr. Taber points out, a number of such attempts were undertaken in the 1960s and 1970s. This type of research can, at best, however, provide only general guidance to decision makers. It might conceivably yield results that would suggest that a particular program approach is preferable to another. Such information would be most relevant in the design stage. While Dr. Taber seems to focus on the design stage as the time when program decisions are made, important decisions are made during all program stages.

It is our contention that large-scale research efforts are unlikely to be the most productive in providing data to guide decision making. On a day-to-day basis, program managers are interested not in data that relate to program theory and program design, but in data relating to how the program for which they have responsibility is meeting its many objectives. Data, relevant to documenting and monitoring program processes and outcomes, are the result not of large-scale research efforts, but of well designed management information systems. Elsewhere (Gabor & Grinnell, in press), we have described how such a system can be built by collecting data that is relevant to the information needs of social workers at the case level and subsequently aggregating these data to provide information pertaining to program processes and outcomes.

Such systems, while not without cost, can be maintained with relative low expense, and the technology to conduct such research is readily available. The approach described can yield a continuous stream of empirical data relating to a variety of program objectives. Such data are likely to be more accurate and less biased than any other sources of information available to the manager. As such, they provide an excellent basis for decision making.

As we made clear in our initial statement, we are certainly not suggesting that *only* empirical data should be used in program-level decision making. We agree with Dr. Taber that other considerations such as values, experience, politics, and so forth are also relevant in arriving at most program decisions. But we cannot accept Dr. Taber's recipe for good beef stew; far from being the seasoning, in our kitchen, empirical data are the meat and potatoes of this dish.

Reference

Gabor, P., & Grinnell, R. M., Jr. (in press). *Evaluation and Quality Improvement in the Human Services.* Boston, MA: Allyn and Bacon.

DEBATE 12

Should Social Work Take Greater Leadership in Research on Total Systems of Service?

Charles A. Glisson is Professor and Chair of the Ph.D. Program in Social Work, University of Tennessee, Knoxville. He is the author of numerous book chapters and articles on research methods, human-service organizations and services to children, and is editor (with David Gillespie) of the forthcoming *Quantitative Methods in Social Work.* He is currently principal investigator of an NIMH R01-sponsored study of the statewide interorganizational coordination of services to children.

Juan Paz is an assistant professor at the Arizona State University School of Social Work, where he teaches courses in human behavior and the social environment and social-welfare policy. His current research and scholarly interests are in the problems of the elderly and substance abuse with adolescents. He is co-investigator with Craig LeCroy of a five-year substance-abuse prevention project that is funded by the Center for Substance Abuse.

YES

CHARLES A. GLISSON

Social work research on total systems of service assesses the impact of social policies and programs on major social problems. It is large-scale research that examines the formal and informal social systems that link needs, services, and outcomes. The research is predicated on the assumption that studies of small components of intervention efforts are valuable, but studies of total systems in the field are necessary to the development of knowledge about policy and program efficacy and the social problems that they are designed to address. For example, it is important to have knowledge of the effectiveness of a particular clinical intervention, the cost of a service provided by a specific organization, or the characteristics of those in a community who are affected by a certain social problem. However, knowledge about the inter-relationships among community characteristics, populations at risk, service structures, activities of direct-practice workers, and outcomes with target groups is necessary to the design of policies and programs that adequately address major social problems.

Social work's roots are embedded in the major social problems and social issues that have confronted the nation since its inception. Historically, social workers have placed a high priority on the amelioration of the social problems that arise persistently amid the nation's affluence and prosperity. The major problems, such as those associated with poverty, immigration, and dependent children, are extremely complex. They involve multiple, overlapping social systems, which include families, communities, service organizations, inter-organizational networks, state-service structures, and federal agencies and policies. As a result, analyses of the major problems must include numerous, higher level systems. If small components of the relevant systems are analyzed separately, the actual complexity of the problem is ignored, the relationships among components remain unknown, and the analyses and subsequent interventions become overly reductionistic and simplistic.

Unfortunately, social work as a profession has become less and less concerned with the big social problems that involve higher level systems. Increasingly, social workers define the units of analyses and the targets of intervention efforts solely in terms of the individual or the family. Although making many positive contributions, the professionalization of social work has contributed to this trend by redirecting the attention of social work practitioners away from the big social issues and major social problems to more myopic concerns. Concerns with such issues as formal credentialing, third-party payments, practice certification, and mastering the popular psychotherapies have become more important as the profession is defined more and more in terms of direct practice with individuals.

This professional trend parallels social work's decreasing involvement in its traditional areas of practice with social problems of major significance such as poverty and child welfare. In most states today, for example, there are no minimum educational or experience qualifications for child-welfare workers and, among those states where there are minimum qualifications, almost no states require a social work degree (Samantrai, 1992, p. 299). Similar trends can be found in the social work research literature. A recent review of all research articles published in five major social work journals *(Social Work, Social Service Review, Journal of Social Service Research, Social Work Research and Ab-*

stracts, Journal of Social Work Education) over a twelve-year period reports an average of one research article per journal per year published in the area of child welfare (Glisson, 1992). Poverty was the subject of one research article in each journal, an average of once every two years. In addition, the review described a 38 percent increase in the proportion of direct-practice articles published in the five journals over the twelve-year period, while documenting a parallel drop in the proportion of articles addressing indirect practice.

At the same time that the practice interests and the research literature of the profession show proportionately more commitment to what Specht (1990) describes as direct practice with "the middle class worried well," other professions and groups have identified an increasing need for more research on the major social problems that involve total systems in social work's traditional areas of practice. For example, recent publications in *American Psychologist* point to the deficits in knowledge about interorganizational systems of care for children, and they describe children served by the child-welfare system as among those in our society who are most at risk as a result of those deficits (Saxe, Cross, & Silverman, 1988; Tuma, 1989). As another example, the National Academy of Sciences National Research Council Panel on Research on Child Abuse and Neglect issued a project announcement in March, 1992, describing the current contributions of some seven different academic disciplines to research and demonstration projects on child maltreatment. Social work was not mentioned in the announcement. Finally, two recent national plans of the National Advisory Mental Health Council of the National Institute of Mental Health, one for child and adolescent mental disorders and one for people with severe mental disorders, both list higher level, service-systems research as among the most needed areas of mental-health research in the country. Unfortunately, only a few social workers nationwide are conducting mental-health service-systems research and only 4 percent of the service-systems research funded by the National Institute of Mental Health (NIMH) was directed by social workers in 1991.

It is disappointing that social work has not assumed a leadership role in the development of research on major social problems that involve total systems of service. Given the profession's traditional interest in systems explanations of psychosocial phenomena and social work's past commitment to the resolution of the big social problems that span families, communities, organizations, states, and even countries, it would be expected that research on these problems would follow. The problems presented nationwide by poverty; immigration; child abuse; drug abuse; and epidemics, such as AIDS, will not be resolved by the development of direct-practice techniques for working with individuals or by the application of the individual psychotherapies that are popular among social workers. These large, complex problems span multiple, higher level systems and, therefore, require interventions that do the same. The systems must become both the objects of social work study and the targets of social work intervention.

In sharp contrast to this need, the current research literature of social work is concentrating not only on the study of direct practice with individuals, but also is depending largely on simple research techniques that are incapable of providing the information necessary to understand major social problems and assess associated interventions in multiple, higher level systems (Glisson, 1992). This means that the research literature reflects both a narrowing definition of social work practice and the use of a narrow range of simplistic research methods. This is particularly relevant to the study of complex social issues because the method and focus of a research effort reflect the level of conceptual complexity upon which the research effort is based. Simple, reductionistic methods reflect simple, reductionistic conceptualizations and provide simple, reductionistic answers. Although simplification is a desirable goal in a research effort, simplicity because of unwarranted reductionism is not. For example, when the analysis of a complex social problem is reduced to a set of bivariate correlations, which have been produced by a nonrepresentative sample of individuals responding to a list of survey questions with answers that range from "strongly disagree" to "strongly agree," the value of the findings must be examined with considerable skepticism.

It is true that the study of small components of a large problem is appealing. The smaller the piece of a problem to which a researcher attends, the more manageable is the research task. That does not mean that the simple surveys popular with social work researchers can in some way begin to control for threats to internal validity, or that their use of nonrepresentative samples can somehow contribute to external validity. It does mean that the smaller the piece of the problem to which a researcher attends, the fewer the sources of variation and the greater the potential for controlling possible confounding influences through design and statistical analysis. Unfortunately, social work research currently concentrates on small pieces of large problems without taking advantage of the potential for increased research rigor offered by the reduced scope of the problem. As a result, the current research literature can boast of few of the advantages of small-scale research, while it suffers from the disadvantages.

As the scope of a research effort becomes larger, the price paid by the messiness and burden of managing the effort is balanced by the potential of addressing a major social need for a large target group. An example is provided by the research that I have directed for the past three years on the coordination of services to children in state custody. Hundreds of thousands of children are placed in the custody of state agencies each year. As a group, these children come from families with high profiles on the major risk factors associated with childhood mental-health problems. These families are characterized by single parents, teenage parents, incomes below the poverty line, community or family violence, family substance abuse, and other problems (Saxe, Cross, & Silverman, 1988; Tuma, 1989). Most of the children and their families are experiencing multiple problems at the time of custody and require multiple services. Because of the organizational and funding structures that exist at the state and federal levels, many of these problems are not addressed, and inappropriate or inadequate services are provided. With support from NIMH (R01-MH46124), this research examines the effect of state-level changes in organizational and funding structures designed to enhance the accessibility, quality, and outcomes of services to children in state custody. If these state-level changes in the organization and funding of services can be shown to affect the actual provision, quality, and outcomes of services, hundreds of thousands of our most vulnerable children may benefit.

Social work's traditional commitment to the amelioration of major social problems, the conceptualization of social work practice as including both direct and indirect practice, social work's approach to understanding psychosocial phenomena in terms of systems, and the current gap in knowledge about total systems of service underscore the need for social work to take greater leadership in research on total systems of service. Other disciplines (i.e., applied sociology, community psychology) have begun to study major social problems and associated interventions through research on higher level systems. For social work to abandon its historical commitment to the problems associated with such traditional social work areas, such as child welfare and poverty, to pursue the development of social work as a profession of direct practitioners and psychotherapists would be to give up areas in which social work can legitimately provide leadership. Moreover, this leadership would be sacrificed while the profession struggles to develop expertise and recognition in areas that will continue to be defined and led by other professions, such as clinical psychology and psychiatry.

References

Glisson, C. (1992). *The state of the art of social work research: Implications for mental health.* Invited paper presented to the NIMH Conference on Building Social Work Knowledge for Effective Mental Health Services and Policies, Bethesda, MD, April 6.

Samantrai, K. (1992). To prevent unnecessary separation of children and families: Public Law 96-272—policy and practice. *Social Work 37,* 295–302.

Saxe, L., Cross, T., and Silverman, N. (1988). Children's mental health: The gap between what we know and what we do. *American Psychologist 43,* 800–807.

Specht, H. (1990). Social work and popular psychotherapies. *Social Service Review 64,* 345–357.

Tuma, J. M. (1989). Mental health services for children. *American Psychologist 44,* 188–199.

Rejoinder to Dr. Glisson

JUAN PAZ

Social work research is still in its infancy. To date, social work research has not been very effective in assessing the impact of social policies and programs on major social problems. Note the fact that most social-policy experts in social work have an extensive background on the theoretical aspects of social policy, yet lack an extensive repertoire in systems research or legislative research. Only recently did NASW recognize the necessity of having a National Center for Social Policy with a heavy focus on research. Social work researchers, for the most part, have not been at the forefront of most major social policy debates in the areas of welfare reform, health care, immigration reform, substance abuse, gerontology, and AIDS. At most, NASW has been the only social work institution signing on to social policy legislation.

The current emphasis on clinical research, with its preference for single-subject design, is producing a generation of technocrats concerned mostly with which treatment methods are most effective in therapy. Students of social work research would do well to study the 1991 report of the NIMH Task Force on social work research. The report reveals that most social work research is being conducted by professors of social work and that there is an anti-research sentiment at some schools of social work throughout the country.

There is a need to expand the units of analysis to subjects as diverse as cohort studies and the analysis of community intervention. I recommend that students who are interested in studying effective models of evaluation research should review the PACE National Replication of On Lok's long-term care model (Hansen, 1992). In the fall of 1992, this model received national attention in the television media for its effectiveness. On Lok is a long-term care model that has created a consolidated system of case management. The On Lok model was begun in 1971 as an agency that was a system by itself. Using effective evaluation research methods, they have demonstrated both the effectiveness of their services, as well as of their financing. In 1986, the Omnibus Budget Reconciliation Act allowed On Lok to mentor the creation of ten other community-based agencies to follow their model. In 1990, the Omnibus Budget Reconciliation Act allowed them to mentor an additional five agencies. Clearly, this is an example where need, intervention, and evaluation have resulted in a model project that has resulted in legislation.

Presently social work has abdicated its claim to community change to the field of public health. Public health has taken up the banner as being the leader in meeting the needs of children, the elderly, and AIDS patients. The public-health field currently has developed some very creative research designs to study the problems of the elderly, children, substance abusers, and persons who are HIV positive.

Social work, with its roots in hygiene, mental health and community change, has the foundation on which to build effective interventions. We can begin by shifting our energies to the evaluation of well conceptualized social work interventions. Part of the problem lies in how we teach research and evaluation. Some theoreticians see evaluation as practice oriented. Others see research as being above evaluation because it focuses on theoretical formulations. The major task here is to fuse the research arsenal with the practice arsenal in order to evaluate social work processes, interventions, and outcomes. Social work is a profession rich in these areas. What the profession needs is an emphasis on the formulation of evaluation and research designs that will creatively measure their impact. We can begin by asking questions, such as: how do we develop process evaluations? how do we develop outcome evaluations? how do they influence each other? how do we measure the impact of a particular intervention?

The task of answering these questions will lead us, we hope, to create a solid research and evaluation design. If we fail to link the theoretically driven arm of research with the body of social work practice, our profession will remain fixated in its infancy.

References

Hansen, J. C. (1992) *PACE, The National Replication of On Lok's long term care model.* San Francisco, CA: On Lok Senior Health Services, 1441 Powell Street, San Francisco, CA 94133.

Task Force on Social Work Research. (November 1991). *Building social work knowledge for effective services and policies: A plan for research development.* Austin, TX: National Institute of Mental Health, Capital Printing.

NO

Juan Paz

Currently, the social work profession is engulfed in its "Nero Era." In this old fable, the Roman emperor, Nero, was said to be self-absorbed and playing the violin while Rome was burning. In much the same way, the social work leadership has been self-absorbed. During the 1980s and now in the 1990s, social work leadership (the National Association of Social Workers and Council on Social Work Education) has been unfolding an agenda controlled by the clinical lobby of the profession. Its focus has been on credentialing, professional recognition, and the evaluation of clinical practice. Social work with groups, community development, and social planning have become stepchildren. Social work research has become a secondary activity in the major national social work institutions. Currently, neither the Council on Social Work Education nor the National Association of Social Workers have a research component nor an agenda that sets research directions for social work knowledge building.

The current crisis in the national health-care system finds the profession ill prepared to compete for resources to conduct research on total systems of service. The professions' leadership historically has been slow in recognizing the need to become meaningfully engaged in the three major fields of social work practice that are inextricably entwined in the national health-care debate. These include 1) the AIDS crisis, 2) the field of gerontology, and 3) the field of substance-abuse prevention. While some individual social workers are involved in each of these areas, social work as a organized profession has been slow to respond to the needs of HIV-positive persons, the elderly, and families with children in crisis.

The fields of AIDS, gerontology, and substance abuse were selected for comment because, in combination, they impact a major cross-section of society. Together, they contribute to the health-care systems' issues of access to health care, quality of care, and finance. The history of the professions' response to each of these problems has been dismal.

The AIDS Crisis

In the field of AIDS, NASW published its first text, *The Social Work Response and Helping Families Cope* in 1987 (Fimbres & Leukfield). This was *eight years* after the AIDS crisis was discovered. These and other ensuing publications have focused on social work service delivery. Through the efforts of individuals, such as Manuel Fimbres, Carl Leukfield, and Gary Lloyd, the social work profession has been involved in responding to the AIDS crisis through training and conducting research on a small scale.

In 1987, The First Annual Conference of the Profession by NASW was held in New Orleans and included several AIDS presentations. However, the social work leadership in the AIDS field felt that they needed a conference to focus specifically on HIV. As a result, they organized their own conference, which highlighted social work practice and research in the AIDS arena. At the 1991 AIDS conference in New Orleans, a recommendation was made calling for large-scale research on women, children, and minorities who are HIV positive (Ryan, 1991). The 1992 conference on AIDS included an institute to help social workers develop evaluation and research skills. A focus that linked practice and research was evident in their conference.

In 1991, a key article by Diaz and Kelly provided a brief overview about the state of the art regarding AIDS-related training in schools of social work nationally. One important finding was that between 20 and 30 percent of graduate programs offered little or no training about AIDS in their curriculum. As a natural outgrowth, the authors concluded that AIDS has challenged social workers to develop innovative interventions, preventive efforts and research protocols (Diaz & Kelly, 1991). Clearly, the AIDS knowledge base requires substantial expansion using sound research methods.

Substance Abuse

Substance-abuse prevention is another field in which the professions' institutions have been slow to assume leadership in knowledge building. In 1991, NASW in collaboration with the Council on Social Work Education (CSWE) received funding from the National Institute of Alcoholism and Alcohol Abuse, through the auspices of the Office of Substance Abuse Prevention, to develop substance-abuse prevention content for infusion into the foundation curricula for schools of social work. The curriculum content was field tested during the fall of 1992. The curriculum materials are expected to be available for use by schools of social work by the fall of 1993.

Nationally, the current focus on substance-abuse prevention is to work with populations that are at-risk of developing patterns of substance abuse. While a great deal of emphasis is made on working with individuals, a considerable amount of attention must be paid to creating changes in the community. One major illustration of this emphasis is the "Community Partnership Program," which has the community as its main target population. The success of these programs often is measured through rigorous evaluation research measures that include a community-needs assessment, process, and outcome evaluation, to name a few.

Social workers have been ill equipped to work in the substance-abuse prevention arena. *Prevention* is a concept that is rarely an integral part of social work education. The social work research curriculum, in general, does not train graduate students to evaluate their practice in the community. As a result, the leaders in the field of substance-abuse prevention are from the public-health sector.

Gerontology

The field of gerontology is one in which social workers have been involved for a slightly longer period of time. In the early 1980s, a loose-knit group of social work educators would hold small meetings during the CSWE conferences to support each other's efforts. From those meetings, the leadership wrote a proposal that was funded by the Administration on Aging to develop gerontology curricula for schools of social work. Since then, gerontology programs have grown in number throughout the country.

Gerontology offers some examples of how social workers can engage in empirical research, while at the same time it reminds us to stay true to our commitment to the disenfranchised. The 1980s was a decade of unprecedented expansion of the elderly population of this country. Yet, statistics from the House Select Committee on Aging revealed that during this decade, the actual number of minority elderly who received services progressively declined. Consequently, the Administration on Aging has developed several initiatives for practice and research to focus on the needs of minority elderly.

One empirical model that offers much potential for social work research is the On Lok model of comprehensive, consolidated services for the elderly. Originally, On Lok was a small community-based agency serving the needs of a predominantly Chinese community in San Francisco. They developed a reputation for qualitative, cost-effective care and became a model for other agencies. In their own efforts to solidify their work, the On Lok staff developed an internal research department that evaluated the services provided. Using sound evaluation research, they have been able to expand the use of their methods around the country.

By demonstrating their services to be effective and efficient, On Lok was made a designated provider of Medicare and Medical services for the elderly. On Lok, in turn, received funding from the Robert Wood Johnson Foundation for the PACE Program, enabling them to establish a network of twelve similar agencies located at various sites around the United States. This model demonstrates how the use of sound evaluation research methods can contribute to creating a partnership between individuals, business, and government. On Lok as a microsystem has been instrumental in the development of several other agencies.

Improvement of Services

These three fields of practice share some commonalities. Social work is a profession that often finds itself at the fringes of the core issues for these fields of practice. Clearly social work is not a leader in these three fields. It is only a novice, which still has to establish its track record. First, social workers will have to lay a foundation on which to build the social work knowledge base in each field. Second, research priorities that focus on the contributions of social work in each field need to be developed. Third, social workers will have to learn sound conceptual, methodological, and research skills in order to be competitive with other professions. By doing so we can become competitive in the larger health-care system.

In today's world, social work is unable to engage in meaningful research in fields of practice such as child welfare. Child welfare, traditionally, has been a stronghold for social workers. However, the child-welfare system is extremely overburdened in many states and falling apart in other states. Research that identifies the contributions of social workers in the child-welfare field is sparse. Instead, national advocacy organizations, such as the Children's Defense Fund and the Child Welfare League, are the leading research institution advocating for children.

Conclusion

The preceding discussion raises further questions that point to the limitations of social workers in their ability to conduct research in several fields of practice. A recent report by the Task Force on Social Work Research recognized the fact that there is a crisis in social work research. Further review of their report indicates that most research in the profession is being conducted by faculty of schools of social work. There is currently no national unifying body organized to promote research development in social work (Austin, 1991).

The fields of AIDS, gerontology, and substance-abuse prevention are components of larger systems, such as the health-care system and the family-services system. Conducting research on total systems would be limited in scope. Any research agenda should include a well conceptualized, multidisciplinary approach to studying the total systems. Such an agenda would provide an opportunity for social workers to establish the parameters and contributions of the social work profession, while placing it in contrast to other professions.

Recommendation

Much can be learned from the research efforts that are being initiated in the fields of AIDS, gerontology, and substance abuse. Experts on AIDS are calling for the development of research protocols to measure the impact of services provided by social workers. The federal Office of Substance Abuse Prevention has several demonstration initiatives directed at developing successful models of substance-abuse prevention for at-risk population. Instead of trying to conduct research on *total systems,* perhaps it would be better to establish a research agenda that uses a *building block* approach to developing social work knowledge. Such an approach would first lay a foundation on which social work interventions would be field tested and evaluated for knowledge and skills building, as well as on model construction. The On Lok model of long-term care, which was initiated and developed in much the same manner, can serve as an example of an incremental building-block approach.

References

Austin, D. M. (1991). *Report: Building social work knowledge for effective services and policies: A plan for research development.* Rockville, MD: National Institute of Mental Health.

Diaz, Y. E., & Kelly, J. A. (1991). AIDS-Related training in U.S. schools of social work. *Social Work, 36,* 38–42.

Fimbres, M., & Leukfield, C. (1987). *AIDS: The social work response.* Silver Spring, MD: National Association of Social Workers.

Ryan, C. (1991). *Recommendations for research on women and HIV infection.* New Orleans, LA: National Conference on HIV Infection, December, 1990.

Rejoinder to Dr. Paz

CHARLES A. GLISSON

The NO paper, offered in counterpoint to my statement, appears to be more in agreement than disagreement with my position. Although welcome, this does make a rebuttal more difficult. Dr. Paz argues that the profession has begun to overemphasize clinical, direct practice with individuals at the expense of a declining emphasis on those types of methods that are included in research on total systems (i.e., community development, social planning, and social policy). Dr. Paz also argues that because of an inadequate emphasis on research by both social work educators and practitioners, the profession is not prepared to conduct research on total systems of service.

Very similar points were made in my YES position statement, and these points continue to be arguments in support of the proposition that social work should take greater leadership in research on total systems of service. It is true, however, that the latter point could be used as an argument against the notion that social work should take greater leadership. That is, if one argued that the research expertise is both lacking and should not be developed further, then leadership would be impossible. That, of course, is not my position, but such a position may be implied in the NO arguments.

There is also agreement between our positions that social work should address the major social problems. Because public and child welfare concern major social problems, a corollary to the point that social work should address the major social problems is that social work should not abandon these traditional areas of practice. Therefore, there is agreement between the two positions that attacking the big problems is important and, moreover, that this requires research on larger, higher level systems. Dr. Paz, however, appears to argue that this should be done, or can only be done, using a multidisciplinary approach to studying total systems. As the principal investigator of a six-year, NIMH-supported, multidisciplinary study of children's service systems at the state level, I would certainly agree with the benefits of multidisciplinary approaches applied to research on total systems of service. However, I would not agree that multi-disciplinary approaches are important because they allow social work participation in total-systems research efforts without requiring the requisite research training. Nor would I agree that multidisciplinary approaches are important because they enable social work participation in that small component of the research effort that is appropriate to the profession's limited practice focus.

Multidisciplinary research efforts require that participants (except those relegated to secondary or subservient roles) be knowledgeable of the methodologies relevant to the research and of the substantive issues addressed. Multidisciplinary research is advantageous to participants because it benefits from the different, and often competing, perspectives offered by various disciplines. This does not imply that some of the perceptions are less informed, although that may be the case. In other words, multidisciplinary research is not an opportunity for a poorly trained researcher or one of limited substantive knowledge to participate in a project that otherwise would be beyond his or her ability. Multidisciplinary research is not a shortcut to research funding that enables one to compensate for training or knowledge deficits. Rather, it is an opportunity for a synthesis of competing positions and perceptions that would not occur in unilateral pursuits.

A number of professions and groups have identified the need for research on total systems of service that assesses the impact of service-system organization, social policies, and social programs on major social problems that are related directly to social work's traditional areas of practice. Social work should take a greater leadership role in the development of the research in these areas, both because of the profession's traditional concern with the major social problems associated with such issues as poverty, immigration, and dependent children, and because of social work's espoused approach to understanding these issues in terms of overlapping social systems that span individuals, families, communities, organizations, and states. However, this will require a change in the current professional trend of defining social work's role solely as that of direct practice and of defining the objects of intervention efforts as only individuals and families. It will also require a broader commitment in the profession to the development of research expertise relevant to the study of complex social issues and inter-related social systems.

In summary, it appears that Dr. Paz and I are in agreement on the need for research on total systems of service, but we disagree on whether social work should assume a leadership role in that effort. Although a leadership role would require changes in the practice and research orientation of the profession, the alternative is to allow other professions to lead the development of service-systems research in areas that have been of traditional concern to social workers.

DEBATE 13

Should Policy Decisions Be Based Predominantly on Empirical Evidence of Effectiveness?

John S. Wodarski is Professor of Social Work at the State University of New York at Buffalo. His current research interests include the areas of preventive health measures for children and adolescents, the effects of social policy on preventive health services, and the evaluation of different types of social work education. He consults with various agencies providing services to children and adolescents.

Walter W. Hudson is Professor of Social Work at the Arizona State University, where he teaches courses in research in the B.S.W., M.S.W., and doctoral programs. His current research and writing interests are in the areas of assessment, evaluation, applied measurement theory, and computer applications for social work practice, evaluation, and administration. He is co-author with Paula S. Nurius of the text, *Human Services Practice, Evaluation & Computers: A Practical Guide for Today and Beyond* (1993), which is published by Brooks/Cole Publishing Company.

YES

JOHN S. WODARSKI

Social work agencies are operating in new complex environments in terms of knowledge and technological explosions. Within the last two decades, the U.S. industrial economy has changed into an economy based on information technology. Consequently, the body of knowledge available to solve social problems is growing and changing and should be incorporated into policy decisions aimed at the eradication or alleviation of these problems. The following five rationales are offered in support of policy decisions being based predominantly on empirical evidence of effectiveness.

Social Work Organizations Must Demonstrate Efficacy with Issues of Public Concern

Efficacy can be derived from developing interventions based on the best available theoretical rationale and subsequently evaluating those interventions. For example, the push to secure employment for Aid For Dependent Children (AFDC) mothers calls for stringent evaluation in terms of monetary policy, training requisites, and support services. In regard to monetary policy, it is evident that disincentives for employment are built into the system. For example, when they become employed, AFDC mothers lose their health benefits in some states, end up with less money because of tax structures, work for inadequate pay, and often lose their public housing. The cost–benefit ratio, likewise, must be considered in employing these mothers. For many, requisite support services are necessary, such as transportation and child care. Special clothing must be purchased in many instances. For some clients, the return to employment may be too costly. Empirical research can isolate which clients can return to work according to an effective cost–benefit analysis. Moreover, a pro-active monetary policy could provide for bonuses when employment is secured.

The most important aspect of returning to work is helping workers secure adequate employment-seeking skills and the relevant job skills necessary to maintain a position once one is secured. Research can determine the effective components of an intervention designed to teach these skills. Moreover, the data derived from this empirically executed research can be used in approaching the public constituencies whose support is imperative.

Social Workers Must Educate the Public on the Cost of Policy Innovations

A timely example of this need for leadership is provided in the area of sex education. Policies concerning sex education must be based on empirical effectiveness. Numbers of approaches to sex education exist in the literature. Few, however, offer a comprehensive empirical analysis of effectiveness. Social work can play a major role in the development of relevant policy to support desired outcomes through participation in the production and implementation of adequate curricula. Intervention to reduce teenage pregnancy will be lengthy and costly. The majority of curriculums currently available are inadequate in terms of their presentation of materials and their failure to use peer structures for the alteration of behavior. Virtually no empirical data exist to support these various curriculums. Thus, the task is substantial in regard to development of curricula on the best theoretical rationale and the subsequent empirical evaluation to convince the public to support the requisite expenditures to implement them.

Social Workers Must Develop, Enhance, and Maintain the Profession's Contribution to Empirically Based Policy Research

Over the last fifteen years, there has been a noticeable decrease in the influence that social work research has had on influencing policy decisions in Washington. Other social scientists (e.g., economists and political scientists) have been far more influential in comparison. Their influence, moreover, in these major policy decisions has been in a conservative direction.

The lack of social work research executed in the area of public policy has resulted in a limited social work perspective in policy decisions. The lack of perspective has further precluded the shaping of a relevant research agenda based on a determination of what program aspects are critical and the determination of how programs can be improved. For example, emphasis in health care is on cost containment rather than on the determination of means for preventing various high-cost conditions. Efforts targeting the adolescent population to prevent them from engaging in high-risk behaviors such as premarital sex, drug use, and the development of inappropriate mechanisms for coping with life's daily stresses, are far less costly than are the cures for the consequences of these behaviors.

Policy Research Should Facilitate the Development of Short-Term and Long-Term Goals

Empirical policy research should be used to articulate relevant short-term and long-term goals. Empirical research should provide the necessary documentation and elucidate the means and costs of attaining these goals. It is estimated that by the year 2000, one in three of our nation's children will be living in poverty. It is essential, for example, that relevant research be executed that will permit a range of goals for the reduction of poverty among children. Studies should be executed to provide the empirical rationale for interventions and, where empirical data are available, position papers should be executed. An example of such pertinent studies is the research to support increased funding for Head Start programs. Such theoretical and empirical support must be provided for each component of relevant short-term and long-term goals.

Both types of goals are necessary if social policies are to be developed. Because the various governments—federal, state and local—do not have unlimited resources, strategic planning is essential. Comprehensive plans will involve difficult decisions; thus, social work policy research must find appropriate forums to facilitate such decision-making processes.

Continued Development of Research Capabilities Is Essential to Empirically Based Policy Decisions

The 1992 Los Angeles riots provided opportunities for the social work perspective to be heard in government circles. It is essential that the profession provide solutions in terms of programs that have empirical rationales. When solutions lacking empirical bases are proposed, the opportunity is lost to establish the necessary influence for developing public policies that will ultimately help our clients. If rhetoric, rather than data, dominates proposed solutions, the contribution that social workers can make will be reduced.

References

Abramovitz, M. (1992). Poor women in a bind: Social reproduction without social supports. *Affilia, 7*(2), 23–43.

American Medical Association. 1990. *Profiles of adolescent health* (vol. 2). Chicago, IL: American Medical Association.

Adolescent Health Care: Use, Costs, and Problems of Access.

Kiesler, C. A. (in press). *The psychiatric care of children: The failure of public policy.* The Harrison Distinguished Visiting Professor Lecture in Mental Health. University of Tennessee, Memphis, September 27, 1991.

Rejoinder to Dr. Wodarski

WALTER W. HUDSON

Dr. Wodarski is correct, I think, in his assertion that the explosive body of knowledge with which to solve human problems should be incorporated into the making of policy decisions. Nor do I disagree with most of his assertions that a well constructed knowledge base must be used to guide policy making—we need to be as well informed as possible. I would suggest, however, that Dr. Wodarski has presented arguments that lean heavily in the direction of the ''proceduralists'' and has done so at the risk of losing sight of core normative issues that ultimately drive all policy making.

Consider, for example, his argument that a program of sex education must be based on empirical evidence of effectiveness. I could not agree more, because it would be silly to offer a program of training that was ineffectual or one whose effectiveness was unknown or questionable. What Dr. Wodarski did not consider is the normative base (the value positions) upon which any program of sex education is predicated. I would argue that the conduct of effectiveness research is a relatively simple matter, technologically speaking. What is far more difficult is the task of shaping a policy of sex education that is based on value positions that could capture broad consensus across the country. Indeed, the value differences are so great with respect to *whether* sex education *should* (the normative issue) be provided, that this issue is nothing short of a politician's nightmare. Similar arguments could be made with respect to the provision of abortion services and the right to use them. This is yet another nightmare for political and community leaders, and these value-driven debates and ''wars'' will not abate in the near future.

Throughout his debate position, Dr. Wodarski placed very great emphasis on the development and use of research and technological expertise. In my judgment, it is correct to argue for such expertise and to support it with educational grants to produce social work researchers who can carry the burden that Dr. Wodarski so well described. But that is not enough, and we dare not pretend it to be so.

The heart and soul of social work practice is value driven at core; and at the highest levels of abstraction, we are attracted to this profession by the impulse to execute value-driven policy positions and services to promote the welfare of those who need and seek professional help. My point is rather simple. We desperately need an enormous cadre of professional social workers who will advocate clearly enunciated value positions in an effort to shape policy that will further the welfare of all clients and needy populations. If this work of our profession is ever removed or is diluted beyond some level of critical mass, that will be the end of us as a profession.

Dr. Wodarski complains that there has been a noticeable decrease in the influence of social work research on influencing policy decisions in Washington. He also could have noted that there is less inclination to be politically active in the promotion of value positions and the dispensing of information to support them, and that this is ultimately what drives the shaping and reshaping of policy. In summary, we need a great press of normatively driven social workers, but we need them also to understand and use the contributions that research can offer to their efforts. We also need to train a group of social workers who can function as highly competent researchers and who identify strongly with a proceduralist perspective. If these two groups can understand and appreciate the contribution that each can make to the other, we might then discover that research evidence will be better used in the future of policy development and management.

NO

WALTER W. HUDSON

Make no mistake, I am an ardent empiricist. If you want to dream about the workings of nature, do so as a form of delicious entertainment. If you want to confirm that your dreams have any explanatory merit, empiricism is your *only* tool. If you want to indulge the fantasy that your interventions are worthy and useful, do so—as an indulgence. If you want to confirm the effectiveness of your interventions, empiricism is your *only* choice. Having made clear an unswerving bent toward empiricism, let me now point out that it is utterly misled to pretend that we can ever build social policy by using empiricism as our principal bedrock of information. The formation of social policy is completely and irrevocably driven by human value positions—*not science.*

Consider just one conspicuous example. Every state in this country runs megabucks social institutions to decide who will be permitted to adopt a child through a public social agency. Every one of these institutions has elaborate rules to decide whether the applicant will be a fit parent. The simple fact is that we do not have a single shred of evidence to confirm that these complex and often terribly restrictive rules result in "better adoptions"—more "fit" parents.

Do you think we shall stop making rules about who will be a better adoptive parent just because we don't have any solid evidence to back up the rules? Indeed not! It simply does not matter that we have no evidence of the effectiveness of adoption criteria. Adoption policy is based first, foremost, and unswervingly upon our values and our beliefs about who we *think* will be a "good parent" or who we think "should" and "should not" be an adoptive parent, and there is no evidence to confirm the truthfulness of those beliefs. Our behavior in this regard strongly suggests that our values and beliefs are even more important than the children whom they are supposed to serve.

Social Policy is a Value Position

If you are driven to form, understand, and use social policy exclusively from the perspective of the policy sciences, you are doomed to frustration and misdirection. Social policy is not science—social policy is merely one means of expressing value positions. And that is the way it must be. Johnston and Pennypacker (1980) clearly pointed out that we have two, and only two, kinds of knowledge—*invented* knowledge and *discovered* knowledge. Invented knowledge consists of rules and procedures that govern the way in which we shall behave and relate to one another within a social order, system, or society. The entire corpus of social policy and codified law is a form of invented knowledge—we make up the rules and then we enforce them. Social policy is indelibly rooted in our "shoulds," ''oughts,'' ''wants,'' and ''needs.'' The stipulation and regulation of our ''shoulds'' and ''oughts'' and the gratification of our ''wants'' and ''needs'' are the two core purposes of social policy. These cannot be based on science, because science is not capable of determining what we *need* or how we *should* behave. Only we can do that—individually or collectively. Like it or not, we are stuck with the creation and use of invented knowledge and social policy. The beauty of it is that *we* make the rules and *we* can change them. The downside of it is that we sometimes make some pretty lousy rules (and judgments about what's ''lousy'' are also based on a value position).

The Consequences of Social Values (Policy)

Adolf Hitler and his henchmen made extensive use of invented knowledge about the value of non-Aryans (how they ''should'' be treated) and on the basis of that ''knowledge,'' they set about to exterminate millions of people. Legend has it that Marie Antoinette lost her head over a policy issue, ''Let them eat cake,'' was a reflection of her value position (social policy) concerning the needs and welfare of the masses within her domain. Every year, our legislators in Congress pass laws that grant special favors to their friends—and the rest of us pay the bill for those favors. The entire corpus of our criminal code is rooted in a single Judeo-Christian value position—retribution. Our criminal-justice system aims solely to punish (hurt) the perpetrator, and it is *not* intended to protect the innocent. Victims of violence are neither protected nor restored (in criminal trials, they do not even have an attorney in court to represent their interests). George Bush recently lost an election because his values were not congruent with those of a substantial portion of the electorate.

The *Declaration of Independence* is a marvelously successful statement of social policy because it was capable of achieving enormous consensus among huge numbers of people over the past two centuries with respect to the assertion that, ''We hold these truths to be self-evident. . . .'' Of course, there are many who do not, and therein lies the root of much bigotry, injustice, and conflict. The conflict among different policy positions (values) is often polite. Quite often it is steamy and rude, and sometimes it becomes violent. It is never rooted with any vigor in scientific debate, except among those who lose sight of the underlying values being represented.

There are two points to be drawn from these and hundreds of other examples of social policy in action. The first is that virtually every social policy is driven by a value position, and the mystery of social-policy analysis vanishes completely when those values are elucidated and understood. The second point is that policy formation and modification ultimately are controlled by those who have the power and authority to implement their beliefs and value positions. Science has little to do with it.

The Nature and Role of Policy Science

Policy science is capable of two achievements. It can be used to describe, and it can be used to compare. Not much else. It certainly cannot determine how we *should* behave and it cannot determine *what we need.* A very large domain of policy science is rooted in the research activities that we call "needs assessment," and it plays a vital role in the arena of social policy. However, it is sheer folly to believe that "needs assessment" research is the basis for creating social policy. Not at all. It is merely a justification for it. The backbone rationale for a new policy is the value position of those who advocate the policy. Needs-assessment studies are conducted for the sole purpose of justifying the policy and, hence, the "correctness" of the value position from which it springs. Needs-assessment studies are examples of descriptive science put to the purpose of serving already well formed value positions.

The second major role of policy science is to make comparisons, and therein lies the basis for conducting evaluation studies to see if one form of policy is "better" than another. But the key question here is "better in relation to what?" The answer rarely is cast in terms of the underlying value positions, but those are the ultimate criteria for drawing preference conclusions (i.e., that one policy is "better" than another). The critical point here is that values shape the policy positions, and comparative science (evaluation research) is merely a tool to help settle arguments about competing value positions. The other side of the coin is equally simple. Comparative research has never been the primary basis for making policy—and it will never be so. What shapes policy? Simple—human value positions—our shoulds, oughts, wants, and needs.

Return for a moment to the adoption example mentioned at the beginning of this paper. Public agencies have their elaborate rules for deciding who will be a fit adoptive parent. That's the public sector. In the private sector, many children are adopted through the use of attorneys and the rules for determining parental fitness are very different. Are the results of comparing these two forms of adoption radically different? Would it matter if they were? If they weren't? To the best of my knowledge, there are no good comparative studies available, and we've been adopting children for many many decades.

Normative and Procedural Approaches

Although the study of social policy is enormously rich and varied, all of it can be reduced to two schools of thought representing a normative and a procedural approach to policy formation and analysis. Normative thinkers are led by the monumental work of Titmuss (1958) and procedural approaches are well represented by Rein (1970, 1976). All of them are well described and summarized by Moroney (1991). Clearly, I am well identified with the normative school in this brief comment about the role of research in social welfare policy. This does not mean that research cannot play an important role in the development and analysis of social policy. It is dangerous, however, to believe that the methods of science can replace the responsibility for creating social policy out of the beliefs and values of a social group. Yes, science can be useful, but beware of the proceduralist who claims that science can replace the normative perspective—in so doing, he or she becomes a wolf in sheep's clothing.

References

Johnston, J. M., & Pennypacker, H. S. (1980). *Strategies and tactics of human behavioral research.* Hillsdale, NJ: Lawrence Erlbaum Associates.

Moroney, R. M. (1991). *Social policy in social work.* Chicago, IL: Aldine de Gruyter.

Titmuss, R. (1958). *Essays on the welfare state.* London, England: Allen and Unwin.

Rein, M. (1970). *Social policy: Issues of choice and change.* New York: Random House.

Rein, M. (1976). *Social and public policy.* New York: Penguin.

Rejoinder to Dr. Hudson

John S. Wodarski

Dr. Hudson and I agree that social policies are based on a variety of values, usually determined by powerful constituencies and, in limited instances, by the majority. The scientific method, however, is essential to developing and evaluating various social policies.

Use of Science to Study How Social Policy is Made

The social work profession is influenced greatly by social policies developed by political leaders and social scientists, particularly political scientists and economists. My position is that we study the policy-making process in an effort to gain information that will enable the profession to effect positive influence on the process itself. For example, accumulated scientifically derived evidence has influenced policy to substantially increase funding for the Head Start program. Moreover, the Family Assistance Act of 1988 mandates that an increased proportion of AFDC clients receive training to remove clients from the welfare rolls. Impressive data indicate, however, that the process and requisites for implementing the policy may be more complex and costly than previously believed. I grant that social policy is based on values; however, relevant research can help us understand the process for formulating and implementing policies and thereby influence the outcome. A profession committed to helping attain higher standards of social functioning cannot ignore the relevance of the application of the scientific method to the study of social policy.

Research Used to Clarify Values

Policies are currently written in vague terms. Examine, for example, policies concerning teenage pregnancy, substance abuse, and provision of services. If policies are vague, their impact cannot be evaluated. Specification of outcomes is critical to the determination of the relevance of policies and the ability to determine which policies work and which ones do not.

Scientific Method as a Means to Develop Adequate Social Policy

The following arguments are offered for the use of science to support the analysis of social-policy formulation.

1. The scientific method can help us to understand the formulation of social policy, thus providing the information to influence it.
2. We can use the scientific method to evaluate social policies to determine their relation to various outcomes.
3. We use a variety of cost–benefit analyses to evaluate various social policies.

In summary, I see empirical evidence as a major tool to be used by social work in understanding, formulating, and influencing social policy.

DEBATE 14

Is Research Training Important to the Development of Analytic Reasoning and Critical Judgment in Social Work?

Lewayne D. Gilchrist is an associate professor at the University of Washington School of Social Work, where she teaches research methods and human behavior in the social environment. She also serves as Associate Dean for Research and Director of the Center for Policy and Practice Research. Her research interests focus on social and health problems in adolescence. She is currently in the midst of a nine-year longitudinal study funded by the National Institute on Drug Abuse, examining the impact on children of inner-city adolescent mothers' drug use and health-compromising behavior. She consults with the Washington State Department of Social and Health Services on evaluating outcomes and quality of life of clients who use publicly funded services.

Howard Goldstein is Professor Emeritus, Mandel School of Applied Social Science, Case Western Reserve University, where he taught direct practice, qualitative research, and philosophy of social work in the masters and doctoral programs. He is author of three books on direct practice and numerous articles on practice and research. He was awarded Richard Lodge Prize (1991) for his contributions to social work theory.

YES

LEWAYNE D. GILCHRIST

By its very nature, social work takes place in the physical or phenomenological world. Social work practitioners cannot—nor can any human-services professional—work solely within their own imaginations, with no requirement to establish explicit links between their mental constructions (ideas, theories, intuitions, hypotheses) and the external situations or problems that they are called upon to address. A responsible, professional practitioner must do more than indiscriminately apply the same theory, interpretation, or intervention to all cases and situations. That practitioner must be able to recognize and consider multiple, alternative hypotheses and approaches for any case. This recognition—that there is more than one way to frame or understand a given issue—is a necessary foundation for the recognition of evidence that may not fit an original theory. Without the recognition of multiple, possible alternative framings and, thus, the possibility of evidence counter to one's first impressions, thinking and behavior are not analytic, but scripted. Scripted thinking and behavior permits little judgment, flexibility, or adaptation to particular circumstances.

Effective professional behavior is not scripted. According to Schön (1987) and other analysts (cf., Gambrill [1990]), effective practitioners in all professional fields have in common a set of very similar skills that constitute enactment of their professional "artistry." Applied in all situations requiring reasoning and professional judgment, these skills are 1) posing a "best guess" hunch (hypothesis) for initial examination, 2) testing that hunch in the action setting, 3) revising the original hunch, and 4) gathering evidence again from the external setting to determine whether the revised hypothesis fits the particular circumstances better than the original one. This posing/testing/revision process may occur as an unconscious, or preferably conscious, process within the practitioner. In any set of circumstances, the process may be conducted several times over, until the best fit of idea (understanding) and test (evidence) is identified. Action then proceeds on the basis of this "best fit" finding. The process also applies across circumstances, so that prior experiences (findings) inform subsequent judgments. Without this explicit and continual movement from hypothesis to evidence to revised hypothesis, the practice judgments and ensuing action choices remain disconnected shots in the dark, a less-than-optimal condition for effectiveness. Further, in the absence of this process, improvement over time in professional performance is slow or nil because initial knowledge, theories, and hypotheses are not systematically revised or enlarged on the basis of relevant new information.

Research training is important to the development of this necessary professional-practice skill set, whether that skill set is called "intuitive artistry" or "empirically based practice." The principle feature of research training—indeed of scientific thinking in general—is the coordination of theory and evidence (Kuhn, Amsel, & O'Loughlin, 1988). This coordination involves the systematic linking of ideas (intuitions, notions, hunches, hypotheses) with indicators of those ideas in the physical world. Research training efficiently teaches students 1) to consciously identify their hypotheses, (ideas, intuitions, notions, hunches), 2) decide on what information or evidence would most persuasively test the viability of a given hypothesis, 3) define the concepts embedded in the hypothesis, 4) link these concepts to the observable world through the process known as operationalization, 5) devise ways to gather unbiased information or to minimize subjectivity of these operationalized indicators (potential evidence), and finally 6) to draw carefully warranted (i.e., with subjectivity controlled as much as possible) inferences about the match between the original hypothesis and the evidence from the world outside the practitioner.

Without explicit training in coordinating hypothesis and evidence, students and practitioners remain vulnerable to a number of common errors in reasoning and judgment that have been identified in many well controlled studies (cf., Gambrill [1990]; Nisbett & Ross [1980]). One common source of professional error can be found in judgments made on the basis of ideology, emotion, or personal preference, rather than on the basis of evidence (independently verifiable observations) from the world outside the practitioner's own mentation (Nisbett & Ross, 1980). Common flaws in analytic reasoning *per se,* include 1) over-generalizing or uncritically applying conclusions from the most immediate, vivid, or available case to all subsequent cases; 2) basing judgments and subsequent decisions on unexamined, irrelevant, or false initial assumptions or premises; and 3) tautological thinking or failing to locate and consider evidence that is separate from the original hypothesis, theory, or idea. Research training on sampling and on probability can diminish reasoning problems related to over-generalization from the most available or most vivid case. Research training that requires overt definition of concepts and operationalization of concepts into observable and verifiable features of the external world (indicators) can mitigate reasoning errors related both to unexamined, irrelevant, or false initial premises and to tautological thinking. Numerous research studies have shown that these kinds of faulty reasoning, including scripted thinking, among adults is remarkably common and remarkably resistant to change (cf., Gambrill [1990]).

Research training is an important means for sensitizing students to the possibility and the nature of flaws in their reasoning and judgment. Further, such training provides a systematic process for improving judgment across a great many professional tasks. However, research training in social work is not always taught in ways that optimize analytical reasoning and critical judgment. Research training can be presented as a memorizable cookbook of mechanical techniques for use in special circumstances, principally for leveraging resources by providing externally required "accountability." The focus of this kind of training is not on the logic underlying research techniques. More importantly, the relationship of this logic to everyday reasoning and a wide array of professional judgments is not emphasized or made clear to students.

In sum, good research training teaches students to think carefully about what evidence would most persuasively argue for *and* against an original idea, theory, hunch, hypothesis, assessment, or choice, and whether the evidence, once collected, does or does not support the original idea. Such training also requires students to recognize counter-evidence and to consider alternative or revised approaches that can better account for the gathered evidence. Research training requires students to make explicit their original hunch/hypothesis/assessment *and* the evidence that supports their judgments about it. Such training constitutes the explicit mastery of inferential thinking. Students who can contemplate multiple, contrasting theories or ideas about a given problem or circumstance; can coordinate the evidence with these different ideas, and can recognize both strengths and weaknesses of the evidence, will be less likely to rely on scripted behavior or on judgmental errors and more likely to generate creative, apt responses in professional practice.

The scientific process entails construction of an argument with supporting evidence that is persuasive to other people and that stands up to public scrutiny. In addition to constructing persuasive arguments of their own, effective professionals should also be able to analyze the quality of reasoning and judgments put forward by others, whether those others be clients, professional practitioners, or authors of lay and professional literature. Demonstrably, teaching students about types of reasoning errors and the desirability of reasoning by means of coordinating theory and evidence is not as effective as systematically engaging students in such reasoning processes. Training in designing and implementing the persuasive coordination of idea and evidence accomplishes this goal. Students are not well served, however, when science (and thus research) is presented as a bag of techniques for providing "accountability" when needed and not as a set of methods to control limitations on inference, reasoning, judgment, and prediction inherent in everyday or garden-variety subjectivity and limited viewpoints. Small wonder that some social work students never see the relevance of research for daily practice. Science is a process for making improved judgments, not for making claims that immutable truths have been found.

References

Gambrill, E. (1990). *Critical thinking in clinical practice.* San Francisco, CA: Jossey-Bass.

Kuhn, D., Amsel, E., & O'Loughlin, M. (1988). *The development of scientific thinking skills.* New York: Academic Press.

Nisbett, R., & Ross, L. (1980). *Human inference: Strategies and shortcomings of social judgment.* Englewood Cliffs, NJ: Prentice-Hall.

Schön, D. A. (1987). *Educating the reflective practitioner.* San Francisco, CA: Jossey-Bass.

Rejoinder to Dr. Gilchrist

Howard Goldstein

Dr. Gilchrist, in her strong YES affirmation, has confirmed my expectation that the term "research training" used in the question was equated with "scientific" or "empirical" orientations to inquiry. To counter her argument would, therefore, be redundant. I have shown that the human and social conditions that are subject to critical social work thought need to be known or understood in naturalistic terms that involve dialogue, interaction, time, history, context, and culture. Subjectivity or reflexivity are essential to discerning judgment; as practitioners or researchers, we cannot exempt ourselves from the phenomenon that we are trying to discover and comprehend.

The empirical mode, as Dr. Gilchrist suggests, follows a standard "how to" system of problem solving; I propose that inquiry must be more inventively concerned with "for what?" questions. Research training, in the first instance, derives from a physical science model focused on *things* (physical, chemical, or biological) that more or less stay put. Qualitative or interpretive research training is focused on *events* (personal, interpersonal, or transactional) that are constantly in process, dialogue, flux, and change. Such events have neither starting points nor conclusions. Thus, to understand the social event, the inquirer must, in some measure, enter its current to partake of its meanings, intentions, and goals.

When it comes to the understanding of the human situation, perhaps the most important part of developing talents of analytic reasoning and critical judgment is casting off the illusion or hope that verifiable truths or categorical answers are possible. This does not disclaim the possibility of understanding and insight; what I propose in common-sense terms is critical "knowing" that is both modest in intent and respectful of the subject. The social worker's insights and wisdom are not one-sided perceptions garnered to test or prove something or to justify an independent treatment plan or intervention. Rather, "knowing" is a collective or mutual enterprise that has meaning not for "what *I* do" but for "how *we* work together and move forward." Two experts collaborate in the attempt to expand understanding and its role in the helping process: the social worker is the expert on the means of growth and change; clients are appreciated as experts on means *and* the ends, on how growth and change might unfold in accord with their values, culture, needs, and goals. Ultimately, common sense should prevail in debating the pros and cons of this question. Clearly, it is the nature of the question and the corresponding reasoning and judgment called for that should determine the method of inquiry and not the other way around.

Conventional research training is restricted to conventional scientific methods of inquiry; these modes are based on assumptions that there is an inherent logic and rationality in human affairs. These conventions are now the target for reconstruction by scientists themselves (Raskin & Bernstein, 1987) that takes account of the ethical and social questions central to the knowledge process. Complementing these movements are new insights about the workings of mind and brain that bear on the development of talents for learning, reasoning and critical judgment (Edelman, 1992). There are many ways of knowing that do not conform to the rational, linear sequences of the scientific method: among these forms are intuition; vicariation; experience; behavior; and, in addition, relational, comparative, and recollective thought. As I proposed, research training should be evocative, offering opportunities not just to realize one's potentials for knowing, but to realize that such potentials are unending.

References

Edelman, G. M. (1992). *Bright air, brilliant fire: On the matter of the mind.* New York: Basic Books.

Raskin, M. G. & Bernstein, H. J. (Eds.) (1987). *New ways of knowing: The sciences, society, and reconstructive knowledge.* Totowa, NJ: Rowman & Littlefield.

NO

Howard Goldstein

An instinctive response to this question would be, "Of course!" Research training that is not limited to the mechanics of statistical operations depends on at least a small supply of analytic and critical thought. Without these aptitudes, how else could one sort out, formulate, differentiate, compare, judge, and otherwise use the mind's ability to pry into a puzzle or problem? The ending phrase, "in social work," however, tends to temper and qualify any confident endorsement. For when it comes to the matters of interest to social work, the more appropriate question is not *if* research training is important but *what kind?* Thus, my negative response is not to what appears to be a forthright question, but to what the question implies, assuming that the question is based on social work's singular infatuation with the "scientific method." My understanding is that it asks if *empirical* research training is the training of choice for social work. To that question, my response is, "No."

"Research," "analytic reasoning," and "critical judgment," the core terms of the question, are constructs: what they mean or refer to depends really on the point of view or perspective of the person who uses them. A closer look at the terms will explain my "No" response and provide a basis for comparison with an alternative research model.

To repeat, *research,* as used commonly in social work, usually refers to *empirical* research, empiricism being one of several ways of "knowing" and understanding the complex world. Briefly, it is a mode of investigation borrowed loosely from the natural sciences, one which separates the researcher from the object of study. Empiricism assumes there is something "out there," an objective reality, perhaps "truths," that can only be "known" through our senses. With the proper devices and instruments, that reality can be measured with enough precision to allow for generalizations and predictions.

The kind of *analytic reasoning* fostered by this controlled and depersonalized mode of "knowing" would necessarily be rational, objective, and systematic in its approach to and analysis of social problems. Such reasoning assumes that for every problem there has to be an identified cause—or at least a linear connection or correlation with some influential agency. It follows that the reasoning or problem-solving task requires splitting or reducing the complex human phenomenon in question into sets of discrete variables. These variables are statistically manipulated and measured to disclose, in probabilistic terms, the sought-for connections or linear cause–effect relations that are presumed to exist among them. Likewise, *critical judgment,* the intent to make sense of findings, also would aim for rational, linear, and objective conclusions.

Because of the rigor and outward precision of empirical methods and the reasoning and judgments that they cultivate, it is unfortunate that they are scarcely applicable to many of the problems and circumstances encountered in social work. The research training implied in the question might be useful for problem situations where clear-cut, impersonal, and undisguised decisions need to be made. But in most circumstances, where a seemingly obvious decision is called for (say, about a frail, aging parent's need for skilled nursing facilities), the attempt to make the decision often is muddled by a complex of moral or value dilemmas, by fear, guilt, or other troubled states of mind. That such sentiments are hardly rational does not mean that they are unreasonable or addle-brained. Rather, they frequently express the competing and confusing voices of culture, experience, need, moral strains, and other tensions that are enmeshed with clients' identity and integrity.

If training in empirical research alone was the source of the practitioner's reasoning and judgment, his or her response to this plight would lean towards an objective and logical solution. Quite possibly, the "scientific" aura and influence implanted in this training may over-ride or put in doubt the practitioner's inclination toward a more compassionate and sensitive reaction to the client's dilemma. At any rate, practice that is restricted to rational or behavioral problem-solving solutions commits the grievous error of misinterpretation and, therefore, of misunderstanding. I am not speaking of direct practice alone. Even in matters of planning, shaping policy, or administrative decisions, rationality may be an illusion; often it is a socially correct veneer that hides the value preferences, personal ideals, and private political agendas, the motives that actually drive the decision-making enterprise.

The language or the social constructions that are imprinted into our ways of knowing—whether they are gender attitudes or ideas about research—release themselves reluctantly, if at all, from our standard world view. Yet to make research training sympathetic to the demands of practice, it is necessary, with whatever sense of disillusionment, to end our romance with the allure of the "scientific method" or the empirical mode. The term, "disillusionment," is apropos because, amid the confusion of our work with chaotic social problems, we want to believe the promise that, oh yes, objective and conclusive answers and prescriptions can be found.

Changing a name sometimes eases the discomfort of transformation: let us therefore speak of ''inquiry'' rather than ''research.'' ''Inquiry'' is a generic term that covers the wide range of ways that we mindfully go about trying to make sense of experience. It is as pertinent to the mundane questions encountered in the course of daily living as it is to the more sophisticated and complex problems of interest to social work practice and investigation. The term also reminds us that the endeavor to understand calls for creativity, imagination, vision, and other talents that are likely to be dampened by reliance on a simple or narrow set of methods. The kit of research tools that we happened to acquire may not only hinder our efforts, but also may lead us to ignore a very rational precept: the nature of the question or problem should suggest the methods of inquiry and not the other way around.

And so, when it comes to the cryptic and ambiguous problems encountered in practice, for which there are few ''right'' or straightforward solutions, proper research training or inquiry should enable learners to forego the need for ''quick-fix,'' final answers. I am not discounting the importance of logical and systematic reasoning. But this reasoning needs to be balanced by the inquirer's access to *reflective* analytic and judgment skills that reject either–or, categorical solutions. Instead, the inquirer comes to terms with understanding and answers that, for the time and place, are not only plausible but capable of generating further insights. Simply put, our understanding of the human predicament is an ongoing process or dialogue; it cannot be reduced to or converted into easy equations or formulas.

I have argued elsewhere (Goldstein, 1991; 1992) that to cultivate reflective thinking, a shift should be made from modes of inquiry that dissect and quantify human experience to those that address the seamless whole, the quality and subjective nature of the lived event. I speak, of course, of research that is variously called qualitative, ethnographic, or naturalistic. The quest, in this instance, is to ''know'' the world as it is in its ever-changing and complex forms, rather than as a composite of lesser categories. It is a respectable form of inquiry in its own right, fundamental to the investigations of cultural anthropology and interpretive sociology. The qualitative perspective shares many of social work's values. Like good social work, it ''begins where the subject is,'' instead of imposing the inquirer's structure or theoretical or technical presumptions. Also, like good social work, it is a case-study approach that seeks to interpret a human event as it presents itself, unlike a statistical approach that devitalizes the event by transforming it into arid, countable frequencies, correlations, or other measures.

Briefly, qualitative inquiry is an expedition of sorts guided by the questions and inquiring mind of the investigator. Depending on what needs to be known and the nature of the circumstances, the researcher may rely—singularly or in combination—on participant observation, open-ended interviews, life histories, or other means that, as Geertz (1983, p. 58) says, reveals "the symbolic forms—words, images, institutions, behaviors—in terms of which, in each place, people actually represent themselves to themselves and to one another."

Doing qualitative research means that the researcher becomes an active part of the social tableau that he or she is studying and trying to understand. Thus, from the outset, if something more than simple description is required, the inquirer must develop the cognitive talents of analytic reasoning and critical judgment required to penetrate and make sense of complex patterns, or what Bruner (1990) calls the "folk psychology" of interaction. What do these talents involve?

Let us say, for purposes of illustration, that the qualitative researcher is curious about students who "drop out" of school. First, the study would take place in the "real world" settings of school, neighborhood, and home. Rather than isolating and attempting to control specific variables, the inquirer would, with an open mind, observe and study the social processes involved in "dropping out" as they unfold over time. Along the course of the study, the question and the problem would be reformulated many times as new information and impressions were gathered.

Analytic reasoning in this approach is not reductive, but is concerned with the complexities of flow, relations, and interaction that characterize human dilemmas. Rather than defining the act of "dropping out" as a dependent variable, it would be understood as a concept or social construct. In these terms, it may be considered as an act that has special meaning for the actor and that occurs within a particular *context* and at a special point *in time.* In this light, that act might be understood in countless ways. It might be a function or expression of a culture, shared beliefs, or family attitudes; it could be a response to failed educational philosophies or competing values; or, for that matter, it may be a mindless act. Thinking analytically, the researcher will search for patterns that allow for some plausible insights and wisdom. Not the least, the researcher follows the *narrative character* of the event, the stories that the key players tell to explain and justify the "why nows?" and "what fors?" of their beliefs and actions.

Complementing these analytic aptitudes is the use of critical judgment or reflection-in-action (Schön, 1983). In effect, over the course of the study, the inquirer is engaged in an on-going process of theory building and reformulation. Constant openness to new impressions and information lead to new and better questions that, in turn, generate more profound impressions. For example, patterns that first appeared to reflect a general state of indifference to education may, with new observations, indicate a sense of cultural isolation that separate families from mainstream attitudes toward education.

Compared to the tidy and settled findings of quantitative investigations, the conclusions of qualitative inquiry are necessarily conditional interpretations of or theories about certain human phenomena: as is the case in our ordinary understanding of fellow human beings, our insights remain tentative, respectful of, and open to the inevitability of human change. Nonetheless, the interpretations generated by the analytic reasoning and critical judgment nurtured by qualitative inquiry are rich and instructive. They are, after all, grounded in the real-life experiences as they are perceived, first hand, by the subjects in question.

A final thought: perhaps a more apt question might ask, "Is social work education important to the development of analytic reasoning and critical judgment in research?" Research, after all, is a means and not an end in itself; as a tool or procedure, its selection and effective use requires the kind of analytic discretion and prudent judgment that social work education fosters.

References

Bruner, J. (1990). *Acts of meaning.* Cambridge, MA: Harvard University Press.

Geertz, C. (1983). *Local knowledge.* New York: Basic Books.

Goldstein, H. (1991). Qualitative research and social work practice: Partners in discovery. *Journal of Sociology and Social Welfare, 18*(4), 101–120.

Goldstein, H. (1992). Should social workers base practice decisions on empirical research? No. In E. Gambrill & R. Pruger (Eds.), *Controversial issues in social work* (pp. 114–120). Boston, MA: Allyn & Bacon.

Schön, D. A. (1983). *The reflective practitioner.* New York: Basic Books.

Rejoinder to Dr. Goldstein

LEWAYNE D. GILCHRIST

I believe that Dr. Goldstein and I agree more than we disagree. We both emphasize the importance of reflective, critical, and analytical thinking in effective social work practice and the usefulness of research/inquiry training for building these skills. Further, we both are wary of the way that research is taught currently. On the surface, our differences appear to lie in our beliefs about the proper methods to use for "evidence gathering" (my term) or "inquiry" (his term). I argue that practitioners should overcome their conceptual blinders by collecting information in a way that will allow the examination of evidence both for and against an initial idea. His argument seems to me to say the same thing, except that he specifies a particular method of evidence gathering—qualitative—as the preferred mode because it is more holistic. He rejects the kind of inquiry called quantitative as too narrow and reductionistic to be of use to practitioners.

Our difference may most fundamentally be one of degree in our acceptance of the utility of quantitative methods in social work. The degree of our acceptance or nonacceptance, in turn, may rest on our beliefs about the nature of the inquiry (questions) that social workers and social work roles require. I agree with his statement that "the nature of the question or problem should suggest the methods of inquiry and not the other way around." I do not reject training in qualitative methods, which are important in direct services for understanding individuals' circumstances and behavior. In fact, most methods courses, particularly in covering techniques of assessment and cross-cultural communication, emphasize methods relevant in qualitative inquiry.

Nevertheless, I believe that there are times, contexts, and particular questions that call for training in quantitative methods. For example, program planners and program administrators are called upon to make decisions affecting a wide variety of individuals with different characteristics and needs. Their decisions may be improved by training in thinking analytically and reflectively about summarized quantified information that was obtained from many individuals over time, regarding service use, client characteristics, and service outcomes, and what changes in these patterns may mean.

Social work is an eclectic profession, and we involve ourselves in a variety of professional roles. We require skills to fit our behavior to the demands of many practice situations. The method of inquiry that a practitioner uses should vary according to the information needed and the resources available. Both Dr. Goldstein and I insist that systematic inquiry, analysis, and reflection routinely take place in professional practice, and we both believe that research/inquiry training can improve these critical skills.

DEBATE 15

Can M.S.W. Students Evaluate Research Critically without Knowledge of Statistics?

Betty J. Blythe is a professor at Florida International University Department of Social Work, where she teaches courses in research and child welfare for masters and doctoral students and is Coordinator of the Master's Program. Her current research and writing interests are in family preservation and the evaluation of social work practice. She also is a member of the Advisory Council of the International Initiative for Children, Youth, and Families and is involved in implementing family-preservation programs in Europe and Israel.

Susan D. Einbinder is an adjunct instructor at Columbia University School of Social Work, where she teaches research methodology, statistics, and social policy and is completing her doctorate. She is currently employed at The National Center for Children in Poverty, Columbia University School of Public Health and is co-editor (with Stuart Kirk) of *Controversial Issues in Mental Health* (Allyn and Bacon, 1994).

Stuart A. Kirk is a professor at the Columbia University School of Social Work. He is the author of many articles on the use of research, services for the severely mentally ill, and on the sociology of psychiatric diagnosis. His recent book (with Herb Kitchins) is *The Selling of DSM: The Rhetoric of Science in Psychiatry* (Aldine de Gruyter, 1992).

YES

BETTY J. BLYTHE

Can M.S.W. students critically evaluate research without knowledge of statistics? My assignment is to argue that social work graduate students *can* critically evaluate research without knowledge of statistics. At the risk of being accused of side-stepping the issue or of being inconclusive, I must confess that my actual response to the above question is that it depends. In this paper, I will argue that the answer to this question depends, to a large extent, on the type of research under review and on the level of statistical knowledge, if any, required for evaluation. Further, I will suggest that much of the research in social work can be critically evaluated by M.S.W. students, without specialized knowledge of statistics.

Research covers a wide range of types of studies. Client-satisfaction surveys, needs assessments, case studies, agencies reports describing clients served, evaluations of program outcomes, census reports, and experimental tests of new treatment techniques are just a few examples of research. These research studies vary on many dimensions, including the complexity of the underlying logic, the research methodology, and the statistical analysis. A case study, for example, is fairly straightforward in its concept and typically requires little or no statistical analysis, but may involve a large amount of complex clinical information which must be analyzed. At the other extreme might be a complicated experimental design to test a hypothesis about certain clinical behaviors, which would require sophisticated statistical analysis.

Tripodi, Fellin, and Meyer (1983) have developed a typology that organizes research into three categories: experimental studies, quantitative–descriptive studies, and exploratory studies. *Experimental studies* are those studies that manipulate an independent variable to test hypotheses regarding cause–effect relationships. Often, these studies involve evaluating the effectiveness of an intervention. *Quantitative–descriptive* studies include a range of types of studies, all of which seek to describe relationships among variables. One sub-type, *hypothesis-testing* or *quasi-experimental* studies, are like experimental studies, except that they do not involve randomly assigning subjects to experimental and control conditions. The two remaining sub-types in the quantitative–descriptive category are *population-description* studies, which seek to describe characteristics of a group of individuals or of an organization or institution, and *variable-relationship* studies, which attempt to identify variables that are related to a particular condition or situation, or to discover relationships among variables. Finally, *exploratory* studies are those studies that use some form of systematic data collection to develop or refine research concepts, questions, or hypotheses. Qualitative data may be gathered alone or in combination with quantitative data. The first sub-type, *exploratory-descriptive* research, involves gathering qualitative and quantitative data to describe a phenomenon such as relapse to drug use. The second sub-type involves following specific research procedures to gather information that can be used to develop conceptual categories for subsequent research. *Content analysis* is an example of this type of research. The final sub-type of exploratory research, *experimental-manipulation* studies, usually involve studying one case (such as a client unit or a social program) to determine if the independent variable(s) seems to represent a feasible approach to dealing with a problem. Single-case designs often are used for this type of research.

Obviously, knowledge of much more than statistics is required when examining the quality of any of these types of research. Statistical analysis, if it is conducted, can only occur after several earlier steps in the research process have been carried out. These research activities vary somewhat according to the type of research being conducted, but they also must be critically evaluated. For instance, one may need to consider whether the hypothesis or research question was appropriately and logically derived from the relevant literature. Is the problem to be studied well specified? Moreover, the instruments have to be examined to determine if they are appropriate for the population and the study. Questions such as whether or not the measures reflect cultural biases, and whether they have sufficient reliability and validity must be asked. Many research courses teach the rudiments of assessing reliability and validity. At a minimum, M.S.W. students without formal training can assess the content validity of the measures. They also can consider whether there is anything about the manner in which the data were collected that might lead to biased findings. The adequacy and appropriateness of the sample to answer the questions of interest also can be assessed without knowledge of statistics, although some simple descriptive statistics, such as the percentages of various subgroups, as compared to the population to which the researcher wants to generalize, may be helpful. If any of the earlier stages of designing the study, or collecting the data have serious flaws, then the quality and appropriateness of the statistical analysis becomes a moot point. Once the data (information) are analyzed in some way, by statistical or other means, the interpretation of the findings also can be critiqued without knowledge of statistics. Clearly, some of these appraisals require research training, but others are simply a matter of applying logical reasoning. Research texts that provide the basic knowledge needed to critique the nonstatistical aspects of research can be consulted (Rubin & Babbie, 1989; Tripodi, Fellin, & Meyer, 1983).

So far, we have discussed the types of research that might be conducted and have observed that more than knowledge of statistics is required to evaluate any research critically. Now, let us consider just what "knowledge of statistics" might entail. In general, statistical analysis is conducted to reduce data to a form that can be understood and interpreted so that, in turn, answers to research questions can be obtained. Statistics are tools for summarizing and manipulating quantitative data to obtain these answers. Most research does involve some form of statistical analysis, with varying degrees of sophistication that range from very elementary calculations, which are easily understood by most people, to more complex and less easily understood operations. For the most part, statistical methods are used to describe a characteristic or set of characteristics of a group of subjects or an individual subject, or to examine relationships among two or more variables.

Statistical methods can be categorized according to the number of variables that are examined at a time (Rubin & Babbie, 1989). Univariate statistics examine the distribution of cases on only one variable at a time. Univariate statistics that are frequently used for descriptive purposes include frequency distributions, percentages, means, modes, and medians. Bivariate statistics examine two variables at a time. An example of a bivariate statistical tool that may be used to describe variables is a contingency table, which compares subgroups using percentages, medians, and so forth. Bivariate statistics also can be used to assess the strength of a relationship. Common examples of these statistical methods are correlation coefficients, chi-squares, t-tests, and analysis of variance. Finally, multivariate analysis involves examining the simultaneous relationships among multiple variables (more than two), or may be used to better understand the nature of the relationship between two variables. If the purpose of the research is descriptive, then contingency tables might be employed. If the purpose is to examine the strength of a relationship, then more complex statistical techniques, such as multiple regression, discriminant analysis, factor analysis, or multiple analysis of variance, are available. The preceding only offers examples of some of the more frequently used statistical methods. It is beyond the scope of this paper to categorize all of them. With all statistical tools, certain characteristics of the data dictate the selection of specific statistical methods.

Most of the univariate and bivariate descriptive statistics are fairly straightforward, and should be comprehensible to M.S.W. students without graduate courses in statistics. In fact, these statistics often are found in articles in newspapers and newsmagazines, as well as in agency reports. The general population can read and understand these statistics, which are taught in high school or even earlier. Thus, research using these statistics should be readily understood and evaluated by M.S.W. students without any specialized knowledge of statistics. On the other hand, the statistical methods that measure the degree of association between or among variables tend to require specialized training in statistics.

Having considered the major categories of research and of statistical analysis, we can speculate about the types of research that M.S.W. students can or cannot critically evaluate. For experimental studies, descriptive univariate and bivariate statistics often depict and compare the experimental and control groups. But, simple t-tests or analyses of variance are most often used to examine cause–effect relationships, although sometimes multivariate tests are used. These latter analyses of cause–effect relationships require more specialized knowledge of statistics, which many graduate students do not possess. The situation is similar with hypothesis-testing studies, which can be analyzed with some simple statistical methods, but often use more complex statistical tests, especially multivariate tests, in part to provide additional control because randomization did not occur. Like experimental studies, most of this research will require more advanced knowledge of statistics. Because there still is some disagreement among statisticians and methodologists regarding quasi-experimental designs and their analyses, these studies are even more complicated to critique.

The two remaining sub-types in the quantitative-descriptive category are population-description studies and variable-relationship studies. Needs assessments, measures of client satisfaction, and agency surveys are among such studies that social workers are likely to encounter in routine practice. When conducted in agencies, they usually rely on univariate and bivariate descriptive analysis strategies, which M.S.W. students will be able to critique. Some published quantitative-descriptive studies, especially surveys, do use bivariate and multivariate measures of association. For example, Butler (1992) surveyed social work graduate students regarding their interest in private practice. In addition to descriptive statistics to summarize the students' values and interest, Butler conducted some statistical tests to examine the relationship between sub-groups of students. In this case, M.S.W. students would require some basic, yet specialized, training in statistics to fully critique her work.

The bulk of the qualitative research in the exploratory studies category does not involve any statistical manipulation of information; hence, M.S.W. students obviously would not require any specialized knowledge of statistics to evaluate them. When statistical analysis is involved, it tends to consist of simple univariate and bivariate descriptive statistics, which also do not require specialized knowledge. As for the single-case studies, quasi-statistical methods are available to analyze single-case data, but visual analysis of graphed data is more common. While there are guidelines for visually analyzing graphed data, these should be covered in the required M.S.W.-level research course, so that M.S.W. students will be familiar with them. As an example of this type of research, Gallant, Thyer, and Bailey (1991) examined the efficacy of a bug-in-the-ear technique for providing clinical supervision in a marriage and family therapy clinic. Most of their analyses consisted of visual inspection of graphed data, although they did calculate some simple percentages to provide summary descriptions of the data and to assess the reliability of the data.

To summarize, M.S.W. students should possess a basic knowledge of statistics, which will allow them to evaluate exploratory studies, and most population-description and variable-relationship studies conducted for agency purposes, and some conducted for scholarly publication. Experimental and hypothesis-testing studies seem to be the categories of research that M.S.W. students cannot fully evaluate because the statistical methods are more sophisticated. As a footnote, some M.S.W. students will possess more specialized knowledge of statistics, that will allow them to evaluate studies that use more complicated statistical tools, with the most frequent case being that of B.S.W. graduates. Further, B.S.W. programs must require that undergraduate B.S.W. students take at least one statistics class. While these classes will vary from university to university, in general they tend to cover many of the more common descriptive statistics, the basic concept of statistical inference, t-tests, and sometimes analysis of variance. Thus, M.S.W. students with B.S.W. degrees will have been exposed to some of these statistics.

Is the fact that M.S.W. students are unlikely to be able to critically evaluate experimental and hypothesis-testing studies a major handicap? I will suggest that it is not. These studies represent a very small proportion of all the research conducted in social work. According to a survey by Tripodi (1984), less than 5 percent of the studies published in major social work journals were experimental and just under 11 percent involved testing hypotheses. Moreover, the statistical power of this research is likely to be very low, thereby making the conclusions questionable. While data are not available for social work research, a recent power analysis suggested that the power of research published in major psychological journals is extremely low (Rossi, 1990). The same is likely to be true for social work. Finally, let us consider the application or potential misapplication of statistics in social work research. Most, if not all, statistical work in social work is derivative. Social workers rarely develop their own statistical methods. According to Glisson and Fischer (1982), social work researchers tend to use incorrect statistical procedures, particularly if they are analyzing more than one dependent variable. Indeed, some of these errors have been identified. Thus, M.S.W. students who are interested in evaluating such research should seek consultation from someone with training in statistical analysis who can critique the statistical methods and examine the power of the study in question.

References

Butler, A. C. (1992). The attractions of private practice. *Journal of Social Work Education, 28*(1), 47–60.

Gallant, J. P., Thyer, B. A., Bailey, J. S. (1991). Using bug-in-the-ear feedback in clinical supervision. *Research on Social Work Practice, 1,* 175–187.

Glisson, C., & Fischer, J. (1987). Use and nonuse of multivariate statistics. *Social Work Research & Abstracts, 18,* 42–44.

Rossi, J. S., (1990). Statistical power in psychological research: What have we gained in 20 years? *Journal of Consulting and Clinical Psychology, 58,* 646–656.

Rubin, A., & Babbie, E. (1989). *Research methods for social work.* Belmont, CA: Wadsworth Publishing.

Tripodi, T. (1984). Trends in research publication: A study of social work journals from 1956 to 1980. *Social Work, 29,* 353–359.

Tripodi, T., Fellin, P., & Meyer, H. J. (1983). *The assessment of social research: Guidelines for use of research in social work and social science* (2nd ed). Itasca, IL: F. E. Peacock.

Rejoinder to Dr. Blythe

Susan D. Einbinder
Stuart A. Kirk

Dr. Blythe recognizes that she may be side-stepping her task, which was to persuade us that M.S.W. students do not need *any* knowledge of statistics to critically evaluate research. She argues, instead, that students do not need *more* knowledge than they already are given, and, further, that the research that they cannot critically evaluate is not a serious concern. Her "it depends" argument, that knowledge of statistics is not needed to understand research reports that do not contain any statistics, is circular. Her tact, however, supports our position. Students do need to understand statistics to critically evaluate research.

Dr. Blythe states that there are many types of research, that knowledge of more than statistics is needed to evaluate research, and that statistical knowledge ranges from the simple to the complex. We agree.

She concedes that students must know some simple statistics and suggests that they often learn these elementary levels while in high school, as undergraduates, or in M.S.W. programs. While this supports our argument by implying that faculty have determined that students do need some statistical knowledge, we are not convinced that social work students enter graduate school with adequate knowledge of statistics. Our experience in teaching research courses suggests that students' desire to work with people co-exists with a fear of numbers, terror at the prospect of taking on research, and anxiety over how to use computers. The social work maxim, "start where the client is," applies to how faculty should approach students as well. But this is not the place to argue about pedagogy or curriculum. Dr. Blythe's next points in her argument are where we begin to sharply disagree.

Dr. Blythe argues that knowledge of research methodology alone will allow students to evaluate the merits of most research. She asserts that "common sense" and a basic knowledge of research methodology are sufficient to critically evaluate some aspects of research. Students versed in research methods can determine if the literature is misused, the research problem was poorly stated, the measuring instruments unreliable or invalid, or the sample inadequate—without any understanding of statistics. A research report with these "problems" will be identified as methodologically flawed and can be rejected immediately. Students need not understand the statistical analysis because it "becomes a moot point." Once they determine that the study is flawed in any of these ways, they do not need to worry about the data analysis.

We disagree. First, understanding the general aspects of a study requires statistical knowledge as well as research know-how. Evaluating the relevant literature requires critically assessing how the authors interpret their own data and the data of others. The validity and reliability of measures are determined by—and reported as—statistical analyses. The generalizability of any study depends upon the method of sampling used. Sampling adequacy should be evaluated, in part, by assumptions derived from probability distributions. And even nonrandom sampling, the most common method in social work research, requires some understanding of probability distributions. Second, even when a study is flawed, the data analysis should be examined. Statistical manipulations can often ameliorate or exacerbate methodological flaws. For students to critically evaluate research, even its methodology, they must understand some statistics.

An unintended danger in Dr. Blythe's argument is that students who understand a little methodology will immediately "pooh pooh" a study that doesn't use random sampling, dismiss any journal article that has a slightly fuzzy problem formulation, and laugh out of the library reports that lack a logically derived hypothesis developed through careful analysis of the literature. Dr. Blythe seems to suggest that students will—and should—only read flawless research. If students are taught that they should immediately dismiss a study at the first sign of any violation of research methodology, they will not read anything. Under this circumstance, not just statistics, but research becomes moot. There is no perfect study, and neglecting research reports because they fall short of methodological perfection is not an example of critical evaluation.

Dr. Blythe's second major point is that what students don't know is not a serious problem. She argues that little research published in social work journals uses complex statistics and, therefore, students who have no statistical knowledge will be unprepared to understand only an insignificant number of research articles. She appears comfortable with the thought that students will be unable to understand the 16 percent of social work research that currently uses multivariate statistics. We are less at ease about this.

Social workers import knowledge from many disciplines, which use increasingly sophisticated statistical techniques in developing and testing their knowledge. Social work research is likely to follow a similar path. We are not prepared to accept a circumstance in which a significant proportion of social work knowledge and a potentially vast proportion of literature from other disciplines, may remain inaccessible to social workers.

We share Dr. Blythe's concern that partial knowledge may be a dangerous thing. It is true that statistical methods may be unwittingly misused and distort research. We feel that the best protection against such problems is prevention: students should learn the meaning of these statistics so that they can critically evaluate research and be informed participants in the knowledge development enterprise in social work.

NO

Susan D. Einbinder
Stuart A. Kirk

On June 6, 1992, the front page of the *New York Times* announced that black and white residents of Queens, New York, had achieved income parity (Roberts, 1992). The accompanying article stated that the 1990 median income was nearly identical for black and white households. For social workers and citizens concerned with social justice, this was good news. But readers unfamiliar with statistics will not know precisely what "median" income is or why this headline may be partially misleading. Worse still, social workers unacquainted with statistics might erroneously conclude that all income disparities associated with race have been eradicated in this New York borough. Based on incomplete information, they might move themselves and their clients to Queens to benefit from this social phenomena.

The "median," a statistical term, is only one way of summarizing a central tendency among a broad distribution of household incomes. Lining up all the household incomes from lowest the highest, the median income is the middle value, the income point at which half of the household incomes are above and half are below. Although using median incomes is an appropriate measure for this comparison, readers might not know that median incomes could be identical, but blacks and whites could have vastly different distributions of income and very different amounts of average (means) incomes. Knowing these additional statistics might lead to another interpretation of the data and an altered headline.

The point is not that there are "lies, damned lies, and statistics," but rather that ignorance of the meaning and uses of statistics leaves one vulnerable to misinformation and tempted unwittingly to draw unfounded conclusions. Statistics, a branch of mathematics dealing with probability theory, are tools for organizing, describing, and making inferences about information that has been gathered systematically. Like any form of conveying information, they can be used to distort or clarify. By themselves, they reveal no truths, nor are they a substitute for skeptical inquiry or careful thought. But as an adjunct to systematic inquiry where information is quantified, they have become indispensable to researchers as a way of analyzing data, and, we will argue, essential to social workers who aspire to be critical consumers of research.

There are forms of systematic inquiry (ethnography, historical studies, etc.) that do not rely on quantitative information, although they require other equally demanding analytical skills. These types of study do not appear as frequently in the social work and behavioral science literature as those inquiries that organize information quantitatively. Therefore, without some knowledge of statistics, social workers would be unable to critically evaluate many research studies. For this reason, some understanding of statistics is implicitly mandated by a basic undergraduate accreditation requirement of the Council on Social Work Education, which calls for students to be prepared as thoughtful consumers of research. At the masters level, according to both the accreditation standards and a recent report from the Task Force on Social Work Research (1991), considerably greater quantitative competencies are needed, although, as others have suggested, most programs probably fall far short of supplying these (Taylor, 1990; Lazar, 1990; Glisson & Fischer, 1987).

Elementary statistical competency can be acquired in several ways: through statistics courses, hands-on research experience, or integrated with content in research methods or other courses. Regardless of the curricula format chosen, students should achieve some familiarity with the following: 1) simple ways of describing distributions of single variables, such as measures of central tendency (median, mean, and mode) and measures of dispersion (e.g., standard deviation, range); 2) basic techniques to describe relationships between two variables (e.g., measures of association and correlation, bivariate tables, and bivariate regression); and, 3) principles used in making inferences about data gathered from samples. The latter require some knowledge of probability theory, the logic of random sampling, and the meaning and uses of tests of statistical significance (e.g., Chi-square, t-tests, F ratio). Although the language and concepts of statistics might seem foreign, without some minimal understanding of them and the theories that support them, social work students will remain strangers in the world of social work research, exiled from intelligently participating or learning from one major component of their profession's knowledge-development enterprise.

There are, of course, qualitative methods of inquiry that rely less on statistics and more on other techniques for understanding data (Glaser & Strauss, 1967; Strauss & Corbin, 1990). (Unfortunately, social work students are often equally unfamiliar with both. Arguing for the importance of one, as we do here, does not in any way diminish the usefulness of the other.) Statistical methods reduce information about a phenomena into numbers representing different facets of the phenomena. Both qualitative and quantitative methods of summarizing data lose information. But they lose information on purpose, trading off details and specificity to detect patterns and nuances that are often not observable by examining each piece of information one at a time, or by looking at all of it at once. The purpose of statistics is not to baffle or disguise; to the contrary, it is to simplify and clarify, to help us understand phenomena and detect relationships among representative parts.

Knowledge of statistics alone will not allow a reader to critically evaluate most research. A research-consumer needs substantive knowledge of the topic under study and basic understanding of the principles of scientific reasoning and research design. But even social workers primed with substantive topical knowledge and armed with an understanding of research methodology are greatly handicapped in reading many research reports if they assume that regression refers to some weakness of the ego, a measure of association has to do with social relationships, or a standard deviation pertains to a psychiatric disorder from DSM-III-R. While knowledge of statistics is not a sufficient basis for understanding research reports, it is certainly a necessary condition for critically evaluating many of them.

Knowledge of statistics is not a mere luxury, needed by a few research specialists who keep their fingers glued to a computer keyboard and their eyes buried in arcane research journals. It is needed by anyone who reads practitioner-oriented journals in social work. A recent study found that over half of the articles in ten social work and related journals were research based and nearly a third of the articles authored by social workers were reports of research (Fraser,

Taylor, Jackson, & O'Jack, 1991). Over the last quarter of a century, there has been a growing proportion of empirical articles in *Social Work,* the major journal of the NASW, by far the most frequently read journal in the profession (Task Force on Social Work Research, 1991). By the late 1980s, approximately a third of all articles in *Social Work* used some form of statistical analysis of information, twice the proportion appearing in the 1960s (Corcorcan, Kirk & Metrey, 1990). The journal literature in the behavioral and social sciences, from which social work imports much of its knowledge, is even more heavily research based (Glisson & Fischer, 1987).

These research articles are inaccessible to practitioners unless they possess the tools to interpret and critically evaluate the quantitative procedures used to reach the conclusions. More troubling than inaccessibility is an inability to judge the scientific merits of published studies. The reader may falsely assume that if a study was published, it must be good. Unfortunately, this is not true. It is not difficult to find published studies that are based on poor samples, weak measures, inadequate designs, and incomplete analytic procedures (Task Force on Social Work Research, 1991). If readers cannot recognize some of these faults, they are at risk of accepting uncritically the author's conclusions. Authors who are themselves statistically impaired can unwittingly overlook important information that may be buried in their data. But a reader with an adequate knowledge of statistics may be able to recognize the statistical shortcomings of an analysis, overly optimistic interpretation of statistical significance (Weinbach, 1989), or omission of a control variable. Without these skills, readers have no choice but to uncritically accept the author's conclusions.

Another reason why statistical literacy is so fundamental for understanding social work research is precisely because the research designs used are often weak and fail to rule out alternate interpretations of the data. Ironically, data from more complex experimental designs are the easiest to analyze, interpret, and understand, often requiring nothing more sophisticated than making comparisons among average outcome scores. These experimental designs allow for more confidence in the conclusions drawn from statistical results. For substantive, practical, ethical, or financial reasons, social work researchers frequently choose to use quasi-experimental and survey designs. When these types of designs are used to explore causal hypotheses, knowledge of statistics becomes even more vital for readers. For if the research design does not rule out rival hypotheses, more complex statistical procedures may be used, and the reader must be able to determine whether the appropriate quantitative procedures were used.

A working knowledge of statistics even helps social workers in critical readings of nonquantitative research (Lieberson, 1991), by sensitizing them to errors that can occur in causal reasoning and in making generalizations. Some research that is qualitative in nature, employing such techniques as field observation, unstructured interviews, and content analysis of documents, will, in the end, reduce and summarize the data by categories. These categories then are ordered in some meaningful way, and manipulated so that general conclusions may be drawn. These steps often parallel those in quantitative research. Likewise, single-subject research that has been designed to be more practitioner-friendly by paralleling the traditional, nonquantitative single-case study, relies on important research assumptions and statistical techniques. Almost all research, both qualitative and quantitative is comparative at its core: it implicitly compares one social group with another, one historical period or culture with some other one, a pre-test score with a post-test score, one scheme for interpreting experience as against some other interpretation of reality, one way of adapting to stress versus some alternative, or the outcome of a treatment group with a control group. Although there are several ways of highlighting possible differences, few techniques are as powerful for making comparisons as statistics.

Social work is a dynamic, resilient, and evolving profession. Its evolution demands that practitioners be able to distinguish fact from fiction, intentions from outcomes, and opinion from evidence. If schools of social work scrimp on training students to assess research critically, the profession's future is compromised. Whatever one may think about the prospects of professional advancement through knowledge-building research, omitting statistics from the M.S.W. curriculum will relegate future practitioners to a world in which they cannot adequately assess the research of others, consciously avoid applying findings that are erroneous, and learn from the knowledge-development process that transpires in the professional journals.

None of us would condone preparing social workers to practice in a setting or with a population in which they did not know the culture, social norms, or even the elementary structure and meaning of the language used. And yet that is what the profession does if it fails to adequately prepare masters students in the customs of science. If we expect social workers to be participants in the intellectual life of their profession, they must have some basic knowledge of the scientific enterprise. Although this enterprise comprises many types of intellectual activities, it is reasonable to assume that social work and the social sciences in the future will continue to rely on various quantitative or statistical techniques. By teaching social work students research methods and statistics, we equip them with tools to evaluate journal articles, research reports, and even the *New York Times,* in the hope that they will critically and appropriately apply the findings to their work of improving the lives of their clients. If we fail in that mission, Queens, New York, may just get overpopulated by the year 2000, full of disappointed people who were expecting full equality. And those who know statistics will know why.

References

Corcoran, K. J., Kirk, S. A., & Metrey, G. D. (1990). Merging *Social Work* and *Social Work Research & Abstracts. Social Work Research & Abstracts, 26,* 6–7.

Glaser, B., & Strauss, A. (1967). The discovery of grounded theory: Strategies for qualitative research. New York. Aldine.

Glisson, C., & Fischer, J. (1987). Statistical training for social workers. *Journal of Social Work Education, 23,* 50–58.

Fraser, M., Taylor, M. J., Jackson, R., & O'Jack, J. (1991). Social work and science: Many ways of knowing? *Social Work Research & Abstracts, 27,* 5–15.

Lazer, A. (1990). Statistics courses in social work education. *Journal of Teaching in Social Work, 4,* 17–30.

Lieberson, S. (1991). Small N's and big conclusions: An examination of the reasoning in comparative studies based on a small number of cases. *Social Forces, 70,* 307–320.

Roberts, S. (1992, June 6). Blacks reach a milestone in Queens: Income parity. *The New York Times,* p. A1.

Strauss, A., & Corbin, J. (1990). Basics of qualitative methodology: Grounded theory procedures and techniques. Newbury Park, CA: Sage.

Task Force on Social Work Research. (1991). *Building social work knowledge for effective services and policies: A plan for research development.* Austin, TX: National Institute of Mental Health, Capital Printing.

Taylor, F. A. (1990). The numerate social worker. *Journal of Social Work Education, 26,* 25–35.

Weinbach, R. W. (1989). When is statistical significance meaningful? A practice perspective. *Journal of Sociology and Social Welfare, 16,* 31–38.

Rejoinder to Drs. Einbinder and Kirk

Betty J. Blythe

In reading the essay by Einbinder and Kirk, I am struck by our different views of the knowledge, previous training, and capacity of social work students. I also realize that we have very different perceptions of the range and relative frequency of the various types of research methodologies and, when appropriate, accompanying statistical tests that are employed in social work. I have identified four areas of disagreement, which I will address here.

My colleagues open with the argument that social work graduate students will not know what a median is. This appears to me to be a grossly insulting suggestion. As I suggested in my earlier essay, students are learning about medians, means, and other such descriptive statistics in high school, if not earlier. Certainly, such knowledge would come with a good liberal arts education, which graduate students should have experienced. To suggest that M.S.W. students would not know what a median is, is to suggest that they are unable to read such common publications as *USA Today* or *Time* magazine, as well as agency and published research reports that describe a sample or population. Do Drs. Einbinder and Kirk really believe that M.S.W. students are inferior to the general population? I think not.

I also find Drs. Einbinder and Kirk's treatment of certain "forms of systematic inquiry" to be troubling. Particularly, I am puzzled by their treatment of qualitative research, which, in my view, is as informative and as rigorous as quantitative research. First, they offer ethnographic and historical studies as examples of research that do not rely on quantitative information. I agree with them that these specific types of qualitative research do not often appear in the social work literature. On the other hand, they apparently overlook case studies, which have been common in social work practice for decades and are a form of qualitative research. And, social work researchers often report findings based on such qualitative methods as participant observation and content analysis to study some aspect of a social problem or its alleviation. Indeed, much recent writing on social work research has called for increased use of qualitative methods. Although Drs. Einbinder and Kirk say that they do not mean to diminish the usefulness of "the other" methods of inquiry (i.e., qualitative research), by mere fact that they omit them from their discussion of research and statistical analysis, they do not treat them as serious and accepted forms of social work research. Could that be because knowledge of statistics is not needed to evaluate qualitative research?

I also disagree with Drs. Einbinder and Kirk's comments about single-subject research. They argue that case studies using single-subject methodology rely on statistical techniques. While it is true that some statistical techniques for analyzing single-case data have been proposed, the primary method of analyzing single-case data is visual analysis of graphic data. Visual analysis is both recommended and most often used in practice, whether the case study is described in an agency report or a published article. And visual analysis clearly is a nonstatistical method of analyzing data.

Finally, I am made curious by the fact that Drs. Einbinder and Kirk open their remarks with the argument that M.S.W. students do not understand a simple statistic such as the median, but end up arguing that they be trained to understand complex statistics such as regression, which is much more difficult to understand and interpret. Moreover, I disagree with their suggestion that the statistics used in experiments are relatively straightforward. For instance, multiple analysis of variance is increasingly used to analyze data from experiments. To this writer, it seems to be a rather substantial leap from understanding a median to understanding the results of multiple analysis of variance, which examines the influence of the independent variable on two or more dependent variables.

DEBATE 16

Should Doctoral-Level Graduates in Social Work Be as Well Trained in Research as Those in Allied Disciplines?

Ram A. Cnaan is an associate professor at the University of Pennsylvania School of Social Work, where he teaches social welfare policy, community organization, research methods, and statistics. His current research and writing interests are in voluntary activity in human services, community organization, community mental health, case management with severely persistent mentally ill individuals and services for dually diagnosed homeless.

Robert J. Wineburg is Associate Professor and Chairperson of the Social Work Department at the University of North Carolina-Greensboro. His teaching and research area is in American social welfare policy. He currently is funded by a three-year grant from the Lilly Endowment to study how religious congregations are involved in human services.

Joseph A. Walsh is Professor and Director of Doctoral Studies at Loyola University, Chicago, School of Social Work. His recent research studies have been on post-adoption problems and on leadership patterns in nonprofit boards of directors. He maintains a private clinical and consulting practice.

YES

RAM A. CNAAN
ROBERT J. WINEBURG

We believe that doctoral education in social work should do more than prepare graduates to pass on the knowledge, skills, and values of the profession. It should also provide training in social-science research methods that is as good, if not better, than that given to students in allied disciplines. We base our argument on five inter-related factors. First, the inability of social work researchers to compete successfully in researching potential solutions to pressing problems may seriously jeopardize their special relationship with the social-service community. Second, researchers from all disciplines are competing with each other for research grants at a time when government and private foundations allocations for research are being cut back. Third, more universities are basing tenure and promotion decisions on research publications that are evaluated by colleagues from many disciplines. Fourth, major research is becoming increasingly interdisciplinary and social workers must have the necessary research skills if they are to be full partners in across-discipline teams and centers. Finally, social workers, as part of the scientific community, should be expected to use scientific principles and methodologies and be judged by the same scientific criteria.

It is our contention that doctoral programs in social work need to do a better job in preparing graduates for their future career as university faculty and as applied researchers who know how to study and solve social problems. The primary goal of social work doctoral education is to prepare a new generation of scholars, who will generate and transmit new knowledge in the field. The importance of this goal is self evident given that more than two thirds of all graduates choose careers in higher education (Kahn, 1983; Patchner, 1983).

Unfortunately, social work academicians, for the most part, have had little training in empirical research. For example, the Task Force on Social Work Research, appointed by the National Institute of Mental Health (NIMH) and chaired by David Austin, found that, although social workers provided a large part of mental-health services in the nation, social work researchers carried out very little research on mental health. This Task Force concluded that at the doctoral level, training for a research career is uneven, too late, inaccessible, and inefficient.

Is this lack of training in research methodology a problem? Yes . . . and for a number of reasons. First, researchers outside the field of social work are producing many of the agency-based and service-focused studies in mental-health and human-service organizations. Meanwhile, investigators in other university programs with applied components such as special education, counselor education, educational psychology, clinical or community sociology, criminal justice, public health, and public administration, are expanding their research to traditional social work settings. This crossover into the domain of social work is certain to continue because funders are demanding practical solutions for complicated service problems. These solutions require service-centered and applied social-science research, and this is where the allied disciplines are focusing their efforts. Social work and social work education, because of the emphasis on the individual, the environment, the service system, and social policy, have had a long tradition of leadership in the practice arena. Now, we must establish our leadership in the research arena. Social work researchers must prove that they are capable both of performing quality research comparable to that in other disciplines and of maintaining the role of practice innovators. This cannot be done without rigorous training in research methods. If our doctoral programs fail to provide such training, social work will not only fall behind those who are waiting to lead; it will be unable to bring its own special perspective to the social-service research agenda. Consequently, social work researchers may become academic dinosaurs in the research universities.

Second, failure to secure external funding for research will jeopardize social work's stature in academe and in the scientific community. Clearly, doctoral graduates in social work face fierce competition in obtaining funding because the number of grants in the public and private sectors is steadily diminishing (Reif-Lehrer, 1989). Most grant providers expect demonstrated ability and rigorous research designs. For example, NIMH is asking that reviewers give a more favorable assessment to those proposals that are designed as controlled clinical trials, double-blind experimental designs, contain random sampling, and base their sample size on power statistics. If social work researchers are to compete successfully, they must be as qualified, if not better qualified, than researchers from allied disciplines.

Third, doctoral graduates are expected to gain academic stature and success, which is traditionally measured in terms of academic tenure and proven productivity (Glisson, 1982). If doctoral graduates are to excel in higher education, they must quickly master the art of productive scholarship. The types of research and publication held in greatest esteem are articles in refereed journals, books, and, to a lesser degree, papers presented at academic conferences. Many universities, especially research universities, give added credit only to empirically based studies and articles. A growing number of journals, especially the leading journals, now require methodological rigor as a condition for acceptance. Today, those who would publish must be able to carry out methodologically sound research and report their findings clearly and effectively. This is particularly important in issues of tenure and promotion and publication in peer-reviewed journals, because faculty from allied disciplines often sit on university review committees and on editorial boards, and they tend to judge an applicant or a manuscript by the more stringent criteria of social sciences.

Fourth, research is becoming increasingly interdisciplinary. It is common nowadays for researchers from various disciplines to be organized within a university as a center, research group, or institute, especially in areas such as gerontology, drug abuse, and mental health. While social workers often are invited to participate in interdisciplinary research in these areas, it is expected that they will have the expertise to carry their weight in such collaborations. Yet, sad to say, we have found that colleagues in the allied disciplines tend to perceive social work researchers as lacking in stature and, therefore, fail to include them in interdisciplinary research programs, which generally have a good record in attracting external funding. Thus, if social workers are to participate in such collaborations as equal partners, they must be at least as well trained in research as their colleagues.

Finally, social workers are part of the scientific community, and, as such, their research must be governed by the same principles and methods common to scientific researchers. There are no valid research methods that are unique to social work. Thus, social workers who study social issues and evaluate human-services programs are rightfully expected to employ methods similar to those used in allied disciplines and at the highest possible level. Thus, mastery of research skills is essential if doctoral graduates are to perform at a level consistent with the standards of a scientific discipline.

The strongest point in our case for rigorous research training may well be the devastating effects that will occur to social work if this area is neglected in doctoral education. The best young minds in the field may have to delay scholarly inquiry because they will have to learn on the job what they were never taught: how to research, write for journals, teach, and solicit grants. The social work field may lose because these beginners are ''learning the ropes'' at a time when their energy could and should be focused on solving major practice problems and transferring those ideas back into the classroom. Ultimately, clients may lose, because these young faculty members must spend much of their creative energy, not in obtaining grants to explore new ideas and in passing these ideas on through publications, teaching, and service, but in compensating for an education that left them poorly prepared.

Although the preparation of the next wave of social work faculty has not yet reached the state of affairs just outlined, we do believe that the stepped-up demands in academe to publish and attract funding, coupled with the need to be accountable and of service to the practice community, necessitate both a thoughtful discussion of the current state of doctoral education in social work and recommendations for constructive changes.

Any discussion, however, must first begin by understanding what is typically done in a doctoral program with regard to research. Most doctoral programs in social work are considered to be two-year programs of study, excluding the time required for preparation and defense of a dissertation (Kronick, Kamerman, & Glisson, 1989). The programs provide broad exposure to social welfare history and policy, a focus on social and behavioral theory, social statistics, and social research methodologies. At the end of the first or second year of study, students are expected to take a comprehensive examination. Subsequently, students write a dissertation, a process that initiates them into scholarly inquiry and solidify basic research skills. Most graduates do master an area of expertise, but, on the average, most lack the ability to compete successfully with doctoral graduates in allied disciplines as far as research is concerned. It is important to note that evaluation studies of research training in social work doctoral education suggest that many students are not adequately prepared for advanced positions in research (Glisson, 1982; Kronick, Kamerman, & Glisson, 1989).

Research training in social work doctoral education usually consists of two research courses, one or two statistics courses, possibly a comprehensive research exam, and a dissertation. Students learn how to conduct literature searches by writing required papers. A most disconcerting experience common to all research professors is that doctoral students claim no previous knowledge of research or statistics, and, therefore, professors have to begin with the basics. Moreover, many students complain about the ''alien substance'' of research and statistics and the pace of instruction, while others overtly ask to be exempted from the courses. In fact, most doctoral programs have no research-related prerequisites other than course work required for the master's degree, nor do they have any formal advanced placement procedures for students with strong research and statistics backgrounds (Jenson, Fraser, & Lewis, 1991). Thus, the level of sophistication in many social work advanced-research courses is minimal. Jenson, Fraser, and Lewis, (1991, p. 33) in their study of research teaching in social work doctoral programs, concluded, ''These results suggest that very few research and statistics skills are taught to students at the mastery or advanced applied level. Further, it appears that content taught at the application level includes only basic research and statistics.''

We believe that doctoral education must go further in preparing new graduates for the increasingly competitive university environment. Caputo (1991) has offered some suggestions for enhancing research requirements; however, we would like to suggest several of our own that we deem to be very important. We recommend that doctoral programs make the following changes: 1) Focus the theoretical approach undergirding the research agenda on finding new ways to solve pressing social problems or developing new theories of application; 2) require all doctoral students to align themselves with an agency early on in their program; 3) doctoral students take courses on quantitative and qualitative research methods and program evaluation; 4) all research projects be geared toward solving clinical, service, environmental, or policy-related problems; 5) each student be required to participate in publishing an article in a scholarly journal; 6) each student be required to participate in a research project; 7) each student be trained in the grant proposal solicitation process; and 8) each student be required to pass a comprehensive examination devoted to research methods and statistics. We realize these changes are profound and comprehensive. Such changes are necessary if doctoral education programs are to guarantee the research competence that the future faculty in social work will need to compete successfully with their colleagues in the allied disciplines.

References

Caputo, R. K. (1991). Doctoral level research: Issues and resolutions in curriculum development. *Arete, 16,* 39–50.

Glisson, C. (1982). Notes on advanced social work education. *Social Service Review, 56,* 629–639.

Jenson, J. M., Fraser, M. W., & Lewis, R. E. (1991). Research training in social work doctoral programs. *Arete, 16,* 23–38.

Kahn, A. J. (1983). *Curriculum issues for doctoral education.* Paper presented at the Annual Meeting, Group for Advancement of Doctoral Education (GADE), University of Alabama, October 10.

Kronick, J. C., Kamerman, S. B., & Glisson, C. (1989). *The structure of doctoral programs in social work: A critical analysis.* Paper presented at the annual meeting, Group for Advancement of Doctoral Education (GADE), Gatlinburg, TN, October.

Patchner, M. A. (1983). The experiences of DSWs and Ph.Ds. *Journal of Education for Social Work, 19,* 98–106.

Reif-Lehrer, L. (1989). *Writing a successful grant application* (2nd ed.). Boston: Jones and Bartlett.

Rejoinder to Drs. Cnaan and Wineburg

JOSEPH A. WALSH

The appeal of debate (narrative or face to face) is to challenge ideas in order to improve, refine, and enrich perspectives on both sides of an issue. Essentially, no one in the field of doctoral education for social workers opposes the wish for graduates to have competent research skills. The debate proper surrounds which goals need to be achieved first and what must be done by whom to achieve them.

Drs. Cnann and Wineburg seem to view the fields of social work as if they form a singular perspective—as though all doctoral students pursue advanced academic preparation coming from the same roots and moving toward identical goals. Nothing could be less true. Many students come as a career transition, to get a "teaching credential," equalize degree levels with colleagues, study a particular topic of special interest, or to pursue a long-held dream of holding a doctoral degree. While most admit to an interest in an academic involvement after obtaining the doctorate, academic involvement may mean teaching one course while carrying on an extensive clinical-practice. To define doctoral candidates as a homogeneous group with common needs and goals (let alone a common developmental life state) is extremely imprecise.

Observations that Drs. Cnann and Wineburg make about social workers having competitors in related academic disciplines who compete vigorously for scarce resources seems a valid observation. As members of a profession, doctorally trained social workers have a vast potential for conducting agency-based research with direct relevance and meaning to a vast array of social-service agencies *and which may not even require deep pockets of special federal funding to conduct.* The implications of Drs. Cnaan and Wineburg's remarks are that if the monies for research do not come by virtue of winning some national interdisciplinary grant competition, they don't count and are irrelevant. That seems *seriously* off-base to me and makes federally funded research seem more like a plume in one's hat than just one method, among many, for supporting research studies.

I have no argument with Dr. Cnann and Wineburg's point that doctoral applicants in social work seem poorly prepared for research studies. The conclusion I would draw is not about the *ability* to do research, but about the academic process in social work doctoral education. Most other disciplines bring students directly from undergraduate studies into an intensive, multifaceted four-year or five-year academic immersion and socialization process, which at its end produces (more or less) a graduate enculturated with the tools and values of the discipline or profession.

It seems prudent for social work to consider this model (which by no accident, parallels that of our more research-sophisticated confreres.) At least a selected number of students could be trained through this model, which, on its face, has vastly more potential that our recruitment of students who, while quite competent, may be in their forties as they start doctoral study and already have a refined, narrowed, and (dare I say) pragmatic point of view in their pursuit of doctoral education.

Lastly, if as Drs. Cnann and Wineburg claim, there are no valid research methods that are unique to social work, why should social workers study them in the relative vacuum of a school of social work? It would make more sense, create an economy of scale, and promote cross-disciplinary commonality and complimentary work to jointly train doctoral students in research skills. At the same time, we could promote both collaboration and benevolent competition at that stage of training, rather than waiting until the post-degree period and then staging jousting matches for funding in the conference rooms at the National Institute of Health (NIH).

References

Caputo, R. (1991). Doctoral level research: Issues and resolutions in curriculum development. *Arete, 16*(1), 39–50.

Chinen, A. (1989). From quantitative to qualitative reasoning: A developmental perspective. In L. E. Thomas (Ed.), *Research on adulthood & aging* (p. 53). Albany, NY: State University of New York Press.

Group for the Advancement of Doctoral Education in Social Work—GADE. (1992, June 12). Guidelines for quality in social work doctoral programs (draft 5). Sheila Kamerman, GADE Chair, School of Social Work, Columbia University, 622 West 113th Street, New York, NY 10025.

Glisson, C., & Fischer, J. (1987). Statistical training for social workers. *Journal of Social Work Education, 23*(3), 50–58.

Jenson, J., Fraser, M., & Lewis, R. (1991). Research training in social work doctoral programs. *Arete, 16*(1), 23–38.

Rose, R. (1977). Disciplined research and undisciplined problems. In C. H. Weiss (Ed.), *Using social research in public policy.* Lexington, MA: Lexington Books.

Task Force on Social Work Research (1991). *Building social work knowledge for effective services and policies: A plan for research development.* Rockville, MD: National Institute of Mental Health.

NO

JOSEPH A. WALSH

For a doctoral-level academician to take the NO position on this question is nearly tantamount to hating apple pie and stomping on the flag. Nonetheless, parsed adroitly, there is ample room to critique the proposition both from the vantage point of the discipline of social work and the purposes of doctoral study.

To delve into the concerns of this proposition, let me first raise a vexing question: why should social work try to be like the "allied disciplines?" For social work, being discussed as a discipline is an incomplete description. It is also a profession with a wide array of meaningful services to people with social needs. Most disciplines do not struggle with a comparable burden. As a discipline/profession, the obligation for social work to fulfill its social mission necessarily may supersede its responsibility to an academic mission. Imbedded in this question are innumerable concerns.

Is social work allied to other disciplines because of a concern with the poor? Probably so, but yet it is unlike the schools of architecture, which stretch to find the ideal design for high-density, low-rent housing. Is social work, then, like other academic disciplines offering doctorates? Must theology and social work, for example, blend approaches to scholarship in order to produce the single entity known as scholars? Probably not.

Imbedded more deeply in the reference to allied disciplines is the intimation that others have found the "right way" to do research, while social work is still groping. Hence, if we imitate others, we will be like them. The obvious flaw, of course, is that the purposes of social work and social work education are not necessarily best served by being like others—but, rather, by finding the most effective way(s) to be our best selves (in the professional sense). If duplicating the techniques, processes, and philosophies of other doctoral disciplines were an answer, the separations among them might better be removed, and simply training doctoral students *en masse* in the rituals of research would be the obvious solution.

The sharper question, it would seem, is: What are the missions, mandates, and tasks of doctorally trained social workers, and are we adequately preparing students for such expectations? Obviously a discipline and profession such as social work is broad enough to have many discrete tasks. Assessing the impact of new welfare models seems substantially different, however, than understanding the correlates between family structure and anorexia and are both removed from the analysis of styles of effective management in nonprofit boards.

Differences being real, yet each research area being a customary bailiwick for social workers, how then should we effectively angle research training? The only sensible answer, it would seem, is to fashion the research questions, tools, and tests to the issues at hand. Hence, a heuristic model is required. Such a model disentangles the scholar from the notion that research rigor is a variable of how many different statistical tests one can access or perform. It allows the perception that rigor is more the skill of finding and choosing the appropriate evaluative processes for the questions that most directly address the problem(s) under study. It is not a question of quantitative or qualitative methodology, but rather—for what purpose, where, and when, is one particular approach better than another (Thomas, 1989).

It seems unlikely, considering the competitive spirit in general, that anyone in social work would publicly support the proposition that we should be "less well trained" than other professions and disciplines. A better focusing of the concern, then, might be on the intensive training of doctoral students for what it is they will be called upon to do, rather than for the breadth of all possible tasks.

For social work, the mission is to do things that have social relevance and positive social impact. To use this as the guiding principle for both teachers and students of research in social work seems the right level of relevance. It permits necessary latitude for the reality that research serves several purposes. In one important way, research training conveys a mastery of specified skills and a desirable intellectual rigor. Without diminishing this, it also should be an expression of scholars' novel insights, powers of persuasion, and grant-procuring acumen. Each is a legitimate and apt use of research prowess if guided, at least in social work, by the beacon of positive and relevant social impact.

In regard to the adequacy of research training in social work doctoral education, there appears to be what is best described as a hodge-podge pattern of preparation. This begins with the simple reality that all schools do not necessarily title courses in the same manner. What is a statistics course in one setting may be enveloped under the rubric of a research course in another (Jenson, Fraser, & Lewis, 1991.)

Most social work doctoral programs do not have research-specific prerequisites other than the course work that is required for the masters degree. Teaching for comprehension with modest application appears to dominate the research curricula in most programs. Only 31 percent of the programs offer research *practica* to promote research skills. Among the many losses resulting from these realities are the ability and readiness of doctorally trained social workers to compete effectively for foundation and federal support when such proposals must reflect the capacity to develop and implement complex research designs (Jenson, Fraser, & Lewis, 1991.)

At the same time, it should be noted that the ability of doctoral-trained social workers to obtain funded research grants is frequently overemphasized and touted as *the* measure of coming of age as a competent investigator. Without rejecting such achievement as a meaningful measure of success, it would be not only prudent, but practical, to suggest that other measures also have value. Some excellent research is generated during the process of teaching research classes, and, frequently, this has been one of the most reliable and significant processes by which both students and faculty in schools of social work contribute to the commonwealth of the community. Moreover, many faculty in schools of social work conduct diverse and meaningful research tasks as part of their scholarly role, independent of special external funding being allocated for it.

One final, niggling issue about the question of the adequacy of research preparedness comes up in the recurrent admonitions that social work doctoral students should be trained as well as (read: in the way same as) their confreres in all aspects of research. While not at all opposing that desire, it raises the general question, "Why?" If some mythical research team were to be established at some mythical point in the future, how would it enhance the team to have every member bring to it the same research skills? Complementarity, unique skills, or in-depth knowledge in a specific area each would appear to be a preferable contribution from a team member rather than sameness or identical contributions. The most recent studies on social work research promote such a team model (Task Force on Social Work Research, 1991).

The point within the point of those who argue the opposite invariably seems to be premised on an assumption: that statistical mastery is the hallmark of research acumen. Such perspective ignores the vast variety of questions, for example, in clinical social work that are not illuminated well at all by the use of statistical maneuvers. Again, without discouraging in any way the achievement of statistical mastery, it does not seem accurate to elevate that one discrete skill (one probably based on a genetic attribute) as the hallmark that confirms that a given doctoral-level individual—or a given profession/discipline—has now passed muster as competent at research. We should look for more complex and interactive measures (cf. Caputo [1991]) to find guidelines for training competent researchers. One specific reference point should be a sufficient knowledge of statistics to understand, learn from and contribute to the social work literature.

To this end, the Group for the Advancement of (Social Work) Doctoral Education (GADE; 1992) has recently been preparing a draft paper to outline criteria for quality in doctoral education. In draft form, these include:

1. Systematic review, critique, and synthesis of a given body of literature
2. Formulation of professionally relevant and theoretically productive research questions and hypotheses

3. Crafting a research design and data collection strategy
4. Drawing of an appropriate sample, using different kinds of sampling methods
5. Systematic analysis of data, using quantitative and qualitative methods
6. Presentation of findings in spoken and written form

What might be added to this list is the capacity to self-educate as the profession continues to mature (Glisson & Fischer, 1987). These are admirable objectives. We clearly are not here yet in terms of having each social work doctoral-level graduate with mastery of these six indicators of research competence.

On the other hand, it would be rash to say we have failed if we were to regularly graduate doctoral students who possessed four or five of these attributes and working knowledge in the remaining ones. High standards for achievement are not only laudable, but necessary. Breast-beating for being at the 70 percent marker on the way to the ideal seems both boorish and without redemptive value.

Let us strive for the highest quality, guided by the social relevance and positive social impact of our research, and be anchored in a sensible reality.

References

Caputo, R. (1991). Doctoral level research: Issues and resolutions in curriculum development. *Arete, 16*(1), 39–50.

Group for the Advancement of Doctoral Education in Social Work—GADE. (1992, June 12). Guidelines for quality in social work doctoral programs (draft 5). Sheila Kamerman, GADE Chair, School of Social Work, Columbia University, 622 West 113th Street, New York, NY 10025.

Glisson, C., & Fischer, J. (1987). Statistical training for social workers. *Journal of Social Work Education, 23*(3), 50–58.

Jenson, J., Fraser, M., & Lewis, R. (1991). Research training in social work doctoral programs. *Arete, 16*(1), 23–28.

Task Force on Social Work Research. (1991). *Building social work knowledge for effective services and policies: A plan for research development.* Rockville, MD: National Institute of Mental Health.

Thomas, L. E. (Ed.). (1989). *Research on adulthood and aging.* Albany, NY: State University of New York Press.

Rejoinder to Dr. Walsh

Ram A. Cnaan
Robert J. Wineburg

In his opening remark, Dr. Walsh acknowledges that ". . . to take the contrary position . . . is nearly tantamount to hating apple pie and stomping on the flag." With all due respect, this is probably the only point with which we agree. We don't disagree so much with his message, we part company on this underlying theme, the subtext of this view. We found four basic ideas in his essay, which we would like to examine to illustrate our differences. First, however, let us make clear that we believe that Dr. Walsh's presentation represents the best values and thinking of the previous era in social work's development. Such thinking was responsible not only for bringing social work into the academy, but also for laying the foundation for its long-term survival in practice. Our perspective, however, essentially is a paradigm shift that represents the next stage of development. On that note, let us point out where we part company.

First, Dr. Walsh asks, ''Why should social work try to be like 'allied disciplines?'. . . It is also a profession with a wide array of meaningful services to people with social needs.'' Here, the discussion subtly shifts from doctoral education to the education for social workers with a masters degree. We basically agree with him on his notion of education for M.S.W. practitioners, but in this discussion, we are assessing the role of education for those who will be responsible for the generation of knowledge. In many academic professions, the division between researchers and practitioners is clear. Take lawyers, physicians, or psychologists, as examples. Often such practitioners serve people by using a combination of practice wisdom and the findings of the researchers in their fields. We find Dr. Walsh's use of theology as parallel to social work rather than any of the above-mentioned three disciplines quite telling. Theology, unlike social work rests on faith as its basic operating principle. Faith can certainly be a starting point for risk taking, innovation, and claims for justice. However, social work not only has to answer to a higher calling, it also has to answer to clients, funders, other disciplines, and the society at large. As such, those who lead the field must be grounded not only in their theoretical and practice specialty, but also in research principles, ways to support that research, and systems of accountability.

Second, it is contended that social work researchers should not follow researchers from other disciplines, but that we should search for our own professional selves. This statement is puzzling for two reasons. First, social work knowledge often comes from allied disciplines, so there is no reason for the research tools to be uniquely different. Second, if we will wait until social work develops its own unique research tools, we will be left behind and our practice will be based on unsubstantiated beliefs.

Third, our counterpoint author calls for a heuristic research model that stresses the skill of finding and choosing the appropriate evaluative processes for the questions that most directly address the problem(s) being studied. We agree. But finding the appropriate evaluative processes requires a familiarity with and thorough understanding of a variety of research methods.

Finally, Dr. Walsh blends research with statistics as if they were the same thing. His criticism is based on what was used to be labeled as ''number crunching,'' and although he does not directly say so, he hints that statistics are antithetical to social work. We see statistics as tools for one kind of research and emphasize that any research curriculum developed based on our ideas include ethnographic, qualitative, and statistical research methods. Social work is clearly at a stage in which the notion of research means more than skills in statistical maneuvers. We believe that with solid grounding in different ways to assess practice-related problems, social work researchers should be well equipped to ask the right questions.

We, too, think that social work's obligation to the tenets of the profession separates us from other professions and distinguishes us from other academic disciplines. We want to maintain that obligation. Unlike, the thesis of the contra position, we are paying attention to the changing contents of both social work and the academy. As such, we feel that preparing future social work scholars to be the best investigators possible will ensure the survival of the profession. What we are looking for is a revision in the way in which social work doctoral education treats research teaching and training. But that revision takes discipline, courage, and willingness to change. Unfortunately, not all social work educators are with us on that point.

DEBATE 17

Should We Have Different Doctoral-Level Research Training Streams for Academia and Practice?

Larry W. Kreuger is an associate professor at the University of Missouri-Columbia School of Social Work, where he teaches program evaluation and policy courses in the graduate school. For the last three years, he chaired the Social Work Doctoral Development Committee and is the chair of the Promotion and Tenure Committee. He has been Visiting Professor at the George Warren Brown School of Social Work at Washington University, St. Louis, Missouri. His research interests include formerly homeless families and their housing needs. He has given numerous papers and presentations on teaching research methods and computer applications in human-services association meetings.

John J. Stretch is Professor and Director of Doctoral Studies at the Saint Louis University School of Social Service in Missouri, where he teaches in the fields of research and nonprofit management. He is a widely sought after consultant in human-service management. He has published extensively in major professional journals and books.

Catheleen Jordan is an associate professor at the University of Texas at Arlington School of Social Work, where she teaches direct practice and research courses and directs the Community Service Clinic. Her current research and writing interests are in clinical assessment and family therapy. She also consults with the Texas State Department of Social Services as a trainer for child protection services (CPS) workers.

YES

LARRY W. KREUGER
JOHN J. STRETCH

The professional responsibilities of academic social workers (professors and researchers), on the one hand, and high-level social work policymakers or advanced practitioners, on the other, are decidedly different. In our opinion, there are distinct, institutionalized norms that govern tenure and advancement; academic pedagogical confrontations; and university curricular subspecializations for these two careers that make necessary differential research training. In substance, the functions served are markedly different.

University faculty holding the Ph.D. degree must be well grounded in the philosophy of science and have, as well, facility with diverse sets of methodological and applicational research strategies, ranging from micro-oriented single-case studies to more broadly based meta-evaluations. We do not see this diverse range of methodological specialization in pure practice settings.

From an institutional perspective, climbing the career ladder for the academician is made easier by conceptual, data-generating, and analytic skills that are not nearly so well institutionalized for the nonacademician. Academic tenure and advancement in rank at the present time are much more likely to require the production of a large number of empirically grounded contributions to the knowledge base of the profession. Such has not been the case traditionally in more purely clinical or policy-making settings.

Academic social workers must therefore possess considerable grounding in the technical aspects of research methods, ranging from procedures as diverse as analytic induction in qualitative methodology to subtle variations in the selection of statistics, based on the Neyman–Pearson Relative Frequency school of probability in quantitative methods. In addition, in order to teach effectively at advanced graduate levels, university faculty must have considerable competence in the epistemological foundations of the discipline. They must be prepared to test a range of substantive problems through rigorous empirical paradigms. They are also likely to face more institutional demands to engage in pure research as well.

Academicians must possess didactic competence, which in many cases (e.g., for the teaching of research coursework) requires considerable pedagogical flexibility and classroom creativity. Both of the authors, as teachers of research methods at the graduate and undergraduate level, spend a considerable amount of time developing and testing new metaphors for teaching statistics, for example. It is our contention that this form of creative endeavor, while part and parcel of academia, is not so likely to be rewarded in advanced clinical or policy settings. From a phenomenological perspective, purely pragmatic (as opposed to theoretical) motives of social work practice anchor the respective cogitations of clinicians and policymakers.

Academicians are relatively more free (and indeed are more likely to be encouraged) to wander creatively in their imaginations through multiple theoretical (as opposed to pragmatic) domains. They are also encouraged to reflect on such nonordinary theoretical mentalisms *(ens rationis)* through both written and spoken word. But on the other hand, how many advanced clinicians or policymakers do you know who can reasonably expect to spend perhaps one third of their time in purely creative or theoretically fanciful pursuits?

Prominent policymakers and advanced practitioners, we would argue, have more straight forward and pragmatic requirements placed on their research. From our experience as consultants in policy development, policymakers need empirical strategies that address very practical decision-making issues. It is our position that advanced practitioners require, perforce, much more pragmatically oriented ''mind work'' to select among intervention protocols to assist them in making reasoned, practiced-based choices among often more compelling alternative theoretical perspectives. In addition, advanced clinicians and policymakers are institutionally much less likely to be able to buffer their time so as to be able to channel their energy into the purely creative didactic pursuits so important to the university-level teacher.

The core research training at the doctoral level for these two advanced levels of practice (policy making and empirically guided clinical intervention) have similar substantive bases. In general, advanced-research, doctoral-level coursework encompasses advanced research design and methods with an ultimate criterion of use as a tool of inquiry in the dissertation. The usual advanced research component of the curriculum for doctoral students builds upon a general requirement of six to nine credit hours in the masters degree experience.

Advanced doctoral-research coursework provides an additional nine to twelve hours, exclusive of dissertation research. Although the majority of doctoral students either immediately or shortly after completing their advanced studies find themselves in the classroom, we feel that explicit attention has not been given to the type of research training required for their future teaching responsibilities at the masters and doctoral level.

One of the reasons for lack of attention to this issue in doctoral curricula is the assumption of a generalist graduate-level teacher in schools of social work. There is not currently an expectation that specially trained graduates of social work Ph.D. programs should devote their energies to research, either exclusively or in a given substantive area.

Thus, it is left to individual preference or happenstance of curriculum for newly trained social work faculty to be assigned a range of research teaching areas. Likewise, we see only occasional attempts in the profession to further research and statistical teaching excellence at the advanced policy-making and clinical-interventive levels.

Advanced practitioners, on the other hand, have a number of sub-specializations and group identities that provide direction for curriculum development and for subsequent continuing education expectations. Within this framework of continuing professional expectations and supportive structures, advanced practitioners have opportunities offered through licensure requirements, most notably Continuing Education Credits (CEC), to refurbish and refresh their subspecialty skills and knowledge-based requirements.

Although this is an area that has not been given the attention that it should, there is no doubt that the differences are so clear and compelling as to argue for structuring differential curricula at the doctoral level for research training for academicians versus advanced practitioners. Likewise, the differences are further manifest as these two arms of the profession pursue their respective career interests and credentials. In the end, advanced practitioners contribute to sound policy and to effective clinical interventions, while university faculty tend to contribute increasingly to the experimentally derived knowledge base of the profession and to its growing theoretical foundation.

Rejoinder to Drs. Kreuger & Stretch

Catheleen Jordan

Drs. Kreuger and Stretch argue in support of differential doctoral-level research training for academicians versus practitioners. Their argument is based on their conclusion that the two have different research interests: practitioners contribute to policy and practice, while academicians contribute to the knowledge base and to theory. Practitioners have pragmatic concerns; academicians have creative concerns.

Even if the assumption that practitioners and academicians do different things is true, the research skills required to contribute to policy and practice versus knowledge and theory are the same skills. Additionally, both must be trained in logical-thinking skills to carry out any analysis . . . policy analysis, assessment and intervention, and so forth. Both must be trained in the scientific method in order to be consumers of research and to contribute to their area of expertise.

But alas, life is not so simple! Doctoral-level practitioners involve themselves in academic pursuits, and academicians practice social work. Practitioners become field supervisors or take on other adjunct faculty roles, while academicians become consultants in agencies. Practitioners contribute to the knowledge base when they have the research skills to evaluate agency activities. Academicians contribute to policy with the implications of their theoretical musings.

Social work is an applied discipline and much of the contributions to theory and to knowledge come from practice research.

Finally, to emphasize a major point in my NO argument, there is a core curriculum that should be required of all doctoral students. This includes theory, research, policy, and practice content. Over-specialization and weakening of the research requirements for practitioners leads to narrowness of thinking and rigidity of action. Watering down the research curriculum is anti-intellectual.

NO

CATHELEEN JORDAN

Schools of social work are the chief employers of doctoral graduates (Shore, 1991). However, no single definition of the goals, purposes, and content of social work doctoral education exists at the present time. The confusion in defining doctoral education is compounded by the recent increase in clinically focused programs, established for the purpose of awarding doctorates to social work practitioners. This gives rise to the current debate: should academics and practitioners be channeled into different doctoral-level research streams? This paper will establish that academics and practitioners should *not* receive differential research training.

Types of Doctoral Programs

Shore (1991, p. 232) reviewed three different perspectives of doctoral education programs. The *traditional academic model* emphasizes ''training for scholarship and pursuit of professional knowledge through scientific research.'' The *practice-oriented model* focuses on acquisition of advanced practice skills, while using a ''scholarly and analytic approach to practice.'' Introduced as a combination of the first two models, the *researcher–practitioner model* emphasizes ''preparation for both advanced practice functions and contributions to knowledge based on scientific research.'' Although these three models emphasize research and practice to different degrees, Thomas (cited in Shore, 1991) reported that research continues to be an emphasis in 83 percent of doctoral programs. This indicates a commitment on the part of social work educators to knowledge building and experimentation. Scholarship and knowledge building through the scientific method define the role of the academic. Therefore, the question becomes: should the doctoral education of the practitioner be the same as that of the academic? More specifically, is the same level of proficiency in research also required of the doctoral-level practitioner?

Arguments Supporting Specialization

Thomas reported that 57 percent of doctoral programs report offering training in direct practice. Shore (1991) asked: ''Since the MSW degree is still considered to be the terminal degree for practice, what additional knowledge and skills do doctoral programs provide for practice?'' (p. 232). Levin (1991) suggested that further training in practice skills beyond the M.S.W. level is required, as a two-year M.S.W. program cannot adequately prepare the practitioner to be competitive in the practice community. Levin argued that the practice doctorate assures social workers a ''more powerful sense of professional authority'' (p. 237). He gave as an example clinical psychologists, who he claimed have ''salaries, status, ability to attract new entrants, and social impact . . . greater than our own.''

Arguments favor further specialization in direct practice methods beyond the M.S.W.-level curriculum. One trend has been the emergence of social work doctoral programs that specialize in clinical practice.

Issues of Clinically Oriented Doctoral Programs

The issues discussed regarding clinically oriented social work doctoral programs are reminiscent of the debates between clinical and experimental psychology doctoral educators. Professional psychology schools sought to train students in practice methods, while maintaining the focus on research.

Barlow, Hayes, and Nelson (1984) reported that psychology faculty decided that doctoral students, regardless of their interest in specialization, should receive training in both practice and research. Their assumption was that specialization ''had certain well-known tendencies to produce narrowness of thinking and rigidity of action'' (p. 17). Stricker (cited in Barlow, Hayes, and Nelson [1984]), in commenting on the clinical psychologist's need for research, said ''the lack of research activity by Ph.D. psychologists was a social and professional tragedy'' (p. 18) and what is needed is a ''clinical psychologist who could solve significant problems, devise new techniques, and evaluate both these new procedures as well as adaptations of older ones'' (p. 18).

Further, Barlow, Hayes, and Nelson (1984) identified the ''scientist–practitioner gap.'' The authors acknowledged that the traditional reasons for emphasizing research—being a consumer of research, adding to the body of knowledge with original research, and evaluating programs—are important. However, problems with integration of research and practice occur in clinically oriented schools because of the perceived lack of relevance of the research curriculum to practice settings. Though committed to research, programs don't offer the details of how to make research applicable to practice. Barlow, Hayes, and Nelson (1984) praised the efforts of Jayaratne and Levy, social work scholars who published a book explaining how to integrate science and practice.

The Problems of Specialization

A further issue is the fear that specialization in practice methodologies will endanger the unique professional identity of social work. Shore (1991) suggested that to train students only in counseling, ignoring the ''broader social welfare system'' is to ''water down the role of social work'' (p. 231). Specht (1991) equated the move toward social work private practice as a move away from social work and toward psychotherapy. His criticisms may be applied to clinically oriented social work doctoral programs. Specht suggested that focusing social workers' training in psychotherapeutic methodologies removes them from the social-context orientation that is unique to the social work profession. Specialization also may remove students from a social work research orientation. According to Specht, a profession ''should develop a body of knowledge and skill to carry out a unique and significant social mission'' (p. 231). Doctoral-level social workers have been charged with this mission. Shore (1991) stated that the ''justification for doctoral education in social work is to contribute to the profession, to build knowledge and theory so that we can be more effective'' (p. 240). Interestingly, Levin, a vocal proponent for the social work clinical doctorate is aware of the dangers of over-specializing. He stated that ''scholarship and research . . . makes for more effective clinicians and that is why I want it included as a central part of a clinical doctorate'' (1991, p. 240).

Therefore, a core curriculum content, which is required of academics and practitioners alike, does exist. Barlow, Hayes, and Nelson (1984) concluded that courses needed by all students include policy and research, as well as practice courses. Additionally, theory must not be separate from application, just as science must not be separate from practice. So the issue becomes how to integrate research with practice in a meaningful way, not whether to do away with research altogether.

Recommendations

Doctoral programs should continue to emphasize traditional doctoral education consisting of scholarship and knowledge building. Specialization may be obtained through other methods, such as a clinical internship for those who wish to specialize further in clinical methodology (Shore, 1991). Patchner (cited in Shore, 1991) recommended that doctoral programs include research, practice, or teaching practica. A curriculum that includes theory, practice, policy, and research assures that doctoral education will meet its purpose, of creating scholars with the knowledge to contribute to the social work profession. At the same time, students who so desire may specialize in advanced, applied clinical methodology.

Alternate research methodologies, such as single-subject designs, that close the gap between science and practice also are recommended (Barlow, Hayes, &

Nelson, 1984). This would ensure that doctoral-level students will be trained in research methodologies that are relevant to the practice setting.

Doctorally educated academics and practitioners, well trained in the scientific method, will strengthen social work as a discipline. In conclusion, *no,* we should not have different doctoral-level research training streams for those who seek to engage in academia and those who seek to engage in practice.

References

Barlow, D., Hayes, S., & Nelson, R. (1984). *The scientist practitioner: Research and accountability in clinical and educational settings.* New York: Pergamon Press.

Levin, A. (1991). Point/Counterpoint: Is there a role for clinical doctoral education? Yes! *Journal of Social Work Education, 27*(3): 235–238.

Shore, B. (1991). Point/Counterpoint: Is there a role for clinical doctoral education? No! *Journal of Social Work Education, 27*(3): 231–235.

Specht, H. (1991). Point/Counterpoint: Should training for private practice be a central component of social work education? No! *Journal of Social Work Education, 27*(2): 102–107.

Rejoinder to Dr. Jordan

Larry W. Kreuger
John J. Stretch

We agree with Dr. Jordan's assertion that there is currently "no single definition of the goals, purposes, and content of social work doctoral education . . . " We further agree that there is " . . . confusion in defining doctoral education . . . " We part company with Dr. Jordan, however, on drawing the conclusion from this lack of consensus that there is no difference between advanced practitioners–policymakers and academicians in their need for research training at the doctoral level.

Despite some initially interesting and well known observations on the present development of doctoral education in social work, Dr. Jordan fails to convince us of the validity of a generalist research-training approach, given the two different functional levels required of doctorally trained leaders of our profession, namely, advanced practice/policy making and academia.

In defense of no differentiation of required research training for advanced practitioners, policymakers and academicians, Dr. Jordan presents a brief review of different types of doctoral programs. The remainder of her exposition discusses the strengths and weaknesses of a hotly debated issue in the profession, which incidentally is focused mostly at the masters-degree level, on the problems of over-specialization.

Dr. Jordan fails to connect, however, on how such observations on this debate are central to the issue of the critical differential roles and research and publishing responsibilities that are of the essence in academic settings. Thus, our argument that academicians have a uniquely different set of organizational expectations regarding role boundaries has not been effectively countered by the arguments that Dr. Jordan sets forth about advanced practice.

In our respective positions as academicians, we have been pained to witness many otherwise competent teachers fail to attain advancement and tenure because of insufficient grounding in complex research methodologies and quantitative and qualitative analysis. Without these essential tools for engaging in rigorous research and the publications that normally follow, many do not attain credible levels of academic prominence and thus find their careers hopelessly truncated. Our position is simply that advanced doctoral-level practitioners/policymakers are not expected to publish, nor are they held by their colleagues to rigid institutional standards for research productivity and the distribution of knowledge. Nonacademicians may be adequately prepared for advanced practice/policymaking, but most are not also institutionally required to participate in the research/publication competition so necessary for survival in an academic sense.

If in the future, the preparatory requirements for advanced practice and policy development demand the same caliber of empirical investigation and production of knowledge as prerequisites for individual advancement, we might be persuaded by the general thrust of Dr. Jordan's reflections. Because this is not the current case, nor does it appear it will be such in the near future, our stronger argument prevails.

The issue that is under debate—the need for differential research training for academicians and practitioners—seems to us to have been missed by Dr. Jordan as she concludes " . . . doctoral-level students will be trained in research methodologies that are relevant to the *practice* setting" (our italics). At no point does Dr. Jordan engage the debatable issue of the relevance of training in the philosophy of science and advanced methodology as background necessary for the complex research methodologies relevant for doctoral students who aspire to succeed in *academic* settings.

Perhaps Dr. Jordan's overemphasis on the practice side of research training, without clear reference to rigorous preparation for future academicians, is a bow to our position that a progressive level of research training is indeed required for university faculty as compared to advanced practitioners/policymakers. *Quod erat demonstrandum.*

DEBATE 18

Are Some Research Methodologies Inherently More Worthy of Professional Endorsement Than Others?

Steven P. Schinke is a professor at Columbia University School of Social Work, where he teaches research methods to doctoral students. His research interests are in the development and testing of interventions to prevent problem behavior and to reduce health risks among adolescents.

William R. Nugent is Associate Professor at the University of Tennessee College of Social Work, where he teaches research and statistics in the M.S.W. and doctoral programs. His research interests include the development and validation of assessment tools, the evaluation of mental-health services, and the development of evaluation research methodology.

YES

STEVEN P. SCHINKE

For social workers to achieve professional recognition, and for social work investigators to have an impact on practice, policy, and the behavioral and social sciences, we must adopt and follow rigorous research standards. Explicitly, those standards express a hierarchy of research methods. Research rigor, therefore, demands that some methods take priority over others. Indeed, to realize the status that we seek within the practice, policy, and research arenas, social workers must eschew certain methodologies altogether. At a future time, when social work is recognized as a legitimate and full partner in the behavioral and social sciences, we can revisit these less preferred methodologies. But until we can hold our own against more established and higher status practitioners, policymakers, and social scientists, we must adhere to respected and exact methods and standards for research.

Against this thematic backdrop, this YES statement affirms the need for a hierarchy of research methods and outlines and illustrates research methodologies that are appropriate for social work. Prior to outlining and illustrating those methodologies, the statement defines what research methodology is and what it aims to accomplish. Whenever possible, examples from social work practice and research are employed to clarify the role of research methods in advancing and edifying the field.

What is research methodology? Put simply, research methodology defines a set of conventionally agreed-upon concepts, principles, and procedures that guide the planning and execution of scientific investigations (Kerlinger, 1986; Kirk, 1982). Scientific investigations, for present purposes, are attempts by social work practitioners, policy analysts, and researchers to evaluate current or planned programs—including client services. Research methodology, therefore, provides the guiding template for such activities as needs assessment, program evaluation, policy analysis, client outcome measurement, and cost-effectiveness analysis. Given its essential role in guiding all evaluation activities, research methodology is of clear importance for social work and for all the professional sciences.

Research methodology then encompasses the following activities: research design, measurement, and data gathering and analysis (Windsor, Baranowski, Clark, & Cutter, 1984). Each of these activities is necessary in most evaluation enterprises; yet, alone, none of the activities is sufficient for evaluation. To understand how the research methodology steps of design, measurement, and data gathering and analysis operate in an applied social work setting, consider how the executive director of a child protective services (CPS) agency would go about evaluating one of her agency's programs.

First, the executive director would choose a strategy for the evaluation. This strategy could range from comparing clients who received agency services to those who did not receive the services, to conducting a prospective study of a new program, to making an association between client outcomes and workers' descriptions of the services rendered to those clients. Each of these three strategies represents a different research design. Respectively, the designs are called case-control, experimental, and correlational.

Measurement in research methodology concerns the choice of instruments and procedures for obtaining information. In our example, the executive director of the CPS agency might consider recording information in narrative fashion directly from client records, observing clients and agency workers during routine clinical sessions, or examining police and other records for information on the problems of the agency's clients after they received services. Respectively, these measurement options are called archival recordings, observational measurement, and unobtrusive measurement (Schinke, Orlandi, & Cole, in press).

Data gathering concerns the manner in which the research methodology dictates how measurements are applied. For example, the executive director could gather data by asking clients about services, giving workers forms to complete on their services, or asking hourly help to rate the extent of client outcomes after services are delivered. These data-gathering procedures are respectively called self-report, questionnaire, and rating.

Finally, data analysis in this example could involve examinations of written material, plotted line graphs of client outcomes, or statistical comparisons of outcomes. These data analysis procedures are called content analysis, visual or graphical analysis, and quantitative analysis. From this simple example, we see that many research methodology options are available for social work.

But, not all methodological options are equal. That inequality is a function of three factors. These factors are confidence in the findings yielded by the evaluation, generalizability of the evaluation's findings, and vulnerability of the methodology and evaluation findings to criticism. Confidence in the findings from an evaluation is determined by the controls engineered into the methodology.

Controls, in turn, are features of the evaluation that methodologically isolate the phenomenon under investigation from other phenomena. For example, in our CPS illustration, controls would involve such considerations as choice of the design, measurement procedures, and data-collection plan. By selecting strategies and procedures that do not lend themselves to outside influence or tampering, the executive director would exert methodological control over the evaluation.

A tactic that would evince low control in this example would involve the interviewing of workers about their past success. Obviously, such a tactic introduces into the evaluation a high degree of subjectivity in assessment, judgment, and conclusion. Greater control would occur if the executive director looked to clients who have received agency services for their impressions. Expectedly, these clients would be less biased by the need to demonstrate that the agency is effective than would the workers.

Generalization of evaluation findings is another sensitive indicator of methodological rigor. If evaluation findings are applicable to other samples that are similar to those involved in an evaluation, the methodologies yielded generalizable results. Thus, findings from the CPS agency study are generalizable to the extent that they apply to other similar agencies.

Generalization is achieved by several methodological principles. These principles are selection of a representative sample; use of unbiased sampling procedures; use of objective measurement tactics; and application of controlled, unbiased data collection methods. Quite simply, all these principles must be in place to achieve generalization. Without the necessary methodological provisions, generalization is limited or nonexistent. Sadly, few evaluations of individual social work agencies or programs can meet generalization criteria and thus are limited in their impact on our field or on large arenas of social and behavioral science.

Vulnerability to criticism may seem to lack the specificity of the other criteria for determining methodological rigor. But, evidence of this criterion is prevalent in the lack of status and dissemination of social work research and evaluation efforts. That evidence often appears in the absence of published findings from social work research. The publication process thus serves as an effective vehicle for criticism. Because journal articles are invariably subjected to anonymous review by a panel of peers prior to acceptance for publication, criticism frequently attends the review process.

Heavily criticized reports, not surprisingly, do not usually find their way into publication. Rather, the authors of the reports are informed that the journal cannot publish the evaluation because of its many weaknesses. Vulnerability to criticism at the publication stage or at any advanced stage of an evaluation is difficult to reduce once methodological plans and procedures are in place. Consequently, the best evaluations are planned mindful of the inevitability of criticism at some future time. By preparing for criticism, the evaluator can build in to the study sufficient methodological rigor to withstand reasonable attacks on the aforementioned grounds of control, confidence, and generalizability.

Having this understanding of research methodology and how it is strengthened and weakened, the central question may be approached. What methodological considerations are necessary for social work to advance the field, gain respect, and compete effectively with other behavior and social sciences practice and research fields? The answer to this question lies in concepts and constructs of methodological rigor. Accordingly, the remainder of this YES statement will define and illustrate methodological rigor.

Methodological rigor is accomplished by a careful design, reliable and valid measurements, unbiased data collection procedures, and quantitative analyses. When each of these elements is present in an evaluation, it has research rigor. A careful design is one that controls competing explanations for the phenomenon under investigation. Often, that control comes from the use of comparison and control groups, sampling representative units (e.g., clients, workers, programs, policies) relevant to the investigation, and the use of tactics that limit bias. Such tactics include randomization, matching, and any procedure that reduces the likelihood of systematic influences toward or away from a particular foregone conclusion.

Reliable and valid measurements are those that have, been shown through prior work to obtain data that are free from major biases and that accurately portray the phenomenon under examination. Frequently, these measures come from the published literature and from other research. But, social workers can freely develop their own measures if they undertake the necessary psychometric procedures to test the measures for reliability and validity.

Unbiased data collection procedures are those absent of influences. In assessing the sources of such influences, evaluators must consider those responsible for data collection, the objects of data collection, and the collection procedures *per se*. Unbiased collection procedures then remove or reduce greatly any subjective influences. Illustrative of unbiased data collection procedures are those that keep data collectors unaware of or blind to the objectives of the evaluation and thereby ensure that anyone else engaging in the same data collection procedures would achieve the same results as the original data collector.

Quantitative analyses, the final component that designates methodological rigor, involves the use of conventional statistics in evaluating data obtained in the investigation. Those statistics, including tests, correlations, and other associations, enable evaluators to rule out the likelihood that chance alone accounted for differences seen in the data. Thus, quantitative analyses allow us to determine empirically the probability of what the evaluation findings show. By subjecting all data from social work research to quantitative analyses, we complete the process of ensuring maximum methodological rigor over every evaluation that we undertake.

In conclusion, this statement argues that social work as a profession and as a behavioral and social science will not achieve its full potential as a contributor of truth, wisdom, and useful services and information unless it adopts standards of rigorous research methods. Indeed, our field will never advance as a viable and persuasive force in society unless we introduce such rigor into every serious evaluation undertaken. By neglecting the tools of science in our research, we will relegate ourselves and our profession to second-class status relative to other practice fields in the human-services and behavioral and social sciences. By adopting and systematically applying rigorous research methods, we will face no limit to what we accomplish as a profession.

References

Kerlinger, F. N. (1986). *Foundations of behavioral research* (3rd ed.). New York: Holt, Rinehart and Winston.

Kirk, Roger E. (1982). *Experimental design: Procedures for the behavioral sciences* Belmont, CA: Brooks/Cole Publishing.

Schinke, S. P., Orlandi, M. A., & Cole, K. C. (in press). Boys and girls clubs in public housing projects: Prevention services for youth at risk. *Journal of Community Psychology.*

Windsor, R. A., Baranowski, T., Clark, N., & Cutter, G. (1984). Evaluation of health promotion and education programs. Palo Alto, CA: Mayfield Publishing.

Rejoinder to Dr. Schinke

William R. Nugent

Dr. Schinke argues that social work interventions and programs must be evaluated and that these evaluations must be conducted using the most rigorous scientific methods possible. Valid and reliable measures must be used and designs controlling for as many threats to internal validity as possible employed.

I agree. The interventions that social workers use must be evaluated for their effectiveness. Further, the designs used must give as much information as possible about the impact of the intervention program. I agree wholeheartedly with Dr. Schinke on these points.

It is a long and inaccurate leap, however, to generalize from this to the assertion that, say, experimental research methods are inherently superior to all other research methods and that the profession should endorse these methods over others. Social work is a multifaceted, diverse profession that is concerned with a wide range of human problems. While intervention and program evaluation are critical research needs, they are by no means the only ones. Other types of research need to be conducted and these endeavors require methods other than experimental.

For example, antisocial behavior in children is a major problem. Somewhere between one third to one half of all out-patient clinic referrals for children are because of antisocial behavior problems. Further, antisocial child behavior is relatively stable and predictive of a host of problems later in adult life. Effective intervention and preventive programs are greatly needed, but no effective programs have yet been developed (Kazdin, 1987). Thus, experimental evaluation research on possible intervention programs in this area is but one type of research that is needed.

If evaluation research using experimental methods were to be given preferential endorsement over other methods and approaches, much needed research likely might not happen. If such a preferential endorsement had occurred in the past, many important discoveries might not have been made, such as the coercive family interaction sequences described by Patterson (1982).

Family violence, verbal and nonverbal, is another critically important social problem area. If experimental, intervention-evaluation research had been given preferential endorsement over other research approaches, our current knowledge base would be much poorer. For example, the evidence suggesting that verbal abuse has more deleterious effects than physical abuse might not have been discovered (Straus, Gelles, and Steinmetz, 1980). Indeed, it might be impossible to find such relationships with experimental methods because of the enormous ethical issues involved.

The need for rigor in research should not be equated with any one particular research approach, and, therefore, implying that that particular methodology is superior to others. All research approaches require the rigorous, systematic application of specific methods, both quantitative and qualitative. The profession should not endorse preferentially one set of methods over another; no research methodology is inherently superior to another. Each set of methods has been created to provide tentative answers to particular types of research questions. These questions are often different, yet they are also very often related to one another. To focus on one type of question to the exclusion or detriment of another can actually hinder the investigation of the research problem of interest.

References

Kazdin, A. E. (1987). *Conduct disorders of childhood and adolescence.* Beverly Hills, CA: Sage.
Patterson, G. R. (1982). *Coercive family process.* Eugene, OR: Castalia.
Strauss, M., Gelles, R., & Steinmetz, S. K. (1980). *Behind closed doors: Violence in american families.* New York: Doubleday.

NO

William R. Nugent

I have been asked to respond to the question: Is there a hierarchy of research methodologies such that some are inherently more worthy of professional endorsement? A key word is "inherently." *Websters Ninth New Collegiate Dictionary* (1990) defines "inherent" to mean: "involved in the constitution or essential character of something . . . : Intrinsic." The question of focus thus implies that there is a hierarchy of research methodologies, such that some methods or approaches are *intrinsically* superior to others and, hence, deserve preferential endorsement by the profession of social work. I have elected to take the NO position in this debate.

First, it is implied that there exists some set of standards or criteria against which different research approaches are compared. However, the questions fail to specify these criteria. Research methodologies are sets of approaches and methods for conducting inquiry. We want answers to important questions about social phenomena. Thus, the merit of a research methodology must be considered within the context in which it arises. Therefore, we might ask: are some research methods superior to others *when used to provide answers to important research questions?* Let us consider this recast of the question under debate.

There are at least two ways in which this question can be considered. First, for a given research question or problem, is there a hierarchy of research methodologies, such that some methods better provide answers than others? That is, within the context of specific research problems and the canons of scientific logic, are there research methods that are more appropriate than others for providing answers? For this context, it might at first seem obvious that there *are* research approaches superior to others. For example, if one wants to know whether or not treatment *X* causes a decrease in both the intensity and frequency of spouse abuse, then, according to the canons of scientific logic, an experiment obviously would be superior to, say, a case study, for providing evidence of causality. The experimental approach offers greater control over threats to internal validity than does the case study. This position seems nothing more than an applicatioon of the old admonition to fit the research method to the research question, and not vice versa.

In one sense I agree . . . an experiment can certainly provide evidence concerning the causal relationship between dependent and independent variables. Moreover, it will do so with a high probability of greater internal validity than will a case study. However, we must keep in mind that ultimately internal validity is established by logically ruling out threats to a causal relationship (Cook & Campbell, 1979):

> Estimating the internal validity of a relationship is a deductive process in which the investigator has to systematically think through how each of the internal validity threats may have influenced the data. Then, the investigator has to examine the data to test which relevant threats can be ruled out. (p. 55)

When it gets right down to it, internal validity is established by hard thinking. An experiment, if properly conducted, can greatly aid in this process. All other things equal, an experiment, will, most of the time, provide greater control over threats to internal validity than will a case study . . . but not necessarily always. A well conceived and planned case study can provide evidence for causality on par with that of an experiment, as Kazdin (1981) has shown. No design or analysis procedures can ever substitute for sound reasoning, as Platt (1963) so aptly pointed out. Thus, the experiment is not *inherently* superior to other approaches.

Further, we must be careful not to view the experiment conducted as a single fixed event in time that is independent of either the research that has gone on before or the research that will follow. An experiment that investigates a possible causal relationship between two variables is a stage in an on-going dynamic chain of investigation. Prior inquiry has been conducted that made the experiment possible. Without this prior inquiry, the experiment could not have been done. Needs had to be identified, perhaps requiring case studies, naturalistic observations, and/or surveys. Constructs had to be created and refined, again, perhaps requiring case studies. Measurement procedures had to be developed, requiring psychometric research and development. Perhaps associational information was required before an hypothesis requiring experimental investigation could even be formulated, requiring correlational studies. Perhaps methodological research needed to be done to help create important methods that were required for the experiment to even be conceived. After the experiment, field studies might be needed to investigate the generalizability of results of the experiment to various practice settings. To say that the experiment is inherently superior in some way to these other research endeavors is to ignore the dynamic processes within which the conduct of social work research is imbedded. All parts of the chain are crucial. If one link is weak, the chain is weak and the value of the experiment to the profession is compromised. Thus, to declare the experiment "superior" and, hence, more worthy of endorsement in social work research than other methodologies would be to undercut the power and value of the very methodology we are praising. In a sense, by declaring that all methods have their place and are important in social work research, we create an interlocking dynamic network that strengthens and reinforces each set of methods. To mix metaphors, we inject strength into the chain. The arguments developed above are not just appropriate to considerations of experiments. They can be applied to all methodologies.

In a more general sense, to suggest that some methodologies are superior to others implies that some so-called types of knowledge are superior to others, and more important to social work, as suggested by Tripodi (1985). If some types of knowledge are superior to others and more important to the profession, then certainly the methods that best provide this type of knowledge should be differentially endorsed. But what type of knowledge can be held as superior to others and thereby more important to the profession? Some might say that cause–effect knowledge holds this distinction. To make this claim, however, again ignores the dynamic processes of knowledge development discussed above. Further, to claim any form of knowledge is superior to others for the profession ignores the tremendous diversity of activity engaged in by social workers. To claim one form of knowledge superior to others, and therefore more worthy of endorsement, would hinder the development of the tremendous diversity of knowledge required by social workers for practice.

Another argument might be that some research approaches are inherently weak relative to others and that little of importance for the profession can come from that methodology. For example, some might say that experimental research is far stronger than naturalistic observations . . . and that naturalistic observations can provide little in the way of important information for the profession relative to experiments. History shows the fallaciousness of such a position. Charles Darwin used five years of naturalistic observation during his voyage on the *HMS Beagle* to develop his theory of evolution, a theory that has had immeasurable impact on thinking and research over the last century. The results of Darwin's naturalistic study can hardly be called unimportant.

It seems to me that we must be very respectful of the richness and complexity of the physical and social world in which we live. We must also be humble and cautious in our estimation of what we can and cannot learn. To begin placing various "types" of knowledge above others, and to place various types of research methodology above others, moves away from humility and caution and towards a brashness that invites error. All methodologies have limitations. All methodologies have strengths. The task for social work researchers is *not* to decide which methodology is superior to others. Rather, it is to learn how to use various methods to complement each other, using the strengths of some to make up for the limitations of others. Further, we must never lose sight of the dynamic social process that is itself social work research. All methodologies play a part in this dynamic process, and the act of elevating some to higher status than others may well hinder the optimal functioning of this dynamic system.

I rest my case.

References

Cook, T., & Campbell, D. (1979). *Quasi-Experimentation: Design & analysis issues for field settings.* Boston, MA: Houghton Mifflin.

Kazdin, A. (1981). Drawing valid inferences from case studies. *Journal of Consulting and Clinical Psychology, 49,* 183–192.

Platt, J. (1963). Strong inference. *Science, 146,* 347–353.

Tripodi, T. (1985). Research designs. In R. M. Grinnell, Jr. (Ed.), *Social Work Research and Evaluation* (2nd ed.; pp. 231–259). Itasca, IL: F. E. Peacock Publishers.

Woolf, Henry B., et al. (eds.). (1990). Webster's Ninth New Collegiate dictionary. Springfield, MA: Merriam-Webster.

Rejoinder to Dr. Nugent

Steven P. Schinke

Dr. Nugent provides a reasoned argument regarding the lack of superiority of various research methodologies. In making his argument, Dr. Nugent weights carefully and appropriately issues of causality, association, and correlation, as they relate to the topic of superiority among research methods. Dr. Nugent devotes considerable attention to the concept of internal validity and how this concept is affected by various methods. Among other assertions, he claims that internal validity is established by hard thinking. Dr. Nugent invokes the words of Cook and Campbell (1979) to strengthen his contention about the inherent logic of internal validity.

Correctly, Dr. Nugent notes that experimental methodology represents "a stage in an ongoing dynamic chain of investigation." Early stages in this dynamic chain include, according to Dr. Nugent, case studies, naturalistic observations, and surveys. Further activities that need to occur before a experiment can be carried out, by Dr. Nugent's account, are the development of psychometrically sound instruments, construct development, and other such procedures.

My opponent additionally calls to task arguments favoring a hierarchy of research methodology by noting the fallaciousness of positions that favor experimental designs over such methods as naturalistic observation. In so doing, he reminds us of the importance of Charles Darwin's observations while traveling on the *HMS Beagle* and so discovering, among other things, his theory of evolution. That evidence and most of the material contained in the argument put forth by Dr. Nugent is persuasive and laudatory in inveighing against a hierarchy of research methodology in social work research.

Still—and the intent of Dr. Nugent's positions notwithstanding—to claim that all methodologies have equal strength for our field is, I believe, to do a grave disservice to the advancement of a legitimate, valued, and applied science in social work. Without question, all methodologies have strength. Dr. Nugent and I agree completely on that point. But equal strength does not connote equal merit. Dr. Nugent admits that various research methods assume different stages in the scientific process. That position seems not incompatible with the notion of hierarchy of methods, with some methods assuming a higher stage than others.

Dr. Nugent's major complaint, according to his statement, with a hierarchy of methods is with the ultimate superiority of experimental designs. Extending his logic of equal strength and importance among all methods, we conclude that experimental methodology is no better than a case study or naturalistic observation. Extending further that logic, we would advise the practitioner or investigator that carrying out one methodology is just as good as carrying out another relative to the value and contribution of the research.

In reality, that advice is wrong. Many of the "lower order," if you will, designs simply cannot address and answer the questions that can be posed of experimental designs. Reviewers for the better journals and for governmental grants certainly do not equate research performed through various methodologies as equal, if we construe what gets published and funded as evidence of the ranking decisions of manuscript and grant reviewers, respectively. Simply put, findings that have emerged from an experimental design carry weight, are accorded status, and influence the development of scientific field.

For social work to compete in the behavioral and social sciences arena, we must recognize and embrace a hierarchy of research methodologies. We must then choose the methods with the greatest rigor and the most payoffs and use them to research problems that are important to us and to society. If we do not, members of other disciplines will quickly fill that need and will eclipse us in science and will preempt us in their evident value to addressing real world problems.

The choice is ours: we can continue to promote such methods as the case study as if it were a rigorous research method and thereby relegate ourselves to answering largely unimportant questions. Or, we can adopt conventionally accepted and truly rigorous methods of research and compete successfully for resources, attention, and prestige in the behavioral and social sciences. By deciding which methodological course we intend to follow and aggressively following that choice, we will change the course of our field and the place that it holds in the behavioral sciences, in shaping public policy, and in answering the pressing questions that face all the human services.

In the social work research arena, no other choice rivals the selection of research methodology in the implications and impact that choice will exert on the field and on the consumers of our findings for many years to come. Consequently, a dialogue between the proponents and opponents of a hierarchy of research methodology has great value. Although Dr. Nugent and I differ in our opinions about that hierarchy, I am sure that we are of one mind about the merits of debating this issue in a scholarly, dignified, and thoughtful manner.

Debate 19

Are Effect Sizes Better Than Traditional Hypothesis Testing for Evaluating Research Findings?

John G. Orme is an associate professor at the University of Maryland School of Social Work, where he teaches introductory and advanced research methodology and statistics courses. His current research and writing interests are in measurement development, applied statistical issues, and single-system design methodology.

Craig Winston LeCroy is an associate professor at Arizona State University School of Social Work, where he teaches direct-practice courses. His research interests include child and adolescent mental health, juvenile corrections, and program evaluation.

YES

John G. Orme

In this paper, I will argue the YES position. When the traditional approach to determine whether a relationship exists between variables is used, a null hypothesis is formulated typically, and the null hypothesis is either rejected in favor of the alternative hypothesis, or not rejected.

Another approach uses the effect size (ES). An ES is a measure of the strength of a relationship between variables or the degree of departure from the null hypothesis. There are a variety of different ways to quantify ES (e.g., r, d-index), but ES will be discussed only in general terms here.

Effect sizes, bracketed by confidence intervals, when appropriate, are better than traditional hypothesis tests for evaluating, interpreting, and planning research in social work (e.g., Hunter & Schmidt, 1990; Rosenthal, 1991). These two approaches provide equivalent information about the statistical significance of a relationship between variables, as detailed below. However, an ES bracketed by confidence intervals provides a more informative description of the relationship between variables than traditional hypothesis tests. In addition, in order to integrate existing research, and to plan future research, it is necessary to conceptualize the relationship between variables in terms of an ES. The traditional approach to hypothesis testing, by itself, is insufficient for these purposes.

Determining Statistical Significance

The statistical significance of a relationship between variables can be determined using either a hypothesis test, or using an ES bracketed by a confidence interval. For example, an investigator may test a nondirectional hypothesis concerning the product–moment correlation between two variables; 90 subjects are sampled. The null hypothesis states that the population correlation equals zero, and the alternative hypothesis states that it does not equal zero. With an obtained correlation of .20 ($F = 3.67$, $df = 1,88$, $p = .06$), and alpha $\leq .05$, the null hypothesis is not rejected.

A 95% confidence interval constructed around the obtained correlation provides equivalent results about statistical significance. In this example the 95% confidence interval ranges from –.01 to .39. If zero falls within this interval, which is the case here, the null hypothesis would not be rejected. If zero does not fall within this interval, the null hypothesis would be rejected.

Describing a Relationship

An ES bracketed by a confidence interval provides a more informative description of the relationship between variables than a test of a null hypothesis. When a null hypothesis is tested, it is either rejected in favor of the alternative hypothesis or not rejected. A dichotomous decision is made that provides minimal and possibly misleading information about the relationship between variables. For example, in the above case of the failure to reject the null hypothesis of a zero correlation in the population, little information is provided about the likely value of the population correlation.

In contrast, an ES provides an estimate of the actual strength of the relationship in the population (i.e., the parameter), not just whether the parameter is some non-zero value. The confidence interval for the ES provides an interval of values within which the population value of the correlation (i.e., the parameter) likely falls. In the above example the parameter estimate is .20; the population value of the correlation probably falls somewhere between −.01 and .39. A more informative picture of the likely relationship between variables is provided by the ES bracketed by the confidence interval than by a knowledge of whether the null hypothesis was rejected.

Integrating Existing Research

An ES provides a better basis for comparing and combining existing research than a test of a null hypothesis because recommended measures of ES are not, in general, biased by sample size. In contrast, rejection of the null hypothesis depends in large part on sample size.

Inconsistent rejection of the null hypothesis across studies may be solely the result of sample size differences among studies. For example, suppose that two studies are conducted to test the null hypothesis that the correlation between two variables equals zero, and the two studies are equivalent in every way except that one study samples 90 subjects and the other samples 100 subjects. If both studies obtain a correlation of .20, the null hypothesis is rejected (alpha ≤ .05, two-tailed) in the study with N = 100 ($F = 4.08$, $df = 1{,}98$, $p = .04$), and not rejected in the study with N = 90 ($F = 3.67$, $df = 1{,}88$, $p = .06$). Results of the two studies are "inconsistent," despite both demonstrating identical correlations.

Comparison across the two studies of the 95% confidence intervals for the respective ESs would more accurately highlight the consistency of the results. The 95% confidence interval ranges from −.01 to .39 for the study with N = 90, and from +0.00 to .38 for the study with N = 100.

The use of ESs is preferable to traditional hypothesis testing even in the unlikely event that sample size is consistent across studies being compared and integrated. If the sample size is consistently small, important relationships will not be detected. If the sample size is consistently large, small and perhaps trivial relationships will be detected. The quantification and aggregation of ESs across studies, although not without limitations, provides a more accurate characterization of the relationship between particular variables across studies.

Effect sizes are preferable to the results of hypothesis tests for comparing and combining existing research for another reason. A hypothesis test, at best, indicates whether a relationship exists, but not how much of a relationship exists. A study in which the null hypothesis is rejected with r = .20 is treated identically as a study in which the null hypothesis is rejected with r = .80, even though most investigators would not consider these results equivalent.

Planning Future Research

A study designed to test a hypothesis cannot be planned appropriately without a consideration of ES. The reason for this is simple: a study designed to test a hypothesis should employ a statistical power analysis to determine the required sample size, and this requires that the minimum ES of interest be specified (Cohen, 1988). The minimum ES of interest may be: 1) estimated from previous relevant research (another reason to compute and report ESs); 2) selected to indicate a population effect that would have either practical or theoretical significance; or, if the previous two strategies are not feasible, 3) selected from suggested conventional definitions of "small," "medium," and "large" ESs. In any case, though, the necessary sample size to test a hypothesis cannot be determined unless the smallest ES of interest is specified, and the necessary sample size will vary considerably depending on the ES specified.

References

Cohen, J. (1988). *Statistical power analysis for the behavioral sciences* (2nd ed.). Hillsdale, NJ: Lawrence Erlbaum Associates.

Hunter, J. E. & Schmidt, F. L. (1990). *Methods of meta-analysis: Correcting error and bias in research findings.* Newbury Park, CA: Sage.

Rosenthal, R. (1991). *Meta-analytic procedures for social research* (rev. ed.). Newbury Park, CA: Sage.

Rejoinder to Dr. Orme

Craig Winston LeCroy

Dr. Orme believes that ESs are useful measures for social work research. His support of this approach rests on the idea that more information can be obtained from effect measures and that such measures are not biased by sample size. On both accounts, he is mistaken.

Interestingly, ESs contain the same information about the data that the F statistic contains. Without going into great detail, it should be noted that the magnitude of effect and the F statistic "can be written as functions of each other" (Murray & Dosser, 1987, p. 70). An ES does not provide information beyond that provided by the analysis of variance (see Murray & Dosser [1987]) and is not independent of sample size. If researchers like Dr. Orme would like to measure a "practical effect," they might consider making the alpha level quite small, as suggested by Murry and Dosser. This would protect against committing a Type I error. Of course, there are problems with this approach—such as, how small should the alpha be? But this is no different from questions, such as, what is a small effect size? More important are the problems with interpretation that Dr. Orme has ignored.

Interpretations using ESs are often very misleading. Consider the following example (Rosenthal & Rubin, 1979). We design an experiment assigning half of our patients in a medical study to a new treatment and half to standard medical treatment. The dependent outcome measure is "alive or dead after one year." Suppose that 30 percent of the patients live under the standard medical treatment while under the new treatment 70 percent of the patients live. Wow! That would be considered a big success. However, the r^2 for these data is a paltry .16. Yet, one is hard pressed to conclude that treatment is unimportant—effect size estimation can be a seriously deceptive measure. Also, as noted in my NO paper, a gross misinterpretation can take place about an effect because the levels of the independent variable are under the control of the experimenter. As a result, the size of the effect is also partially controlled by the researcher. This can lead to problems in interpretation regarding how practical or important an effect really is.

Particularly problematic with Dr. Orme's suggestion for the use of ESs is his statement that "measures of ES are not, in general, biased by sample size." Several studies have found this statement simply inaccurate. Results from a study of the sampling characteristics of two measures of ES found that there are indeed problems with small sample sizes (Carroll & Nordholm, 1975). The standard errors of ES measures were sizable, which raises doubts about their utility. Another study (Lane & Dunlap, 1978) found that there was severe overestimation of experimental effects with small sample size. They concluded their findings "support the conclusion that published estimates of magnitude contain little or no valid information" (p. 111). These results are critical because effect sizes are often misinterpreted to have little sensitivity to sample size.

Even if researchers could learn to interpret the effect size properly, it is doubtful it would be a useful measure because social work researchers do not know what their major independent variables are (Dooling & Danks, 1975). As a result, experiments are limited to hypothesis testing, as opposed to parameter estimation. Should we go "beyond tests of significance?" My conclusion is no different than that arrived at by Dooling and Danks more than fifteen years ago. Our research questions seek to answer the question: "Does this variable have an effect?" Tests of significance can answer this question. However, when we ask, "What is the strength of the relationship between the two variables?" a magnitude of effect estimate will only mislead the researcher.

References

Carroll, R. M., & Nordholm, L. A. (1975). Sampling characteristics of Kelley's and Hays'. *Educational and Psychological Measurement, 35,* 541–554.

Dooling, J. D., & Danks, J. H. (1975). Going beyond tests of significance: Is psychology ready? *Bulletin of Psychonomic Society, 5,* 15–17.

Lane, D. M., & Dunlap, W. P. (1978). Estimating effect size: Bias resulting from the significance criterion in editorial decisions. *British Journal of Mathematical and Statistical Psychology, 31,* 107–112.

Rosenthal, R., & Rubin, D. B. (1979). A note of percent variance explained as a measure of the importance of effects. *Journal of Applied Social Psychology, 9,* 395–396.

NO

Craig Winston LeCroy

The researchers of today are much more sophisticated in their use of statistical methods. Along with that use comes misuse and misunderstandings about a number of fundamental issues concerning the application of statistics. Cowger (1984) suggests that these abuses form a scientific ritualism, in contrast to thoughtful and appropriate use of statistics. Researchers all too often accept statistical methods as routine, without understanding the limitations that are inherent in the application of the methods.

Such misunderstanding is portrayed poignantly in the use of statistical methods that attempt to measure the "strength" of a relationship. Increasingly, researchers have been called to incorporate this measure into their analysis. An influential source came from a statistics book common to most of us, Hays's *Statistics for Psychologists* (1963). In his book, Hays notes, "The occurrence of a significant result leads to the inference that some associate exists, but in no sense does this mean that an important degree of association necessarily exists. Conversely, evidence of a strong statistical association can occur in data even when the results are not significant" (p. 342). Estimates of strength of the relationship are based on the correlation ratio computed on a sample or some of the other estimators of the population correlation ratio. Originally, a measure known as the correlation ratio or n^2 (eta squared) was developed to give a descriptive index of the total relationship into a single factor, fixed effect design. This is in contrast to r^2, which only indicates a linear relationship. Kelley (1935) proposed another estimate of the population correlation ratio, e^2 (epsilon squared), recommended by Cohen (1965). Hays (1963) derived another measure of the strength of relationship between a categorical variable X and the dependent variable Y, referred to as w^2 (omega squared).

Although there is merit in the attempt to derive measures of strength, I take a position in opposition of their use. I do not fault the reasoning provided by Hays or the computational formulas. Indeed, knowledge of the strength of the association would add new information that is not available with the use of traditional significance testing. The critical problem with measures of association or effect sizes is their interpretation and their likely misinterpretation. Furthermore, the current state of social work research speaks against the use of such statistics in most instances.

Serious problems arise when w^2 is used within a fixed-effects design because there is no naturally occurring population corresponding to the various levels of treatment groups. As Dooling and Danks (1975) aptly point out, the selection of the levels of the independent variable is not sufficiently well defined to permit reasonable inferences about the strength of that independent variable's effect. In many (if not most) research designs employed by social work researchers, the researcher is interested in whether or not a particular independent variable has any effect at all on the dependent variable. Therefore, two or more levels of the independent variable are selected for manipulation. However, factors controlling the selection are not always evident (Dooling & Danks, 1975; Keppel, 1991). The design of the experiment may lead to various conditions: extreme values selected to maximize differences, little choice due to replication, or constraints regarding the ability to manipulate the variables. In none of these common situations did the researcher randomly select the level of the independent variable, therefore, the fixed-effects model is the appropriate design for the analysis. As a result, "w^2 appropriately describes only the strength of the *particular* levels of the independent variable on the dependent variable, not the influence of the independent variable *in general*" (Dooling & Danks, 1975, p. 16). What's interesting about this example is how clearly one can see that the strength of the effect is to some extent under the direct control of the researcher (Keppel, 1991). The researcher who chooses extreme values for the independent variable will likely obtain strong effects, another researcher who chooses related values of the independent variable is likely to end up with a smaller w^2. Studies that may differ with regard to heterogeneity of their samples or in the reliability of their measures may result in different effect sizes not as a result of differentially effective treatments, but because these other factors vary. How can we make a correct interpretation of w^2? We can't, because the underlying population of values on the dependent variable has not been randomly selected. Thus, one of the serious limitations of using w^2 is the potential for misinterpretation of their true meaning. As Maxwell, Arvey, and Camp (1981, p. 531) point out, "researchers may derive conclusions as if their measures of association were derived from a random-effects design rather than a fixed-effects design and thus attach more meaning to the measures than is warranted."

Indeed, meaning is difficult to assess when using measures of association. Many experienced researchers do not have an intuitive sense of what "explained variance" means in practical or theoretical terms (Rosenthal & Rubin, 1979). Also, w^2 is misleading as an index of the influence of systematic factors because it underestimates the practical effects of individual influences that can accumulate to produce meaningful outcomes (Abelson, 1985; Rosnow & Rosenthal, 1988). Furthermore, philosophical issues are of importance in defining and interpreting effect sizes. As Krauth (1983) notes, Is an effect size taken to indicate the treatment effect on an individual or typical subject within the population or to indicate the treatment effect on a population as a whole?

Another consideration is that in some situations small values of association may be more important than large values (Keppel, 1991). All too often, large values simply reflect obvious treatment effects, whereas smaller values may reflect important advances in understanding. Clearly, the decision of importance cannot be made exclusively on statistical grounds.

Also problematic with regard to measures of association such as w^2 is that these measures are point estimates and, therefore, ignore the sampling error of the resulting estimate. Carroll & Nordholm (1975) conducted Monte Carlo simulations and found that the standard error of these measures is substantial, particularly when dealing with small sample sizes. This is a serious concern because most of social work research is based on small sample sizes (Orme & Tolman, 1986). Unfortunately, the sample value of w^2 does not reflect the inherent sampling variability. This is critical when there is a statistical test of marginal significance with a small sample size and the researcher pleads for a meaningful treatment effect by reporting a substantial value of w^2 (Maxwell, Arvey, & Camp, 1981).

Some statisticians and researchers suggest w^2 is useful because of two common circumstances. One is when a nonsignificant F is obtained, but there might be a strong relationship present in spite of this. The second circumstance is when a significant F is obtained, but there is interest in determining if the relationship is nonetheless trivial. Research examining these two situations (Carrol & Nordholm, 1975; Murray & Dosser, 1987) reports only moderate utility for these purposes.

In summary, there are serious problems with measures of strength of association because of difficulties in interpretation. This has lead several researchers to conclude, ''published estimates of magnitude of effect, expressed in terms of w^2 or simply as the difference between group means, contain little or no valid information'' (Lane & Dunlap, 1978, p. 111). Carroll and Nordholm (1975, p. 541) reach a similar conclusion: ''It is questionable, however, whether the need for 'practical significance' is best served by estimates of strength of the relationship such as the correlation ratio computed on a sample or the other estimators of the population correlation ratio.'' However, the analysis of data must remain flexible. Information that may be just as meaningful and easier to interpret can result from confidence intervals for mean differences or simple graphic and numerical displays (Maxwell, Avery & Camp, 1981). A flexible and multifaceted approach is needed to fully understand research data.

References

Abelsen, R. P. (1985). A variance explanation paradox: When a little is a lot. *Psychological Bulletin, 97,* 129–133.

Carroll, R. M., & Nordholm, L. A. (1975). Sampling characteristics of Kelley's and Hays.' *Educational and Psychological Measurement, 35,* 541–554.

Cohen, J. (1965). Some statistical issues in psychological research. In B. B. Wolman (ed.). *Handbook of Clinical Psychology* (pp. 95–121) New York: McGraw-Hill.

Cowger, C. D. (1984). Statistical significance tests: Scientific ritualism or scientific method? *Social Service Review, 58,* 358–372.

Dooling, J. D., & Danks, J. H. (1975). Going beyond tests of significance: Is psychology ready? *Bulletin of Psychonomic Society, 5,* 15–17.

Hays, W. L. (1963). *Statistics for psychologists.* New York: Holt, Rinehart & Winston.

Kelley, T. L. (1935). An unbiased correlation ratio measure. *Proceedings of the National Academy of Sciences, 21,* 554–559.

Keppel, G. (1991). *Design and analysis.* Englewood Cliffs, NJ: Prentice-Hall.

Krauth, J. (1983). Nonparametric effects size estimation: A comment on Kraemer and Andrews. *Psychological Bulletin, 94,* 190–192.

Lane, D. M., & Dunlap, W. P. (1978). Estimating effect size: Bias resulting from the significance criterion in editorial decisions. *British Journal of Mathematical and Statistical Psychology, 31,* 107–112.

Maxwell, S. E., Arvey, R. D., & Camp, C. J. (1981). Measures of strength of association: A comparative examination. *Journal of Applied Psychology, 66,* 525–534.

Murray, L. W., & Dosser, D. A., Jr. (1987). How significant is a significant difference? Problems with the measurement of magnitude of effect. *Journal of Counseling Psychology, 34,* 68–72.

Orme, J. G., & Tolman, R. M. (1986). The statistical power of a decade of social work education. *Social Service Review, 60,* 619–632.

Rosenthal, R., & Rubin, D. B. (1979). A note of percent variance explained as a measure of the importance of effects. *Journal of Applied Social Psychology, 9,* 395–396.

Rosnow, R. L., & Rosenthal, R. (1988). Focused tests of significance and effect size estimation in counseling psychology. *Journal of Counseling Psychology, 36,* 203–208.

Rejoinder to Dr. LeCroy

JOHN G. ORME

Dr. LeCroy presents several arguments against the use of ESs. His paper provides some guidance in the interpretation and use of ESs, but not a basis for repudiating their use. There are several reasons for this conclusion.

First, Dr. LeCroy notes that "researchers all too often accept statistical methods as routine without understanding the limitations that are inherent in the application of the methods." He then goes on to note that "such misunderstanding is poignantly portrayed in the use of statistical methods that attempt to measure the 'strength' of a relationship.'' Even if these assertions are accurate, they don't constitute an argument against the use of ES. If they are accurate, they provide a basis for arguing that researchers should be educated better about the limitations and appropriate applications of statistical methods in general and ES in particular.

Second, Dr. LeCroy's argument against ES is illustrated in part by a discussion of the potential limitations and possible misinterpretations of omega squared, one of many ESs (e.g., Cohen, 1988; Hunter & Schmidt, 1990; Rosenthal, 1991). Certainly, this is understandable, given space limitations. However, the potential limitations and possible misinterpretations of omega squared are not common to all ESs. For example, omega squared provides an estimate of explained variance, and Dr. LeCroy cites arguments from Rosenthal that estimates of explained variance can be problematic. However, Rosenthal has presented numerous ESs that are not based on explained variance, and he is, in fact, a major proponent of ES (Rosenthal, 1991).

Third, in addition to arguing against ESs because they can be misinterpreted, Dr. LeCroy asserts that ''the current state of social work research speaks against the use of such statistics in most instances.'' If he means by this that social work researchers are likely to misinterpret and misuse ESs, again I would argue that better education is in order, given the advantages of ESs that I detailed in my YES statement. Beyond the issue of possible misinterpretation and misuse, however, Dr. LeCroy does not provide any explicit basis for this assertion. Only two of his thirteen references are from the social work literature, and one of those references is to an article that I wrote with Tolman, in which we advocated the use of ESs.

Finally, Dr. LeCroy argues that point estimates of ES are misleading because they do not account for sampling error. This is true. It is also true for any type of point estimate, however, and it does not constitute an argument against the use of ESs. Effect sizes can be, and I argue should be, bracketed by confidence intervals in order to characterize the uncertainty in a point estimate due to sampling error.

In conclusion, I agree with Dr. LeCroy that ''a flexible and multifaceted approach is needed to fully understand research data.'' However, ESs bracketed by confidence intervals should be an integral part of this multifaceted approach.

References

Cohen, J. (1988). *Statistical power analysis for the behavioral sciences* (2nd ed.). Hillsdale, NJ: Lawrence Erlbaum Associates.

Hunter, J. E. & Schmidt, F. L. (1990). *Methods of meta-analysis: Correcting error and bias in research findings.* Newbury Park, CA: Sage.

Rosenthal, R. (1991). *Meta-analytic procedures for social research* (rev. ed.). Newbury Park, CA: Sage.

DEBATE 20

Should More Rigorous Quantitative Measurement of Service or Treatment Interventions Be a Part of Agency Evaluation and Research?

Steven L. McMurtry is Associate Professor of Social Work at Arizona State University, where he directs the child-welfare specialization and teaches macro practice and research. His recent research has focused on policies affecting foster children and child victims of sexual abuse. He also recently co-authored *Social Work Macro Practice* with F. Ellen Netting and Peter M. Kettner (White Plains, NY: Longman Publishing Group, 1993).

Kevin Corcoran is a professor in the Graduate School of Social Work at Portland State University, where he teaches courses in clinical social work and research. His M.S.W. and Ph.D. are from the University of Pittsburgh, and he is currently completing a J.D. from the University of Houston. His areas of interest include clinical practice, practice evaluation, measurement, and mediation. He maintains a small private practice in clinical social work and dispute resolution.

YES

STEVEN L. MCMURTRY

Perhaps the best way to defend the YES position is to consider the alternatives. Should we abandon quantitative measurement? Should we use quantitative measures that are less rigorous than those now used? Should we maintain the current rigorousness of the measures that we use, but advance no further? Should we do away with agency-level evaluation and research entirely?

It will be argued here that the answer to each of these questions is no. Social work agencies have made substantial progress in their use of quantitative measures to evaluate services, and there is no reason to believe that this progress should suddenly cease. To explain these assertions, the discussion below will review the rationale for quantitative measurement, highlight promising advances in the measures themselves, and identify means by which they can be more effectively employed in human-service agencies.

The Logic of Quantitative Measurement

There are three basic reasons for emphasizing quantitative measurement of social work interventions—one practical, one professional, and one epistemological. The practical reason is that most people think in terms of quantitative measurement (ranging from automobile gas mileage to the "scale of 1-to-10" attractiveness of a romantic interest), and they tend to accept the validity of such measures. This is also true of funding sources for human-service agencies, as was made all too clear in the accountability movement that began in the late 1960s. It remains true today, and most social work agencies recognize that if they hope to continue providing services they believe are worthwhile, they must be prepared to demonstrate this using quantitative methods. The only thing that has changed is that many funding bodies have become more sophisticated in distinguishing simple "bean-counting" from legitimate measures of service effectiveness, thus, there is likely to be growing pressure not just for more but for better quantitative measurement.

The professional reason for quantitative measurement addresses the fact that agencies need to be able to demonstrate their effectiveness not only for the benefit of funders but also for the benefit of their clients. One aspect of this is noted by Carter (1988) who argues that in the aftermath of the Reagan/Bush years, measurement of outcomes is critical for documenting the effect of budget cuts on clients. Other aspects of the professional need for quantitative measurement are expressed in the "effectiveness-driven management" movement that began in the mid-1980s. As elaborated by Patti (1988) and others, the key to the movement is the notion that management decisions in human-service agencies should be oriented toward maximizing service effectiveness. This means that management is, in turn, dependent on the ability of the agency to accurately evaluate effectiveness. As Hudson (1988) points out, managers must move toward more rather than less rigorous measurement in order to 1) clearly define client problems in a consistent way and 2) monitor change toward resolution of these problems as the means for determining service effectiveness.

Finally, the epistemological argument for quantitative measurement involves the quest for "objective" or mutually observable results. An individual practitioner may be able to make qualitative assessments of a particular client that are both informative and internally consistent when restricted to that client or to that practitioner. However, the same procedures applied to many clients across many practitioners would tend to produce results that are either useless or misleading. This point is addressed by Royse (1992) in his introduction to program evaluation. He argues that the subjectivity of assessment that may be acceptable when evaluating an individual client creates enormous problems when spread across the large number of clients in the course of evaluating entire agency programs. Quantification of measurement promotes standardization of measurement, and this is critical in making macro-level assessments.

Improvements in Quantitative Measures

Though the rationale for the use of quantitative measures of service outcomes in agencies seems persuasive, it does not mean the job is an easy one. The development of measures has been slow in some areas, and a number of difficulties have been encountered in evaluating results across different clients, problems, and workers. Fortunately, a variety of advances have been made in this area during the past twenty years, and recent literature holds examples of opportunities for further improvement.

One area of advancement involves improved training of social work students in research and measurement techniques. A number of studies of research use have indicated that practitioner evaluations of clients using quantitative measures and structured research designs can be made much more likely by proper professional training. One example is a study by Blythe (1983) of graduates of an M.S.W. program that focused on training students to integrate practice and research. Her results showed that 40 percent reported having used at least one research design for evaluating their practice during the past year. Many schools of social work have now adopted a similar emphasis, meaning that a much larger proportion of social workers now can be expected to have basic skills necessary to use research and measurement tools.

More importantly, measurement tools themselves continue to improve, and a number of examples are worthy of note. One of the most important is the increased availability of rapid-assessment inventories for use with clients. Hudson's *Clinical Measurement Package* (1982) is the best example of a set of instruments designed specifically for social work practice, but many others have since appeared. These scales have improved dramatically the speed and ease with which practitioners can measure clients across a variety of problem areas and compare them with established norms.

Other examples of improvements in quantitative measures relate directly to the issue of evaluating outcomes across numerous clients in agency settings. One approach is goal-attainment scaling (GAS), which was first elaborated in the early 1970s, but has since been championed by evaluation specialists such as

Rossi and Freeman (1989). Using GAS, an agency can be evaluated on the proportion of its clients who have achieved specified outcome goals. Similarly, individual clients can be compared on the amount of progress that they have made toward individual goals (e.g., one client may have completed 80 percent of tasks required for achievement of a goal whereas another has achieved only 40 percent). The advantage to this approach is that it establishes a standard basis of comparison and also facilitates the process of clinical goal setting.

A related advance, called the Reported Resolution Ratio (RRR), is described by Fanshel, Marsters, Finch, and Grundy (1992). The RRR is the "ratio of the number of problems reported resolved at the end of a case to the number of problems expected to be reported resolved based on the problem-specific rates observed" (p. 310). In other words, an agency first determines the average number of clients who are successful at resolving particular types of problems, then these averages become the basis of comparison for progress on the part of individual clients. As with GAS, this ratio also allows comparisons across clients in aggregate, and it also allows comparisons of individuals and groups with norms established within the agency and on a wider basis.

Enabling More Rigorous Quantitative Measurement in Agencies

An unfortunate fact of quantitative measurement is that it often has been less than wholeheartedly embraced by all agencies and practitioners. To the contrary, many workers still resent collecting data for the purpose of agency evaluation, seeing it as a task that serves the needs of managers rather than line-level staff. This problem has been compounded by the accompanying implementation of management-information systems, which were also seen as serving only administrative purposes.

Still, recent studies have demonstrated that measurement strategies and computerized data systems can be combined into an effective means of gathering and disseminating information on client progress across organizational levels, provided that the studies are designed and implemented correctly. One example is reported by Grasso, Epstein, and Tripodi (1988) in which a system was developed in a youth treatment and residential center to expand research use on the part of staff members. The centerpiece of the project was a computerized information system that collected demographic information, case history data, and measures of case progress (including standardized scales). The system had the advantage of having been in trial use for several years, but its most important feature was that it was designed to produce reports and other desired products not only for managers but for line-level staff as well. Results of the study of the system's implementation indicated that staff made moderate-to-high research use of the products of the system, and although initially they were critical of the system's implementation, their attitudes toward research improved after its inception.

This work illustrates the importance of *how* quantitative information is collected and returned to practitioners if it is to be used successfully at the agency level. A demonstration project by Kuechler, Velasquez, and White (1988) addressed the *what* of the measures to be used. Three types of measures were examined: 1) existing standardized scales; 2) a level of functioning (LOF) scale created especially for use in the agency studied; and 3) numerical counts of criteria, such as the number of clients functioning well at the time of follow-up. Results showed that agency staff rated all three types of quantitative measures as useful, but the straightforward numerical counts "were considered by managers, planning team members, and practitioners to provide the most credible evaluation data" (p. 78). The authors also echo Grasso and colleagues in noting that a key to the success of all three types of measures was that results from each had to be made available across organizational levels and not just to administrators.

A number of conclusions can be drawn from these and related studies. First, quantitative measurement of client outcomes *can* be used effectively in human-service agencies. Second, the potential usefulness of these measures extends across agency levels to workers, planners, managers, and evaluators. Third, a variety of quantitative measures can be successfully used, from numerical counts to standardized scales to aggregate measures such as GAS. Fourth, as social workers become more knowledgeable of quantitative measures, they also become more likely to use them and more likely to find value in their use. Fifth, the means by which these measures are employed and the results disseminated appears to be critical to their success. Measures used exclusively for administrative purposes or program evaluation and that simply are imposed upon workers are most likely to succeed only in providing poor results, generating conflict, and diminishing rather than enhancing the quality of agency evaluation and research. Quantitative measurement is not easy to do well, but until a demonstrably superior alternative is found, the difficulty involved in doing it right should not be used as an excuse for its abandonment.

REFERENCES

Blythe, B. J. (1983). *An examination of practice evaluation among social workers.* Unpublished doctoral dissertation, University of Washington.

Carter, R. K. (1988). Measuring client outcomes: The experience of the states. *Administration in Social Work, 11*(3/4), 73–88.

Fanshel, D., Marsters, P. A., Finch, S. J., & Grundy, J. F. (1992). Strategies for the analysis of databases in social service systems. In A. J. Grasso & I. Epstein (Eds.), *Research utilization in the social services: Innovations for practice and administration* (pp. 301–323). New York: Haworth.

Grasso, A. J., Epstein, I., & Tripodi, T. (1988). Agency-based research utilization in a residential child care setting. *Administration in Social Work, 12*(4), 61–80.

Hudson, W. W. (1982). *The clinical measurement package: A field manual.* Homewood, IL: Dorsey Press.

Hudson, W. W. (1988). Measuring clinical outcomes and their use for managers. *Administration in Social Work, 11*(3/4), 59–71.

Kuechler, C. F., Velasquez, J. S., & White, M. S. (1988). An assessment of human service program outcome measures: Are they credible, feasible, useful? *Administration in Social Work, 12*(3), 71–89.

Patti, R. (1988). Managing for service effectiveness in social welfare: Toward a performance model. *Administration in Social Work, 11*(3/4), 7–22.

Rossi, P. H. & Freeman, H. E. (1989). *Evaluation: A Systematic Approach.* Newbury Park, CA: Sage.

Royse, D. (1992). *Program evaluation: An introduction.* Chicago, IL: Nelson Hall.

Rejoinder to Dr. McMurtry

KEVIN CORCORAN

I have long admired the work of Dr. McMurtry and have always found his arguments crisp, cogent, and persuasive. Such is the case for his assertion that more rigorous measurement is needed in agency evaluation. I am puzzled, however, by his affirmative response because his argument is the very basis for the conclusion that more rigor is not needed. This rejoinder will consider how Dr. McMurtry and I could use similar evidence while reaching opposite conclusions, and will question two minor points, which are presented as facts but are not in the evidence.

Controversial Conclusions

While a controversy is like a pancake—every one of which has two sides regardless of how thin it is—Dr. McMurtry and I seem to be advancing similar evidence only to reach contradictory conclusions. This is because what Dr. McMurtry considers "more rigorous" is only so in contrast to the relative dearth of quantification used by practitioners. The role of GAS, for example, is indeed more rigorous than practice wisdom and clinical judgment. The problem is not the use of clinical judgment itself, but when it is the sole bases for assessing whether a client's problem is changing or a goal is being met. To assert that such rudimentary assessment tools are more rigorous is only plausible in comparison to no measurement.

Facts Not in the Evidence

I must quarrel with two of Dr. McMurtry's assertions, ones that are presented as if they are facts, but are not supported by the evidence. He, like many other proponents of single-system design (SSD), assembles assurance from Blythe's (1983) finding that 40 percent of a sample used at least one element of SSD over the previous year. There is cold comfort, indeed, in this finding in that *all* subjects were exposed to the methods of single-case evaluation and the majority did not report using this new technology. In light of the fact that most clinicians see dozens of clients each year, use of SSD with at least one client over the year should not be considered an index of success.

Dr. McMurtry also advances his position by asserting that standardized instruments continue to be improved. While this is correct, the improvement has done little to "improve the speed and ease" of measurement in daily practice. As disputatious as this may sound to researchers, almost everyone who sees clients several hours a day, day in and day out, admits that using even a single 25-item instrument simply takes too much time! It remains to be seen if computers and creative methods of administering, scoring, and interpreting rapid-assessment instruments will, in fact, help or will simply be an added burden to the over-worked practitioner. In essence, to think that more rigorous measurement is a simple addition to clinical practice is a position that is advanced by academics and not by practitioners, who might see six or more clients a day, five days a week, for forty eight or more weeks a year.

In summary, Dr. McMurtry and I agree more than we disagree: that is, of course, with the important exception of our conclusions. The common ground between his YES and my NO might best be seen not as a need for "more rigor," but a need for "any rigor" in the measurement of practice interventions.

NO

KEVIN CORCORAN

Students enrolled in social work research frequently consider empirical courses to be difficult obstacles to the completion of their practice degree, obstacles that concomitantly have an adverse affect on their grade-point average. Even those students with a proclivity for and interest in social work research struggle to see the relevance to the daily routine of agency or private practice. Therefore, to assert that more rigorous quantitative measures should be part of practice evaluation may simply further the perceived dissonance between research and practice; it would make practice evaluation more difficult, and indirectly defeat its goal of promoting the use of research as practice.

When considered, however, in light of the fact that quantitative measurement—whether rigorous or not—is rarely used by practitioners (Mutchschler, 1984), more rigorous measurement is needed. After all, because so little quantitative methodology is used in the first place, more rigorous measurements are needed; or, at least, any measurement is needed, regardless of the degree of rigor. This chapter, however, will argue that rigorous measurement really is not necessary and is not very helpful to practitioners.

Purpose of Research and Practice

The point of departure for my NO position is the distinguishable purposes that guide research and practice. This is not an endorsement of the extreme position that research has nothing to offer practitioners, that it does not contribute to our understanding of practice, or that interventions cannot be empirically validated (e.g., Heineman-Piper, 1981). While measurement has been considered to be a futile attempt to approximate an observational language (Witkin, 1991), it is simply the process of applying a number to something. In the case of practice this ''thing'' is most likely an intervention, a client problem, or a treatment goal. To measure clinical events is, in fact, quite valuable and is simply quantification. Quantification actually adds to the valuable qualitative observations made by social workers every day in treatment. In essence, data without descriptions is as problematic as simply having practice wisdom without any empirical support.

As Thomas (1978) articulated, research and practice have fairly distinguishable purposes. The purposes of practice is to help clients change by decreasing a particular problem or attaining a specified goal. The purpose of research, on the other hand, is to demonstrate the effects of an independent variable on a dependent variable. Of course, research intends to establish causal relationships between the variables. The practitioner strives to meet his or her purpose with a variety of techniques that range from planned and strategic interventions to such nebulous notions as the therapeutic relationship, transference, empathy and, yes, even luck. Research, in contrast, attempts to establish causality by experimental controls.

To illustrate the difference between these two important activities of social work practice, consider ''reactivity.'' Reactivity is defined as a confounding variable, where the very act of measuring a presenting problem or goal itself changes the variable. When the act of measuring a problem or goal changes it, one cannot discern if the observed change is a result of a treatment (i.e., the independent variable) or simply assessment. Moreover, the changes that are noted by the act of measurement are usually short-term and not meaningful clinically. If simply measuring a problem actually changes it, we would not need clinicians, just measurement tools.

Because reactivity confounds the relationship between an independent variable and dependent variable, researchers strive to eliminate it. For the clinicians, however, the researchers' problem may facilitate change and may be an aid to practice, even if only slightly. As Gingrich (1990) argues, because reactivity is going to occur, clinicians should select measurement tools that produce a reaction toward the goal. For example, a clinician who is working with a couple who are having problems with sexual arousal, such as hyposexuality, should use a measure that itself may be sexually arousing. Similarly, a client attempting to quit smoking should use assessments that—while reliable and valid—are also adverse to the client; one example is measuring the frequency of cigarette smoking by keeping the butts in a jar and counting them each morning, afternoon, and evening may facilitate cessation.

Practical Impediments to Rigorous Measurement

There are additional, practical reasons for not using rigorous measurement. Many of these have been identified by Levy (1981) and include the lack of time available to the practitioner for purposes of evaluation. All too often, clinicians have large caseloads and see several clients every day, often with sessions scheduled back to back. While such time demands are not ideal and may, if fact, be detrimental to clients, most agencies have a waiting list.

In light of the demands of overworked practitioners, to attempt to use rigorous measurement is simply not feasible. This is especially so for the novice at evaluation. What a researcher may consider to be an elementary procedure, such as scoring a scale, can initially be confusing and, therefore, even more time consuming to the inexperienced social worker. Once familiar with the various steps of measuring practice and evaluating outcomes, the time demands become much less; initially, however, they are an impediment to routine practice because the clinician must have some research design, locate suitable measurement tools, reproduce the instrument, score them and then try to figure out what the results truly mean. To professors of research, this may be second nature, but to the practitioner all of it is difficult, demanding, and most of all a time-consuming activities of questionable utility.

To use more rigorous measurement is also somewhat expensive. While it may seem trivial to consider photocopying a stack of measurement tools, to administrators one of the first targets of pecuniary problems is photocopying. Consider, for example, a small-size agency with twenty five clinicians, each of whom sees twenty five clients per week. If they measure only one problem with a single instrument, at 7¢ a page to copy, the result would be over $2000 a year. Many agency workers would prefer to see these funds used for a holiday bonus or a few social functions. These allocations may actually be better for the client by enhancing staff morale, decreasing stress and burnout, and validating workers' sense of importance to the agency.

As further noted by Levy (1981), some agencies and treatment approaches simply are not suited for rigorous measurement of a client problem. Examples include hospital-setting, crisis-intervention, or single-session therapy. It is impossible to imagine the value of times-series data when a hospital client may be discharged only a few days after admission, or what to do with single baseline data for a client whose insurance carrier only approves three or four sessions of treatment for a particular problem.

Needless to say, these practical impediments to rigorous measure are far from an exhaustive list. Practitioners who have attempted to evaluate their treatment are familiar with numerous other arguments for not using measurement. Some include lack of client cooperation and a general aversion to anything that even sounds like research. Most of all, though, many simply conclude that it is not worth the time, toil, or trouble.

If Not More Rigorous Measurement, What?

While it has been argued that practitioners do not need to use more rigorous measurement, this is not meant to imply that social work practitioners should once again return to practice that is ill defined; lacks specified problems and goals; and uses unstructured, nebulous treatment interventions (i.e., ''flying by the seat of your pants''). If, however, practitioners are to actually use any measurement—whether rigorous or not—the process and product must assist them in their efforts to help clients change. As Kazdin (1977) noted over fifteen years ago, in order for practitioners to use empirical procedures, these procedures must address therapeutic issues and have utility.

Therefore, while more rigorous measurement may not be necessary, some measurement is helpful and necessary for effective practice. Specifically, what is needed are simple observational systems of the client problems or treatment goals; two viable measurement systems are self-anchored rating scales and GAS. These simple, nonrigorous measurements are useful to guide practice by using retrospective baseline data or post-intervention baseline data, which serve as the referent point to determine if change has occurred. Clearly, such rudimentary elements are accompanied with many problems of reliability and validity. Nonetheless, these simple methods—while a far cry from rigorous—are actually helpful to clinicians when combined with other therapeutic tools, such as clinical judgment, hunches, intuition, and practice wisdom. With these nonrigorous measurements, clinicians are able to fulfill the purpose of practice: to help clients decrease problems and obtain goals.

In summary, the social worker should use more rigorous measures, in that any good measurement is more rigorous than relying solely on clinical judgment. The degree of rigor in measurement, then, does not need to be rigorous, but relevant. Practice may actually help the client by simply using a simple design, individualized observations of problems and goals, and a simple graph to see if clinically significant change has occurred. Thus, nonrigorous measurement is what is needed to facilitate the purpose of practice, not rigorous measurement.

References

Gingrich, W. J. (1990). Rethinking single-case evaluation. In L. Videka-Sherman, & W. J. Reid (Eds.), *Advances in Clinical Social Work Research.* Silver Spring, MD: National Association of Social Workers.

Heineman-Piper, M. D. (1981). The obsolete scientific imperative in social work. *Social Service Review, 55,* 371–397.

Kazdin, A. E. (1977). Assessing the clinical and applied importance of behavior change through social validation. *Behavior Modification, 1,* 427–452.

Levy, R. L. (1981). On the nature of clinical-research gap: The problem with some solutions. *Behavioral Assessment, 3,* 235–242.

Mutchschler, E. (1984). Evaluating practice: A study of research utilization by practitioners. *Social Work, 29,* 332–337.

Thomas, E. J. (1978). Research and services in single-case experimentation: Conflicts and choices. *Social Work Research and Abstract, 14,* 20–31.

Witkin, S. L. (1991). Empirical clinical practice: A critical analysis. *Social Work, 36,* 158–163.

Rejoinder to Dr. Corcoran

STEVEN L. MCMURTRY

In the popular television series, ne'er-do-well Homer Simpson tells his son Bart that "anything hard to do is probably not worth doing anyway." Unfortunately, this sentiment seems to be the gist of Dr. Corcoran's arguments with regard to improving quantitative measurement of practice in social work agencies. For example, Dr. Corcoran cautions that because students "struggle to see the relevance" of research methods, any attempt to make it clear to them "may simply further the perceived dissonance between research and practice." By analogy, teaching school children that the earth revolves around the sun should also be avoided, lest it interfere with their perception that precisely the opposite is true.

Simply stated, the difficulty involved in learning or applying good methods of measurement is not an acceptable rationale for avoiding them. Instead, this difficulty means that we must work even harder to improve our means of teaching this content. As noted in my YES statement, there is persuasive evidence to indicate that improved instruction *can* increase research utilization (Blythe, 1983), which in turn suggests that students *can* see the relevance of its use if given proper training.

In addition, distinctions between practice and research to which Dr. Corcoran alludes (e.g., Thomas [1978]) are not universally accepted. For example, Siegel (1984) illustrates clearly that the same logical reasoning that characterizes good research closely parallels the reasoning in good practice. Research techniques, including rigorous quantitative measurement, are tools available to social workers to improve their practice. It makes no sense to suddenly declare that these tools should not be improved further, or that no attempt should be made to use better ones that already exist.

Other points raised by Dr. Corcoran also follow this sort of unconvincing reasoning. For example, his arguments concerning measurement reactivity are not really arguments against quantitative measures at all; instead, they simply point out the need for finding and using the *right* measure. As he correctly notes, many measures actually enhance rather than interfere with practice goals.

Even more important, Dr. Corcoran's arguments against using good quantitative measures because they are expensive, time-consuming, or difficult to score are either outdated or overstated. Numerous rapid-assessment instruments have become available in recent years, and so have well known compilations of these instruments (as Dr. Corcoran is well aware). More recently, software for both administering and scoring these instruments has become easily available at the same time that social worker's access to desktop computers has increased dramatically (Hudson, 1992). Finally, with regard to cost, the $2,000-per-year expense of a standardized instrument that Dr. Corcoran uses in his example seems a small price to pay for the quality of measurement that it would afford the agency in question. Such a sum is but a fraction of what the same agency likely pays each year to ensure itself against liability claims for malpractice, thus the improved practice afforded by use of the instrument may be a real bargain.

In conclusion, the question must be raised: what is the alternative to continued efforts to improve quantitative measurement of social work services? Are we to endorse either poor measurement or no measurement at all simply because it takes time and resources to locate, learn, and score these measures? With apologies to Homer Simpson, the only viable answer is a resounding, "No."

References

Blythe, B. J. (1983). An examination of practice evaluation among social workers. Unpublished doctoral dissertation, University of Washington.

Hudson, W. W. (1992). *Computer assisted social services (version 2.0).* Tempe, AZ: WALMYR Publishing Co.

Siegel, D. H. (1984). Defining empirically based practice. *Social Work, 29*(4), 325–331.

Thomas, E. J. (1978). Research and services in single-case experimentation: Choices and conflicts. *Social Work Research and Abstracts, 14,* 20–31.

DEBATE 21

Are Social Work Journals Requiring Adequate Empirical Justification for Claims of Effectiveness?

Nancy A. Humphreys is Dean at the University of Connecticut School of Social Work and a former President of the National Association of Social Workers. She also teaches in the Smith College School of Social Work doctoral program and is on the visiting faculty at the George Warren Brown School of Social Work at Washington University in St. Louis, Missouri.

Eileen Gambrill is a professor of Social Welfare at the University of California at Berkeley. Her areas of interest include decision-making processes used by professionals, the use of behavioral methods in social work practice, and social skills training. She teaches practice methods and research courses to graduate social-welfare students. Her recent publications include *Critical Thinking in Clinical Practice* (1990, Jossey-Bass) and *Controversial Issues in Social Work* (series editor with Robert Pruger, 1993, Allyn and Bacon).

YES

NANCY A. HUMPHREYS

The adequacy, or lack thereof, of standards for determining the effectiveness of social work practice remains one of the most controversial subjects in the profession. Nowhere is this controversy more heated than in the disagreement about the standards for publication in social work journals. Recently, there has been a dramatic proliferation in the number and type of journals catering to social workers. This development has led some to fear that greater opportunities to publish means a significant and dangerous reduction in standards for scholarship. Rather than welcoming new publishing opportunities as a way of increasing our scholarship, some have argued that we have weakened standards, because fewer opportunities to publish would enhance competition and produce a better quality of work.

Concerns about the quality of journals generally have been a reflection of our shifting attitudes toward our uses and appreciation of research. In social work, the pendulum has swung from a profession that has had little interest in research to one in which today many argue that only through rigorous science can the profession justify its value. Too often, practice wisdom has been replaced by the view that if a practice technique cannot be measured and quantified, it does not exist and should not be used. Today, there is a belief in the preeminence of one model for knowledge development, which has become so powerful and ubiquitous that it has altered the whole of our understanding of professional knowledge.

Quantification, coupled with concern for objectivity, verification, and replication of results have shaped a view of knowledge that urges social workers to mimic the standards and empirical methods of other social scientists. In our effort to gain status and credibility, we have aligned ourselves with a scientific model used in the academic disciplines. Nowhere is this more clear than the profession's efforts to educate and train the practitioner–scholar. In my view, training and expectations held out for such a position probably result in a reversal of the emphasis in the position's title. Rather than "practitioner–scholar," those who advocate this development are really calling for a "scholar–practitioner," one whose practice is defined and determined by skill as a researcher.

Weick (1992, p.) asks, "Has our obsession with respectability become more important than asking ourselves what kind of a profession we want to be?" Put another way, we might ask if we are in danger of letting our standards of knowledge distort who social workers are and what they do.

Social workers require knowledge that is applicable and usable in the real world of practice. While the scientific approach involves a specific method of knowledge production, professions need a broader spectrum of knowledge generation formats to meet the demands of practice. This is especially true for our profession because our practice responsibilities cut across many scientific disciplines and fields.

Social workers also need knowledge grounded in the profession's traditions and values. This must incorporate such issues as our emphasis on seeking to eradicate barriers of all sorts by recognizing diversity and practice principles that respect client wisdom. Intellectually rigorous inquiry that relies heavily or exclusively on empirical validation may serve the needs of practice less well than knowledge development that relies on multiple strategies of inquiry. We often have become more concerned with the reliability of method, rather than the validity of the outcome of our inquiry. Validity as measured by utility in practice should be of at least equal, some would argue greater, importance to concerns about reliability of method.

It is ironic that the greater demand for publication and scholarship as a condition of promotion and tenure is advocated by the very critics of the intellectual standards of the new journals. In effect, we have demanded that people publish more as a condition of promotion and tenure, while some are too ready to criticize the quality and value of those publications.

Linsey and Kirk (1992) argue that journals are one way of measuring the knowledge development of the profession. Therefore, a primary purpose of journals is the creation and transmission of new knowledge. Kirk (1991, p.) claims that "faculty are the trustees of the knowledge base of the profession." Similarly, Marsh (1992, p.) argues that "the role of a professional school is precisely to develop and disseminate the knowledge and analytic tools to enable practitioners to reduce uncertainty and to execute professional responsibility." In their work, both Kirk and Marsh have argued that more rigorous standards for empirically based practice is the most important task confronting social work faculty. This position assumes that faculty should be the standard setters of knowledge, while practitioners are the recipients and beneficiaries of journals. In my view, this promotes an artificial separation between schools and practice; faculty and worker; and ultimately, knowledge and practice. All represent false dichotomies.

While faculty members make up the majority of the contributors to journals, they are a small proportion of the readership. Individual journal subscribers consist of scholars and practitioners or practitioners-to-be. The notion that journals are the primary territory of academics is not borne out in the readership. While journals serve important purposes for authors, the primary beneficiary is the reader whom the authors seeks to inform and influence. Accordingly, the standards of journal publications ought to give at least equal weight to question their usefulness to readers in practice. In this view, the wisdom and validity of journals must be assessed and based on their relevance in meeting the needs of practice.

Practice involves learning while doing; it involves testing out new ideas; and it requires a range of techniques, methods, and ways of validating. Relying on elegant statistical models of analysis that ensure reliability may have little utility in the real world of practice, which is much less ordered. The purpose of rigorous science is to order the world and make it clear and predictable. The needs of practice, however, center on methods of inquiry that enable practitioners and clients alike to make meaning out of significant activities and events that occur in the unpredictable real world. Good practice research requires regular and in-depth collaboration with agencies and practice organizations and must be usable to practitioners and useful to practice organizations. The world of practice requires a cultivation of many ways of knowing, rather than a perpetuation of rigorous empirical standards that represent only one way of knowing. The standards for good practice research should be very different from those associated with good social-science research. Knowledge for practice must follow an heuristic approach and support a variety of different research and practice methodologies. Knowledge for practice must be rooted in practice.

Behaviorism, for example, represents one model in which research and practice are joined through on-going empirical validation. Many other practice paradigms used by social workers, such as those grounded in psychodynamic theories are less amenable to empirical verification. Interestingly, scholars exploring psychodynamic paradigms have discovered that the belief in the purity of empiricism is being challenged by students of the "hard" sciences:

> ". . . the belief that it may be possible to obtain certain, indubitable knowledge grounded in presuppositionless, unshakeable foundations, verifiable by empirical findings, and supported by internally consistent, complete logical systems has come to be seen by most, if not all, workers in the philosophy of science as a mistaken ideal, unattainable in principle." (Berger, 1991, pp. 82)

Ironically, while social work research tries belatedly to emulate the other sciences, the very foundation of scientific research is being challenged by those same fields.

Nowhere is the dilemma of how to integrate practice and research more obvious than in social work education, where recent changes in Council on Social Work Education standards require that those who teach practice must have a prescribed number of years of post-masters practice experience. In a practice-based profession, whose educational history has been closely linked to practice, the separation of practice and research is no more evident than in this particular requirement. Too many well trained, advanced quantitative researchers, newly awarded Ph.D.s are entering Schools of Social Work to teach practice or a practice-related content area. Often, however, their careers are not rooted in practice. Instead, they have been steeped in the ways of rigorous scientific methods of quantification and experimental research. While these individuals may be well prepared to teach knowledge about practice, they are not prepared to teach practice itself.

The schism between research and practice would be worse if journals were required to adhere to more rigorous empirical standards, which could produce knowledge of little or limited value to the world of practice. The standard of good scholarship ought to be the extent to which it informs practice: application to practice should be the primary criteria of quality. The demands of scientific and academic respectability, coupled with the evolution of extremely sophisticated methods of scientific inquiry aided by the advances in computer technology, have moved the research mission of the profession further away from the needs and requirements of practice.

A 1991 report issued by the National Association of Deans and Directors set forth a list of criteria for assessing quality scholarship (McMahon, Reisch, & Patti, 1991). This list holds that the relevance of questions asked and problems studied to the world of practice should be a primary consideration in research. A second criterion is whether the methods of inquiry used are rigorously applied and appropriate for the question under study. A third criterion is if the dissemination of the results is adequate and appropriate. These criteria recognize a combination of quantitative and qualitative methods, rather than setting one method against another.

The practice world of social work does not lend itself to a single method, our focus on the interface between person and environment does not lend itself to only one approach. Rather than focusing on a single approach to knowledge and to excellence in scholarship, the multiplicity of our purposes and the range of our practice responsibilities require that we value variation in our knowledge and research methods, and respect the synergy that occurs in the interaction of multiple and conflicting variables in the real world. Rather than limiting ourselves to one definition of rigor, we should value our diversity and concentrate on ensuring that social work research advances practice in its many forms. Empiricism is one important way of justifying our claims of effectiveness in practice, but it is not the only way.

References

Berger, L. S. (1991). *Substance abuse as symptom: A psychoanalytical critique of treatment approaches and the cultural beliefs that sustain them.* Hillsdale, NJ: The Analytic Press.

Kirk, S. A. (1991). Scholarship and the professional school. *Social Work Research and Abstracts, 27*(1), 3–5.

Lindsey, D., & Kirk, S. A. (1992). The role of social work journals in the development of a knowledge base for the profession. *Social Service Review, 66*(2), 295–310.

Marsh, J. C. (1992). Should scholarship productivity be the primary criterion for tenure decisions? Yes! *Journal of Social Work Education, 28*(2), 132–134.

McMahon, M. O., Reisch, M. & Patti, R. J. (1991). *Scholarship in social work: Integration of research teaching and service.* Washington, DC: National Association of Dean and Directors of Schools of Social Work.

Weick, A. (1992). Primary criterion for tenure decisions? No! *Journal of Social Work Education. 28*(2), 135–139.

Rejoinder to Dr. Humphreys

Eileen Gambrill

As in most controversies, there are areas of agreement. I agree with Dr. Humphreys that research should have practice relevance and that there are ‘‘different ways of knowing.'' We differ in our views of the usefulness of ''different ways of knowing'' in assessing the credibility of claims about practice effectiveness. What are credible grounds? One could be the degree to which the data presented decreases social workers' uncertainty about how to help clients attain real-life outcomes that they value.

If helping clients is the major function of social work, we have to ask, ''How do we know if we help clients?'' How do we know that attempting to ''empower clients'' really results in ''empowerment?'' Certain ''ways of knowing'' are more likely, compared to others, to yield answers to such questions. We should guess and test (the process inherent in a scientific approach) rather than guess and guess again or, simply assert that ''X'' is helpful. Anecdotal experience may suggest promising directions for further exploration, but is not a sound guide on which to base claims of practice effectiveness (Dawes, 1987). Different ways of knowing differ in the extent to which they can weed out biases and distortions that may influence assumptions. The very purpose of experimental studies and certain kinds of single-case designs is to avoid unwarranted assumptions about effects achieved. (Whether they offer information about the role of methods used in the reported effects, depends on the particular design used.)

There is no agreement (as Dr. Humphreys claims) on ''one way of knowing'' in social work, and it is certainly *not* scientific reasoning that is accepted, as shown by the extensive literature in social work on ''different ways of knowing.'' Quite the opposite. Many presentations of science in social work journals misrepresent what science is and what it is not, confusing it with naive empiricism, essentialism, and pseudoscience. As Phillips (1987) remarks, many who write about the philosophy of science have not done their homework (see also, Phillips [1992]). Science uses multiple strategies of inquiry. Some of the most fruitful ones are those that are least represented in social work journals. Reviews of research reported in social work journals show that most (about 60 percent) involve surveys. Experimental studies and single-case designs are rarely reported, about 5 percent and 1.7 percent, respectively (Glisson, 1990; Fraser, Taylor, Jackson, & O'Jack, 1991).

Dr. Humphreys (as well as others) seem to equate rigor with *rigor mortis.* It is assumed that careful exploration of claims and beliefs requires a distortion of events studied and produces data of little practice value. Rigor does not have to result in *rigor mortis* (i.e., results of little value in decreasing uncertainty about questions posed), although it may, as perusal of social work journals suggests. Systematic inquiry and the discovery of valuable practice knowledge does not require the use of complex statistics (examine, for example, the *Journal of Applied Behavior Analysis).*

If social work journals are interested in helping social workers to help their clients, they should require authors to provide credible evidence for claims made. They would help readers to understand problems with questionable grounds, such as anecdotal experience and unfounded authority that permit biases and distortions to flourish unchecked. Giving attention to whether or not outcomes of concern to clients are achieved is one way to honor the profession's traditions and values of focusing on client needs.

References

Dawes, R. M. (1987). *Rational choice in an uncertain world.* San Diego, CA: Harcourt Brace, Jovanovich.

Fraser, M., Taylor, M. J., Jackson, R., & O'Jack, J. (1991). Social work and science: Many ways of knowing. *Social Work Research and Abstracts, 27,* 5–15.

Glisson, C. (1990). *A systematic assessment of the social work literature: Trends in social work research.* Knoxville, TN: University of Tennessee, College of Social Work.

Phillips, D. C. (1987). *Philosophy, science and social inquiry.* New York: Pergamon.

Phillips, D. C. (1992). *The social scientist's bestiary: A guide to fabled threats to, and defenses of, naturalistic social science.* New York: Pergamon.

NO

EILEEN GAMBRILL

What is the role of social work journals in relation to the stated aims of social work? On the masthead of *Social Work,* it states, "*Social Work* is a professional journal committed to improving practice and expanding knowledge in social work and social welfare." Thus, it would seem that the aim is to help social workers keep up with practice-related research about what works with which clients and with what problems.

Clarifying Terms

Practice prescriptions refer to recommendations regarding actions that social workers should take in certain situations. They are in the form of "You should do A with B in C situation to attain D outcome." Empirical justification concerns the credibility of claims. How credible is a claim? What kind of evidence is presented to support a claim? What evidence is presented that one method is better than others? How is it known that a method will not result in more harm than good? Let's say that a writer claims that "focusing on client strengths helps clients to achieve their aims." What evidence is offered to support this claim? Is "focusing on client strengths" clearly described, so that we can assess the extent to which this occurred? Has an experimental study been conducted in which clients were randomly assigned to different groups and social workers in one group focused on client strengths and in the other this was not done, all else being kept equal? Are there any single-case studies exploring whether a focus on client strengths is related to positive outcomes? Empiricism and scientific exploration are hallmarks of a scientific approach. Empiricism refers to making observations (i.e., looking and seeing). Empiricism represents the factual component of science. In naive empiricism, the role of the scientist is to observe and record. In this kind of empiricism, the further step is not taken of testing the accuracy of theories or assumptions by manipulating conditions to determine if predictions are accurate. Critics of scientific thinking often confuse this with naive empiricism.

Questionable appeals include reliance on testimonials (I tried it; it works), anecdotal experience (I use it with my clients), authority (e.g., Dr. [name] said . . .) and manner of presentation (e.g., a confident demeanor). Other questionable appeals are reliance on popularity (everyone's doing it), influence on *ad hominem* grounds (you like or dislike the author), reliance on tradition (we've always done it this way), or on newness (it's the latest thing) (see, for example, Gibbs [1991]; Gambrill [1990]).

Differences of opinion about criteria that should be used to justify claims of effectiveness and prescriptions for practice abound in social work. These range from those who may argue that anecdotal experience and testimonials are sufficient grounds on which to base claims to those who believe that claims of effectiveness should be supported by empirical research, such as experimental studies comparing the effectiveness of a method, with no intervention, or with another kind of intervention. One way to explore what one means by "adequate empirical justification" is to make the general personal—ask what kind of evidence you would like when making decisions that affect you personally. I often ask my students what kind of evidence they would like their dentist or doctor to rely on when making recommendations. They hasten to tell me that they want them to rely on the best validated methods. Isn't what's sauce for the goose, sauce for the gander?

Examples of Lack of Documentation

Illustrations of the lack of documentation for claims made in social work journals are given below. Some statements appear in conclusion sections and make claims that are not warranted by data described. All "beg the question" by asserting that a claim is true rather than providing supportive evidence. Key terms often remain undefined, making it impossible for readers even to know how to implement methods claimed to be effective.

> By rekindling the belief that people can continue to grow and change and should have equal access to resources, social workers can aid mentally challenged people in their efforts to reclaim the community as their legitimate life domain. (Sullivan, 1992, p. 205)

> The group serves as a protective factor contributing to the positive adaptation of Hispanic/immigrant youth. (Lopez, 1991, p. 39)

> Implementing and institutionalizing programs such as the one formulated in this article serve to enhance the well-being of adolescents in ways that are institutionally feasible, developmentally appropriate, and culturally syntonic with their value system. (Land & Levy, 1992, p. 174)

> The worker can capitalize on the game's opportunities to aid children in conflicts in interpersonal relations and in the acquisition of adaptive social skills. (Zayas & Lewis, 1986, p. 62)

> This subjectively directed model of dream analysis is an effective adjunct for social workers facilitating life review groups. (Magee, 1992, p. 172)

Some lapses in supporting claims may be a result of poor scholarship—not taking the time to document claims—or, if they cannot be documented, to say so. It is not uncommon for an author to refer the reader to a theoretical description to support an assumption, when what is needed is credible evidence.

Other Concerns About Evidence Quality

Concerns about the adequacy of support for claims also arise in relation to advertisements in social work journals. Many ads in *Social Work* are for residential care programs for youth. What evidence is offered in support of claims? Investigations of such residential centers suggest that hospitalization may deprive residents of their due process rights and cause harm (e.g., Schwartz, 1989). Isn't inclusion of ads a tacit endorsement for these programs? Do disclaimers guard against undue influence? Even if these are read, readers may forget the caution and recall only the slickly marketed ad. We are often influenced without our awareness (Forgas, 1991; Nisbett & Ross, 1980).

What I Am Not Saying

I am not saying that only studies that demonstrate evidence of effectiveness should be published. This would rule out publication of innovative exploratory approaches to problems as well as many other valuable contributions. What I am saying is that *if* a claim to effectiveness is made, *if* a prescription for practice is made in the form of "you *should* do this . . ." or "this is best" or "this achieves ________ with ________" then some empirical evidence should be presented. We should be offered more than appeals to popularity, common practice, anecdotal experience, unfounded authority, or testimonials. These may be fine when trying to sell soap. Professional journals should be more discriminating. They serve a gatekeeper role in transmitting content to professionals. Excessive claims could be avoided through proper wording. A writer may say, "This group therapy method offers a valuable contribution to practice," when what is meant is, "This group therapy method *may* offer . . ." or, its potential effectiveness should be explored. Whenever a claim is made such as "X works," "workers should do this," or "this helps clients," some credible evidence supporting the claim should be provided. How about using real-life outcomes of interest to clients as indicators of effectiveness? Do clients locate needed housing? Do neglectful parents provide proper care to their children? Is a couple's communication skills enhanced as assessed in role plays and in real life? Is credible evidence presented to support claims?

Editors, reviewers, and authors should assume more responsibility for reviewing the quality of evidence for claims made in manuscripts. Isn't it their job to help readers sift out bogus claims from those that can be supported? Clients will be affected by the actions that social workers take based on unfounded claims of effectiveness. Uncritical espousal of claims about what is useful and what is not may result in use of methods that are harmful, as well as in the neglect of methods that are helpful. This kind of writing erodes rather than helps readers to hone their critical thinking skills in evaluating claims. Practice prescriptions are not always spelled out in detail, leaving it up to the reader to try and determine what was meant by vague phrases such as "focus on client strengths." Vagueness may be viewed as a virtue, allowing different social workers to carry out prescriptions in accord with their unique styles. This is fine if all styles result in positive outcomes. But do they? Here, too, reviewers and editors could assume greater responsibility for encouraging authors to clarify terms.

Weak appeals are often accepted (or offered) because people have not been trained to examine the basis for claims critically. Many goals compete with informing readers, such as sounding profound through reliance on obscure language, gaining status by unsupported claims of effectiveness, and saving time. It takes so much less time simply to assert a position than to support it. We live in a culture in which pseudoscience and bogus science are rife both in professional and lay sources. The average person does not know what science is and what it is not (Miller, 1981).

In Summary

Social work journals are not doing their job as discerning gatekeepers of knowledge, which is defined here as information that decreases uncertainty about how to attain a certain outcome (Nickerson, 1986). This is the kind of knowledge that is of unique value to clients and, it is hoped, to social workers. We could develop an index for reviewing the credibility of claims in journals:

$$\frac{\text{number of claims supported}}{\begin{array}{c}\text{number of claims not supported/unsupported claims}\\ \text{that violate empirical generalizations/claims supported}\end{array}}$$

This "formula" could be calculated for articles as well as for advertisements. Progress in enhancing the evidence quality base for claims could be monitored and shared with readers. We are a profession and, therefore, should be concerned about the credibility of claims made about effectiveness, *if* our goal is to help clients attain outcomes that they value.

References

Forgas, J. P. (Ed.). (1991). *Emotion and social judgments.* New York: Pergamon.

Gambrill, E. D. (1990). *Critical thinking in clinical practice.* San Francisco, CA: Jossey-Bass.

Gibbs, L. E. (1991). *Scientific reasoning for social workers: Bridging the gap between research and practice.* New York: Macmillan.

Land, H. & Levy, A. (1992). A school-based prevention model for depressed Asian adolescents. *Social Work in Education, 14*(3), 165–176.

Lopez, J. (1991). Group work as a protective factor for immigrant youth. *Social Work with Groups, 14*(1), 29–42.

Magee, J. J. (1992). Dream analysis as an aid to older adults' life review. *Journal of Gerontological Social Work, 18,* 163–173.

Miller, J. D. (1987). The scientifically illiterate. *American Demographics, 9,* 26–31.

Nickerson, R. J. (1986). *Reflections on reasoning.* Hillsdale, NJ: Erlbaum.

Nisbett, R., & Ross, L. (1980). *Human inference: Strategies and shortcomings.* Englewood Cliffs, NJ: Prentice Hall.

Schwartz, I. (1989). *(In)justice for juveniles: Rethinking the best interests of the child.* Lexington, MA: Lexington Books.

Sullivan, W. P. (1992). Reclaiming the community: The strengths perspective and deinstitutionalization. *Social Work, 37*(3), 204–209.

Zayas, L. H. & Lewis, B. H. (1986). Fantasy role-playing for mutual aid in children's groups: A case illustration. *Social Work with Groups, 9*(1), 53–66.

Rejoinder to Dr. Gambrill

Nancy A. Humphreys

Dr. Gambrill and I agreed that the primary purpose of social work journals is to serve the needs of readers and practitioners and through them to improve practice. From this purpose, she concludes that the aim of journals is to help social workers "keep up with practice-related research about what works with which clients and with what problems." I agree. But must all practice-based research meet rigorous standards for empirical justification? I think not.

Success in practice-based research occurs when there is a balance between empirical research in its most rigorous form and a positive recognition of the contribution of other types of scientific inquiry. Anecdotal experience may be all that is possible, at a particular stage of formal inquiry, and it may be very valuable. Even more important is the fact that good empirical research often happens after tentative, exploratory, and anecdotal reports. Anecdotal evidence is the first step to rigorous study and, therefore, must be included in our professional journals.

Dr. Gambrill and I agree on the desired outcome, but disagree on the means to achieve it. Sometimes our professional disagreements occur because we define terms differently. Dr. Gambrill defines empiricism as "the factual component of science" and divides it into two types: naive empiricism, which includes simple observation and recording; and empirical studies that test and manipulate conditions. Rather than thinking of the two types of empiricism as competitive, one good and one not good, perhaps they are really two phases in the long-term process of validating practice. Anecdotal evidence can be the basis for later testing and manipulation. Unless our journals include articles derived from anecdotal observations, they will not become the basis of further testing.

My definition of empiricism had a slightly different meaning. I referred to the scientific approach that rejects all evidence if it cannot be measured, and the further corollary that if evidence cannot be measured, it probably does not exist and, therefore, should not be employed in practice.

Not only was our definition of empiricism slightly different, but we have also defined the issue of justification differently. Dr. Gambrill argues against anecdotal experience as a sufficient basis for justifying claims. I agree that it is insufficient, but as a first step or as a beginning in a long-term investigation, it may well be appropriate. But how can it be a first step if it is never reported? Rather than one or the other method as better, use of both approaches feel more productive to me.

I agree with Dr. Gambrill that in reporting on efforts to improve practice, the highest standards of documentation must apply. Examples of faulty documentation cited in her statement read to me more like examples of less than desirable reporting, rather than problems of inadequate standards. Adding conditional language (i.e. "may"), remembering and being true to the anecdotal nature of reports would, in my view, take care of the several troublesome examples that she notes. Perhaps one outcome of this debate might be a new agreement that the definition of key terms and the respect given to the nature of the data must be more exact; and our standards in this area should be more rigorous.

It bears noting, however, that disclaimers do not always work. Dr. Gambrill expresses concern that disclaimers about advertisements in journals may not be enough to alert the careless or unsuspecting reader. Maybe we need to spend more time training readers to note and respect cautionary notes not only in advertising, but in the actual report of research findings themselves.

DEBATE 22

Must Social Workers Continually Yield Current Practice Methods to the Evolving Empirically Supported Knowledge Base?

Cynthia Franklin is an assistant professor at the University of Texas at Austin School of Social Work, where she teaches clinical practice with a special emphasis on children and family services. Her current research and writing interests are in school social work, clinical assessment, and family therapy. She is a clinical member of the American Association of Marriage and Family Therapy and maintains a part-time practice.

John S. Brekke is Associate Professor at the University of Southern California School of Social Work. He teaches diagnosis and psychopathology in the M.S.W. program and clinical research methods in the Ph.D. program. He is currently the principal investigator on a longitudinal investigation of the effectiveness of community-based treatment for individuals with schizophrenia, which is funded by the National Institute of Mental Health.

YES

CYNTHIA FRANKLIN

> It is clear, then, that science "has something." It is a unique intellectual process which yields remarkable results. (Skinner, 1953, p. 11)

> Today's science fiction is tomorrow's science facts. The technology now exists to replicate genes. Beam me up, Scotty, is no longer a joke. (David

M. Susarret, Technological Inventor, President and Founder of DMSAT Satellite Communications [1990])

This chapter discusses a controversial issue in social work research. Must social workers be willing to continually yield current practice methods to the evolving empirically supported knowledge base? This author says YES, definitely, for five strong reasons.

First, social workers claim that the profession is a science as well as an art. By definition, a scientifically based profession adapts current practices to evolving empirical knowledge. Some social workers have argued that there are many "ways of knowing" (Hartman, 1990) outside of those that fall under empirical or scientific methods. The empirical knowledge base, however, remains critical if social work is to be a scientific profession.

Like medicine, social work's practice methods have been developed from a combination of empirically based knowledge and "practice wisdom." The scientific knowledge base of the social work profession has borrowed from many disciplines, because social workers have failed to produce its own empirical knowledge base.

Although not all social workers view the profession as empirically based, there are those who disagree. This is evidenced by the recent work of the National Institute of Mental Health (NIMH) Task Force on Social Work Research. The task force's report expresses confidence that a larger pool of social work researchers can be developed and that these researchers can contribute to the evolving empirical knowledge base of the profession, particularly in the area of mental health (Austin, 1992).

Current social work practice methods, therefore, must not be viewed as the "end all" or "absolute way" to help clients. Rather, current practice methods must be viewed as "the state of the art" at any point in time and context (Franklin & Jordan, 1992). The "state of the art" will likely progress a considerable amount during a social worker's career. For example, we currently have more effective behavioral technologies for treating clients with simple phobias, anxiety disorders, and obsessive compulsive disorders than existed in the days of Freud. There also have been advances in psychopharmacology, such as the development of drugs like Anafranil, which is used to treat obsessive compulsive disorders.

Second, technological advances from many fields may change the way social workers practice, and also provide new opportunities for developing empirically supported innovations in service-delivery systems. Social workers must be willing to yield practice methods to new knowledge and skills in accordance with these developments. Our willingness to use new technologies helps us remain current and provides opportunities to discover the full potential of these technologies as practice tools. The advent of the microcomputer is an example. Computer-based technologies, such as those found in computerized assessment systems, expert systems, and data management systems are becoming pervasive in social work practice. Research on the use of these methods also indicates that new technologies like computer-based assessments can result in reliable and sometimes more valid assessments than practitioners can arrive at without the use of those tools (Nurius, 1990). Computer-based systems have also been demonstrated to be an effective tool for single-subject research and practice evaluation. And, despite the misgivings of some social work practitioners, research indicates that clients like using the new computer technologies (Hudson, 1990; Nurius & Hudson, 1989).

Who knows what opportunities new technologies may bring to social work practice in the not-so-distant future. Hudson (1990), for example, reports that a "thinking" computer that learns from its own mistakes is on the way. Revolutionary technology in telecommunications has also been developed, which will allow us to send our image in a holographic form (Susarret, 1990). What advances might happen in social work practice when this new telecommunications technology meets up with the thinking computer?

Competence is a third reason why social work practitioners should yield current practice methods to the evolving empirically supported knowledge base. Competence is the social worker's adequacies, capabilities, proficiencies, qualifications, and overall mastery of skills. Social work practitioners function like skilled craftpersons and their overall mastery is greatly contingent on their knowledge base, skills development, and practice experiences. Knowledge, skills, and practice experiences are believed to build on one another in a type of recursive, positive feedback loop. That is to say, the more effectual the knowledge base that we have, the greater our skills level is likely to become; and the greater our skills level becomes, the more new knowledge and skills we are likely to gain from our practice experiences. Further, the more new knowledge and skills that we are able to learn from our practice experiences, the more effectual the new knowledge base that we may develop, and so forth.

A common adage in social work has been that "theory (empirically supported knowledge) guides practice." Thus, Blythe and Briar (1985) state that a practice model "prescribes what a practitioner should do in a given situation" (p. 483). In the process of learning and applying practice models, we develop the "artistry" and practice wisdom of social work practice. Rather than the science of social work being distinct from the art of the profession, there is a crucial link between them that engenders competence.

Currently, we live in a age of rapid infiltration of new information. Vast opportunities exist to incorporate developing, empirically supported, knowledge into our repertoire of practice skills. For example, behavioral genetics and pharmacology, new discoveries in human development, and the ever-expanding fields of the brain sciences provide empirically supported knowledge that social workers may use for developing new and more complex understandings of person and environment interactions. Competent social work practice may increase in proportion to the extent that we open our minds and transcend to the new and empirically supported knowledge.

Professional accountability explicit in our social work practice ethics provides a fourth reason that social workers must yield current practice methods to the evolving empirically supported knowledge base. As members of a profession, social workers are bound together by a code of ethics (National Association of Social Workers [NASW], 1980). The code of ethics mandates that we contribute to the knowledge base of our profession. As is stated in the code of ethics: V.O. "Development of knowledge—The social worker should take responsibility for identifying, developing, and fully utilizing knowledge for professional practice." The code of ethics states under O, number 2: "The social worker should critically examine, and keep current with emerging knowledge relevant to social work." Number 3, under O, further states: "The social worker should contribute to the knowledge base of social work and share research knowledge and practice wisdom with colleagues." It is impossible for social workers to embark upon research and new knowledge building without giving credence to the evolving empirically supported knowledge base. Professional accountability toward our clients and colleagues demands no less from us. Our code of ethics requires that we embrace new, empirically supported practice methods as they are developed.

Finally, effectiveness of practice methods is the fifth reason that social workers must yield current practice methods to the evolving empirically supported knowledge base. Effectiveness of practice methods has been a subject of intense interest and heated debate in the social work literature for the past fifteen years. For example, during the 1980s, a voluminous literature on practice evaluation was amassed, with a focus on single-subject research in particular. Fortunately, empirical research into the usages of practice evaluation methods have helped us broaden our perspectives concerning the utility of these methodologies.

Despite our increased interest on the subject of practice effectiveness, our concerns about this issue are unresolved. To achieve effectiveness, empirical research must undergird and guide our practice decisions. When research guides our practice, we adopt new practice methods if the research literature clearly indicates that the new methods are more effective. For example, it has been demonstrated in a number of empirical studies that psychoeducational family methods are a more effective approach for treating families of clients with schizophrenia than traditional family-treatment methods, such as those relying on communication and psychoanalytic theories (Simon, McNeil, Franklin, & Cooperman, 1991). Current practice with families of clients with schizophrenia should be changed to reflect these empirically supported methods.

Social workers must change in order to yield current methods, "pet theories," and "professional turf" to new empirically supported knowledge and methods. To choose not to change is a major obstacle to the development of effective practice methods. Refusal to adopt new methods and technologies, as they emerge, will ultimately produce negative consequences for both our profession and our clients. Metaphors and storytelling are techniques that developed out of practice wisdom. The author will leave the readers with some practice wisdom that illustrates this point.

Once upon a time, not so long ago, in a kingdom not so far away, Technology Person suddenly appeared in the streets. "Listen and look at me," she said. "I have all the knowledge possessed in the science and wisdom of humans. My talents are available to you to use as you wish for the good of others or for the good of only yourself."

The Keepers of Social Justice said to Technology Person, "How can you help us?" Technology Person said, "I have new knowledge and tools that will improve your work." But the Keepers of Social Justice scoffed and said, "We serve the poor and oppressed who would not understand your ways." "But I can help you empower the poor and oppressed and enable you to find solutions to their problems," said Technology Person. "No," said the Keepers of Social Justice. "To use your talents, we would have to change the way we do our work to accommodate your ways." Technology Person insisted, "My ways will make your work more efficient and effective." But the Keepers of Social Justice said, "No, thank you, Technology Person. You are too costly for us. In addition, the poor and oppressed people whom we serve would not like you."

Technology Person reluctantly retreated from the Keepers of Social Justice. A short time afterwards she was invited to a feast at the home of a rich young ruler in the kingdom. The rich young ruler ask her to stay with him. He saw many profits in her talents. Technology Person now lives with the rich young ruler, and she is mostly known among the elite class in the kingdom.

The Keepers of Social Justice now complain to the rich young ruler, saying, "What gives you the right to keep Technology Person in your home as your very own servant? Why not share her profits with others? You are using her talents to get richer and to exploit the poor and oppressed." The rich young ruler, however, does not reply.

References

Austin, D. M. (1992). Findings of the NIMH task force on social work research. *Research on Social Work Practice, 2*(3), 311–322.

Blythe, B. J., & Briar, S. (1985). Developing empirically based models of practice. *Social Work, 30,* 483–488.

Hartman, A. (1990). Many ways of knowing. *Social Work, 35*(1), 3–4.

Hudson, W. W. (1990). Computer based clinical practice: Present status and future possibilities. In L. Videka-Sherman, & W. J. Reid (Eds.), *Advances in clinical social work research,* pp. 105–117. Washington, DC: NASW Press.

Franklin, C. & Jordan, C. (1992). Teaching students to perform assessments. *Journal of Social Work Education, 28*(2), 222–241.

National Association of Social Workers (NASW). (1980). NASW code of ethics. *NASW News, 25,* 24–25.

Nurius, P. S. (1990). A review of automated assessment. *Computers in Human Services, 6*(4), 265–282.

Nurius, P., & Hudson, W. W. (1989). Workers, clients and computers. *Computers in Human Services, 4*(1/2), 71–83.

Skinner, B. F. (1953). *Science and human behavior.* New York: Macmillan.

Simon, C. E., McNeil, J. S., Franklin, C., & Cooperman, A. (1991). The family and schizophrenia: Toward a psychoeducational approach. *Families in Society, 72*(6), 323–333.

Susarret, D. M. (1990). *Using technology to achieve America 2000 Goals for all students.* Plenary presented at the conference, ''New Directions in Education III,'' Texas A&M University, College Station, TX.

Rejoinder to Dr. Franklin

JOHN S. BREKKE

Dr. Franklin presents five cogent (albeit, not new) reasons why social workers must yield their clinical methods to the evolving empirical knowledge base. Her arguments sound True, Good, Just, and Right. Why, then, haven't more practicing social workers believed them? My suspicion is that scientists try to oversell their product to those who are not yet converted. As a result, the arguments lack balance on the practice of science, and lack self-consciousness as to the process of knowledge building and testing in science.

My argument is that science is a methodology of progress, regress, sometimes outright error and redress. The only way for its findings to be accepted by those who are untrained in its methods is by honestly assessing its costs and benefits, strengths and limitations. Dr. Franklin presents science as I want it to be, but it seems too much like a science from a mythical land. While I cannot disagree with Dr. Franklin's points, as a practicing social scientist I am far more interested in the interface between scientific knowledge and methods and the clinical wisdom of the experienced social work practitioner. As I have tried to illustrate in my NO paper, clinical research methodology evolves at this interface, and, therefore, the best knowledge results from it.

Finally, when I look to practice wisdom to guide the science I do, I ask two questions: 1) what does your experience tell you; 2) what do your intuitions say? Therefore, in my opinion, the contribution of clinical wisdom to the evolving scientific knowledge base is inestimable.

NO

JOHN BREKKE

The question under discussion suggests that empirical research on clinical interventions can influence the progress of clinical practice. In fact, there is little doubt that empirical research has already influenced the landscape of clinical practice for more than two decades. However, during this period, it is also clear that clinical research methods have evolved and that this has dramatically influenced the quality and relevance of the knowledge generated. The thesis of my argument is that while the evolution of clinical research methods has increased the meaningfulness of empirically based knowledge, it also significantly tempers the degree to which social workers should continually yield their currently held practice strategies. Specific instances will be presented in which advances in clinical-research methodology led to dramatic differences in the conclusions that could be drawn from research on clinical practice.

The evolution of clinical research methods is evident in the work of Garfield and Bergin (1978; 1986), Kazdin (1980), and Beutler (1990). Significant advances have been made in the areas of design, measurement, and statistical analysis. To illustrate the degree to which these advances can influence the findings and conclusions from studies on clinical practice, five controlled clinical studies will be briefly examined. These studies illustrate methodological advances in four areas: 1) the use of multidimensional outcome measures; 2) the use of post-treatment follow-up periods; 3) establishing the potency of treatments; and 4) the assessment of treatment processes.

Multidimensional Outcomes

The use of multidimensional outcomes measures allows for the assessment of the generalizability of intended and unintended treatment effects across client-functioning domains, as well as the assessment of differential treatment effects. In a controlled study of the effectiveness of three treatments for bulemia nervosa, Fairburn, Jones, Peverler, Carr, Solomon, and O'Connor (1991) found that while cognitive-behavioral treatment was superior to behavior modification and interpersonal therapy in certain attitudinal and behavioral measures relevant to the dynamics of over-eating, there were no differences among the treatments on actual over-eating, weight gain, social adjustment, depression, or overall symptomatology. The assessment of multidimensional outcomes provides a basis for examining treatment effects in a rich context and will influence the judgment as to which treatment strategy is better relative to the different outcomes measured.

Follow-Up Periods

Concerning the use of appropriate post-treatment follow-up periods, Stein and Test (1980) randomly assigned a sample of chronically mentally ill patients to either an intensive and continuous treatment modality or to regular community care. They found that the gains accrued in many areas of psychosocial functioning in fourteen months of intensive treatment disappeared during a fourteen-month follow-up period.

Snyder, Wills, and Fletcher (1991) examined the effectiveness of twenty five sessions of insight-oriented or behavioral marital therapy. They found that while the treatments showed no differences at the end of treatment or at a six-month follow-up, by the four-year follow-up period there was significantly greater deterioration in the behavioral condition.

These two studies illustrate the dramatic influence of follow-up periods on the findings from clinical outcome studies. In the case of the Stein and Test study, a treatment that was extremely efficacious, remained so only for as long as it was in place. In the Snyder, Wills, and Grady-Fletcher study, it took up to four years for significant differential effects to surface that would alter the judgment about the relative efficacy of the two treatments.

Establishing Potent Treatments

Another methodological issue concerns the time necessary to establish a potent treatment. For example, in a study of the effectiveness of medication and psychosocial intervention with schizophrenics, Hogarty, Goldberg, Schooler, and Ulrich (1974) found that it took up to eighteen months for the effectiveness of the psychosocial treatment to manifest. A design that used a shorter treatment period could have resulted in the abandonment of an efficacious treatment.

Investigating Treatment Processes

The study of the process and integrity of treatment has received considerable attention (e.g., Beutler 1990). In a study of the impact of insight-oriented versus supportive therapy in the treatment of schizophrenia, Gunderson, Frank, Katz, Vanicelli, Frosch and Knapp (1984) found no differences in the impact of the two treatments on overall outcome. In a subsequent analysis of these data, Glass, Katz, Schnitzer, et al. (1989) examined the relationship between the quality of the treatment implemented and patient outcomes. They found that skillfully conducted psychodynamic explorations had a significant impact on treatment-resistant symptoms. These findings suggest that the study of the processes of treatment can yield findings that might be obscured by straightforward between-group analyses.

Conclusion

The examples discussed above are not meant to highlight the equivocal nature of findings from increasingly sophisticated methodologies. Quite to the contrary, these studies are more relevant to clinical practice because of the improvements in their empirical methods. What is clear, however, is that advances in research methodology can dramatically alter the character of findings, and, therefore, the influence that these findings will have on clinical practice. So, while clinicians must be willing at some point to yield their clinical practice methods to findings from clinical research, they must do so with great caution.

In the real world of clinical practice, do we then wait for the "gold standard" in methodologies to arrive before we allow research to influence clinical practice? This is an extreme position that could delay the impact of important findings. Conversely, the notion that any seemingly rigorous empirical findings are sufficient for the abandonment of current clinical practices is equally extreme. Type I and Type II errors are not only embedded in the samples that we draw, but also in the evolution of our empirical methods. The impact of these inevitable "errors" can be diminished with informed caution. Because a clinician's judgment about the relative effectiveness of treatments is a potentially serious one, this caution is exercised in the best interests of the clients that social workers serve.

References

Beutler, L. E. (Ed.) (1990). Special series: Advances in psychotherapy process research. *Journal of Consulting and Clinical Psychology, 58*(3): 263–304.

Fairburn, C. G., Jones, R., Peverler, R. C., Carr, S. J., Solomon, R. A., O'Connor, M. E., et al. (1991). Three psychological treatments for bulimia nervosa: A comparative trial. *Archives General Psychiatry, 48,* 463–469.

Garfield, S., & Bergin, A. E. (Eds.) (1978). *Handbook of psychotherapy and behavior change.* New York: Wiley.

Garfield, S., & Bergin, A. E. (Eds.) (1986). *Handbook of psychotherapy and behavior change.* New York: John Wiley & Sons.

Glass, L. L., Katz, H. M., Schnitzer, R. D., Knapp, P. H., Frank, A. P., and Gunderson, J. G. (1989). Psychotherapy of schizophrenia: An empirical investigation of the relationship of process to outcome. *American Journal of Psychiatry, 146,* 603–608.

Gunderson, J. G., Frank, A. F., Katz, H. M., et al. Effects of psychotherapy in schizophrenia, II: Comparative outcome of two forms of treatment. *Schizophrenia Bulletin, 10,* 564–598.

Hogarty, G. E., Goldberg, S. C., Schooler, N. R., & Ulrich, R. F. (1974). Drug and sociotherapy in the aftercare of schizophrenic patients: II. Two year relapse rates. *Archives of General Psychiatry, 31:* 603–618.

Kazdin, A. E. (1980). Research design in clinical psychology. New York: John Wiley & Sons.

Snyder, D. K., Wills, R. M., & Grady-Fletcher, A. (1991). Long-Term effectiveness of behavioral versus insight-oriented marital therapy: A 4-year follow-up study. *Journal of Consulting and Clinical Psychology, 59,* 138–141.

Stein, L. I., Test, M. A. (1980). Alternative to mental hospital treatment: I. Conceptual model, treatment program, and clinical evaluation. *Archives General Psychiatry, 37:* 392–397.

Rejoinder to Dr. Brekke

Cynthia Franklin

"Where there is knowledge it will pass away."

St. Paul—I Corinthians 13:8

Dr. Brekke has made six important points concerning the limitations of current empirical clinical-research methods. He is also wise to caution practitioners about the risks of yielding their current practice methods to the expanding empirical knowledge base. While I generally agree with Dr. Brekke's criticisms of the clinical research methodologies, I would take a different view concerning some of the conclusions that he draws from these limitations.

First, Dr. Brekke's main concern is that empirical research results cannot be trusted because they may change as we expand our methodologies. I emphatically agree that results will change, and we can even change those results by selecting one research design over another, or changing our clinical measures or statistical procedures. Evolving changes in methodology may seem to produce contradictory results, which make it difficult for practitioners to know what clinical methods to use. I would contend, however, that these contradictions are an integral part of normal science and cannot be removed from the research process (Kuhn, 1970). Follow-up studies that produce varying results over different periods of times or studies that indicate the efficacious results of treatments not previously assessed as being effective for a particular population should be welcomed and come as no surprise. Clinical experience indicates that diverse treatments may impact clients positively but in unique ways, and clients may change in one area of their functioning and not in another. Multiple measures will naturally lead to complexity of outcomes. The result of this complexity is that a myriad of different results must be incorporated into our knowledge development.

Knowledge development through the scientific method is complex, ladened with controversy, and forever progressing (Passmore, 1978). The clinical research process, similar to the human process of change, cannot be thought of as absolute or complete, but rather as a continuous effort at quality improvement. We cannot wait for "gold standards" before we yield our methods to the evolving empirical knowledge base, because no "gold standard" exists. Although, some innovations may serve as a gold standard for a time, they will be replaced with methods or newer interventions that are demonstrated to be more effective. Contradictions that emerge from evolving changes in methodologies, therefore, should not be seen as a threat to the integrity of practice but rather as a significant controversy to be analyzed, synthesized, and incorporated into the current clinical paradigm.

The processes inherent in the scientific method facilitate the incorporation of existing knowledge and helps us to ask the most pertinent and relevant questions. Practitioners are not unfamiliar with the evolving and sometimes contradictory nature of progress in that they are constantly challenged by the changing needs of their clients. In the same way, it is up to practitioners to be knowledgeable about the scientific method and to be able to critique, analyze, and become consumers of the evolving empirical knowledge base. In this regard, Dr. Brekke and I agree that clinical practitioners are best suited for developing and evaluating the effectiveness of clinical interventions. Unfortunately, however, many clinical practitioners are not involved in the research process and some lack the expertise to critique and become consumers of research. Likewise many clinical researchers in our profession do not work with clients, further building a gap between practice and research (Festinger, Turnbull, Moncher, 1992; Franklin & McNeil, 1992).

Rather than developing a reluctance toward yielding current methods to the empirical knowledge base, it seems more appropriate for clinical practitioners to learn to become competent consumers of research so that they can judge how and when to incorporate empirical knowledge (Thyer, 1991). Clinical researchers also should take responsibility, not for the burden of proof of their findings, as suggested by Dr. Brekke, but for being a part of the real world of practice and as fellow clinicians helping their colleagues make informed decisions.

Second, Dr. Brekke also criticizes linear research methods for their inability to capture the circularity and fluidity of clinical practice. Likewise, he criticizes current clinical assessment measures for their lack of relevance and clinical utility. It is obviously true that there are limitations to the current research methodologies. Rather than being an impediment to our knowledge base, the very fact that we know that those limitations exist may become an impetus for the development of better methodologies. In fact, through continuous clinical research, better methodologies have emerged. For example, in the last ten years, the field of family therapy has produced a number of relevant, standardized clinical assessment measures to assess family structure and processes (Grotevant & Carlson, 1989). These measures emerged as the result of the limitations of previous clinical measures in their abilities to assess systemic processes. The on-going debate regarding the validity and reliability of the "state of the art" family-assessment measures will likely lead to even further improvements in the assessment of complex family processes (see, for example, Franklin & Streeter [1993])

Third, Dr. Brekke expresses concerns that the research process may alter the practice being observed. He also asserts the belief that clinical interventions are partly based on an implicit knowledge about such interactions as the client–worker relationship that cannot be assessed by scientific methods. It is true that studying a phenomenon may change that phenomenon, and it is impossible to totally separate the observed from the observer. Clinical researchers are well aware of this fact and try to design studies that minimize reactivity. I would also argue, however, that clinical research that inadvertently changes the practice being observed may not be ineffective insomuch as researchers are aware of these changes and can help practitioners incorporate the changes into their practice. Concerning the implicitness of clinical knowledge, I would agree that it may be true that such personal characteristics as empathy, warmth, genuineness, and the belief in the potential of others may be resonant in some individuals more than others. However, all knowledge concerning effective clinical interventions is implicit until its technology is made known, and much of what we know and teach practitioners about demonstrating these characteristics toward clients emerged from empirical studies on the social work and the counseling process (see, for example, Kanfer & Schefft, [1988]; Schulman [1991]). Despite current limitations, empirical research methodologies have contributed significantly to our understanding of the clinical process.

References

Brekke, J. S. (1994). Must social workers be willing to yield current practice methods to the evolving empirically supported knowledge base? No. In W. W. Hudson, & P. Nurius (Eds.), *Controversies in social work research.* Boston, MA: Allyn & Bacon.

Festinger, T., Turnbull, F., & Moncher, M. S. (1992). Workshop 1: Training the clinician researcher. *Research on Social Work Practice, 2,* 324–337.

Franklin, C., & McNeil, J. S. (1992). The cassata project: A school–agency partnership for practice research integration. *Aretê, 17*(1), 47–52.

Franklin, C., & Streeter, C. L. (1993). The validity of the three dimensional circumplex family assessment model. *Research on Social Work Practice, 3,* 258–275.

Grotevant, H. D., & Carlson, C. (1989). *Family assessment: A guide to methods and measures.* New York: Guilford Press.

Kanfer, F. H., & Schefft, B. K. (1988). *Guiding the process of therapeutic change.* Champaign, IL: Research Press.

Kuhn, T. S. (1970). *The structure of scientific revolutions.* Chicago, IL: The University of Chicago Press.

Passmore, J. (1978). *Science and its critics.* New Brunswick, NJ: Rutgers University.

Schulman, L. W. (1991). *Interactional social work practice: Toward an empirical theory.* Itasca, IL: Peacock.

Thyer, B. A. (1991). Guidelines for evaluating outcome studies on social work practice. *Research on Social Work Practice, 1,* 76–91.

DEBATE 23

Are Professional Guidelines Needed Regarding the Appropriate Use of Research in Practice?

Paula S. Nurius is Associate Professor of Social Work at the University of Washington, where she teaches research and practice in the master's and doctoral programs. Her areas of interest include use of research and computer tools as decision and reasoning supports for practice, as well as social cognition, particularly with respect to self-concept change, violence against women, and critical thinking in practice. Recent publications include *Human Service Practice, Evaluation and Computers* (1993, Brooks-Cole, with Walter Hudson) and *Social Cognition and Individual Change* (1993, Sage, with Aaron Brower).

Bruce A. Thyer is Professor of Social Work and Adjunct Professor of Psychology at the University of Georgia, and Associate Clinical Professor of Psychiatry and Health Behavior at the Medical College of Georgia. He is the founding editor of *Research on Social Work Practice* (Sage). His major interests involve the promotion of behavior analysis within the field of social work and in the design and conduct of evaluation research.

Dianne F. Harrison is Professor and Director of the Ph.D. program at the Florida State University School of Social Work. She teaches courses in research, behavioral methods, and human sexuality. Her current research and writing interests are in HIV prevention, gender issues, and cultural diversity.

YES

PAULA S. NURIUS

''Need'' is a difficult qualifier to weigh with this issue. Are the repercussions serious if social work does not undertake this agenda? It is difficult to know. I will maintain in this YES statement that *if* social work wants to maximize benefits and minimize costs associated with research in practice, *then* it "needs" to establish guidelines to facilitate the former and to avoid and effectively contend with the latter. I will first identify the context that I have in mind in taking this position, and then identify a number of factors that argue for the utility of guidelines, concluding with a recommendation to move forward, carefully, but to move forward nonetheless.

It is important to identify some of the assumptions upon which this statement builds. Because this book is about controversies in *social work* research, I assume that we are speaking about research conducted in social agencies, within the context of social work practice, under the auspices of agency decision makers (although, clearly, this practice often involves multiple disciplines and varied types of settings). This leads to the assumption that social work staff are playing central roles in defining and grappling with issues related to research in practice, rather than implicitly relying on others—whether they be social work academics or other disciplines—to set the standards and to provide the oversight. This is not to suggest that others are not or should not be useful contributors. Rather, my point is to focus on the modal social-agency scenario and to weigh the issues within that context.

The conduct of research is an integral part of the social work profession. But it is not necessarily an integral part of either agency operations or direct-service provision. Concern for the potential of risk to research subjects has long been recognized formally and provided for in institutions that routinely sponsor research, such as colleges and universities; funding sources; and large service settings, such as hospitals (e.g., through human-subjects review and monitoring mechanisms). In many social agencies, however, these norms and guidelines often either have not been incorporated or are insufficiently clear to provide guidance in unclear situations.

The need for guidance is reflected in the periodic publications that offer guidelines of various sorts. For example, Caputo (1985) examined six major roles that research can play in family-service agencies. Within these prescriptions, he identified sources of conflict and the means of problem solving that moved situations to the benefit of the agency's goals. Turnbull, Saltz, and Gwyther (1988) offer a framework for implementing research in health-care settings with an emphasis on the creation of administrative contexts that facilitate research. Literature resources such as these are useful and could be drawn upon as part of the basis for crafting professional guidelines. It is not realistic or fair, however, to expect practitioners to continuously comb the social work literature to help piece together these guidelines, any more than this would be reasonable as a basis for establishing a professional code of ethics.

Toward avoiding a "headless machine" approach to research in practice, Marsh (1983) offers three directions to better anchor research in agency life and to enhance practitioners' capacity to contribute to social work research: knowledge generation, knowledge aggregation, and knowledge validation. This framework includes recognition of the increasing availability of automated information systems that enable agencies to more easily, systematically, and reliably capture, store, aggregate, and manipulate data in order to address questions, such as the relation of client characteristics, problem types, and intervention success. One advantage noted by Marsh is that "use of practitioner-generated data for addressing important *research* questions establishes a *research* role for the practitioner that better utilizes the full range of practitioner experience" (p. 592, italics added).

Marsh's point that automation assists knowledge building by supporting better use of the routinely collected data bases of social agencies is well taken and will be discussed further. This point also illustrates the fuzzy boundaries in social agencies and in the social work literature about what constitutes "research." That is, where should we draw the line in agency (or individual practitioner) information gathering, manipulation, and use in order to distinguish research from other activities (such as assessment, testing, planning, monitoring, and evaluating) and distinguish activities that do and do not require the special oversight and safeguards normally associated with research?

This is not meant to be a pedantic question. In efforts to persuade and assist practitioners to become more empirically supported in their reasoning and decision making, research has become an increasingly broad concept. Add to this the increasing pressures on agencies and practitioners to be accountable, demonstrate their effectiveness, compete with other (generally more research-oriented) disciplines for fewer and fewer resources, and to essentially re-form their professional identities and practice habits in the direction of scientist–practitioners, and, not surprisingly, we find a resulting amalgam of ambivalence, ambiguity, and anxiety.

Indeed, I have been among the educators and writers who have argued that the goals and tasks of social work practice and research have much that is inherently in common; that, rather than all or nothing, "research" can be usefully thought of as a multiform set of tools (e.g., principles, methods, instruments). There is, however, a considerable gulf between this flexible, integrative view of an academician and the present operative context of many social agencies in defining, conducting, and overseeing research activities in practice. In striving to translate research into terms more compatible with practice, we have blurred important responsibilities and failed to respond to significant caveats. Having a set of guidelines developed with the mission of social work and the realities of social agencies in mind could be useful to further illuminating the common ground between research and practice, while also educating and providing guidelines to protect all involved. Yet the preparation typical at the bachelors and masters level of training, which includes the vast majority of social workers employed in social agencies, often is insufficient to prepare social work staff to anticipate the varied risks, develop and evaluate creative yet credible plans, and oversee the on-going conduct of formal research in the harried world of social services.

Thus far, I have been speaking of the notion of "appropriate" primarily with respect to ethical considerations and the use of "correct" research (principles, methods, or instruments). If one also factors in issues of appropriateness relative to the motivations for the venture in the first place, one would consider questions, such as: Is this a suitable match of research methods to the motivating practice question or task (will what you'll get from this be what you're needing or expecting)? Are there important considerations or variables that have been overlooked? Is the degree of intrusion into service provision or conflict with service priorities acceptable? unavoidable? Is there an undue risk of placing direct practitioners (the typical data collectors) in unfair or jeopardizing positions? No single source can anticipate all of the myriad of complexities in the use of sound research tools in social work practice. (Kirk [1990] and Proctor [1990] offer the principles of purpose and utility as decision-making guides for whether and how to use research in practice.) A carefully developed set of guidelines, however, can help to spotlight what might otherwise be overlooked; inform decision makers about trade-offs that may not have been obvious; and suggest directions that may be more, rather than less, likely achieve desired means and ends.

Now, let us briefly turn our attention to the future, to emerging issues related to research in practice, for which we have few if any prior referents to draw upon. This, of course, could include a wide sweep of issues. But two have broad applicability and are gaining a great deal of attention: 1) under-attended process-related variables in effective practice, and 2) the increasing prevalence of computer technology in social agencies and its effects on practice. Advances in both these areas have provided clearer frameworks than were previously available. For example, recent research on inference, reasoning, and decision making from an information-processing perspective has identified several aspects of "process" that demonstrably have significant influence on practice (Gambrill, 1990). Similarly, we are now on the cusp of a new era, in which we will need a critical eye in gauging the influences of computerization of "information management" (which increasingly houses the managerial basis of research activity) on direct practice and in guiding the use of this technology as a tool for research in practice (Grasso & Epstein, 1987; Murphy & Pardeck, 1988).

As with any practice question, familiarity with the substantive knowledge base is essential. Yet there is typically a gap that the social worker must traverse between the practice question and the best research means of addressing this question. Again, although no resource can do or be all things, guidelines that offer rationales and "traversing principles" for how to translate from the question to the method and back can be an important aid to overcoming inertia and to guiding stronger inquiry efforts (see Gibbs [1991] and Nurius & Hudson [1993] for beginning attention to this).

Finally, in any prescription, one needs to study and weigh the "con" factors. In this case, I have the benefit of colleagues who will undoubtedly point out far more factors than I alone am likely to have considered. So here I will be brief. Guidelines should be just that: guidance lines. These neither need be nor should be an all-or-nothing undertaking. Nor is it useful or in keeping with the spirit of guidelines (as opposed to regulations or mandates) that guides be developed and applied in a rigid or irresponsible manner. Perhaps such concerns suggest the utility of a step-wise approach (e.g., to establishing an initial set of guidelines, getting feedback as to their clarity and utility, revision based upon this feedback, and so forth), and to prefatory statements as to what the purpose and purview of such guidelines would and would not be. As the field evolves, so one would expect the need and form of guidance would evolve as well. The ultimate goal is the strengthening of social work practice and so doing within a thoughtfully considered set of referents. To this end, guidelines appear far more a "pro" than a "con."

References

Caputo, R. K. (1985). The role of research in the family service agency. *Social Casework, 66,* 205–212.

Gambrill, E. (1990). *Critical thinking in clinical practice.* San Francisco, CA: Jossey-Bass.

Gibbs, L. E. (1991). *Scientific reasoning for social workers: Bridging the gap between research and practice.* New York: Merrill.

Grasso, A. J. & Epstein, I. (1987). Management by measurement: Organizational dilemmas and opportunities. *Administration in Social Work, 11,* 89–100.

Kirk, S. A. (1990). Research utilization: The substructure of belief. In L. Videka-Sherman, & W. J. Reid (Eds.), *Advances in clinical social work research.* Silver Springs, MD: National Association of Social Workers.

Marsh, J. C. (1983). Research and innovation in social work practice: Avoiding the headless machine. *Social Service Review, 57,* 582–598.

Murphy, J. W. & Pardeck, J. T. (1988). Technology in clinical practice and the "technological ethic". *Journal of Sociology and Social Welfare, 15,* 119–128.

Nurius, P. S. & Hudson, W. W. (1993). *Human services practice, evaluation, and computers: A practical guide for today and beyond.* Pacific Groves, CA: Brooks/Cole.

Proctor, E. K. (1990). Evaluating clinical practice: Issues of purpose and design. *Social Work Research & Abstracts, 26,* 32–40.

Turnbull, J. E., Saltz, C. C., & Gwyther, L. P. (1988). A prescription for promoting social work research in a university hospital. *Health and Social Work, 13,* 97–105.

Rejoinder to Dr. Nurius

Bruce A. Thyer
Dianne F. Harrison

We would like to respond to several points made by Dr. Nurius in her arguments that favor the establishment of professional guidelines for the appropriate use of research in practice. The issues for rebuttal concern: 1) social workers' roles in setting standards; 2) the separation of practice and research activities; 3) preparation of B.S.W. and M.S.W. graduates; 4) the extent of professional agreement regarding research approaches; and 5) the necessity for flexibility and change in standards, should any such guidelines be developed, and the basis and outlook for change.

Dr. Nurius assumes that "social work staff are playing central roles in defining and grappling with issues related to research in practice, rather than implicitly relying on others to set the standards and provide the oversight." She also suggests that in many social agencies, there are no existing guidelines nor clear guidelines for conducting research. We believe that this position overlooks existing guidelines that govern the practice and research activities of social workers, including state legal regulations (in all 50 states) and the NASW Code of Ethics. We would also suggest that guidelines exist from other contexts that can be used by social workers seeking standards for research. For example, a social-service agency that did not have its own institutional review board (IRB) could certainly use standards and guidelines established by other agencies, including both local institutions (e.g., college or university) and federal institutions (e.g., National Institute of Mental Health).

We agree with Dr. Nurius that it is difficult to separate what constitutes practice activities from research activities. We would further point out that because of this lack of distinction, most practice activities should require the special safeguards and oversight normally associated with research studies—especially informed consent, and the benefits and risks associated with intervention and confidentiality. In fact, it seems to us that more ethical practice may result from social workers applying the same standards to practice as are mandated by most agencies and state and federal regulatory bodies for research.

Dr. Nurius points out that the preparation of B.S.W. and M.S.W. graduates is often insufficient in regard to the conduct of research in applied settings; hence, another argument for a new set of guidelines for social agencies. Our response is that inadequacies in curricula require improvement in social work educational programs, not the promulgation of new guidelines.

It appears that Dr. Nurius' proposal for guidelines that would address practice questions and the best research means for addressing such questions assumes there is agreement in our profession regarding epistemologies, research approaches, and methods of inquiry. Even a casual perusal of recent journal articles and the controversial issues presented in this book should convince the reader otherwise. Not only is there disagreement, some readers might label the advocates of certain views as openly hostile toward the opposing side (see, for example, Tyson [1992]). Further, certain guidelines related to research design may serve to discourage innovation or diversity in methodology.

Lastly, Dr. Nurius recommends "guidance lines" versus rigid regulations or mandates. Such guidelines, she suggests, might evolve over time as the field of social work evolves. Should any such guidelines be developed, we would agree with the necessity for change as appropriate. We would add that any changes should preferably be made in response to the empirical investigation of the assumptions and efficacy of such standards in relation to ethical issues. In fact, we would suggest that such studies evaluate the need for new guidelines and, if guidelines are needed, empirical investigations should play an important role in their development. (See Stanley, Sieber and Melton [1987]), for a discussion of these same issues in the field of psychology.)

Finally, at the risk of being called cynics, we are not quite as confident as our colleague, Dr. Nurius, that the profession would be responsive and willing to change once some set of guidelines was in place. Recall, for example, the time lapses between changed versions of the NASW Code of Ethics (nineteen years) and the CSWE Curriculum Policy Statement (ten years).

References

Stanley, B., Sieber, J. E. & Melton, G. B. (1987). Empirical studies of ethical issues in research: A research agenda. *American Psychologist, 42*(7), 735–741.

Tyson, K. B. (1992). A new approach to relevant scientific research for practitioners: The heuristic paradigm. *Social Work, 37*(6), 541–556.

NO

Bruce A. Thyer
Dianne F. Harrison

The perspective that we have taken on the question, under debate is that of "Is it desirable to develop some form of universal written guidelines that address different aspects of the implementation of research in practice?" Our response to this question is, "NO!" We have taken the NO position to the question for reasons centered around three major themes: 1) protection of clients, 2) research design issues, and 3) impracticality. We shall address each of these objections in turn.

Protection of Clients

There presently exist a number of inherent safeguards for the protection of clients who may be involved in research on practice. The NASW *Code of Ethics* contains a number of guidelines regarding the ethical involvement of persons in research, as do analogous codes of other professional associations such as the American Psychological Association, the American Association for Marital and Family Therapy, and so forth. While not binding on nonmembers, these codes nevertheless provide suitable guidance regarding admissible and inappropriate practices.

The practice of social work is legally regulated in all fifty states and most statutes relating to social work contain provisions regarding the confidentiality of clients, including granting social workers the right of privileged communication in some instances. Apart from practice issues, the right of confidentiality would seem to be a further safeguard that identifying information about clients would not be revealed in the course of research or in related publications. Indeed, violations of client confidentiality, regardless of whether they occurred within the context of practice or of some research project, would render the social worker liable to civil prosecution. This is an existing and built-in legal safeguard for the protection of clients, at least with respect to confidentiality.

Formal Institutional Review Boards IRBs exist at all agencies that receive federal funds (hospitals, universities, etc.) as oversight committees charged with prospectively examining proposed research projects and ensuring that subjects/clients' rights are protected. Also, IRBs have been established at some facilities that are not required legally to have them. Many practice-based research projects undertaken by social workers (but admittedly not all) are subject to IRB scrutiny. For social workers employed in agencies that lack IRBs, the nearest one (say, at a local university) is available to provide informal consultation at no cost. Thus, IRBs are an existing, nationwide resource providing for the protection of client/subject rights and whose services are freely available to all social workers involved in research, should such consultation be warranted. (See Grigsby and Roof [in press] for a further discussion of the role of IRBs in research on social work practice.)

Not to be overlooked are the professional training experiences undergone by social work students at all levels, B.S.W., M.S.W., and Ph.D. No set of abbreviated guidelines can substitute for formal classes on research design, on the values and ethics of the profession, for field instruction that contains a practice-research assignment conducted under supervision, and for the study of professional journals that publish research on social work practice. Our students should be (although admitted, imperfectly) reasonably well trained in the competent and ethically appropriate design of research when they graduate with their professional degree in social work.

Research Design Issues

The very concept of "guidelines" is alien to the process of scientific inquiry, which depends upon constant innovation and the free-ranging application of diverse methodologies to differing research questions. To some extent, the choice of research methodology is driven by one's conceptual or theoretical orientation. A behavior analyst and a psychoanalyst would likely employ differing outcome measures and research designs to assess the efficacy of some novel form of psychosocial intervention. Although the authors, as dedicated empiricists with a behavioral orientation, have their own views as to what may constitute suitable research designs, we would not dream of imposing such views upon our social work colleagues. We are confident that the Darwinian process of natural selection will gradually shape the field into the adoption of conceptual frameworks and research methodologies that have demonstrated value. Theories and methodologies that are of little value will gradually be relegated into the file marked,

"Discarded Approaches to Social Work Research and Practice." No set of official guidelines are needed to facilitate this process.

One lesson derived from history consists of the adoption within the Soviet Union of "Lysenkoism," a biological theory and set of research practices held to be consistent with Marxism that became the official dogma of Soviet agriculture for decades. Unfortunately, the principles of Lysenkoism were incorrect (that characteristics acquired through environmental changes can be transmitted by heredity). Despite the repeated failure of inappropriately planted and cultivated crops, the Soviet central planners held on to ineffective agricultural policies for many years, driven by their earlier adoption of a set of stifling (and erroneous) rules that were politically unwise to jettison. This is not ancient history. Lysenko died in 1976. The adoption of any set of professional guidelines for research on social work practice poses a similar danger.

Impracticality

It is impossible to disentangle social work research from social work practice. For example, one of the authors recently conducted a program evaluation of the effectiveness of a local homeless shelter. This involved tracking down former shelter clients, nine to twelve months after they left the facility, and ascertaining their housing and employment history since placement by the shelter's case manager. Given our profession's mandates for accountability, we would argue that such studies are simply a part of good social work practice and could be appropriately labeled program evaluations or quality-assurance studies, not as "research" as this is typically construed. Similarly, when one of the authors conducted a single-system research study on a ten-year-old boy with severe mental retardation, examining the effects of a psychosocial treatment program on aggression, this, too, could be arguably contended to be an evaluation effort, with such evaluations being an integral part of all contemporary models of social work *practice* (not simply as "research").

A further impediment to the adoption of professional guidelines for research consists of the failure on the part of our profession to agree upon a unifying set of principles for practice research. Empiricists, such as the authors, have their own views (e.g., Harrison & Thyer [1988]; Thyer [1989; 1991]), which are shared by mainstream science and the majority of social workers. However, the whole notion of empirically based clinical practice is being assailed by a minority of qualitative researchers, constructivists, certain feminist researchers, the shrill advocates of an amorphous "heuristic approach," and other social worker counterparts to the inventors of "cold-fusion." Leaders within the profession advocate "many ways of knowing," but ignore the most fundamental way of knowing at all, knowing truth from fantasy (Hartman 1990). Apart from the undesirability of professional guidelines for research, we feel that it is most unlikely that the profession could coalesce around some central set of principles for research on social work practice.

The concept of "professional guidelines" conjures up images of "Research Police," with attendant review boards, monitoring function, professional sanctions imposed by NASW for violations of guidelines, and the like. Few things could be more stifling of the process of conducting research.

One final point. Social work research shares many features with other academic disciplines and helping professions. There are no counterparts to any proposed professional guidelines for research on social work practice within clinical psychology, psychiatry, medicine, education, nursing, counseling, and so forth. Rather, these fields draw upon a common base of behavioral and social science research methodologies, which cuts across all professional boundaries, theories of practice, and questions relevant to applied research. We should follow this example and not waste precious time and limited resources on the development of specific mandates regarding research on social work practice.

References

Grigsby, K., & Roof, H. (in press). Federal policy for the protection of human subjects: Applications to research on social work practice. *Research on Social Work Practice.*

Harrison, D. F., & Thyer, B. A. (1988). Doctoral research on social work practice. *Journal of Social Work Education, 24,* 107–114.

Hartman, A. (1990). Many ways of knowing (editorial). *Social Work, 35*(1), 3–4.

Thyer, B. A. (1989). First principles of practice research. *British Journal of Social Work, 19,* 309–323.

Thyer, B. A. (1991). Guidelines for evaluating outcome studies on social work practice. *Research on Social Work Practice, 1,* 76–91.

Rejoinder to Drs. Thyer & Harrison

PAULA S. NURIUS

In their argument against professional guidelines for the use of research in practice, Drs. Thyer and Harrison raise a number of issues that—although presented in terms of near-disastrous outcomes—do warrant careful attention. I will conclude this rebuttal with a view of our common ground on some of these issues. First, however, I will first speak to some of their specific points that I found perplexing and unfounded.

The broadest point of confusion relates to their view of the relative "goodness" or "badness" of guidelines. Drs. Thyer and Harrison seem to argue both ways—guidelines are sufficiently important that social work should be governed by those already in existence (e.g., in hospitals and universities), yet, for some reason, should not undergo its own parallel process of articulating, examining, and deciding upon these issues within the context of its own professional priorities and needs. This is especially odd in that my debators cast review mechanisms, such as IRBs, as credible and respected resources, yet argue that guidelines developed explicitly by social workers would constitute some sort of "research police" with stifling, verging on facist, tendencies. It is frankly amazing to see, based on absolutely no data, the assertion that *any set* of professional guidelines for research in social work practice poses a danger comparable to the methods of national oppression formerly characteristic of the Soviet government's blind adherence to communist dogma. It would be useful for them to explicate what they see as the source of such a rigid, choking, and incompetent disposition in the profession of social work.

A second point of confusion is the assertion that the very concept of guidelines is "alien to the process of scientific inquiry." Really . . . *alien?* This raises the question of what exactly is going on in the classrooms of the professional training to which Drs. Thyer and Harrison refer, and in the conference rooms wherein review groups are writing and applying, well, *something* as they determine whether any set of research activities proposed for their institution is appropriate. Is this a semantic hair being split between "guidelines" being bad, but regulations, safeguards, codes, appropriate methods, review boards, and the like being okay?

Very troubling also is their notion of a "Darwinian process of natural selection" as the force that we should rely upon to shape outcomes in this arena. How is this in the best interest of the welfare of our clients? What is the link between this survival-of-the-fittest notion and their earlier statement of concern for client safeguards? How does this approach guide or assist social work practitioners and students, who are struggling to figure out viable means through which to undertake research efforts in the context of their practice realities? I know that I and many of my colleagues would certainly love to get our hands on that file marked, "Discarded Approaches to Social Work Research and Practice." What a resource it would be for clarifying which methods are *un*likely to be fruitful with certain types of populations, problems, or settings . . . but this sounds rather like guidelines!

Perhaps most perplexing is the image that my debators portray of social workers as just not being up to the job. Or at least, not those wrong-headed social workers. Drs. Thyer and Harrison tell us that their own views are "mainstream" and characteristic of "the majority of social workers." Some, of course, would differ with this nonevidence-based assertion. But, in characterizing professionals whose views differ from their own as "shrill advocates" who can't seem to distinguish "truth from fantasy," I can see why they are so pessimistic. What is less clear is how this derisive view of differences serves as an argument *against* efforts to generate aids and guides regarding use of research tools. Surely they would be useful within the admittedly complex, diverse, and messy realm of everyday social work practice, wherein the cost for errors or misjudgment are high and the decision supports are few.

There are several points of agreement in our debate positions. I agree with Drs. Thyer and Harrison that precious time and limited resources should not be wasted. I agree that perspective differences can be very trying to contend with, and that some individuals and groups within social work have engaged more in diatribe than dialogue around issues of research and practice. I agree that existing codes, regulations, and review criteria can be useful resources to draw upon. I certainly agree that a rigid, ''Big Brother-ish'' approach to the notion of guidelines is not useful. But is this honestly at issue? Further, I agree that attention to flexibility and safeguards on multiple levels is essential.

What I do not agree with is that social workers presently have the guides and supports that they need to undertake this extrapolation process—about *how* to best translate textbook teaching of research tools and methods into *their* practice; *their* agency; *their* working context of limited stability, resources, or controls. This is not to argue that social workers are devoid of preparation or resources for this task. But, as the recent survey report from the Task Force on Social Work Research (1991), the vast majority of social workers simply do not yet have either the preparation or the resources needed.

Drs. Thyer and Harrison's vision of plentiful, free, easily accessible, nationwide resources contrasts sharply both with these survey findings and with my own and others' experience of phone calls from former students and field colleagues who are trying to determine how they can realistically undertake and sustain meaningful research activities as a part of their on-going agency life. It contrasts with the experience of allied professions, as evidenced by the recent editorial by the president of the American Psychological Association (Wiggins, 1992), which stated that guidelines are sorely needed ''for translating principles of basic science into the delivery of efficacious health services'' (p. 3). Codes of ethics and licensing regulations simply do not provide guidance that extends much beyond the important yet obvious issues, such as client confidentiality.

In closing, it may be that I am using a more heuristic-oriented notion of guidelines, whereas Drs. Thyer and Harrison are assuming a more policing or governance-oriented approach. They seem to frame guidelines as requiring a stance of absolute right and wrong answers. This has not been true in other fields, so I am not sure why it should be so in social work. I would frame guidelines more in terms of goals; as criteria and principles to support planning and decision making about the incorporation of research tools and activities into practice in varying forms, as appropriate to the motivating questions, setting factors, and so forth. Rarely is there only one right answer to a question, and I maintain that guidelines could help social workers generate stronger solutions.

References

Task Force on Social Work Research (1991). *Building social work knowledge for effective services and policies: A plan for research development.* Austin, TX: National Institute of Mental Health, Capital Printing.

Wiggins, J. G. Jr. (1992, December). Practice guidelines: We sorely need them, *APA Monitor,* 3.